MW01713107

SCOTTISH STUDIES 37

Chuidich Comhairle nan Leabhraichean am foillsichear
le cosgaisean an leabhair seo.

Scottish Studies

The Journal of the School of Scottish Studies
University of Edinburgh

vol. 37 2014

EDITED BY
VIRGINIA BLANKENHORN

Published by The School of Scottish Studies
University of Edinburgh
2014

Articles are invited and should be sent to:

Dr John Shaw
The Editor, *Scottish Studies*
The School of Scottish Studies
The University of Edinburgh
27 George Square
Edinburgh EH8 9LD

All articles submitted are sent out to readers for peer review. Enquiries may be made by email to: j.w.shaw@ed.ac.uk.

Subscription requests should be sent to The Subscription Secretary, *Scottish Studies*, at the address above.

Cover image: Orchard in the grounds of the Royal Edinburgh Hospital. Photograph by Virginia Blankenhorn.

Frontispiece: Photograph of John MacInnes by Virginia Blankenhorn.

Printed in Great Britain by Airdrie Press Services.

ISBN 978-0-900949-04-3

CRAOBH NAN UBHAL

A Festschrift in Honour of
John MacInnes

Contents

Contributors

Margaret Bennett, Folklorist, writer, singer and broadcaster.

Virginia Blankenhorn, Celtic and Scottish Studies, University of Edinburgh.

Angela Bourke, Professor *(emeritus),* School of Irish, Celtic Studies, Irish Folklore & Linguistics, University College Dublin.

Aonghus Pàdraig Caimbeul, Gaelic novelist, essayist and poet.

Hugh Cheape, Professor, Sabhal Mór Ostaig, University of the Highlands and Islands.

Edward J. Cowan, Professor of History *(emeritus)*, University of Glasgow.

Ailean Dòmhnallach, Royal Conservatoire of Scotland, Glasgow.

Robert Dunbar, Professor of Celtic, University of Edinburgh.

Ian Fraser, Celtic and Scottish Studies, University of Edinburgh.

William Gillies, Professor of Celtic *(emeritus)*, University of Edinburgh.

William Lamb, Celtic and Scottish Studies, University of Edinburgh.

Emily Lyle, Celtic and Scottish Studies, University of Edinburgh.

Dòmhnall Mac Amhlaidh, Poet; Professor of Celtic *(emeritus)*, University of Glasgow.

Caoimhín Mac Giolla Léith, School of Irish, Celtic Studies, Irish Folklore & Linguistics, University College Dublin.

Raghnall MacilleDhuibh, Writer and journalist.

Margaret A. Mackay, Celtic and Scottish Studies, University of Edinburgh.

Colin Scott MacKenzie, D.L., F.S.A. Scot., Sheriff of Grampian Highland and Islands.

Wilson McLeod, Professor, Celtic and Scottish Studies, University of Edinburgh.

Donald Meek, Professor of Scottish and Gaelic Studies *(emeritus)*, University of Edinburgh.

Michael Newton, Writer and researcher.

Lillis Ó Laoire, National University of Ireland, Galway.

Roibeard Ó Maolalaigh, Professor of Gaelic, University of Glasgow.

John Purser, Sabhal Mór Ostaig, University of the Highlands and Islands.

Iain Seathach, Celtic and Scottish Studies, University of Edinburgh.

Domhnall Uilleam Stiùbhart, Sabhal Mór Ostaig, University of the Highlands and Islands.

John MacInnes
A Biographical Note

Chraobh nan ubhal, gheug nan abhal,
Chraobh nan ubhal, gu robh Dia leat,
Gu robh Moire 's gu robh Crìosda,
Gu robh ghealach, gu robh ghrian leat,
Gu robh g[h]aoth an ear 's an iar leat,
Gu robh m' athair fhìn 's a thriall leat.[1]

Childhood and Education

John MacInnes – Iain Mac Aonghuis (Iain mac Ruairidh mhic Iain mhic Iain mhic Nèill mhic Mhaol Mhoire mhic Iain mhic Mhaol Chaluim) – was born on 3 April 1930 in Uig, Lewis, when his father Ruairidh was minister in the Established Church – *an Eaglais Stéidhte,* the Church of Scotland – in the parish of Uig. The MacInneses, however, came not from Lewis but from the Isle of Skye, and originally from Morvern. His father's mother's people – Andersons (Clann mhic Annraisg) – lived in Torrin, and his father's ancestors, swordsmen with the MacDonalds of Sleat, once held the tack of Leitir Fura. One of them, Maol Caluim, fought with the Jacobite forces at the Battle of Sheriffmuir in 1715.

If, as many Gaels believe, tenacity and the warrior spirit have a genetic basis, then Ruairidh MacInnes inherited them in full. An outspoken supporter of the Land League, his passion for social justice animated his life. He was also a steadfast defender and ardent proponent of the Gaelic language. As a minister, he possessed not only the rich Gaelic of his Skye forbears but also the powerful lexicon of theology and religion, the language of erudition and philosophy, and could fashion a compelling argument in trenchant and uncompromising fashion. Perhaps because he was in his forties when he first became a parent, his values – like his Gaelic – were those of an older generation, and he disapproved of a growing trend for parents to speak only English to their children. Ruairidh MacInnes's tireless advocacy of the human rights of the Gaels, and his love of the Gàidhealtachd, its language and its culture, were to exert a potent influence upon his son.

John's mother Morag (Morag Alasdair 'ic Mhurchaidh) was a MacAskill, and grew up in Clàdach Circebost in North Uist. Her grandfather, Murchadh Mac Asgaill, had moved to Uist from Skye, and had married a Uist woman. Morag's mother's people were MacCorquhodales: her grandfather Calum Mac Còrcadail had worked as a schoolteacher in Tiree, where he married Mór Nic Fhionghain, a Tiree woman. Like her husband, Morag was committed to the use of Gaelic at home. As John told Michael Newton:

> By far the most important element in my background was the fact that at home we spoke Gaelic all the time. My parents, from Uist and Skye, both of them equally, had a wonderful command of rich, idiomatic Gaelic. To the present day, my sister and myself, like a great number of our relatives, would never dream of conversing in any other language than Gaelic.[2]

When John was eight years old, the family left Lewis and moved to Raasay, where John immediately felt at home. Raasay's proximity to Skye afforded him an opportunity to get to know members of his father's extended family: his father's paternal uncles, in particular, would

[1] J. L. Campbell and F. Collinson (eds), *Hebridean Folksongs: A Collection of Waulking Songs Made by Donald MacCormick in Kilphedir in South Uist in the year 1893.* Oxford 1969: 146.

[2] M. Newton (ed.), *Dùthchas nan Gàidheal: Selected Essays of John MacInnes.* Edinburgh 2006: xxv.

eventually help to ignite his appreciation for Gaelic song and tradition. From the beginning, however, the topography of Raasay – and particularly the fact that it was forested – strongly appealed to him:

> Bha mi trì bliadhna a's a' sgoil ann an Bhaltois, ann an Sgìr Ùige, ach chan 'eil ann ach...gu bheil na bliadhnaichean sin 'nan aisling, 'nam bruadar dhomhsa. Ach chaidh an teaghlach a Ratharsair an uair sin, agus gad a tha Ùige Leodhais, gad a tha an dùthaich cho àlainn 's a gheibh thu anns na h-eileanan – tha beanntan Ùige ann, 's tha iad ainmeil, tràighean móra, Tràigh Mhór Ùige fhéin – 's e àite lom a tha ann. Tha na h-àiteachan lom, mar gum b'eadh, gu nàdurra.
>
> Thàinig sinn a Ratharsair, agus bha ceann-a-deas Ratharsair fo choille. Agus bha buaidh anabarrach aig a' choille ormsa, feumaidh mi ràdh. Bha i, cha mhór, 'na diamhaireachd. ... 'S bha buaidh aig a h-uile dad a bha sin ormsa, agus riamh bho'n uair sin 's toil leam a bhith measg nan coilltean. Chan eil dad cho cofhurtail ann ri bhith 'gabhail fasgadh aig bun craoibheadh, na ann an coille, na ann an doire, ma tha stoirm, gaoth mhór, ann, gaillean is dòcha, agus tha thu cho seasgair 's a ghabhas tu. [3]
>
> *I was at school for three years in Valtos, in the district of Uig, but those years are little more than a dream to me. But then the family went to Raasay; and although Uig, Lewis, and the country round there is as beautiful as any you'd find in the Islands – the hills of Uig, which are famous, the wide beaches – it's basically a bare place. The places are bare, as it were, by nature.*
>
> *We came to Raasay, and the south end of Raasay was forested. And the forest had a remarkable effect upon me, I have to say. It was almost magical. And it all had a great effect upon me, and ever since then I have loved to be in the midst of a forest. There's nothing as comforting as to be sheltering at the foot of a tree, or in a forest, or in a wood, if there's a big storm brewing, with gales maybe, and you're as snug as can be.*

When the MacInneses moved to Raasay in 1938, the forests were those that had been planted by George Rainy some eighty years before to provide habitat for deer: oak, beech, ash, elm, spruce and pine. All of these trees were cut down during the Second World War. Today, Raasay's forests are plantation softwoods, and are nothing like the trees John remembers with such fondness, and that Somhairle MacGill-Eain celebrated in his poem 'Coilltean Ratharsair'.

After completing his primary education in Raasay, John was sent as a boarding pupil to Portree School, where he lived in the boys' hostel. His memories of this time are not sunny, as he greatly missed Raasay. Because the school regime was conducted entirely through the English language – even the playground, peopled in large majority by native Gaelic-speaking children, was English-speaking – John's main opportunity to speak Gaelic was provided by visits to a house in Portree where his sister Christina was lodging:

> Ann an Port Rìgh, nuair a bha mise 'sa' *hostel*, bha boireannach ('na banntraich an uairsin), agus 's e *Mistress Beaton* a chanamaide rithe an comhnaidh. Bha i pòsda aig fear Iain Peutan, agus 's ann à Tròndairnis a bha i, agus bhiodh i gabhail loidsearan, cuid dhiubh clann sgoile. Bha mo phiuthar, a bha na bu shine na mise, cha robh i 'sa *hostel* ann, 's ann 'san taigh aice-sin a bha i. Agus nuair a thànaig mise a Sgoil Phort Rìgh, chuireadh an aithne a chéile sinn, agus thubhairt *Mistress Beaton* a bha seo riumsa, 'Thig thusa a-nuas a-seo an deaghaidh na sgoile latha sam bith 's a h-uile latha thogras tu.' Agus 's e Gàidhlig a bh' againn fad an t-siubhail. Boireannach laghach – cha b'urrainn dhomh gu leòr molaidh a thoirt oirre; bha an taigh aice-se dìreach 'na

[3] From 'Air mo Chuairt', a series of interviews with John MacInnes conducted by Fiona MacKenzie of the BBC, first broadcast in 2009; Programme 1.

dhachaidh dhomhsa fad na bliadhnaichean a bha sin. Agus chùm e Ghàidhlig agam a' dol cuideachd, chionn 's gur h-e Beurla a bha a' dol anns a' *hostel* an comhnaidh.[4]

In Portree, when I was in the hostel, there was a woman, then a widow, whom we always called 'Mrs Beaton'. She had been married to a man, John Beaton, and was from Trotternish, and she provided lodgings for some of the students. My sister, who was older then myself, never stayed in the hostel, but lodged in her house. And when I came to Portree School, we were introduced and Mrs Beaton said to me, 'You come down here after school any day, as often as you like.' We spoke Gaelic all the time. A generous woman – I couldn't praise her highly enough; her house was like a home to me throughout those years. And it kept my Gaelic going, for it was all English that was spoken in the hostel.

John MacInnes's experience of the educational regime at Portree School came to colour his understanding of what it meant to be a Gael in the context of the British Empire:

Bha prógram na dhà...air an teilibhisean bho chionn ghoirid, agus daoine a' bruidhinn…air a bhith beò ann an *hostel* ann an Port Rìgh na ann an Inbhir Nis; agus 's a h-uile dad a bha iad a' ràdh dh'aontaichinn riutha ach gum bithinn, tha mi 'smaoineachadh, fada nas truime air an t-siostam uile gu léir a rinn ùdaras Alba agus Bhreatainn air na Gàidheil.

Rinn a' foghlum fada fada barrachd millidh air a' Ghàidhlig na rinn na Fuadaichean riamh. Can an-dràsda – chan eil mi a' dol a dh'àicheadh idir nach robh brùidealachd 's nach robh anaceartas eagalach fuaighte ri na Fuadaichean – ach can gu robh mìle duine ann am baile...agus gun deach cóig ceud dhiubh a ruagadh a-null fairis a Chanada na dh'Astràilia na dh'àite sam bith eile. Cha robh seo a' ciallachadh ach gu robh cóig ceud air a' fàgail gus an dèanamh Gallda tron an fhoghlum. Agus 's e Achd an Fhoghluim 1872 – nuair a dh'fheumadh a h-uile duine dol dhan a' sgoil aig aois chòig bliadhna, agus gu feumte am foghlum ann am Beurla fad an t-siubhail – 's e sin a' bhuille, 's e buille cho goirt 's cho cruaidh 's a thàinig air a' Ghàidhlig 's air a' Ghàidhealtachd riamh.

Nise, dh'ainmich duine na dìthis a bh' air na prógramman a tha seo cho iongantach 's a bha e gur h-e Beurla a bha sinn a' bruidhinn fad an t-siùbhail. Agus 's e sin a bh'ann. Nuair a chaidh mise a Phort Rìgh 's e Ghàidhlig a bha againne a-staigh an comhnaidh, agus bha lethcheud gille anns a' *hostel*,…agus 's e Ghàidhlig a bhiodh a-staigh aig cuid mhór mhór dhiubh fad an t-siùbhail. Ach bha, mar gum b'eadh, a' Bheurla air a spàrradh oirnn. Agus gad a bhiodh tu ag iarraidh – agus bha mise feuchainn ri seo a dhèanamh – a' Ghàidhlig a chumail, 's gum biodh i againn comha ri chéile, bha a h-uile duine a' géilleadh air a' cheann thall.

Bha rud ann mu na tidsearan nach deach ainmeachadh [a's na prógramman] idir. Ann an Port Rìgh, a-mach air Iain Stil, Sgitheanach – 's esan a bha a' teagasg Gàidhlig – a-mach air a leitheid sin de dhuine, 's e Goill a bh' annta, à caochladh àiteachan ann an Alba. Agus bha cuid aca a bha, mar gum b'eadh, a dh'aon ghnothach a' cur sìos air a' Ghàidhlig. Bha feadhainn eile a bha…ga dhèanamh ann an dóigh na bu shuaraiche. 'S bha sin a' cur air shùilean dhuinn, ann an dòigh sheòlta, nach robh feum sam bith a's a' Ghàidhlig. Chan e sin a-mhàin, ach gu robh e, mar gum b' eadh, nach robh innte ach rud a bha gad chumail ar ais. Bha iad gad chur an suarachas. Bha iad a' cur na cainnt' agad an suarachas, a' cur a' chànain agad an suarachas, agus uime sin bha iad gad chur fhéin an suarachas. Agus tha mise a' smaoineachadh gu robh buaidh eagalach

[4] *Ibid.*, Programme 4.

aige sin air a' Ghàidhlig agus air na daoine a bha bruidhinn na Gàidhlig air feadh na Gàidhealtachd.[5]

There were a few programmes on television recently in which people spoke of living in the hostels in Portree and in Inverness; and I would agree with everything that they said, except that I would be far harder on the whole system which the Scottish and British authorities imposed upon the Gaels.

Education brought a great deal more destruction upon the Gaelic language than the Clearances ever did. Now I am not going to deny that there was brutality connected with the Clearances, that there was not terrible injustice done; but say that there were a thousand people in a village...and that five hundred of these were driven abroad to Canada or to Australia or somewhere else. This only meant that there were five hundred remaining to be Anglicized through the educational system. And it was the Education Act of 1872 – which required everyone to attend school from the age of five, and to learn exclusively through the medium of English – that struck the real blow, a blow as sharp and severe as any ever dealt to the Gaelic language and to the Gàidhealtachd.

A few of the people interviewed on these programmes mentioned how amazing it was that we all spoke English all the time. And that is indeed what happened. When I went to Portree, it was Gaelic that we invariably spoke at home; and there were fifty boys in the hostel and the same was true for most of them. But it was as if English had been thrust upon us. And even if you tried – as I did – to keep Gaelic going, so that we'd be speaking it amongst ourselves, everybody gave way to English in the end.

One thing about the teachers was not mentioned in the television programmes. In Portree, apart from John Steele, a Skye man – he was the Gaelic teacher – apart from the likes of him, they were all Lowlanders, from various places in Scotland. Some of these intentionally disparaged the Gaelic language, while others did so in a meaner way. It was made clear to us, in a subtle fashion, that Gaelic was of no use, that it would keep you back. They were belittling you – belittling your speech, belittling your language and, by implication, belittling you. And I think that that had a dreadful effect on Gaelic and the people who spoke Gaelic throughout the Gàidhealthachd.

While most of the schoolmasters made little impression upon John, and he describes hostel life as nothing short of imprisonment, it was during his time at Portree School that he first became acquainted with the poetry of Somhairle MacGill-Eain. As a child in Raasay, John was familiar with the Maclean family, known locally as 'Clann an Tàilleir'; but because of the difference in their ages – Somhairle was born in 1911 – John did not get to know him well until much later, when he moved to Edinburgh to attend university. But his appreciation of Maclean's poems, surely intensified by his own love of Raasay, dates from this period.

John's feeling of being culturally cast adrift undoubtedly increased in 1943, when his father was called to serve a parish in Durness, Sutherland; and his mother's untimely death in Durness the following year dealt a further severe blow. His parents' move to Durness, however, enabled John to further his exploration of the Gàidhealtachd during school holidays, and he recalls his interest in the linguistic differences between the Gaelic of Durness and what he had previously encountered:

Cha deach mise a dh'fhuireach ann – bha mi 'sa *hostel* ann an Port Rìgh, agus cha robhar aig iarraidh mo ghluasad, bhithinn a' dol ri saor-laithean – ach 's e cheud rud a ghabh mise beachd air, cho diofraichte 's a bha Gàidhlig nan Caoidheach bhon a' Ghàidhlig a chuala mi roimhe sin. Ged a bha i na bu choltaich ann an iomadach dòigh ri Gàidhlig Leodhais na ri cainnt eile a chuala mi gu ruige sin, cha robh i ach aig na

[5] *Ibid.*, Programme 4.

seann-daoine. Na daoine có-dhiubh a bha caran ann an meadhan an aoise, cha robh Gàidhlig aig a' chloinn idir aig an àm sin fhéin.[6]

I didn't go there to live – I was in the hostel in Portree, and they didn't want to move me, I used to go [to Sutherland] for holidays – but the first thing I noticed was how different the Gaelic of the Mackay Country was from what I had heard before. Although it bore greater resemblance in a number of ways to the Gaelic of Lewis than to anything else I'd heard up to then, it was spoken only by the old people. At any rate, the people who were more-or-less middle-aged – even then, their children had no Gaelic at all.

John MacInnes returned to the Mackay Country in the late 1950s to conduct fieldwork under the auspices of the School of Scottish Studies. In addition to recording a number of the songs of Rob Donn Mackay and the stories connected with them, he also began to develop his thinking about why Sutherland Gaelic shared some of the features of Lewis Gaelic, and to get a sense of how valuable such linguistic evidence could be in helping to unravel the complicated history of Scotland's Gaelic-speaking clan society.

After leaving Portree School in 1948, MacInnes enrolled at the University of Edinburgh. His undergraduate studies began with English Literature, where he completed Junior Honours and was awarded the J. Logie Robertson Prize; shifted to English Language (Anglo-Saxon, Old Norse, Old High German, Old Saxon and Gothic); and included Philosophy and British History as his minor subjects. (Indeed, his studies in Philosophy earned him the Class Medal, in a class of nearly 400 students, as well as the James Seth Prize in Moral Philosophy in 1950, with the result that the faculty in that department tried to recruit him.) His language studies also included the study of phonetics with David Abercrombie, whose ideas about metre and rhythm greatly influenced his own understanding of the accentual character of Gaelic verse. Upon receiving his M.A. in 1953 he was awarded the Gatty Scholarship, which allowed him to undertake postgraduate study in any aspect of Anglo-Saxon or Germanic languages. His academic studies provided him with a rich understanding of and an abiding interest in the structure and etymology of words in both English and in Gaelic – an interest which, as any of his friends can attest, is undiminished sixty years later.

It was during the two years immediately following graduation that he began formal study of Gaelic, completing the first two years of the undergraduate degree in Celtic under the direction of Prof. Kenneth Jackson and the Rev. William Matheson, who at that time were the only two faculty members in the Department of Celtic. He eventually satisfied the terms of the Gatty Scholarship by completing work on the topic 'The Gaelic element in Lowland Scots'.

The shifting of MacInnes's academic focus towards Gaelic, along with his growing interest in his native culture and traditions, was no doubt encouraged by the founding of the School of Scottish Studies in 1951, whilst he was an undergraduate. Following graduation, he took advantage of the School's willingness to lend out recording equipment and began to record songs, stories and traditional lore in the Gàidhealtachd, initially from family members in Skye and from families he knew in Raasay, where his father was once again living.

In 1955, all of these postgraduate activities were interrupted by the necessity of fulfilling his National Service requirement. He was enlisted in the Gordon Highlanders, who assigned him to the Intelligence Corps and posted him to Cyprus, where he spent eighteen months sitting at a desk and, in free moments, cultivating friendships with the Greek Cypriot population. During this period he managed to learn Modern Greek, a language which he still enthusiastically deploys whenever he gets a chance:

> Learning a people's language always opens doors, and I was offered the warmest of hospitality, being invited to weddings, baptisms and all sorts of social

[6] *Ibid.*, Programme 7.

gatherings. I used to hear songs of the *Klephts* – the Greeks who fought in the mountains against the Ottoman Empire – and ballads of the great *Digenes Akritas*. There were some fascinating parallels between these songs and the Gaelic panegyrics, and between the balladry and *Duain na Fèinne*.[7]

Demobilised at the end of 1957, MacInnes returned to Edinburgh where he continued his study with Professor Jackson, who quite exceptionally took him on as a single student. (MacInnes's connection with the Department of Celtic continued until 1975, when he was awarded the Ph.D. for his dissertation entitled 'Gaelic Poetry'.) Early in 1958 he began work at two University jobs, the first as a tutor in Old and Middle English, a post he held until 1963; and the second as a text transcriber in the School of Scottish Studies. In 1959 he was promoted to the position of Junior Research Fellow at the School, and he remained at the School of Scottish Studies until he retired as a Senior Lecturer in 1993.

During these early years in Edinburgh, John MacInnes laid out a course for the rest of his life. It was an exciting time to live in Scotland's capital city. Beyond the University, beyond the enormous potential of the new School of Scottish Studies, Edinburgh's postwar intelligensia included some of Scotland's greatest twentieth-century writers, thinkers and poets: Hugh MacDiarmid, Derick Thomson, George Mackay Brown, George Campbell Hay, Iain Crichton Smith, Sidney Goodsir Smith, Norman MacCaig (the latter two became particularly close friends) and many others. Sorley Maclean, invalided out of the Army following the North Africa campaign, had resumed his pre-war teaching job at Boroughmuir School; in 1951 his brother Calum I. Maclean became one of the first Research Fellows hired at the School of Scottish Studies. In this intellectual ferment, John MacInnes matured as a creative and imaginative scholar, committed to championing the Gaels' right to learn about and to take pride in their cultural heritage.

Cultural Background

The world in which John MacInnes grew up was one in which traditional learning – historical anecdotes, legends and stories about the otherworld, songs, placename lore and family history – passed through many generations, formed the bedrock of a person's cultural identity in childhood. This knowledge was subsequently overlaid by the teachings of the Church and, ultimately, by the official curricula of school and university. As he himself acknowledges, the educational authorities made it their business to detach their pupils from their early cultural heritage, to set the traditional learning of the Gàidhealtachd – along with the language in which it was transmitted – at nought, and to replace it with a mindset that would ensure that these young people identified themselves ever after as 'British' rather than as Gaels.

By the middle of the 20th century, the majority of Portree residents, whether through choice or necessity, had become English-speakers. This fact was reflected in the off-campus cultural offerings available to pupils at Portree School. Concerts, held mainly in the Drill Hall, frequently featured performances of classical music and song – something which MacInnes likened to an alien encounter. There were, however, occasional concerts of Gaelic song, parlour-songs of the sort made popular by Marjory-Kennedy Fraser, performed by platform-singers with Mòd credentials. The boys were so glad to be released from school for a short while that they were all too glad to attend any sort of entertainment; and John naturally assumed that the Gaelic singing he heard in the Drill Hall was the best Gaelic singing there was.

It was when he was about sixteen, home in Raasay (where his father was once again living) during school holidays, that he first began to take a conscious interest in Gaelic song in its traditional habitat. Returning to the house one evening, he overheard his father singing to himself. Enquiring about the song, John learned from his father that his grand-uncles in Skye – Ruairidh's own paternal uncles – had the best store of songs in the family. MacInnes's subsequent visits to

[7] As told to Michael Newton, *op. cit.*, xxvii.

these elderly uncles – particularly Calum and Niall, born between 1850 and 1870[8] – were a revelation to him, and ignited a deep love of Gaelic song, traditionally sung, that remains with him today. It was at this time, as John set about absorbing the hundreds of songs held in the memory of family members and others in his community, that his mature understanding of traditional knowledge and of its transmission in the Gàidhealtachd began to take shape.

Once his interest in such matters was aroused, other Gaels – both at home and in Edinburgh – were on hand to feed it. Dr Allan MacDonald, general practitioner in the north end of Skye, was a noted piper and an excellent Gaelic singer – and as he possessed a car, was a handy source of transport round the island. Tradition-bearers in Raasay included a family of Gilleses at Baile Chùirn – *'bha Baile Chùirn mar gum b'eadh dìreach na theis-meadhan seanchais ann an Ratharsair'* – and and two MacLeod brothers in Baile Mèadhanach.[9] These people, whom John had known for most of his life, told him stories about Mac Gille Chaluim Ratharsair and the Baintighearna Dhubh. They told him about old people whom they had known, people so old that they had been able to describe *'Ratharsair 'na theine an deaghaidh a' Phrionnsa'* – Raasay in flames, burnt by the redcoats in retribution for Raasay's support of the Jacobite cause. They told him about the land raiders, whose families had been cleared to the north of Raasay and to Rona, and how their return to claim their ancestral lands following the Great War made international headlines.

In Edinburgh, John got to know Calum and Annie Johnston from Barra, who worked and lived in the city. Annie Johnston had been recorded by the redoubtable Marjory Kennedy-Fraser, and both possessed wide repertoires of stories, traditions, songs and – in Calum's case – piping. Another Edinburgh resident and Barra native, Flora MacNeil, was gaining a wide reputation as an excellent Gaelic singer. The Morningside home of Mrs Kim Dunn, whose family came from Bernera, Harris, was a port-of-call for many Gaels in the capital, including Somhairle Maclean, once again teaching at Boroughmuir School, and his brother Calum, returned from Ireland and working at the School of Scottish Studies. John became a frequent visitor to the Dunn home, and eventually married Mrs Dunn's daughter Wendy, who has been his wife for over fifty years.

Professional Life

The life of an academic is in many ways predictable – teaching, reading, research, conferences, publication. John MacInnes's life certainly included all of these. Michael Newton has listed more than 170 of his publications at the beginning of *Dùthchas nan Gàidheal: Selected Essays of John MacInnes*, which was named Scottish Research Book of the Year by the Saltire Society in 2006. But unlike many scholars, MacInnes has not limited his scholarly activities to a single narrow focus. On the contrary, his writings, in both English and in Gaelic, include essays on the history of the Gàidhealtachd, drawing upon local and family traditions as well as from more conventional written sources; Gaelic literature – traditional and modern, oral and written; Gaelic song, music and dance; religion, belief-systems and the supernatural world; language and dialect studies; onomastics; politics; and the ways of life in traditional Gaelic society.

As a teacher, MacInnes got a late start, owing to the fact that the School of Scottish Studies did not become a teaching department until it was subsumed within the Faculty of Arts in the late

[8] Trained as an advocate, Malcolm MacInnes spent most of his life working as a civil servant in South Africa, where he was Secretary of the Johannesburg School Board. He published books of songs, based musically on traditional material, as well as two operettas with Gaelic and English lyrics. After retiring to Sleat in Skye, he prepared a new edition of Sheriff Alexander Nicolson's collection of *Gaelic Proverbs*, which appeared in 1951. Neil MacInnes had a croft at Drumfearn.

[9] 'Baile Chùirn was, as it were, the centre of *seanchas* in Raasay.' The Gillieses were *clann Iain Iain Raghnaill* – Seoras, Seumas, and their sisters – and the MacLeods were Seonaidh and Dòmhnall Ruadh Dhòmhnaill Iain Bhàin; BBC, *Air mo Chuairt,* Programme 2.

1960s.[10] Even so, his students, both undergraduates and postgraduates, describe him as an engaging and generous teacher, someone for whom every class presented an opportunity for him to learn something new, or to learn to see something familiar from a new perspective. He encouraged students to challenge what they heard from him, not simply to write it down. Roibeard Ó Maolalaigh, now Professor of Celtic in the University of Glasgow and a contributor to this volume, recalls MacInnes's generous gift of his time and knowledge:

> Thachair mise air Iain MacAonghuis an toiseach a's a bhliadhna 1988 nuair a thàinig mi a dh'Oilthigh Dhùn Éideann 'nam iar-chéimeannach. Bha esan air a bhith 'g obair fad deich air fhichead bliadhna ann an Sgoil Eòlais na h-Alba an uair sin. Agus bhitheamaid tric a' coinneachadh airson biadh a ghabhail, aig àm diathaid, agus bhiodh còmhraidhean snog againn a h-uile làtha, cha mhór. Bha e riamh, tha cuimhn a'm, gu math math taiceil do na sgoilearan òga, dìreach mar a bha mi fhìn aig an àm. Bha e gu math math fialaidh ri ùine, agus gu seachd àraid ris an fhiosrachadh a bh' aige – bha e uamhasach fhéin deònach a' fiosrachadh a bh' aige a thoirt seachad. Feumaidh mi aideachadh gun do dh'ionnsaich mi torr mór mun a' Ghàidhlig agus mu dhualchas nan Gàidheal Albannach bho Iain 'sna làithichean sin.[11]

> *I first met John MacInnes in 1988, when I came to Edinburgh University as a postgraduate. He had been working in the School of Scottish Studies for thirty years by that time. We often met for a meal at lunchtime, and had great conversations together nearly every day. I remember him as always being very supportive of young scholars, as I was at the time. He was very generous with his time and especially with his knowledge – he was extremely willing to share the knowledge that he had. I have to admit that I learned a very great deal about Gaelic and about the traditions of the Gaels of Scotland from John in those days.*

For a number of his colleagues in the School of Scottish Studies, 'research' meant the usual academic thing, enquiry based on published and unpublished written works, or derived from carefully-planned studies designed to test a theoretical proposition. All of John MacInnes's work is, indeed, underpinned by constant study, careful reading and thoughtful consideration of the work of previous scholars. But there is one important difference between MacInnes and most other scholars of his generation, and it derives from the fact of his upbringing in the Gàidhealtachd and his inheritance of a Gaelic mind-set that sets great store by knowledge that has stood the test of time. As a consequence, he has been able to assess his own and others' scholarship against the background of his knowledge of the Gàidhealtachd and the Gaelic language. Whereas many of us, having been raised as English-speakers, can only make dim surmises about the life and cultural heritage of the Gaels, MacInnes has the benefit of insider knowledge, gained over a lifetime of listening to people from all parts of the Gàidhealtachd, including members of his own family, at his own hearth. His instincts are sure, and his gift for lateral thinking allows him to deploy those instincts in a variety of relevant contexts to draw multiple and often remarkable conclusions – thoughts that others might have expressed at greater length, but probably not to greater effect. His colleague and former student Dòmhnall Uilleam Stiùbhart, another contributor to this volume, remarks:

> Uairean, nuair a bhios mi ri rannsachadh, bidh beachd-smaoin a' tighinn chugam mu eachdraidh, na mu dhualchas – 's dòcha cuspair a dheanadh deagh *article*. Ach nuair a

[10] For details of the School's founding, see John MacInnes, 'Reminiscences of the School of Scottish Studies of Edinburgh University' in K. Campbell *et al.* (eds), *A Guid Hairst: Collecting and Archiving Scottish Tradition. Essays in Honour of Dr Margaret A. Mackay.* Edinburgh 2013: 229–38.

[11] BBC, *Air mo Chuairt*, introduction to Programme 6.

bheir mi sùil air obair Mhic Aonghuis, chì mi gu robh an aon bheachd air a bhith aige bliadhnachan roimhe, ach gun do dhèilig esan ris ann an aon *sentence*, na eadhon ann an aon nóta.[12]

Sometimes, in the course of my research, I'll get an idea about history, or about tradition – maybe a topic that would make a good article. But when I look at MacInnes's work, I will see that he had the same idea years before, but dealt with it in a single sentence, or even in a single footnote.

There is nothing casual about MacInnes's prodigality. Only too aware of his inclination to grasp at the big ideas, he has disciplined himself to pay close attention to detail. One of his first projects upon joining the staff of the School in 1958 was to provide English translations of stories in *More West Highland Tales,* the second volume in the collection made by J. F. Campbell of Islay. Morag MacLeod, who worked alongside John in the School of Scottish Studies for many years, recalls his approach to translation:

Tha e air leth math air e fhéin a chuir an céill ann am Beurla, agus 's ann ainneamh a thachair duine rium a b'fhearr a smuaintean eadartheangachadh bho Gàidhlig gu Beurla. Ach tha barrachd obrach air cùl na h-obrach seo na shaoileas duine: tha cuimhin agam e ràdh rium gur iomadh duilleag a bhiodh e a' caitheamh air falbh mus biodh e riaraichte leis an oidhirp.[13]

He is extraordinarily good at expressing himself in English, and it's only rarely that I have met anyone better at translating his thoughts from Gaelic to English. But there is more to that sort of work than meets the eye: I recall him telling me that he would have thrown away a lot of paper before he would be satisfied with a project.

Another aspect of MacInnes's scholarly life must be mentioned, as it formed the background to a great deal of his research and publication. This was his fieldwork. As he himself has pointed out, the founders of the School were unclear to what extent fieldwork should be considered 'research'; but for MacInnes and a number of his other colleagues, the work of collecting traditional material in Gaelic and in Scots was of paramount importance.[14] Whereas fieldwork nowadays tends to be more specifically designed to address a particular problem or question, in the early days MacInnes and his colleagues recognized the urgent need to collect as much as possible, across the widest possible range of categories, before the inevitable loss of the older tradition-bearers made such an undertaking impossible:

Thanks to the persistence of individual staff members in pursuing such collecting, often in their spare time and on holiday, the Sound Archive now ensures that today's scholars have a broad corpus of material upon which to base their own research – material that was collected for no immediate purpose other than its own preservation.[14]

MacInnes's own collecting activities reflected his keen awareness that the material he sought was ephemeral. Rather than focusing, as others did, on the Western Isles, which still supported a relatively large Gaelic-speaking population, MacInnes made the early choice to head for areas, many of them on the Scottish mainland, in which Gaelic was spoken only by older people. His recordings from Sutherland and from Perthshire preserve echoes of the speech of these districts as it must have been for centuries, as well as of the traditions that his informants considered important and interesting. His collecting among Gaelic-speaking travellers in the Northeast and in Lewis – *na*

[12] BBC, *Air mo Chuairt*, introduction to Programme 3.

[13] *Ibid.,* introduction to Programme 1.

[14] MacInnes, *op. cit.*, 232.

Torgairean – introduced him to a culture-within-a-culture, and in gaining the trust of these people he was even allowed to learn some of their secret language, the *Beurla Reagairt*. He sought out the remaining natives of St Kilda, now living on the mainland following their evacuation from the island in 1930, and asked them about their traditions and their way of life. He travelled to Canada and interviewed Gaelic-speakers in Cape Breton. His fieldwork in Ross and Cromarty, Inverness-shire and Argyll took in not only the island communities, but also mainland areas where Gaelic was losing ground. In a recent interview for the BBC, he recalled a memorable encounter during a fieldtrip to the Loch Ness area:

> Chaidh mise air feadh na Gàidhealtachd, cuid mhath dhe na h-eileanan, ach bha mi feuchdainn ri dhol a dh'àiteachan ann an tìr mór far nach deach móran a dhèanamh. Agus bhithinn suas mu thaobh Loch Nis, agus nuair a bha mi ann an Cille Chuimein bha mi 'bruidhinn ri Ailig Caimbeul, nach maireann. Agus 's esan, air réir coltais, an duine a thug Béist Loch Nis gu follais an t-saoghail tro na pàipearan naidheachd. Bha Ailig ag innse dhomh mu sheann-duine a bha, an oidhche a bha seo, a' tighinn à Inbhir Nis, agus bha ceum ri taobh a' Loch agus ghabh esan an ceum, anmoch a dh'oidhche, agus chunnaic e 'n creutar air réir coltais ana-ghnàthaichte a bha seo. Bha fhios aige mun a' bhéist có-dhiubh. 'S bha e 'g innse do dhaoine, a's bha maighstir-sgoile 's an àite, agus leabhar aig a' maighster-sgoile far a robh dealbhannan de bheothaichean dhen a h-uile seòrsa. Agus sheall e dhan a' t-seann-duine na dealbhannan agus "O, cha b'e, 's cha b' e, 's cha b' e" gus an tàinig e chon an t-*salamander*. "Siud e!" arsa a' bodach. "Siud a' beothach a chunna mise!" "O, ged-tà," arsa a' maighister-sgoile, "chan eil ann an *salamander* ach beothach beag." "À, ma-tha," ars esan, "'s e a' *salamander* mór a chunnaic mise." Agus cha do thug e riamh ach 'A' *Salamander* Mór' air Béist Loch Nis.[15]
>
> *I travelled throughout the Gàidhealtachd, to a good many of the islands, but I was trying to go to places on the mainland where not much had been done. I used to go up to Loch Ness-side, and when I was in Fort Augustus I was speaking to the late Alec Campbell. It would appear that he was the one who brought the Loch Ness Monster to the world's notice through the newspapers. Alec told me about an old man who, this particular night, was coming from Inverness, and he took a path by the side of the Loch, late at night, and he saw this unnatural-looking creature. He knew about the Beast, anyway. And he was telling people about it. And there was a schoolmaster in the place who had a book containing pictures of all sorts of animals. He showed the pictures to the old man, who said "No; no; it's not that one" until he came to the salamander. "That's it!" he cried. "That's the animal that I saw!" "Oh," said the schoolmaster, "but the salamander is only a small creature." "Even so," said the old man, "it's the big salamander that I saw." And all he ever called the Loch Ness Monster after that was 'The Big Salamander.'*

One of MacInnes's favourite informants was Donald Sinclair (Dòmhnall Chaluim Bàin) of Baile Phuil, Tiree. The *Tobar an Dualchais* website contains 618 items recorded by MacInnes from Donald Sinclair between 1960 and 1970 – songs, stories, verse, Fenian lore, historical accounts and anecdotes involving Tiree people. The man had an extrordinary grasp of all sorts of traditional material, and a wonderfully vivid way of expressing himself:

> Bha e anabarrach math air e fhéin a chur an céill, Dòmhnull Chaluim Bàin. Nuair a bha e 'na bhalachan bha e 'g obair aig dìthis bhràithrean – Maighstir Niall agus Maighstir Calum. Agus tha e coltach gur h-e duine anabarrach mór a bha ann am

[15] BBC, *Air mo Chuairt*, Programme 8.

Maighstir Calum. Agus bhiodh e aig bòrd a' chidsin a' sgrìobhadh cùnntaisean 's rudan. Agus "bha na crògain aige cho mór" bha Dòmhnull a' ràdh, "shaoilidh tu gur h-e snathaid mhór a bha 's a' pheann." Turus eile, chunnaic e seann-duine. Bha a duine a bha seo, bha e 'fàs gu math aosda, 's cha robh e tighinn a-mach idir. "Ach chunnaic mise e," arsa Dòmhnull, "a's b' e sin an coltas," ars esan, "duine mór lomachnàmhach lachdunn granna, coltach ri leannan a bhiodh aig taidhbhs'!" Agus bha e an còmhnaidh cho beòthail 'na chainnt.[16]

He was remarkably good at expressing himself, Dòmhnall Chaluim Bàin. When he was a boy he worked for two brothers – Mr Neil and Mr Calum. It would appear that Mr Calum was an extraordinarily large man. He used to sit at the kitchen table writing accounts and so forth; and "his hands were so big", Donald said, "that you'd think that the pen was nothing but a bodkin." Another time, he saw an old fellow. This old man was getting old, and he didn't come out at all. "But I saw him," said Donald, "and I'll tell you what he looked like," he said: "a big, raw-boned, dun-coloured, ugly man, like a sweetheart that a ghost might have!" His conversation was always so lively.

One could fill pages with anecdotes like this. Indeed, anyone who knows John MacInnes will be aware of his considerable gifts as a raconteur, a skill that was long ago recognized by the BBC and other broadcasters. His distinctive speaking voice has been a presence on the airwaves for many years, as the former Managing Editor of BBC Gàidhlig, Jo MacDonald, recalled in her introduction to the final programme in the series *Air mo Chuairt*, from which we have been quoting throughout this introductory sketch:

Thairis air na seachdainnean a dh'fhalbh tha sinn air cluintinn mu Iain Mac Aonghuis mar shàr-sgoilear Gàidhlig, mar sheanchaidh, mar eòlaiche litreachais is eachtraidh, mar dhuine aig a bheil eòlas farsaing air iomadach cuspair, mar dhuine a bha – agus a tha – fialaidh leis an eòlas sin, agus a tha taiceil do sgoilearan òga, agus do sheinneadearan agus do luchd ciùil. Agus tha e taiceil cuideachd do chraoladairean. Cha b'ann an-dé a thoisich Iain Mac Aonghuis a' sgaoileadh fiosrachadh mu litreachas, mu bheul-aithris, mu dhùthchas 's mu dhualchas nan Gàidheal, gu h-àraid air rèidio. Có-dhiubh bha e 'g innse dhuinn mu òrain a bu toil leis – nam measg sin, tha cuimhn' a'm bha òrain leithid *Smeòrach Chlann Raghnaill*, *Cumha Mhàrtainn a' Bhealaich,* agus *Nan ceadaicheadh an tìde dhomh* ann an aon phrògram. Neo, is dòcha gura h-ann air bàrdachd a bha e 'bruidhinn – bàrdachd na seachdamh 's na h-ochdamh linn deug, mar eisimpleir, bàrdachd leitheid *Òran Gaoil do Bhràigh Mhàr* no *Dàn do Sheumas Mór, Mormhair Shléite*, no *Latha Inbhir Lóchaidh*. 'S iomadh neach mun cuala sinn bhuaidhe, 's saoil leam fhìn gun cluinn mi e an-dràsda fhìn ag innse mun Tirisdeach bha 'na sgiobair air an tì-*clipper* an *Teiping*, a's mun a' duine mu dheireadh aig a robh Gàidhlig air Eilean Arainn, a's mu *John the Bard* ann an Loch Abar. 'S iomadh leabhar is taisbeanadh thairis air na bliadhnaichean air an do rinn e léirmheas do luchd éisdeachd Radio nan Gàidheal. 'S iomadh bàrd air an tug e iomradh – bho Dhunnchadh Bàn 's Mac Mhaighstir Alasdair gu Somhairle Mac Gill-Eàin 's Iain Crichton Mac a' Ghobhainn. Tha mi an dòchas gum bi a ghuth ri chluintinn air Radio nan Gàidheal airson iomadh bliadhna fhathast.[17]

Over the past weeks we have heard about John MacInnes as a pre-eminent Gaelic scholar, as a seanchaidh, *as an expert in literature and history, as a man of wide*

---

[16] *Ibid.*, Programme 8.

[17] *Ibid.*, Introduction to Programme 8.

knowledge on many topics, as a person who was – and is – generous with that knowledge, and who is supportive of young scholars, and of singers and musicians. He has also been supportive of broadcasters. It wasn't yesterday that John MacInnes began broadcasting on the literature, oral tradition, and heritage of the Gael, especially on the radio, whether he was telling us about his favourite songs – I recall him once discussing Smeòrach Chlann Raghnaill, Cumha Mhàrtainn a' Bhealaich, *and* Nan ceadaicheadh an tìde dhomh *in the same programme – or talking about poetry – the poetry of the seventeenth and eighteenth centuries, for example, poetry like* Òran Gaoil do Bhràigh Mhàr *or* Dàn do Sheumas Mór, Mormhair Shléite, *or* Latha Inbhir Lòchaidh. *And it's many a person we first heard of from him. I can still hear him telling about the Tiree man who was master of the tea-clipper* Taeping, *about the man who was the last Gaelic-speaker in the Isle of Aran, and about 'John the Bard' in Lochaber. He has reviewed countless books and exhibitions for Radio nan Gàidheal listeners, and discussed many a poet – from Duncan Bàn MacIntyre and Alasdair Mac Mhaisghstir Alasdair to Sorley Maclean and Iain Crichton Smith. May his voice be heard on Radio nan Gàidheal for many years yet.*

The late Rev. William Matheson famously remarked of John MacInnes that he was 'the last of our native scholars'. This assessment contains a world of meaning, and one that may not be apparent at first glance. MacInnes is not the last Gael to have achieved distinction in academic life – there have been plenty of others in his own and subsequent generations. What distinguishes him from these is that the knowledge upon which his scholarship is based – of the Gaelic language, of the Gàidhealtachd, of its history and its culture – was gained not through formal study in an academic setting, but primarily from his own home and from the communities in which he grew up. The academic regimen that he endured in school was designed to discourage pupils from even speaking their native language, let alone taking a scholarly interest in it or in the cultural heritage that depended upon it. As an undergraduate at Edinburgh University, MacInnes studied English literature, English language, linguistics, philosophy and history – study that undoubtedly sharpened his mind and imparted the mental rigour necessary to a successful academic career. But his formal study of Gaelic or 'Celtic' subject matter did not begin until he was a postgraduate, when he was supposedly engaged in research in English and Germanic languages. It was therefore his own upbringing that supplied the knowledge upon which his academic career ultimately rested, knowledge to which he then applied the mental tools that his formal education had given him.

In following this path MacInnes was not unique. Many Gaels followed professions that encouraged thoughtful and rigorous habits of mind. His own father, like most ministers, was a learned man, deeply engaged with questions and causes requiring thoughtful scrutiny and articulate response. His grand-uncle Malcolm, an advocate who, in retirement, took up the scholarly re-edition of Alexander Nicolson's *Gaelic Proverbs*, was also a highly-regarded piper and competition adjudicator who was not afraid to take on the piping establishment at long distance – from Durban, South Africa – in the columns of the *Oban Times* and the *Inverness Courier*. Men like these published volumes of sermons or poetry, engaged in philosophical debate, and shaped the Gaels' response to the political and social forces that impinged ever more urgently upon the Gàidhealtachd. At the most basic level, they were the *seanchaidhean,* those whose prodigious memories and intellectual gifts gave them authority in matters relating to their communities' historical and cultural heritage.

Generations of such men were undoubtedly the 'native scholars' whom William Matheson had in mind, and the models for John MacInnes's own life. In contrast to most of the academic Gaels of his own and preceding generations – men like W. J. Watson, Derick Thomson, Angus Matheson, and William Matheson himself – MacInnes derived his scholarly authority not from years of formal study of the Celtic languages and of Gaelic literature, but from what he had learned before he entered university at all. He was fortunate in possessing a scholarly inclination; he excelled at academic study; he became a prodigiously persuasive writer, lecturer, and broadcaster; and he recognised – at just the right moment, when the founding of the School of Scottish Studies made such a career trajectory possible – that he could live an academic life while putting these skills to the service of his own people. By helping his fellow Gaels gain a deeper understanding of and love for the linguistic and cultural heritage which their education had deemed irrelevant; by helping his academic colleagues appreciate the broad sweep and rich subtlety of Gaelic literature, history, song and *seanchas* and their important contribution to the identity of the Scottish people; and by raising awareness of these riches among non-Gaels, John MacInnes has performed a unique service to his country, to his people, and to his friends.

In grateful recognition that he did so, and in thanksgiving for his work, his scholarship and his excellent company, this volume is offered to John MacInnes – Iain Mac Aonghuis – Iain mac Ruairidh mhic Iain mhic Iain mhic Nèill mhic Mhaol Mhoire mhic Iain mhic Mhaol Chaluim – with love and affection.

Acknowledgements

A book of this nature is a collaborative effort. The editor's gratitude to the following people goes well beyond her ability to express:

- To Michael Newton, who in 2011 pointed out to me the lamentable fact that a volume celebrating John MacInnes's life and achievements was well overdue;
- To my colleagues in Celtic and Scottish Studies at the University of Edinburgh, for their encouragement and support, not least of which was the provision of work-space for this project;
- To the Gaelic Books Council / Comhairle nan Leabhraichean Gàidhlig for supporting costs of publication;
- To BBC Radio nan Gàidheal for allowing quotation of passages from their series *Air mo Chuairt* in the brief biography of John MacInnes provided here;
- To all of those (you know who you are) who served as 'peer reviewers' for the articles in this volume;
- To Rachel Meek, Ronald Black, and John Shaw, whose editorial advice and careful proofreading prevented many an error;
- To the Editorial Board of *Scottish Studies* for allowing publication of this book as a volume in that journal, and to Dr John Shaw, its permanent editor, for allowing me a free hand in editorial decision-making, for his painstaking help in the editing of Gaelic-language material, and for his sure guidance on a wide variety of matters arising in the course of this project;
- To all of John MacInnes's friends, students and colleagues who contributed articles to this *Festschrift*, and who patiently put up with my pestering, cajoling, and threats over many months;
- And above all to John himself, and to his wife Wendy, whose active participation in this project – in suggesting the names of possible contributors, in answering endless questions, and in putting up with countless hours of my company over the past three years – has greatly increased the chances that this volume will stand to his credit as a work of scholarship in its own right.

Tapadh leibh.

Virginia Blankenhorn
Edinburgh, February 2014

‘Recorded by the School of Scottish Studies…’ The Impact of the Tape-Recorder In a Rural Community

MARGARET BENNETT

Most people in Scotland interested in traditional songs and stories will have heard the phrase ‘they were recorded by the School of Scottish Studies’. From 1951, when the School was founded, those whose songs, stories and oral traditions were of interest to collectors and research staff enjoyed the prestige of having their names linked with what has become our national collection. For many years, the fact that a singer or story-teller had been ‘recorded by the School of Scottish Studies’ would often form part of an introduction at a ceilidh or a concert. Today, with much of the archived material available on the website *Tobar an Dualchais / Kist o’ Riches*, singers of a younger generation still mention that the song they are about to perform was ‘recorded by the School of Scottish Studies’, and may even mention the name of the ‘source-singer’ from whose recording they learned it.

Growing up in Skye, I first became aware of the School’s activities in the 1950s, though I did not encounter the phrase until 1960, when there appeared on the market a twelve-inch LP entitled *Gaelic and Scots Folksongs*, accompanied by a booklet of notes by Hamish Henderson and James Ross. One of the singers featured on this LP was Duncan Beaton – *Donnchadh Peutan,* who had been recorded for the Linguistic Survey of Scotland in the late 1940s. He was a crofter in Uig who had been a neighbour of my grandparents, and whose remarkable singing is still remembered though he died in 1955.[1] Since my family had known Duncan, and because of the high esteem he had enjoyed in our community, our copy of this LP became well-worn at Band 4: *’S mi air m’ uilinn ’sa’ leabaidh’* – and almost as often as it was played, it was followed by a comment on the man himself, his repertoire, his remarkable breath-control (‘a whole verse in one breath!’), and how wonderful it was that he had not only been recorded, but that his singing had been chosen for inclusion on this record. Despite the fact that Duncan had been recorded before the School of Scottish Studies came into being, this commercially-available recording inevitably linked his name with that of the School and its growing collection.

In 1953, several years before his appointment to the School of Scottish Studies, John MacInnes made a fieldtrip to Skye, during which he recorded several singers, adding a significant contribution to the archive. In a recent conversation with me, he recalled:

> I don’t remember a time when Gaelic songs weren’t one of my greatest interests.... I had uncles who sang – there were singers everywhere and from the age of sixteen I started learning [songs], collecting them.... So [in June 1953, after finishing at University] I borrowed a tape-recorder from the School of Scottish Studies, and they gave me blank tapes.... The only training was on how to use the machine, as I had done an earlier recording for the Linguistic Survey.[2]

[1] Duncan Beaton was recorded in the late 1940s by the late Derick Thomson for the Linguistic Survey of Scotland, whose recordings subsequently became part of the Archives of the School of Scottish Studies. Only one of these recordings, of the song *Allt an t-Siùcair*, has so far been made available through the *Tobar an Dualchais* website, but it gives a sense of why this singer enjoyed the reputation he did; see www.tobarandualchais.org., Track ID 88148.

[2] Private conversation, 19 December 2012.

Although John's trip coincided with the Portree Mòd, he did not confine himself to recording the Mòd singers, but also took the opportunity to visit other tradition-bearers in the community, people from whom – as the archived tapes reveal – he recorded a significant number of local legends, tales and traditions. It was on this fieldtrip that John MacInnes recorded my mother, Peigi Bennett (née Stewart, b.1919) – *Peigi Iain Phàdruig* – whom he had heard singing at the Mòd that year. The song she sang, *Fhleasgaich òig ma chuir thu cùl rium*, was one that John had not heard before, and he recalls that she told him she had learned it from Katie Anne Nicolson from Braes.[3]

My mother is now 94 years old, and, as far as I know, the only one of those whom John MacInnes recorded at that time who is still living. Although she claims to have a poor memory, she was able to recall the occasion when I asked her about it recently:

> MB: Do you remember John MacInnes recording you in Portree?
>
> Peigi: Yes, it was in Ina Douglas's house. There was a flat attached to the Drill Hall and the Douglases lived in it. .... John and Dr Allan [Macdonald] heard me singing this song at the Mòd and wanted to record it because they'd never heard it before.... [*She hums the song*] But it wasn't a good place that we were recording in, because it was a sort of attic and it was closed in and I felt that my voice was coming back at me. It wasn't a good place [acoustically]...
>
> MB: Where did you learn that song?
>
> Peigi: I might have learned it at school. You see, there used to be a singing teacher going round, the *Bodach Seinn,* so it could have been then. That's a long time ago [mid-1920s to mid-30s].

As John remembered Peigi telling him where she learned the song, I returned to the topic several weeks later and resumed the conversation:

> MB: Do you remember a Katie Ann Nicolson?
>
> Peigi: Oh yes! She was a lovely singer. Miss Nicolson – she used to teach the seniors in Uig School – she was my teacher too. She was from Braes and she was full of songs. She used to get us ready for the Mòd... (*begins to sing) A' fhleasgaich ùr, leanainn thu.* I believe that was one of them.
>
> MB: Oh yes, you taught me that. And what about *Fhleasgaich òig, ma chuir thu cùl rium?*
>
> Peigi: Oh yes, I believe that was one of Miss Nicolson's songs. Oh, she was a lovely teacher.... Have you got my notebook, Margaret? It's in that. And that's the song I sang for John MacInnes.

[3] The 7-inch reel is archived at the School of Scottish Studies. On the lid of the box is SA 1953/167, Reel No. 6, a list of names of singers, titles of songs, and dates of recordings (June 24 and 25). Neither the name of the fieldworker (John MacInnes) nor place recorded (Portree) appears, but both were noted in the tape-index and transcription book. The first track was Mrs Bennet [*sic*]: *Fhleasgaich òig ma chuir thu cùl rium.* To hear the song, go to www.tobarandualchais.org, Track ID 12329. This is the only recording of this song that exists in the School of Scottish Studies Archives.

Hò rinn ò hi rì ho rò u
Hao ri rì ho rò u éile
Hò rinn ò hi rì ho rò u.

1	Fhleasgaich òig ma chuir thu cùl rium Feuch gur h-ì an diugh a thréig thu.	*Young lad, if you have turned your back on me / You can be sure (in the first place) that it was she who betrayed* you.
2	Ghabh thu ’n t-seann té leis an stòras Ged a’ bha sin òg le chéile.	*You took the old[er] woman with the wealth / although we were young together.*
3	Càch a’ dannsa aig do bhanais ’S mis’ ’gam sgaradh o mo chléibhe.	*Others [are] dancing at your wedding / and here I am tearing my heart out.*
4	’S beag a shaoil mi anns an àm sin Gum biodh do luaidh air aon té eile.	*Little did I think at the time / That you would give your love to any other.*[4]

The notebook to which Peigi referred was one she began keeping in her teens. In it she wrote certain songs, including this one,[5] though well-known songs such as *Fear a Bhàta* would not be included, as the notebook was kept only for the songs she heard that had not been published – ‘it was important not to lose them.’[6] Peigi also jotted down the melody of some songs in sol-fa notation, ‘just in case someone else happened to want the tune’. When the songs began to appear in print, the notebook began to lose its value to her. In 2012, however, Ainsley Hamill, a student at the

[4] The text and translation given here were recently (2013) supplied from memory by Peigi herself, and the text was found to be identical to what she wrote in her notebook when she first learned the song. Regarding the second line of the first stanza, she explained: ‘The young woman singing the song is sure that it was the older woman who put him up to the betrayal – in other words, she set him up to forsake his first love.’ Referring to the expression *Feuch gur...*, she said, ‘That’s what we’d say to someone, in the sense of “you can be darned well sure that something or other went on”. It’s a kind of a warning, a caution.’

[5] Alan Bruford notes that ‘A typical song notebook...seems to have been one written mainly when the compiler was young, probably under twenty....’ (Bruford 1986: 102).

[6] On a fieldwork trip to Arisaig in 1906, Lucy Broadwood (1858–1929) noted that 30-year-old Kate MacLean, whose home contained copies of MacKenzie’s *Sar-Obair* (1841) and Sinclair’s *An t-Oranaiche* (1879), was ‘singularly intelligent at avoiding published songs’ for the recording (Broadwood *et al.* 1931: 281).

Royal Conservatoire of Scotland, compared my mother's notebook texts to those of the same songs in published collections, and discovered no identical versions.[7]

Peigi shared her interest in Gaelic song with her grandson, composer and musician Martyn Bennett (1971–2005), who himself recorded several Gaelic tradition-bearers, including Flora MacNeil and John MacInnes (Bennett 2006: 59–63). He was deeply interested in the older styles of Gaelic singing, and regretted the demise of tradition with the new generation's preference for songs easily accompanied by three chords on the guitar. When Peigi told Martyn that her grandfather, Peter Stewart, had been recorded on wax cylinder by Marjory Kennedy Fraser, he was inspired to create a song cycle to include this recording as well as the 1953 recording of Peigi singing *Fhleasgaich òig, ma chuir thu cùl rium.* Within a soundscape of old and new, he hoped to reflect the evolution of family music-making across five generations.[8]

Though the Kennedy Fraser recording had been made before Peigi was born, the act of being recorded had clearly made an impact, as Peigi could remember being told about it from a very early age:

> She was collecting old songs, and my grandfather must have known a lot of old songs. And she was staying in the shooting lodge, 'Conon Lodge' (it became the doctor's house later on) and she was wanting people to sing so that she could record them – you know, so people would remember all the old songs. So she *sent* for him – she didn't go to Glenconon; my grandfather went along to the Lodge and she recorded him there. [Peigi begins to sing one of them] *Air maduinn dhomh 's mi sràideaireachd …* Oh, yes my father used to sing that too – and so did Doctor Allan. Now he had a lot of old songs – I believe he might have got that one from my father.

Although none of the singers or their families ever heard wax cylinder recordings until the end of the twentieth century, and very few had access to Mrs Kennedy Fraser's *Songs of the Hebrides*, it was the very act of being recorded that lent distinction to these singers and their communities. In Kennedy Fraser's day, Skye crofters with their 'great genius for music and mechanics' (Martin 1716:199) would have been just as fascinated with the wax-cylinder recorder as later generations were with the reel-to-reel tape recorders of John MacInnes's time. Fieldworkers of the tape-recorder era remember the external microphones, stands, heavy batteries, adapters (13 amp, 15 amp, round pins, square pins, and, just in case, a two-pin), extension cables and spare reels, not to mention the crawling behind couches to look for plugs, fixing fuses, sitting on the floor and changing reels mid-sentence. To those who were recorded, however, the lasting memory is that they were 'recorded by the School of Scottish Studies'. For sixty years that has helped validate tradition-bearers – for some, it has even become something of a badge of office, as it is the fact of *being recorded* that carries the weight – and helped them to realise that the songs, stories and traditional lore that they inherited from previous generations were of value not just to them, but to people beyond the Gàidhealtachd, to the people of Scotland as a whole, and to the world beyond.

---

[7] Ainsley Hamill, unpublished research paper, Royal Conservatoire of Scotland, 2012.

[8] Martyn Bennett's CD 'Glen Lyon' includes this track from SA1953/ as well as two of the songs recorded c. 1910 by Marjory Kennedy Fraser.

Sources

BENNETT, MARGARET.

1999 'From Kennedy-Fraser to the Jimmy Shandrix Experience in Five Generations'. Fintan Vallely *et al.* (eds), *Crosbhealach an Cheoil – The Crossroads Conference 1996: Tradition and Change in Irish Traditional Music*. Dublin.

2006 *It's Not the Time You Have: Notes and Memories of Music-Making with Martyn Bennett.* Edinburgh.

BROADWOOD, LUCY E., FRANK HOWES, A. G. GILCHRIST AND A. MARTIN FREEMAN.

1931 'Twenty Gaelic Songs'. *Journal of the Folk-Song Society* 8/35: 280-303.

BRUFORD, ALAN.

1986 'Song Manuscripts and the Acquisition of Song Repertoires in Orkney and Shetland'. Ian Russell (ed.), *Singer, Song and Scholar*. Sheffield: 95–116.

GRAINGER, PERCY.

1908 'Collecting with the Phonograph'. *Journal of the Folk-Song Society,* 3/12: 147–162.

MACINNES, JOHN.

2006 'The Choral Tradition in Scottish Gaelic Songs'. Michael Newton (ed.), *Dùthchas Nan Gàidheal: Selected Essays of John MacInnes*. Edinburgh: 211–29.

MARTIN, MARTIN.

1716 *Description of the Western Isles of Scotland circa 1695.* Edinburgh.

SMITH, THÉRÈSE.

2003 'Untranscribed Voices from the past: Music and Folklore'. *Béaloideas* 71: 55–74.

Sound Recordings

BENNETT, MARTYN AND MARGARET BENNETT.

[1998] 2010 *Glen Lyon: A Song Cycle.* CD with notes. Grace Note Publications GNPCD0009.

SCHOOL OF SCOTTISH STUDIES, UNIVERSITY OF EDINBURGH.

1960 Gaelic and Scots Folk Tales; Gaelic and Scots Folk Songs; Scottish Instrumental Music. Selection by Calum Maclean and others. Set of three LPs with accompanying booklet of notes by John MacInnes (tales), James Ross and Hamish Henderson (songs), and Francis Collinson (instrumental music). Edinburgh.

'Griogal Cridhe'
Aspects of Transmission in the Lament for Griogair Ruadh Mac Griogair of Glen Strae

V. S. BLANKENHORN

With the advent of *Tobar an Dualchais* (www.tobarandualchais.co.uk), the online trove of materials recorded from oral tradition during the last century and held by the National Trust for Scotland, the BBC, and the sound archive of the School of Scottish Studies, it has become easier to integrate study of published and manuscript versions of traditional materials – most of which date from the nineteenth and early twentieth centuries – with more recent orally-transmitted versions of the same materials. Such study has the potential to help us understand the workings of oral transmission over time, to evaluate the printed and manuscript sources of an earlier day, and to understand the complex inter-relationship between written and orally-transmitted traditional materials in the Gàidhealtachd itself.

The song commonly known as *Griogal Cridhe* offers an excellent opportunity for such study. Thanks to an important article by Glasgow historian Martin MacGregor, we know when, by whom, and in what circumstances the song was composed.[1] It survived solely in oral tradition – perhaps (but not necessarily) supported by manuscript sources now lost – for some 243 years, from its probable composition in 1570 until its appearance in Patrick Turner's *Comhchruinneacha do dh' Orain Taghta, Ghaidhealach* in 1813. Subsequently, the song has been regularly anthologised, and the relationship between the published versions and ongoing oral transmission will be a focus of our discussion here. Judging from the evidence of sound recordings, variants of the song and accounts of its composition remained current throughout the Gàidhealtachd into the middle years of the last century, and even today the song remains a popular choice among platform-singers, Gaelic choral societies, and recording-artists in the 'traditional' genre.

1.0 Historical Background

Long the subject of scholarly speculation, the circumstances that inspired the lament for *Griogair Ruadh* – red-haired Gregor MacGregor of Glen Strae – have now been thoroughly investigated. Martin MacGregor's study shows that the events mentioned in the poem can be substantiated from contemporary records, and supports the view that the most likely author of the verses was Marion Campbell (*Mór nighean Dhonnchaidh*), daughter of Duncan Campbell of Glenlyon *(Donnchadh Ruadh na Féile),* who was widowed by those events. The value of MacGregor's investigation lies not only in its documentation and determination of the facts of the case, but also in its confirmation of the tenacity and accuracy of the oral tradition, which appears to have preserved the essence of the poem with remarkable fidelity despite the passage of nearly two-and-a-half centuries between its composition and its earliest appearance in written records.

While our topic here is not history *per se*, a brief summary of MacGregor's case may be useful. The relationship between Griogair Ruadh and his wife was, from beginning to end, shaped and conditioned by the turbulent relationship between their two kindreds: the MacGregors of Glen Strae and the Campbells of Glenlyon, a branch of the Campbells of Glenorchy. While it has been long

[1] Martin MacGregor, '"Surely one of the greatest poems ever made in Britain": The Lament for Griogair Ruadh MacGregor of Glen Strae and its Historical Background'. E. J. Cowan and D. Gifford (eds), *The Polar Twins*. Edinburgh 1999: 114–153.

assumed that the Campbells had always been at loggerheads with their MacGregor neighbours, in fact the MacGregors had, for much of the 130 years prior to the execution of Griogair Ruadh, lived in accommodation with the Campbells, and held their ancestral lands in Glen Strae 'as vassals of the Campbell chiefs' (MacGregor 1999: 118). The Glenorchy Campbells' appropriation of lands to the east, which by 1513 had given the Campbells control of a large portion of Breadalbane, was facilitated by the support of the MacGregors.

After 1513, however, the power of the Campbells of Glenorchy fell into something of a decline, and the Earl of Argyll assigned the services of the MacGregors to Iain Campbell of Cawdor, whose own expansionist efforts they likewise supported. During this period the MacGregors continued to flourish as clients of the Campbells, although no longer bound to serve the Campbells of Glenorchy.

In 1550 Colin Campbell – *Cailean Liath* ('Grey Colin') as he is referred to in the poem – became chieftain of the Glenorchy Campbells. Under his leadership and that of his son *Donnchadh Dubh a' Churraic* ('Black Duncan of the Cowl'), the Campbells of Glenorchy emerged from their period of stagnation and went on the offensive once again, using all manner of means – most of them perfectly legal if not particularly humane – to ensure the subjugation of rival kindreds. As events were to prove, they took particularly seriously the threat posed by their lively and prosperous neighbours and erstwhile military supporters, the MacGregors.

In order to regain control of this troublesome kindred, Cailean Liath sought by various means to push the chief of the MacGregors into a corner. He pressed some of the MacGregor kin-groups to accept bonds of manrent, thereby ensuring their loyalty to him; he evicted an important member of the clan from a MacGregor stronghold at Balloch *(Bealach)*, the subsequent site of Cailean Liath's own fortress and of Griogair Ruadh's beheading; and he persuaded the Earl of Argyll to reassign the services of the MacGregors to himself. Most crucially, he 'purchased the superiority of Glen Strae, and the ward and marriage of Griogair Ruadh' from Argyll, thereby ensuring his legal right to the MacGregor homelands and giving him the tools he would need, as he supposed, to turn the young chieftain of the MacGregors into a toothless client who could pose no threat to him (MacGregor: 120).

In late 1562, when the young Griogair Ruadh had newly come of age and assumed leadership of his kindred, Campbell of Glenorchy placed before him an awful choice: the MacGregors would be permitted to retain possession of their ancestral lands in Glen Strae, but only on condition that Griogair accede to 'certain unspecified legal restrictions' and that he surrender to Cailean Liath two clansmen who had recently killed one of Campbell's servants. This dilemma, as Martin MacGregor makes clear, could not have been more painful, for 'if he wished to retain Glen Strae, the *dùthaich* of his clan, it would be at the price of accepting conditions which would reduce him to a degree of vassalage unknown to any of his predecessors, and manifestly compromise his authority as chief' (MacGregor: 120). Cailean Liath's proposal came with a deadline: 1 January 1563.

Griogair Ruadh sent his answer on the night of 7 December 1562, when he and a band of his clansmen attacked two groups of Campbells and their followers as they returned to Glenlyon from a fair in Perth. In the first attack they set fire to an inn, killing eight men; and later the same night they fired a barn and captured the men sleeping there, one of whom was later killed. (This latter group was led by Pàdraig, brother of Duncan Campbell of Glenlyon, who a few years later became Griogair Ruadh's father-in-law.) So began a period of intense conflict between the Campbells and MacGregors, which lasted – with one brief hiatus – until 1570, when Griogair Ruadh was executed.

It was probably during the brief normalisation of relations between the two clans, which lasted from late in 1565 until the summer of 1567, that Griogair Ruadh married the daughter of Duncan Campbell of Glenlyon, an uncle and close ally of Cailean Liath, and a man to whom some of the victims of the 1562 MacGregor raids had been connected.[2] Even if there were no other evidence for

[2] This cease-fire had nothing to do with a genuine rapprochement, but rather resulted from a complex political situation that brought a temporary halt to the feud; see *ibid.*, 121.

it – and there is – the emotionally charged quality of the poetry strongly argues that this was a love match.[3] Martin MacGregor suggests, in fact, that it was the initial refusal of Marion's father to countenance the marriage which may have prompted Griogair Ruadh to respond to Cailean Liath's 'offer' by launching raids not against Glenorchy but against the Campbells of Glenlyon (MacGregor 1999: 125).

Conflict between the two kindreds resumed in late July, 1567, following the fall of Mary Queen of Scots and the outbreak of civil war in Scotland. Two years later, on 1 August 1569, Griogair Ruadh was taken unawares by a group of Campbells that included his father-in-law, Duncan Campbell of Glenlyon. He was held for the next eight months in Cailean Liath's stronghold at Balloch, while the Campbells petitioned the Scottish crown for legal sanction to execute him. This they finally obtained, and Griogair Ruadh was beheaded – apparently by Cailean Liath himself – at Balloch, at the east end of Loch Tay, on 7 April 1570.[4]

Before he died, Griogair Ruadh's wife had borne him one son, Alasdair Ruadh. On the day of his execution, she was pregnant with a second, Iain Dubh. Given the length of time involved, she must have conceived this child on a date very close to that of Griogair's capture, and given birth very near the time of his execution. Her suffering during those eight months can only be imagined.

Not least of Martin MacGregor's achievements in the article summarized here is his persuasive identification of Raibeart Menzies of Comrie, second husband of Griogair Ruadh's young widow, as the mysterious *'baran crìon na dalach'* mentioned in the poem. Comrie lies on the south bank of the Lyon near its junction with the River Tay, occupying the sort of alluvial land to which one might refer as *na dalach,* 'of the river-meadow' – land which the Menzies family had possessed for at least a century prior to these events. Contemporary documents reveal that both Raibeart Menzies and his father were styled 'baron', and it is likely that the family enjoyed the sort of comfort and prosperity mentioned in the poem. The Menzies family were loyal supporters of the Campbells, and so offered a safe repository for Campbell of Glenlyon's troublesome daughter and her children. MacGregor suggests that this marriage may have taken place shortly after the execution of Griogair Ruadh, and therefore that the poem reflects not only her grief at the loss of her first husband, but also her unhappiness in the home of her second (MacGregor 1999: 132–5).

2.0 The Text

In the following paragraphs we shall survey the published and unpublished versions of the text, along with associated textual materials such as background notes, in order to determine what conclusions we can legitimately draw regarding the relationships among them.

2.1 Published versions

As noted above, the poem first appears in writing in the collection of Gaelic songs published by Padruig Mac an Tuairneir in 1813, where it is preceded by the following headnote (Turner: 286):

> *Cumha le nighean do Dhonnacha dubh, Moirfhear Bhraigh-dealbunn, an uair a thug a h-athair, agus a brathair an ceann deth a fear, Griogair Mac Griogair, agus a ciad leanabh air a glùn.*
>
> A lament by a daughter of Black Duncan, Lord of Breadalbane, when her father and her brother beheaded her husband, Griogair Mac Gregor, while her first child was on her knee.

[3] An earlier poem attributed to Mór Chaimbeul, *Righ gur mór mo chuid mhulaid*, expresses the intensity of her longing for Griogair and her rage at being forbidden to marry him; see *ibid.,* 116–8 (discussion) and 140–1 (text and translation).

[4] MacGregor 1999: 124 and n. 31. Balloch was located at the site of what is now Taymouth Castle.

Turner's identification of the author as a daughter of Donnchadh Dubh, son of Campbell of Glenorchy, is impossible, as Donnchadh was only 20 years old at the time of Griogair's execution. Further confusion arises when he identifies *nighean an Ruthainich* – Katherine Ruthven, wife of Cailean Liath and mother of Donnchadh Dubh – as the *poet's* mother, presumably under the impression that Katherine was Donnchadh's wife rather than Cailean's. Martin MacGregor argues that Turner's genealogical confusion led him to transpose the second couplets of stanzas 6 and 7 in order 'to bring the reference to *nighean an Ruadhanaich* into the same verse as the reference to *m'athair,* "my father", thereby creating a stronger impression that these two were man and wife' (MacGregor: 129–30). In fairness, the error may have appeared in the text as Turner collected it – his source is unknown – and may be understandable given the frequency with which the same given names tend to occur in highland genealogies and the length of time which had elapsed since the events occurred.

In what follows, stanza-numbers are preceded by a letter indicating the source of the text – in this case, 'T' for 'Turner' – in order to facilitate subsequent comparison with other versions we shall be examining.

T1	*Moch maduinn air la lunasd',* *Bha mi sugradh marr-ri m' ghradh;* *Ach mu 'n d' thainig meadhon latha,* *Bha mo chridhe air a chradh.*	Early on the first of August I was sporting with my love, But before midday had come, my heart was left in ruins.
T2	Ochain, ochain, ochain uiridh, 'S goirt mo chridhe laoigh, Ochain, ochain, ochain uiridh, Cha chluinn t-athair ar caoidh.[5]	*Ochain, ochain, ochain uiridh, sore is my heart, my dear child;* *Ochain, ochain, ochain uiridh, your father won't hear our cries.*[5]
T3	*Mallachd aig maithibh 's aig cairdean,* *Rinn mo chradh air an doigh;* *Thainig gun fhios air mo ghradh-sa,* *'Sa thug fo smachd e le foill.*	A curse on nobles and relations who have destroyed me thus; Who came upon my love unawares, and took him prisoner by treachery.
T4	*Na 'm biodh da fhear-dheug deth chinneadh* *'S mo Ghriogair air an ceann* *Cha bhiodh mo shuil a sileadh dheur,* *No mo leanabh fein gun daimh.*	Had there been twelve of his kinsmen, with my Gregor at their head, My eye would not be weeping tears, nor my child left friendless.
T5	*Chuir iad a cheann air ploc daraich,* *'S dhoirt iad fhuil mu lar* *Na 'm biodh agam-sa 'n sin cupan,* *Dh' olainn d'i mo shadh.*	They put his head on an oaken block and spilled his blood on the ground, If I had had a cup there, I'd have drunk my fill of it.
T6	*'S truagh nach robh m' athair an galar,* *Agus Cailein ann am plaigh;* *Ged bhiodh nighean an Ruthainaich* *Suathadh bas a's lamh.*	It's a pity my father was not taken in illness, and Colin with the plague, Even though Ruthven's daughter would be left wringing her hands.

5 Remarkably, both T2 and T17 are refrain stanzas – one reflecting the lament function of the song, and the other the lullaby function. We cannot say whether Turner heard both from a single informant; his text may represent a conflation of variants he heard from several people. Later variants recorded from tradition contain only one or the other – not both.

T7	*Chuirinn Cailein liath fo ghlasaibh* *'S Donnacha dubh an laimh* *'S gach Caimbeulach th'ann am Bealach* *Gu giulan na 'n glas lamh.*	I would lock Grey Colin up, and put Black Duncan in prison, And cause every Campbell in Balloch to endure hand-cuffs.
T8	*Rainig mise réidhlein Bhealaich* *'S cha d' fhuair mi ann tamh;* *Cha d' fhag mi ròinn do m'fhalt gun tarruing,* *No craiceann air mo laimh.*	I reached the plain of Balloch, but I gained no repose there; I left no hair on my head untorn, nor skin upon my hands.
T9	*'S truagh nach robh mi 'n riochd na h-uiseig,* *Spionnaidh Ghriogair ann mo laimh* *'S i chlach a b'airde anns a chaisteal* *Chlach a b' fhaisg do 'n bhlar.*	A pity I couldn't rise like the lark, with Gregor's strength in my arm: The highest stone in the castle would be the closest to the ground.
T10	*'S truagh nach robh Fionnlairg na lasair,* *A's Bealach mor na smal,* *'S Griogair ban na 'm basa' geala,* *Bhi eidear mo dha laimh.*	A pity Finlarig wasn't in flames, and great Balloch in embers, And fair Gregor of the white palms close in my two arms.
T11	*'S ged tha mi gun ubhlan agam,* *'S ubhlan uil' aig cach;* *'S ann tha m' ubhal cùraidh grinn,* *A's cul a chinn ri lar.*	Though now I have no apples, and others have them all: My own apple, fragrant, handsome – and the back of his head on the ground.
T12	*Ged tha mnaithibh chaich aig baile,* *Na 'n luidhe 's na 'n cadal seimh* *'S ann bhios mis' aig bruaich mo leapa,* *A' bualadh mo dha laimh.*	Though other men's wives are at home, sleeping sweetly, Here am I at the edge of my bed, beating my hands in grief.
T13	*'S mor a b' annsa bhi aig Griogair,* *Air feadh coille 's fraoich* *Na bhi aig Baran crion na dalach,* *Ann tigh cloich a's aoil.*	I'd much prefer to be with Gregor among woods and heather Than with the mean little Baron of the river-meadow, in a house of stone and lime.
T14	*'S mor a b' annsa bhi aig Griogair,* *Cuir a chruidh do 'n ghleann* *Na bhi aig Baran crion na dalach,* *'G ol air fion 's air leann.*	I'd much prefer to be with Gregor, driving his cattle to the glen, Than with the dry old Baron of the river-meadow, drinking wine and ale.
T15	*'S mor a b' annsa bhi aig Griogair* *Fo bhrata ruibeach ròinn* *Na bhi aig Baran crìon na Dalach,* *Giùlan sìoda 's sròil.*	I'd much prefer to be with Gregor with only a rough, hairy mantle for covering, Than with the small-minded Baron of the river-meadow, suffering in silk and satin.
T16	*Ged bhiodh cur a's cathadh ann,* *A's latha nan seachd sion;* *Gheibheadh Griogair domh-sa cnagan* *'Sa 'n caidlimid fo dhìon.*	Although there would be storm and snow-drift, a day of seven gales, Gregor would find me a little nook where we would sleep in shelter.

T17	Ba hu, ba hu, àsrain bhig, Chan eil thu fhathast ach tlath; 'S eagal leam nach tig an latha Gu 'n diol thu t-athair gu brath.[5]	*Ba hu, ba hu, little orphan, you are only young yet;* *But I fear the day will never come that you will avenge your father.*

Much as we might be tempted to treat this text as some sort of 'original', it is worth reminding ourselves that Turner himself had it from a traditional source – perhaps more than one.[6] Alasdair Duncan, in an excellent discussion of metre and related matters, suggests a number of possible changes wrought by tradition-bearers over the long period since the poem's composition (Duncan: 71–80). Turner's unexamined text has, however, been treated as an authoritative source by generations of editors and anthologists. The following list includes publications in which the text given is ultimately derived from Turner's version:

Date	**Item Title**	**Anthology Author/Title**	**Stanzas**	**Also includes**
1848	'The Maid of Lochawe'	Finlay Dun, *Orain na 'h-Albain,* 46–7 and note.	T1–4, 8–9, 17	Translation; musical setting; background note
1874	'Seann Sgeulachdan mu Bhraid-Albann II: Donnchadh Dubh'	*An Gaidheal III*: 48–9.	T1–17	Background note
1881	'Gregor MacGregor's Lament'	*The Highlander*, July 1881: 32–3.	T3–4, 8–9, 17	Translation; musical setting; background note
1884	'Cumha Ghriogair MhicGriogair'	Charles Stewart, *The Killin Collection of Gaelic Songs*, 60–2.	T1–17	Translation; musical setting; background note
1890	'Cumha Ghriogair Mhic-Griogair'	A. MacLean Sinclair, *The Gaelic Bards from 1411 to 1715,* 18–21.	T1–17	Background note
1890	'MacGregor's Lullaby'	Thomas Pattison, *Gaelic Bards and Original Poems,* 116–19.	T1–17	Translation only (no Gaelic text); background note
1893	'Cumha Ghriogair MhicGriogair'	*The Celtic Monthly*, 1: 39.	T1–3, 9, 12	Translation; musical setting; background note
1895	'Maighdean Loch Otha'	Keith Norman MacDonald, *The Gesto Collection of Highland Music,* Appendix, 46.	T1–4, 8–9, 17	Musical setting and background note
1908	'Cumha Ghriogair MhicGriogair'	Calum Mac Phàrlain, *Binneas nam Bard,* 48–50.	T1, 3–12, 14–17	Musical setting
[1918] 1932	'Cumha Ghriogair MhicGhriogair Ghlinn Sreith'	W. J. Watson, *Bardachd Ghàidhlig,* 244–6 and notes.	T1–9, 11–17	Background note

[6] A native of the Cowal peninsula, Turner was an itinerant collector and seller of Gaelic poems and songs; see D. Maclean 1915: 361.

1913	'Air Madainn Lùnasdainn'	Angus Morrison, *Orain nam Beann,* 20–1.	T1–2, 4, 13–16	Musical setting
1913	'Bardachd nam Ban'	Calum Mac Phàrlain, *Guth na Bliadhna* X/3: 347–50.	T1–17	Background note

Relationships among these published sources can most easily be traced through comparison of the song-titles, background notes, and musical settings included. Although these relationships represent a tangled and somewhat incestuous web whose unpicking is not central to our purpose here, the genealogical gist can be summarized as follows:

- The titles alone would indicate that K. N. MacDonald's 'Maighdean Loch Otha' in the *Gesto Collection* (1895) is nothing more than a reprinting of Finlay Dun's 'The Maid of Loch Awe' in his *Orain na 'h-Albain* (1848). The Campbells were an important presence in Argyll, and Kilchurn Castle commands the length of Loch Awe; but the poet in this case belonged to the Campbells of Glenlyon and was not, as Dun had it, 'the daughter of Sir Duncan Campbell of Lochawe.' Gesto's background note also includes a shortened version of the Victorian melodrama described by Dun.[7]

- The background note given in Charles Stewart's *Killin Collection* – whose Glenlyon provenance makes it by far the most credible of the accounts given in these anthologies – is echoed in MacLean Sinclair's *Gaelic Bards* (1890) and in the *Celtic Monthly* (1893).

- The air included in the *Celtic Monthly* is reminiscent of the one included in Dun, with some modifications; the *Celtic Monthly* version of the air is also given (with very slight alteration) by Calum Mac Phàrlain in *Binneas nam Bard* (1908). We shall have more to say about the musical settings in these anthologies in due course.

- The background note given by Mac Phàrlain in *Guth na Bliadhna* (1913) hearkens back to the tale as it appeared in both Pattison's *Gaelic Bards and Original Poems* (1890) and *The Highlander* (1881): all three base their historical notes on a faulty account given in Cosmo Innes' 1861 book, *Sketches of Early Scotch History and Social Progress* (355–8), in which Innes quotes the curate of Fortingall, but unfortunately misses the 1570 entry regarding Griogair Ruadh and cites instead an entry for June 1552 in which an entirely different Griogair Mac Griogair was beheaded, along with his brother Malcolm and his father Duncan.

- The version of the poem published in *An Gàidheal* (1874) and the version given by Watson in *Bardachd Ghàidhlig* (1918, 1932) derive directly from Turner. Both of these, along with Mac Phàrlain's article in *Guth na Bliadhna* (1913), also quote Turner's pitiful phrase

[7] Dun's fanciful note reads as follows (1848: notes p. 3):

> The authoress of this Gaelic song was the daughter of Sir Duncan Campbell of Lochawe. She was "cag'd in" Balloch (Taymouth) "castle's dungeon dark" by her father, for having married a chief of the Clan Macgregor, with whom the Campbells were at feud.
>
> Macgregor often visited his young bride secretly at the castle, by rowing across Loch Tay in a small boat. These visits were, however, not unknown to Sir Duncan, who determined to be revenged on the bold intruder. Accordingly, an ambush was one day laid for the unsuspecting Macgregor, in a wood near the spot where his boat was moored; and, as he was returning to it, he was suddenly attacked by several men and wounded. He, however, fought his way through them, and was just stepping into the boat, when he was struck down by some one and stunned. His pursuers coming up shortly after, finished their cruel work. The verses were composed by the lady after learning the sad fate of her husband.

describing the author's having composed the lament *'agus a ciad leanabh air a glùn'* ('and her first child on her knee').

Returning to the poem itself, we must note three other published versions that appeared within the same hundred-year time-frame as those just listed. These derive not from Turner but from more recent oral tradition:

Date	**Item Title**	**Anthology Author/Title**	**Also includes**
1895	'Griogal Cridhe. Lament of the wife of an outlawed MacGregor'[8]	Keith Norman MacDonald, *The Gesto Collection of Highland Music*, Appendix, 25.	Musical setting
1911	'Griogal Cridhe'[8]	Frances Tolmie, *Journal of the Folk-Song Society*, No. 16: 196–7.	Musical setting; background note
1911	'Taladh'	A. and A. MacDonald, *The MacDonald Collection of Gaelic Poetry*, 325; note liii–liv.	Background note

The versions in *Gesto* (G) and *JFSS* both originate with Frances Tolmie, who says in the latter volume that she recalled the stanzas and air 'from earliest days' in Skye – likely sometime before 1850, given her birth in 1840. We should note, however, that one of the stanzas in *Gesto* (stanza G5 below) does not appear in *JFSS*. The very few stanzas of *Griogal Cridhe* which appear in Miss Tolmie's surviving notebooks shed no light on this omission;[9] and the simplest explanation may be that she sent Keith Norman MacDonald the words as she recalled them from childhood at the time, but inadvertently omitted G5 from the stanzas that she subsequently sent to Dr George Henderson, from which the collection eventually published in *JFSS* was compiled (Bassin 1977: 151).

Here is the version which Frances Tolmie contributed to *Gesto*. Corresponding (sometimes only roughly corresponding) stanzas in Turner (T) and the MacDonald Collection (M) are indicated for purposes of comparison.

G1 (T16, M2)

'S ioma h-oidhche fhliuch 'us thioram
Sìde na seachd sian
Gheibheadh Griogal dhomhsa creagan
Ris an gabhainn dion.

Many's the night, wet and dry, seven gales blowing,
Gregor would get me a rocky nook where I could get shelter.

G2 (T2)

Obhan, obhan, obhan i ri,
Obhan i ri ò
Obhan, obhan, obhan i ri,
'S mór mo mhulad, 's mór!

Obhan, obhan, obhan i ri,
Obhan i ri ò
Obhan, obhan, obhan i ri,
Great is my sorrow, great!

[8] Martin MacGregor (PC) suggests that *Gesto* may represent the first occasion of this song being given the title 'Griogal Cridhe', perhaps owing to the appearance of this phrase in two of the verses supplied to K. N. MacDonald by Frances Tolmie. The title has been widely used in subsequent publications (many of which are based on Tolmie), and is also the title attributed to many of the versions held in the School of Scottish Studies Archive. It is unclear whether the singers themselves used this title, or whether it was subsequently applied to the songs by fieldworkers familiar with Tolmie's version. John MacInnes has told me that he believes the pronunciation 'Griogal' for 'Griogair' derives from Miss Tolmie's informants in Skye; it is certainly not a variant found in Perthshire.

[9] National Library of Scotland, Tolmie Collection 14904: 27

G3[10]	*Dhirich mi dha 'n t-seòmar mhullach* *'S theirinn mi 'n tigh làir,* *'S cha d'fhuair mise Griogal cridhe,* *Na shuidhe mu 'n chlàr.*	I ascended to the uppermost room and descended to the lowest, But I did not find dear Gregor seated at the table.
G4 (T5, M5)	*Eudail mhor a shluagh an domhain!* *Dhoirt iad d' fhuil o 'n dé;* *'S chuir iad do cheann air stob daraich* *Tacan beag bho d' chré.*	Darling of all the world's people, they spilt your blood yesterday; They put your head on an oaken block and took it from your body.
G5 (T9)	*'S truagh nach mis a bha nam dhorsair* *An dorus an tigh bhàin,* *A chlach a b' airde bhitheadh san oisean* *Si b' fhaisge dh' an làir.*	A pity I wasn't the door-keeper at the door of the white house: The highest stone at the corner of the house would be closest to the ground.
G6 (T14/15, M8)	*B' annsa a bhi le Griogal cridhe,* *Tearnadh chruidh le gleann* *Na le Barainn mór na Dallaich* *Sioda geal mu 'm cheann.*	I would rather be with dear Gregor, driving cattle down the glen, Than with the big Baron of Dall, with white silk round my head.
G7 (T11, M4)	*Ged nach eil ùbhlan idir agam* *'S ùbhlan uil' aig càch* *'S ann tha m' ubhlan 's cùbh 'r ri caineal* *'S cùl an cinn ri làir.*	Although I have no apples, and others have them all, My own cinnamon-scented [?] apples are lying on the ground.
G8 (T12, M3)	*Nuair a bhitheas mnathan òg a bhaile* *An nochd 'n an cadal sàimh,* *'S ann bhitheas mis' air bruaich do lice* *Bualadh mo dhà laimh.*	When the young women of the village are sleeping soundly tonight, I shall be at the edge of your grave-slab, beating my hands in grief.

Finally, the *taladh* ('lullaby') included in *The MacDonald Collection of Gaelic Poetry* also contains eight stanzas. The editors tell us that it was 'taken down in Uist':[11]

M1 (T17)	Bà, bà, bà, mo leanabh, Bà, mo leanabh, bà; Bà, ho i o, mo leanabh, Cha 'n 'eil thu ach bà.	*Bà, bà, bà,* my baby, *Bà,* my child, *bà;* *Bà, ho i o,* my baby, You are only *bà.*

[10] While G3 has no obvious counterpart in either Turner or MacDonald, Martin MacGregor (PC) points out that it does include the 'high/low contrast' found in T9; it also may bear some relation to the migratory stanza M6/T8; see below n. 12.

[11] A. and A. MacDonald (1911), liii. In his copy of *The MacDonald Collection*, now lodged in the National Library of Scotland, the late Rev. William Matheson has pencilled a note at the bottom of page 325: '(from Isabella MacRury, Benbecula)'. We cannot presently confirm Matheson's identification of the informant, beyond saying that he undoubtedly had the information on what he considered good authority.

M2 (T16, G1)	*Is iomadh oidhche fliuch is tioram,* *Sìde nan seachd sian,* *A chuir Griogal ormsa fasgadh,* *A chumadh orm dion.*	Many a night, wet and dry, in seven gales of weather Gregor found shelter that kept a roof over my head.
M3 (T12, G8)	*'S buidhe mhnathan òga 'bhaile,* *Fhuair an cadal seimh;* *Mise so air bruaich do leapa* *'Bualadh mo dha làmh.*	Lucky young women of the village who slept sweetly, While I was here at the edge of your bed, beating my hands in grief.
M4 (T11, G7)	*Ged tha mi gun ùbhlan agam,* *'S m' ùbhlan uil' aig càch,* *'S ann tha m' ulaidh, cùbhraidh, caineal,* *'S cùl a chinn ri làr.*	Although I have no apples – my apples gone to others, My treasure, fragrant and cinnamon-scented, lies with his head on the ground.
M5 (T5, G4)	*Fheudail a dh' fhearaibh an domhain,* *Dhòirt iad t' fhuil an de;* *Chuir iad do cheann air stob daraich,* *Tacan beag uam fein.*	Darling of the world's men, they spilt your blood yesterday: They put your head on an oaken block a small distance from myself.
M6 (T8)	*Dhìrich mi 'bheinn mhòr gun anail,* *Mu 'n do ghlas an là,* *Chuir mi gruag mo chinn ri talamh* *'S craicionn mo dha làmh.*[12]	I climbed the big mountain breathlessly before the sun arose; The hair of my head I left on the ground, along with the skin of my two hands.
M7 (T6–T7, T10)	*'S truagh nach robh m' athair 's an teasaich,* *'S Iarl Adhull an laimh;* *Griogal cridhe nam bas gealla* *Eadar mo dha laimh.*	A pity my father wasn't ill with fever, and the Earl of Atholl captured; Darling Gregor of the white palms close in my two arms.
M8 (T14/15, G6)	*B' annsa 'bhi aig Griogal cridhe,* *'G iomain chruidh 's a ghleann,* *Na aig Baran crionda, gallach,* *'S sioda dubh mu m' cheann.*	I would rather be with dear Gregor driving cattle in the glen Than with the withered, cursed Baron wearing black silk round my head.

Judging from the published evidence of Miss Tolmie's version (Skye) and that collected by the MacDonalds (Uist), it is clear that over 70 percent of the stanzas – or important elements of them – published by Turner in 1813 were still preserved in oral memory at the end of the nineteenth century, more than three hundred years after their composition. As we shall now see, however, this is not the end of the story.

2.2 Unpublished versions

The following summary includes all known unpublished versions of the text collected since the middle of the nineteenth century.[13] With the exception of one BBC recording, the audio recordings listed below are available through the Sound Archives of the School of Scottish Studies. For

[12] M6 is a *rann fuadain,* a migratory stanza, found in numerous Gaelic songs; T8 and G3 are probably related to it. The poet probably tapped into this tradition when composing her verses.

[13] Exceptionally we have included the version published by Anne Lorne Gillies in her 2005 collection *Songs of Gaelic Scotland*, which she learned from the Rev. William Matheson. The reasons for this inclusion are discussed below.

recordings available on the *Tobar an Dualchais* website (TD), track ID numbers given here can be entered into the website's search engine to gain access to the recording itself. For School of Scottish Studies recordings not yet available on *Tobar an Dualchais*, original Sound Archive (SA) identification numbers are given.

Place	**Date**	**Contributor (Recorder)**	**Reference**	**Corresponding Stanzas**
GROUP 1				
Scalpay Harris	1954 1959	Angus MacLeod (School of Scottish Studies)	SA 1954/071/B6 SA 1959/114/08	M1, G4(M5), G5, G7
Skye	1954 1958	Kirsty Munro (School of Scottish Studies)	SA 1954/069/B2 SA 1958/043/B8	G2, G4, M7, G1, G8, G6(M8), G7(M4)
Lewis	1956 1957	Jessie MacKenzie (School of Scottish Studies)	TD ID No. 54954 TD ID No. 94452	New stanza, M1, G1(M2), G7, G5, new stanza[14]
Scalpay Harris	1963 1971 1971	Flora Cunningham (School of Scottish Studies)	TD ID No. 76047 TD ID No. 77277 SA 1971/100.01–2	M1, G6, G4(M5), new stanza, G5, G7, G8, G1[15]
GROUP 2				
Iochdar, S. Uist	1869	Seonaid Churraidh (Alexander Carmichael)	Edinburgh University Library, CW MS 244 fos. 490–1, item 170	M1, M6, M3, M2(G1)
Eriskay	1896	Mrs Ronald O Healy[16] (Fr Allan MacDonald)	Glasgow U. Library, MS Gen.1090/28: 96–7	M1, M4, M3
Eriskay	1896	Ewen M'Lennan (Fr Allan MacDonald)	Glasgow U. Library, MS Gen.1090/28: 104	M2(G1), M8
Eriskay	1905	Unnamed Singer[17] (Amy Murray)	National Library of Scotland, Acc. 9711, Box 3	M1, M8
Eriskay	1951	Flora MacInnes (School of Scottish Studies)	SA 1951/04/01	M1, M4
S. Uist	1956	Agnes Currie (School of Scottish Studies)	TD ID No. 84577	M1, M6, M4

[14] Stanzas sung in MacKenzie's 1957 recording.

[15] Cunningham knew and sang all of these verses, although no more than seven of them appear in any one recording.

[16] Martin MacGregor (PC) suggests that this might be an error for O Henl(e)y, a surname still found in the southern part of South Uist.

[17] Possibly Penny Campbell, housekeeper to Fr Allan MacDonald, from whom Murray collected a large number of songs; see McGuire 1999:84.

Barra	1959	Mary MacNeill and Peigi MacNeill (School of Scottish Studies)	SA 1959/066	M1, G8(M3), M4
Barra	1959 1965 1966	Mary Morrison (Màiri Eòghainn Mhóir)[18] (School of Scottish Studies)	SA 1959/68/02 SA 1965/152/05 TD ID No. 98765	M1, M6, M4, M8, M3
Barra	1965	Calum Johnston (School of Scottish Studies)	TD ID No. 24923	M1, M6, M4(T11)
Barra	1965	Catherine MacNeil (School of Scottish Studies)	SA 1965/105/17	M1, M6, M4
Barra	1965	Jane MacDonald (School of Scottish Studies)	TD ID No. 95860	M1, M4, M2(G1), M6, M3
Barra	1965	'Barra Waulking Women' (School of Scottish Studies)	TD ID No. 24925	M1, M6
Grimsay	1966	Peter Morrison (School of Scottish Studies)	SA 1966/093/02	M1, M4
S. Uist	1966	Mary Munro (School of Scottish Studies)	SA 1966/097/05	M1, M6, M4, M2(G1), M8, M1
S. Uist	1967	Mrs Hugh MacEachen (School of Scottish Studies)	SA 1967/008/A5	M1, M6, M4, M8, M2
Scalpay Harris	1970	Mary MacLeod (School of Scottish Studies)	SA 1970/005/02	M1, M2
Berneray Harris	1970	Margaret MacLeod (School of Scottish Studies)	SA 1970/082/B6	M1, M6
GROUP 3				
N. Uist/ Edinburgh	1959 1960s 1975	Rev. William Matheson (School of Scottish Studies) (Anne Lorne Gillies) (School of Scottish Studies)	TD ID No. 85852 (SA 1959/055) 2005:140–2 SA 1975/221/B5	M1, G6, G1, T8, T5, M4 M1, G4, G3, G1, G6, T11, G8 M1, G6, M5, T11, M3
Acharn, Tayside, Perthshire	1964	Christopher MacDonald (School of Scottish Studies)	SA 1964/23/B2 Tocher 2/11 (1973), 81 (text) and 100 (air)	T13–15, T17
Harris	n.d.	Peggy Morrison (BBC Scotland Gaelic Archive)[19]	"Sia Òrain" programme 6, broadcast 29/03/2012	T1–4, T6, T13

[18] With regard to the 1966 recording, the singer's name is listed on the website as 'Unknown (female)'. Comparison with her other performances of this song nonetheless indicates that the singer in this recording is Mary Morrison.

Vatersay	1956 1967	Nan MacKinnon (School of Scottish Studies)	TD ID No. 27170 TD ID No. 56989	T2, G1, G3, M3

Our analysis suggests that these recordings be divided into three groups. Group 1 contains recordings that appear to belong to the strand of tradition exemplified by Frances Tolmie's Skye version, while the recordings in Group 2 appear closer to that encountered by the MacDonalds in the Uists.[20] Group 3 contains recordings that for one reason or another cannot be assigned to either of the other groups; we shall discuss these presently.

Because the versions in the *MacDonald Collection* and in *Gesto* are in many ways similar, and because only thirteen of our twenty-four singers remembered more than three stanzas of the song, there are some cases in which we cannot be hard-and-fast about assigning a singer to Group 1 or 2 on the basis of textual evidence alone. There are nonetheless a number of small differences between *Gesto* and MacDonald that are worth noting, and that I believe allow us to express some confidence in the differentiation outlined above. The most significant of these are:

1. **Unique stanzas.** As noted above, *Gesto* contains three stanzas (G2, G3, and G5) which do not appear in MacDonald; and MacDonald in turn contains three stanzas (M2, M3, and M8) which do not appear in *Gesto*. It seems logical to assume that the appearance of one or more of these unique stanzas in a given performance may help us identify the strand of tradition to which that performance belongs.
2. ***'Ar bhruaich do...'.*** Both *Gesto* (G8) and MacDonald (M5) contain a stanza in which the poet complains of sleeplessness. The interesting difference is in line three, where *Gesto* has the poet mourning at her husband's grave (*air bruaich do lice* 'at the edge of your gravestone'), whereas MacDonald has her in her bedroom (*ar bhruaich do leapa* 'at the edge of your bed'). We shall have more to say about this difference shortly. For the moment, however, this distinction may help us decide to which group a recording should be assigned.
3. ***'sioda geal' / 'sioda dubh'.*** The colour of silk head-dress worn by the poet is given as 'white' in *Gesto* (G6) and as 'black' in MacDonald (M6); our recordings show evidence of both traditions, and the singer's choice may help us decide to which group a recording may belong.

Variants included in Group 2 clearly support the notion that a distinct version of *Griogal Cridhe* predominated in the Uists, Eriskay and Barra, while those in Group 1 suggest that the versions collected in Skye, Harris and Lewis have features in common with Frances Tolmie's Skye version as given in *Gesto*. Tolmie learned *Griogal Cridhe* as a child growing up near Dunvegan, home of the MacLeods, whose clan alliances in Harris and Lewis were manifold and of long standing. Granted the fact that by Tolmie's time the MacLeods of Skye/Harris and the MacLeods of Lewis were politically independent of each other, it nonetheless stands to reason that such relationships could account for the similarity between the version sung in the northernmost Outer Hebrides and the one Tolmie learned in childhood.

---

[19] BBC Scotland Gaelic Archive 138, Volume 94, track 11. The singer's identity, not given in the broadcast, was determined by comparison with other recordings from the same singer held in the Scottish Studies Archives, and subsequently confirmed by the BBC.

[20] There is obviously some overlap; and one should note that Peter Morrison (Grimsay), Mary MacLeod (Scalpay) and Margaret MacLeod (Berneray) are, despite belonging geographically and culturally (as least as regards religion) in Group 1, are included in Group 2 because they failed to sing any of the Gesto/Tolmie stanzas favoured by Group 1 informants. None of these three, however, sang more than two stanzas, and it is impossible to say if they had heard others that they omitted to sing on the occasion of recording.

As we shall presently discuss, the musical evidence also supports the distinction between Group 1 and Group 2 as outlined here.

2.3 Anomalous versions

As indicated, Group 3 contains four versions (*i.e.* versions from four singers) that cannot be confidently assigned to either of the first two groups. In each of these cases, it seems possible or even likely that the singers had recourse – either personally, or at a near remove – to a printed version of the text.

The Rev. William Matheson, late Reader in Celtic at the University of Edinburgh, recorded over 400 items for the School of Scottish Studies, some of which display evidence of his having collated textual and musical elements from his own North Uist background with material he encountered in published and manuscript sources during a lifetime's study of Gaelic song. Intensely interested in understanding and replicating the performance practices of past generations, Matheson was open and straightforward about his use of material from multiple sources in his performance of Gaelic songs. It is thus not surprising that his recordings of *Griogal Cridhe* contain stanzaic elements unique to each of our main printed sources, including Turner as well as *Gesto* and MacDonald.[21]

Although Peggy Morrison of Ardhasaig, Harris, was recorded on several occasions by researchers from the School of Scottish Studies, it was for the BBC that she recorded *Griogal Cridhe*, several stanzas of which were recently incorporated into a half-hour programme on BBC Radio nan Gàidheal.[22] Thanks to colleagues at the BBC, I subsequently heard this recording in full: it includes all but two of Turner's stanzas, and presents them in the same order as given in Turner. From the halting character of the performance, it seems clear that she was singing from a printed text; indeed, most of Turner's stanzas do not appear in living tradition in the twentieth century. Why she should have preferred singing Turner's text to the one doubtless known to her – as the evidence of the air confirms – from Harris tradition we are unfortunately no longer in a position to enquire, as Peggy Morrison died in 1988. John MacInnes tells me that he often encountered, in the course of his fieldwork, informants who revered the printed word, and who would declare their own version of a song 'wrong' if it did not accord with a printed version subsequently shown to them.

Not only was Christopher MacDonald of Acharn, Perthshire, among the last generation of native Gaelic speakers from that county, but he also lived only a few miles from the east end of Loch Tay, where the events lamented in the poem occurred. It is therefore a pity that his version of *Griogal Cridhe* clearly derives from the text published in Turner. John MacInnes, who recorded Christopher MacDonald in his home, tells me that the family owned a copy of Stewart's *Killin Collection*, which includes all of Turner's stanzas. Whether Christopher MacDonald learned his four stanzas directly from a printed source or from someone else who had done so it is not possible to say; it is remarkable, however, that MacDonald's stanzas are virtually word-for-word as they appear in print, that they occur in the same order, and that (with the exception of the hybrid stanza G6/M8, which combines elements of T14 and T15) these stanzas occur in no other variant recorded in the twentieth century.

Finally, Nan MacKinnon (*Nan Eachainn Fhionnlaigh*) of Vatersay was undoubtedly one of the most extraordinary informants who ever recorded for the School of Scottish Studies, contributing hundreds of songs, stories and examples of traditional lore to the Sound Archives. One might hazard a guess that, given her intense interest in the material, she might have consulted printed works; indeed, both *MacDonald* and *Gesto* were well-subscribed volumes that found their way into many homes in the Gàidhealtachd, as did other publications that printed all or parts of Turner's text.

---

[21] For an analysis of his reconstructive method in connection with songs in so-called 'strophic' metres, see Blankenhorn (2013).

[22] The programme on 'Griogal Cridhe' was the sixth and final programme in a series entitled 'Sia Òrain' broadcast on BBC Radio nan Gàidheal between 23 February and 29 March 2012.

If we could assume that some of these sources were to be found in Nan MacKinnon's home, we might understand how – unlike those of other singers from Barra, Eriskay, and the Uists – Nan's performance strayed beyond the southern stanzas that we would expect her to know, and contained elements drawn from all three of the traditional strands we have so far identified.

Unfortunately, however, we can assume no such thing. John MacInnes tells me that, as far as he knew, Nan MacKinnon was not literate in Gaelic. The most we can say is that, while Nan credited her mother as the source of most of her songs, she surely picked up some of them from other singers. She may have learned *Griogal Cridhe* from someone who was literate in Gaelic, and who had had access to Turner and to the more recently-collected texts in *Gesto* and MacDonald. This case, as well as that of Christopher MacDonald, illustrates the complexity of the relationship between oral and literary versions of a given text, and the danger of drawing conclusions based on evidence that can never be complete.

2.4 'New' stanzas and interesting variants

Three of the stanzas collected from recent oral tradition are hitherto unattested from any other source. Do these stanzas represent authentic traditional memories of the original text as Mór Chaimbeul composed it – keeping in mind that 243 years elapsed between the events of 1570 and the first appearance of the text in Turner? Or have they become associated with the song at a later time? It is impossible to know for certain, but it is surely worth considering the possibilities.

The first of these unique stanzas, from Jessie Mackenzie's 1957 performance, is as follows:

Dh'iarr iad mise chun na bainis	They asked me to the wedding
Bainis nach robh ann	A wedding that never took place;
Bha do cheann ac' air an dealg	They had your head on the pin
Air a' phost ud thall.	On that post over yonder.

This stanza, with its reference to the image of the victim's severed head, is likely to be a remote variant of the text as given in Turner (T5), although the ghastly idea that the head was then displayed on a spike is not attested elsewhere. The reference in the first couplet to a wedding-that-never-was may represent an attempt, by a tradition-bearer unfamiliar with the actual events, to dramatise the circumstances of Griogair's beheading.[23]

In both of her performances, MacKenzie also sings this:

Nam faiceadh tu Griogal Crìdhe	If you saw beloved Griogair
'S e 'na shuidhe air tom	Seated on a hillock
Gaol nam ban òg, gràdh nan nigheann	The love of the young women, darling of the girls
'S currac beag m'a cheann.	With a small hood over his head.

Here we have a reflection of what could have been Mór Chaimbeul's genuine experience. The stanza depicts Griogair seated on a raised hillock *(tom)*, a typical place of execution, wearing a hood *(currac)* presumably placed there in preparation for the event.[24] If this chilling image truly originates with Mór Chaimbeul herself, it would support the idea that the poet was indeed an eyewitness to her husband's judicial murder – a notion most credibly floated by Charles Stewart, whose background note to the *Killin Collection* is based upon Glenlyon tradition.

[23] Interestingly, Martin MacGregor (PC) tells me that he will be arguing in a forthcoming article that the poet 'had refused an attempt to marry her off to another before the feud began'.

[24] John MacInnes tells me that such executions were generally carried out with the victim being placed on a small knoll or bit of rising ground referred to as a *tom (tom na croicheadh, tom an dìcheannaidh)*. MacGregor cites J. Christie, *The Lairds and Lands of Loch Tayside* (Aberfeldy 1892: 21) as a source helpful in identifying the 'probable precise location' of the execution (1999: 145, n. 31).

Another such stanza is the following, recorded by Flora Cunningham in 1971:

Chuir iad ruigheadh air do chasan[25]	They stilled your legs
Is glas air do chainnt,	And silenced your speech;
'S nuair a lùb iad thu 's an anart	And when they wrapped you in the shroud
'S e mo chreach-sa bh'ann.	That was my undoing.

Here we get a sense of Mór's despair at Griogair's capture and execution, vivid and specific details which convey a physical sense of her heartrending loss. Indeed, it is the vividness and specificity of these two stanzas – not to mention their consistency with what we now know of the actual circumstances – that I believe argue for their having been part of Mór's original poem, as opposed to later accretions to it.

Glenlyon tradition notwithstanding, a recent article by Kate Louise Mathis expresses the view that Mór Chaimbeul was unlikely to have personally witnessed her husband's execution. While Mathis eventually concludes that the matter 'cannot be decided conclusively with the available evidence' (60, n. 24), she discusses the reference to blood-drinking, and specifically mentions the appearance of the cup in T5, describing it as a 'foreign object' which 'implies distance from instead of proximity to the event described' (59). Surely, however, we may imagine Mór having been present, but physically restrained from rushing to her husband's body and drinking the blood directly from his wounds in the approved traditional manner. Whether she was physically present or not, however, is immaterial; the important thing is that by mentioning the drinking of blood, Mór invokes a theme and image long associated with the rhetoric of women's lamentation, thus reminding listeners that her poetry draws from a deep well of tradition going back centuries.[26]

In addition to these unique stanzas, recent recordings contain other variant readings that may be significant in light of what we now know to be the truth of these events. Earlier we mentioned the stanza in which the poet expresses envy of other young women who sleep soundly at night. Turner (T12) gives it as follows:

Ged tha mnaithibh chaich aig baile,	Although the wives of all the others are at home,
Na 'n luidhe 's na 'n cadal seimh	Sleeping soundly in their beds,
'S ann bhios mis' aig bruaich mo leapa,	I am here at the edge of my bed,
A' bualadh mo dha laimh.	Beating my two hands.

The image here is of a young woman so beset by grief that she can get no rest, but sits up on the edge of her bed, rocking back and forth, her hands beating together as tears flow down her cheeks, her face a rictus of despair. Of the nine singers who recorded this stanza, three – Nan MacKinnon, Jane MacDonald, and William Matheson in his 1975 recording – give this stanza in the form Turner expressed it: *aig bruaich mo leapadh* 'at the edge of my bed'. Three others accord with the

[25] Cunningham's pronunciation in three of her recordings is *ruigheadh* or *ruitheadh*, the meaning of which is obscure; in SA1971.100.01–2, where she sings the song twice, it sounds more like *luigheadh*. While the confusion of /l/ and /r/ is commonplace, it seems likely that she was uncertain about this word. Could the original form have been *luighe*, for which Armstrong's *Gaelic Dictionary* (Mid-Perthshire) gives 'death' as one meaning? This feature, and the naming of the poet's second husband as 'Pàdruig Baron' – whom William Matheson identified to John MacInnes as 'Patrick Menzies, petty baron of Dull' – suggest that Cunningham's version of the song may have a closer connection to its Perthshire origin than some of the other variants collected in the Western Isles appear to do.

[26] Consider the behaviour of Eibhlín Dhubh Ní Chonaill, widow of Art Ó Laoghaire, who licked her husband's blood from her hands after discovering his fallen body (Ó Tuama 1961: 35, ll.82–4); also the story of Deirdre, who 'began drinking Naoise's blood copiously' following his murder (Mac Giolla Léith 1993: ll. 766–7).

MacDonald text (M5) in having in the third line *do leapadh* 'your bed'; and four others reflect *Gesto* (G8) in rendering the line as *air bruaich do lice* 'at the edge of your grave-slab'.[27] Clearly *air bruaich do leabadh* makes no sense: whose bed are we supposed to imagine here? As for the 'grave-slab', we must ask ourselves how likely it would have been for the Campbells of Glenorchy and Glenlyon, having dispatched their troublesome in-law, to accord him so costly a burial-plot as this image suggests, or how likely it would have been for Mór Chaimbeul – a re-married woman with two children – to have visited her first husband's grave in the middle of the night whilst other women were asleep in their beds. The 'grave-slab' image seems to me to carry a whiff of Victorian melodrama about it, whereas the image of the woman in sleepless agony in her bedroom has the piercing ring of truth.[28] Were it not for the fact that Tolmie's version, having been frequently reprinted, is now popularly regarded as canonical, it would perhaps be unnecessary to point out that Turner's informant is likelier to have had the better text.[29]

Finally, one further stanza merits our attention in this respect. It appears in both of Jessie MacKenzie's recordings:

Bha mi 'n oidhche ud na mo sheasamh	That night I stood
'N dorus an tùr bhàin	In the door of the white tower
A' chlach a b'àirde bh' air a bhalla	The highest stone in the wall
'S i b' fhaisg air an làr.	Was the one closest to the ground.

Meanwhile, both Flora Cunningham and her brother Angus MacLeod sing this:

Nach truagh nach bu mhise 'n dorsair	It's a pity I wasn't the door-keeper
An dorus taigh-bhàis,	At the door of the death-house
'S a' chlach a b' àirde bha 's an ursainn	The highest stone in the door-frame
'S i b' fhaisge dha làr.	Would be the one closest to the ground.

This stanza clearly corresponds to G5 (which gives *dorus an taigh bhàin* in the second line) and to a lesser extent to T9 (whose second couplet reads *'S i chlach a b'airde anns a chaisteal / Chlach a b' fhaisg do 'n bhlar*). So our question should be: do either the Cunningham/MacLeod or the MacKenzie versions contain anything we might consider original to the poem? MacKenzie's reference to a 'white tower' *(tùr bhàin)* is unique, as is *Gesto*'s to a 'white house' *(tigh bhàin).* The Cunningham/MacLeod version's *taigh-bhàis* ('death-house' – or perhaps even 'death's abode') is appropriately creepy, and may represent some later tradition-bearer's inventive attempt to explain why the poet might wish to tear down the walls. But even so, what 'death-house' would this be? Should we take the phrase literally or metaphorically? *Taigh-bhàis* is no less mysterious than the other two.

A clue may be found in castles named in the text. Balloch – *Caisteal a' Bhealaich* (T7–8, T10) – whose foundations lie under Taymouth Castle today, was the home of Mór's cousin, *Cailean Liath*, Colin Campbell of Glenorchy. *Fionnlairig* (T10) contained a chapel and burial-ground that

[27] Including a second performance by William Matheson; the text credited to him by Anne Lorne Gillies contains the line *'s ann bhios mis' aig bruaich do lice*; see Gillies 2005: 141.

[28] The image of grief drawn here – sleeplessness, the beating of one's hands in distress, dishevelment of hair and other motifs – is a common one in Gaelic poetry; see Mathis 2008: 61n., also Partridge 1980–1: 29–31. It is also one which must have its origins in the physical experience of intense grief, as anyone who has had such an experience can attest.

[29] Tolmie's text and air appear in *Coisir a' Mhòid* (An Comunn Gàidhealach 1932–37: 4/51–4); *Orain a' Mhòid* (An Comunn Gàidhealach 1935: XII/13); J. N. McConochie, *Gaelic Calling "Ghaidhlig a' Gairm"* (1960: 30–1); Francis Collinson, *The Traditional and National Music of Scotland* (1966: 87); *Ceol nam Beann: The Ceilidh Song-Book* (An Comunn Gàidhealach 1972: 29); Bruce Campbell, *Orain nan Gàidheal* (1989: 2: 37), and no doubt elsewhere. The Mòd collections have been particularly influential.

was also associated with the Glenorchy Campbells.[30] Remarkably, however, the poem makes no reference to the residence of Mór's father, Duncan Campbell of Glenlyon. Given the prominent role her father played in Griogair's arrest and execution, and her expressed wish that he become seriously ill (T6), one might expect a reference to his dwelling place.

Charles Stewart, reporting Glenlyon tradition, may provide a relevant clue here. His background note to the song begins (Stewart: 60) :

> In the latter half of the sixteenth century lived Duncan Campbell, of Glenlyon, who was so celebrated for his hospitality that he was known as 'Donnacha Ruadh na Feileach.' His residence was 'Caisteal a Curin-bhàin,' about two miles above the pass.

Chaisteal a' Chùirn-bhàin (Carnbane Castle) did indeed belong to the Campbells of Glenlyon at the time in question: W. J. Watson notes that 'its first stone was laid in 1564' by Donnchadh Ruadh na Féile, Mór Chaimbeul's father (Watson 1939: 287). While Mór herself may not have lived there, she would have known that the castle was important to her father – perhaps because of its newness, because he had built it himself from scratch, because he would have been pleased with it.[31] Accordingly, if we may invoke the principle of *lectio difficilior potior*, we may entertain the idea that Jessie MacKenzie's *tùr bhàin* retains an echo of what could have been *Chùirn Bhàin* in the original poem. If so, we may have solved the mystery posed by the variant *taigh bhàin / tùr bhàin / taigh-bhàis* readings. The restored stanza would then read something like this:

Nach truagh nach bu mhise 'n dorsair	It's a pity I wasn't the door-keeper
An Caisteal a' Chùirn Bhàin:	At Carnbane Castle:
'S a' chlach a b'àirde bha 's an ursainn	The highest stone in the door-frame
'S i b' fhaisge dha làr.	Would be the one closest to the ground.

If we accept such a reading, there is of course the problem of how we should regard T9. This I happily leave to others, with the reminder that nearly two and one-half centuries passed between the poem's composition and its first appearance in print. The vagaries of oral transmission are well-known, and there is little reason, apart from its date, why Turner's version should enjoy greater authority than other orally-transmitted versions of the poem. Two and one-half centuries is a long time, and the poem could have been subjected to any number of alterations, misconstructions, accretions and omissions between its composition and the date when Turner noted it down.

3.0 The Music

In our examination of the musical settings associated with *Griogal Cridhe* we shall mainly be interested in three questions:

- Can we manage to separate, in the published versions of the 19th century, the genuine traditional elements from the Victorian 'improvements'?

[30] Cf. *Chronicle of Fortingall* entries for 12 August 1523 and 26 July 1524, which note the burials of 'Sir Colin Campbell Knight Laird of Glenuruquhay' and 'Margaret Stewart Lady of Glenuruquhay' 'in the chapel of Finlarg.' Martin MacGregor informs me (PC) that this chapel was added in 1516 to a larger fortification at Finlarig, purchased by Donnchadh, second chief of the Campbells of Glenorchy, around 1500. He argues that Finlarig was the Glenorchy Campbells' main fortress from then until the building of Balloch, and believes that Griogair Ruadh could well have been imprisoned there for a time in 1569–70. If so, there is ample reason for Mór Chaimbeul to have singled it out as a place she would like to have seen destroyed.

[31] Martin MacGregor tells me (PC) that the Glenlyon Campbells' 'first and main fortress' at Meggernie is far more impressive than Carnbane, and stands in a more prominent location. In his 1999 article he points out that he has been 'unable to establish with certainty the order in which these fortresses were built' (1999: 127 and nn. 54–55).

- Does the distribution of musical variants collected from oral tradition support our conclusion, outlined above, regarding two strands of tradition in the Hebrides, *i.e.* one strand which predominated in the Uists and Barra, and another which includes versions collected in Skye, Harris, and Lewis?
- Will scrutiny of both published and unpublished versions of the air allow us to draw any conclusions regarding the character of the 'original' air?

3.1 Published settings

We have already mentioned a number of the anthologies that included a musical setting alongside the poem, beginning with Finlay Dun's 1848 collection. A total of nine musical settings appeared in print in the first century following Turner's publication of the poem.

3.1.1. Dun and followers.

The tendency of Victorian anthologists to indulge in melodrama is, it must be said, no less marked in their musical settings than in the fanciful background notes which they often supplied. They wanted to sell copies of their works to a middle-class audience, schooled in mainstream western art-music; and in order to do so they felt that they needed to titivate their raw material to make it more commercially viable. The Rev. William Matheson calls them 'systematizers and improvers' (1955:75):[32]

> They were inclined to think, because the people who sang folk-songs were innocent of musical theory, that therefore their singing of their own music was imperfect: it was quite legitimate for a person of taste and refinement to see to it that imperfections were removed, and that the music was made to conform to the style which was fashionable in the drawing rooms of the day. What they failed to realise was that the folk-singer, by a combination of tradition and intuition, can achieve effects which elude the mere theorist or rationaliser, and which are of great value for that very reason.

Prior to the publication of Tolmie's air, the most influential of these musical renditions was that of Finlay Dun (1848), whose setting was reprinted, with minor modifications, in *The Highlander* (1881), *The Killin Collection* (1884), under the title 'Maighdean Loch Otha' in *The Gesto Collection* (1895), and – with an additional melodic flourish – in Morrison's *Orain nam Beann* (1913):[33]

[32] While it is easy to deplore the practices of these 19th-century 'improvers', it is worth noting that twentieth- and twenty-first-century performers continue to 'arrange' *Griogal Cridhe* and hundreds of other Gaelic songs, regularising the rhythm, obscuring the integrity of the text, removing tonal ambiguity, and adding instrumental accompaniments and all sorts of electronic effects, for exactly the same social and commercial reasons. For those who prefer their Gaelic songs (and perhaps their single-malt whiskies) 'neat', the ongoing assumption that this unique art-form requires such adulteration to be rendered acceptable is a source of some dismay.

[33] Matheson (1955: 73–4) notes that Dun, an Edinburgh musician, 'provided most of the accompaniments' to this volume, whose 'provenance is somewhat obscure'. The introduction says that the source of the melodies was a manuscript collection 'made by a native of the Highlands'; Matheson points out that, although Grove's *Dictionary of Music* identifies this person as Miss G. A. Bell of Edinburgh, 'it is more than doubtful whether she could be described as a native of the Highlands.' He goes on to suggest that the collector might have been Lachlan McLaine of Scalasdale, Mull; or possibly Miss Breadalbin Maclean, daughter of Alexander Maclean of Coll. It is unfortunately impossible to know for certain where the songs gathered by Finlay Dun were first noted down.

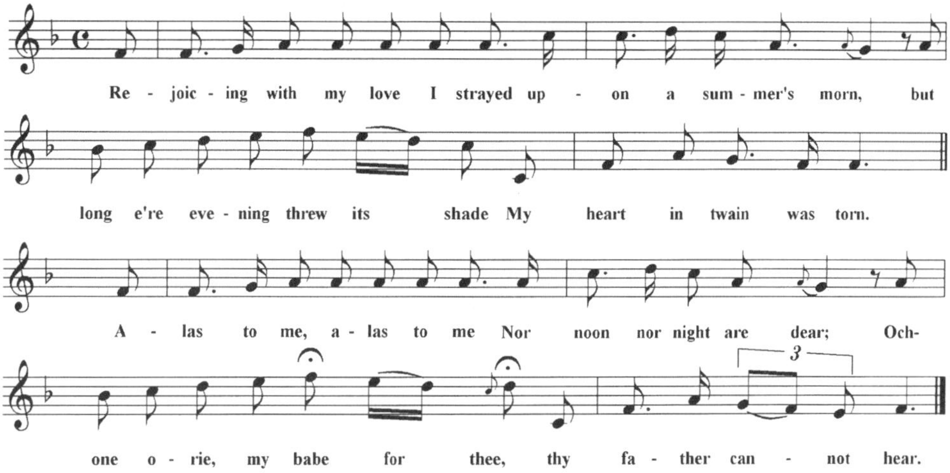

Dun's air illustrates the 'improving' tendency – perhaps best described as a sort of emotional inflation – in its second strain, where the melody soars to a high point before descending by a full octave in preparation for the final bar. The use of the *fermata*, directing the singer to linger pathetically on certain notes, provides another insight into the composer's artistic intent. The character of the traditional air – if we are correct in assuming that Dun based his melody upon a traditional air and did not compose the entire melody out of his own imagination – has been thoroughly swamped by these grandiose effects, and by the fact that it has been rhythmically re-designed to suit the English text.

3.1.2. *Celtic Monthly* and followers.

The two-part air provided in *The Celtic Monthly* (Fig. 2) is of a similar character. Like Dun's air, it contains a soaring second strain inappropriate to the Gaelic traditional context; indeed, whoever composed (or adapted) this air was probably familiar with Dun's version.

The difference between Dun and the *Celtic Monthly* version may stem from the fact that, while both are settings not of the Gaelic poetry but of the English verse translations, Dun's translator ('Delta') has remained true to the metrical structure of the Gaelic poetry, in which there are fourteen syllables in each couplet. Whoever composed the English verses for the *Celtic Monthly,* however, has created a metre in which each couplet contains fifteen syllables rather than fourteen. Compare the following:

Gaelic text	**English text: Dun ('Delta')**	**English text: *Celtic Monthly***
Moch maduin air la lunasd' Bha mi sùgradh mar ri 'm ghràdh; Ach m'un d' thainig meadhon latha, Bha mo chridhe air a chràdh.	Rejoicing with my love I stray'd Upon a summer's morn, But long ere evening threw its shade My heart in twain was torn.	Early on a Lammas morning, With my husband I was gay, But my heart got sorely wounded, Ere the middle of the day.

The result is that the melody given in the *Celtic Monthly* requires the artificial stressing of a normally-unstressed syllable when the song is sung in Gaelic:

The *Celtic Monthly* setting appears to have inspired the even more florid arrangement supplied in MacPhàrlain's *Binneas nam Bard* (1908). Remarkably, it may also be the ultimate model for the air sung by Christopher MacDonald of Tayside whose version of the song, as we mentioned earlier, appears to derive from a published source. The next illustration is a transcription of Christopher MacDonald's performance, as it appeared in *Tocher* 11. Significantly, MacDonald's air resembles the *Celtic Monthly*'s only in the first strain, where the artificial stress on *agus* creates the impression that the entire phrase is a beat too long; the second strain, by contrast, accords with the verse-structure, and as a result seems entirely appropriate in metrical terms:

3.1.3. Tolmie and followers.

Frances Tolmie's air, first published in *Gesto* (1895) and subsequently in her own collection in *JFSS* (1911), has become the most popular over the past century, undoubtedly through its having been republished in the 1930s in *Coisir a' Mhòid* and *Orain a' Mhòid* as well as in other anthologies as noted above. Fortunately, it avoids the grandiosity of the airs considered above, presumably because Tolmie had enough regard for the traditional melody to leave it alone. Here is how it appears in *JFSS:*

3.2. Unpublished settings

We earlier noted some 34 versions of *Griogal Cridhe,* collected from the oral performance of 25 informants between 1869 and 1975. While the earliest of these, taken down in South Uist and Eriskay by Alexander Carmichael and Fr Allan MacDonald, do not include the airs, we still have a good deal of material to consider. In addition, we now have easy access to two additional versions of the air collected during the 19th century: *The Elizabeth Ross Manuscript*, which contains an air for *Griogal Cridhe* recorded by Elizabeth Ross (Lady D'Oyly) of Raasay no later than 1812 – a setting that is contemporary with the Turner collection, and by far the earliest version of the air that we possess; and *Moch air maduinn latha Lunaisd* ('Early on Lammas day morning'), included in a manuscript compiled by Angus Fraser around 1870.

3.2.1 Elizabeth Ross.

Because Ross's manuscript was not intended for publication, it is mercifully free of the commercially-motivated improvements that make other nineteenth-century collections seem dated. Ross includes two versions of the melody (the editors suggest that one would have been used for the stanza and the other for the refrain), plus an additional two iterations following the double-bar; these latter two are probably intended to suggest how the air might be varied and elaborated in an instrumental performance.

Notwithstanding its Raasay provenance, Ross's air bears a closer resemblance to Dun's than it does to Tolmie's Skye melody. Not only is the final cadence (bar 4) identical to Dun's, but the medial cadence (bar 2 above) falls, like Dun's, on the second degree of the scale *(re)* rather than the third *(mi),* as in Tolmie's version.[34] It may be, therefore, that in Ross's air we come somewhat nearer to the way people were singing this melody at the time Dun first heard it – before he inflated the second phrase out of all recognition:

[34] Even so, it is worth noting also that Ross's third bar – in which the melody dips down to low *d* – is reminiscent of the Tolmie's third bar, except that in the latter the tune dips to *e*-flat.

3.2.2 Angus Fraser.

In his manuscript *Collection of the Vocal Airs of the Highlands of Scotland* (c. 1870) Fraser gives an air entitled *Moch air maduinn latha Lunaisd* ('Early on Lammas day morning').[35] Fraser includes two versions of the melody, and we must entertain the possibility that he heard both sung, perhaps one used for the stanza and the other for the refrain. It is perhaps more likely, however, that the second strain, following the double-bar, was composed by Fraser himself and intended to suggest to the instrumental performer how the melody might be varied in performance:

Published versions of the melody fall into two main categories: (1) settings directly descended from, or at least related to, Dun's 1848 melody; and (2) republications of Tolmie's Skye air. Fraser's air appears related to both of these strands: like Tolmie/Gesto, Fraser's medial cadence (*i.e.* the end of the first phrase) ends with the notes (in sol-fa) *la –so – mi* (the notes *a – g – e* in bars 3–4 above), while its final cadence – like those of Dun and all the other Victorian settings – ends with *do – mi – re – do – do* (bars 7–8 above). It seems likely that, despite their differences, all three of these versions were ultimately based upon airs gathered from oral sources. It is a pity that more such airs were not noted down at a time when the song was a living tradition in all parts of the Gàidhealtachd – especially in those mainland areas that might have provided a link to the Perthshire air with which Mór Chaimbeul might have been familiar.

[35] Angus Fraser was an illegitimate son of Captain Simon Fraser of Knockie (1773–84), a violinist, whose own *Airs and Melodies peculiar to the Highlands of Scotland* was published in 1816. The family lived at Errogie on Loch Ness-side, and Angus Fraser may have gathered his own collection in the same vicinity. Fraser's manuscript was published for the first time in 1996.

3.2.3 Twentieth-Century Airs.

Having considered the printed and manuscript evidence for the melody of *Griogal Cridhe*, we may be able to draw some conclusions about the variants of the air collected from oral tradition in the last century. Given our findings with regard to the text, it comes as no surprise that the melodic variants appear to reflect the same division into two distinct strands, a northern strand associated with Skye, Harris and Lewis, and a southern strand associated with the Uists and Barra (see §2.2 above):

GROUP 1: Northern Hebrides	
Skye	Kirsty Munro (1954, 1958)
Berneray Harris	Margaret MacLeod (1970)[36]
Scalpay Harris	Mary MacLeod (1970)[36]
Scalpay Harris	Angus MacLeod (1954, 1959)
Scalpay Harris	Flora Cunningham (1963, 1971)
Harris	Peggy Morrison (recording date unknown)
Lewis	Jessie MacKenzie (1956, 1957)
N. Uist/ Edinburgh	Rev William Matheson (1959, 1960s, 1975)[37]
GROUP 2: Southern Hebrides	
Eriskay	Unnamed Singer (1905)[38]
Barra	Mary MacNeill and Peigi MacNeill (1959)
Barra	Mary Morrison (1959, 1965, 1966)
Barra	Calum Johnston (1965)
Barra	Catherine MacNeil (1965)
Barra	Jane MacDonald (1965)
Barra	'Barra Waulking Women' (1965)
Vatersay	Nan MacKinnon (1956, 1967)
Eriskay	Flora MacInnes (1951)
South Uist	Agnes Currie (1956)
South Uist	Mary Munro (1966)
South Uist	Mrs Hugh MacEachen (1967)
Grimsay	Peter Morrison (1966)

[36] Although both Mary MacLeod (Scalpay) and Margaret MacLeod (Berneray) were included in the southern grouping for textual reasons (see §2.2), their choice of melody firmly places them, alongside other Harris informants, in the Northern Hebrides group.

[37] William Matheson's air is included here because of its clear relationship to others in this group. Whether this is an air that he heard in boyhood in North Uist or one that his later studies led him to choose cannot, unfortunately, be confirmed; see §2.3 above.

[38] See above, n. 17.

The northern group contains performances by eight singers, some of whom recorded the song multiple times, and whose recordings reflect a certain amount of variability. All of these, however, reflect a number of features in common not only with one another, but also with the manuscript and published versions we have been discussing. The above comparison, which includes a representative sample from the modern recordings, illustrates these similarities. Note that for ease of comparison we have transposed all examples into the same key, and have represented the airs as simply as possible, eliminating rhythmic features and ornamental notes which would, in any case, vary from stanza to stanza in accordance with the demands of the text.

The twelve singers in the Southern group clearly represent a different melodic tradition. The above illustration compares four representative performances, which stand apart most significantly from those in the Northern group in having a medial cadence on the dominant, or fifth degree, of the scale (bar 4), and in having a predominantly dorian modal character, as opposed to the mixolydian modality of the airs in the Northern group.[39] When – and where – the southern tradition began to manifest itself it is of course impossible to say; it does, however, seem likely that it was an air from this tradition that the Reverends Angus and Archibald MacDonald heard when they recorded this particular *taladh* for their collection of Gaelic poetry.

4.0 Conclusions.

While we have been at pains here to point out the differences between the various versions of *Griogal Cridhe* – text and music, published and unpublished, northern Hebridean variants and southern ones – the clearest impression overall must remain one not of difference, but of similarity. None of the versions we have encountered here truly stands at odds with the others. Even Finlay Dun's romantic inflation of the melody does not wholly obscure its traditional origins; even the severe truncation of the text over the course of four centuries – only a few of our twentieth-century informants recorded more than four stanzas – does not disguise the fact that *Cumha Ghriogair Ruaidh* continued to hold an important place in the Gaelic repertoire some four centuries after its composition.

Why should this be the case? To suggest an answer, it may be helpful to imagine how the song first entered the living tradition. Mór Chaimbeul herself was clearly a strong character: her determination to marry Griogair Ruadh demonstrates that fact, as does her earlier poem, *Rìgh gur mór mo chuid mhulaid*, in which her love for him – and her feelings about the opposition of her father and other Campbell relations – are manifest. She clearly knew herself to possess a voice, and

[39] The so-called 'church modes' differ from the conventional major and minor tonalities that our ears are commonly attuned to. The *mixolydian* mode most resembles a typical major scale, except that the leading-note – the seventh degree of the scale – is flattened; the *dorian* mode most resembles a melodic minor scale, except for a raised sixth and (again) a flattened leading-note. Complicating matters in the latter case is that several of these supposedly 'dorian' melodies from the Uists and Barra exhibit what William Matheson called the 'variable third' – in this case, the note *a* which in some cases is expressed as *a-flat* and in others as *a-natural*; see Matheson (1955: 77–8) and the performances by Nan MacKinnon and Mary Morrison in the examples given here.

to be a poet. Equal parts love and rage, her lament for Griogair and her violent denunciation of his murderers demanded an audience.

But women in sixteenth-century Gaelic Scotland were not generally granted the right to be heard.[40] Their lives were circumscribed and dictated by the roles granted to them in society: dutiful daughter, loyal wife, nurturing mother. Following Griogair's execution, the Campbells understandably wanted to keep Mór under control, and the best way of doing so was by marrying her off as quickly as possible and keeping her close at hand. Assuming that Martin MacGregor is correct in identifying her second husband as Raibeart Menzies of Comrie, we can visualise Mór's life with him as respectable, comfortable – and suffocating. Her one release would be her private grief, alone and sleepless in her bedroom at night. But we can also imagine her lulling her two small sons, Alastair Ruadh and Iain Dubh, with the lament she had composed for their father.[41] Indeed, the act of composition itself, possibly begun at the time of Griogair's capture, may have continued even after her marriage to Raibeart Menzies.

So how did a song composed and sung in such oppressive circumstances become known? The simplest answer must lie in the comfortable household in which Mór latterly found herself, a household peopled with her husband's female servants. Whether she would have taken any of these directly into her confidence or not, the power of Mór's story and of the lament she composed must have compelled members of this unregarded audience to carry the song home with them, sing it to their own children, and set the tradition in motion. Recent recordings of the song, captured far from Loch Tayside and all too often fragmentary, show that even in its barest manifestations it continued to function as a lullaby – a function that probably preserved it long after the details of its composition (and many of its stanzas) had fallen into oblivion.

Singers choose songs which appeal to them at some deep emotional level. Singing is the purest distillation of emotional meaning in aural form: the expression of emotion is what song is *for*. Lamentation, panegyric, love, faith, sheer *joie-de-vivre* – in Gaelic society, all of these emotions were realised in song, giving emotional release to both singer and listener. In a society which regarded the manifestation of strong feeling as socially risky, such an outlet was essential. We must be grateful for the extraordinary chain that has linked our own emotional reality to that of a spirited young widow, tragically bereaved, whose life otherwise would surely have been overwhelmed by the weight of her husband's epitaph, recorded by the Curate of Fortingall: 'The vij da of Apryill Gregor McGregor of Glenstra heddit at Belloch anno sexte an ten yeris.'

Acknowledgments

I am grateful to my former colleagues in the School of Scottish Studies, Dr John MacInnes and Morag MacLeod, for reading this article in draft, and for the lively discussion and helpful suggestions that emerged; to Fiona MacKenzie at BBC Radio nan Gàidheal for sharing with me the recording of Peggy Morrison; to Nancy R. McGuire for sending me a scan of the variant of 'Griogal

---

[40] John MacInnes has tried to persuade me that women have long been strong and articulate members of Gaelic society, and should not be regarded as having been mere chattels, repressed and without a voice. I do not doubt the sincerity of his belief. Nevertheless, the fact that women – including a number of notable women poets – have left their indelible mark on Gaelic society should not be allowed to obscure the fact that they, unlike men, would have had to fight for the right to be heard. As Alasdair Duncan points out (1979: 70), 'there have been...cases of adverse circumstances producing poetry, the most celebrated perhaps being Màiri Mhór nan Oran with her line, *"'S e na dh' fhulaing me de thàmailt a thug mo bhàrdachd beò"* ["It's all the disparagement I've endured that has brought my poetry to life"].'

[41] The number of lullabies that also function as laments suggests that the lullaby genre provided women a rare opportunity of expressing strong feelings in a manner that was not too disruptive to the male-dominated society in which they lived; see Hillers 2006.

Cridhe' collected by Amy Murray in Eriskay; and particularly to Dr Martin MacGregor of Glasgow University, whose painstaking comments upon my draft article have substantially enriched my own understanding of this song, its author, and the circumstances of its composition.

Sources

AN COMUNN GÀIDHEALACH / THE GAELIC LEAGUE OF SCOTLAND.

1932–37 *Coisir a' Mhòid: The Mòd Collection of Gaelic Part-Songs,* 4: 51–4. Glasgow.

1935 *Orain a' Mhòid,* XII: 13. Glasgow.

1972 *Ceol nam Beann: The Ceilidh Song-Book.* Stirling.

AN GÀIDHEAL III (1874).

BASSIN, ETHEL.

1977 *The Old Songs of Skye: Frances Tolmie and her Circle.* Derek Bowman (ed.). London.

BLANKENHORN, V. S.

2013 'The Rev. William Matheson and the Performance of Scottish Gaelic "Strophic" Verse'. *Scottish Studies* 36: 15–46.

CAMPBELL, BRUCE.

1989 *Orain nan Gaidheal* 2: 37. Glasgow.

CAMPBELL, DUNCAN.

1886 *The Lairds of Glenlyon.* Perth.

1910 *Reminiscences and Reflections of an Octogenarian Highlander.* Inverness.

CARMICHAEL-WATSON Ms. 244 No. 170, Edinburgh University Library.

CELTIC MONTHLY, THE: A MAGAZINE FOR HIGHLANDERS. Vol. 1. 1893.

COLLINSON, FRANCIS.

1966 *The Traditional and National Music of Scotland.* London.

DUN, FINLAY.

1848 *Orain na 'h-Albain: The Vocal Melodies of Scotland.* Edinburgh.

DUNCAN, ALASDAIR.

1979 'Some MacGregor Songs'. Unpublished M.Litt dissertation, University of Edinburgh.

FRASER, ANGUS.

1996 *A Collection of the Vocal Airs of the Highlands of Scotland.* Breakish, Isle of Skye.

FRATER, ANNA C.

1997 'Women of the Gàidhealtachd and their songs to 1750'. E. Ewan and M. Meikle (eds), *Women in Scotland c. 1100 – c. 1750.* East Linton: 67–80.

GILLIES, ANNE LORNE.

2005 *Songs of Gaelic Scotland.* Edinburgh.

GILLIES, WILLIAM.

1976–78 'Some aspects of Campbell history'. *Transactions of the Gaelic Society of Inverness* 50: 256–95.

HIGHLANDER, THE. Series 2. I: 32–3.

HILLERS, BARBARA.

2006 'Dialogue or monologue? Lullabies in Scottish Gaelic tradition'. Michel Byrne, T. O. Clancy and S. Kidd (eds), *Litreachas & Eachdraidh: Rannsachadh na Gàidhlig 2 / Literature & History: Papers from the Second Conference of Scottish Gaelic Studies, Glasgow 2002.* Glasgow: 33–55.

INNES, COSMO.

1861 *Sketches of Early Scotch History and Social Progress.* Edinburgh.

KERRIGAN, CATHERINE.

1991 *Anthology of Scottish Women Poets.* Edinburgh.

MAC AN TUAIRNEIR, PARUIG.

1813 *Comhchruinneachadh do dh'orain taghta Ghaidhealach.* Edinburgh.

MACDONALD, A. AND A.

1911 *The MacDonald Collection of Gaelic Poetry.* Inverness.

MACDONALD, FR ALLAN.

Ms. Gen 1090 (28), No. 92. Glasgow University Library.

MACDONALD, KEITH NORMAN.

[1895] 1997 *The Gesto Collection of Highland Music.* Burnham-on-Sea.

MAC GILL-EAIN, SOMHAIRLE.

1985 'Realism in Gaelic Poetry'. *Ris a' Bhruthaich.* Stornoway: 15–47.

1985 'Aspects of Gaelic Poetry'. *Ris a' Bhruthaich.* Stornoway: 75–82.

2008 'Five Gaelic poems – regional, national or European?'. Paper read to the Gaelic Society of Glasgow, January 1940. *Aiste* 2: 1–29.

MAC GIOLLA LÉITH, CAOIMHÍN.

1993 *Oidheadh Chloinne hUisneach.* Irish Texts Society 56. Dublin.

MACGREGOR, A. G. M.

1898 *History of the Clan Gregor.* Vol. I: 160. Edinburgh.

MACGREGOR, MARTIN.

1999 '"Surely one of the greatest poems ever made in Britain": The Lament for Griogair Ruadh MacGregor of Glen Strae and its Historical Background'. E. J. Cowan and D. Gifford (eds), *The Polar Twins.* Edinburgh: 114–53.

2013 PC (Personal Communication) to the author, by email, 8 September 2013.

MACLEAN, DONALD.

1915 *Typographia Scoto-Gadelica: Books Printed in the Gaelic of Scotland.* Edinburgh.

MACLEAN SINCLAIR, ALEXANDER.

1890 *The Gaelic Bards from 1411 to 1715.* Charlottetown, P.E.I.: 18–21.

MAC PHÀRLAIN, CALUM.

1908 *Binneas nam Bàrd: leabhar anns am bheil dàin, òrain is duanagan nan Gaidheal Albannach air am foillseachadh maille ri'm fuinn.* Struibhle (Stirling): 48–50.

1913 'Bàrdachd nam Ban'. *Guth na Bliadhna* X/3: 347–50.

MATHESON, WILLIAM.

1955 'Some early collectors of Gaelic folk-song'. *Proceedings of the Scottish Anthropological and Folklore Society* 5/2: 67–82.

MATHIS, KATE LOUISE.

2008 'An Ulster tale in Breadalbane? Personae and literary allusion in the poetry of Mòr Chaimbeul'. *Aiste* 2: 43–69.

MCCONACHIE, J. N.

1960 *Gaelic Calling "Ghàidhlig a' Gairm".* Glasgow.

MCGUIRE, NANCY R.

1999 'Amy Murray's Eriskay Collection'. *Scottish Gaelic Studies* 19: 83–92.

MCLEOD, WILSON AND MEG BATEMAN.

2007 *Duanaire na Sracaire / Songbook of the Pillagers: Anthology of Scotland's Gaelic Verse to 1600.* Edinburgh.

MORRISON, ANGUS.

1913 *Orain nam Beann.* Glasgow: 20–1.

NEWTON, MICHAEL.

2000 'The MSS of Donald MacGregor'. *Transactions of the Gaelic Society of Inverness* 61: 280 ff.

Ó TUAMA, SEÁN.

1961 *Caoineadh Airt Uí Laoghaire.* Baile Átha Cliath.

PARTRIDGE, ANGELA.

1981 'Wild men and wailing women'. *Éigse* 18: 23–37.

PATTISON, THOMAS.

1890 *The Gaelic Bards and Original Poems.* Glasgow: 116–19.

ROSS, ELIZABETH.

2011 *The Elizabeth Ross Manuscript: Original Highland Airs collected at Raasay in 1812 by Elizabeth Jane Ross*. Peter Cook, Morag MacLeod and C. O'Boyle (eds). Edinburgh University Celtic and Scottish Studies: www.ed.ac.uk/polopoly_fs/1.100545!/fileManager/ERossfacsimilesm.pdf

SHARP, ELIZABETH A.

1891 *Lyra Celtica: an anthology of representative Celtic poetry*. Edinburgh.

SINCLAIR, ALEXANDER MACLEAN. SEE MACLEAN SINCLAIR, ALEXANDER.

STEWART, ALEXANDER.

1928 *A Highland Parish, or, the History of Fortingall*. Glasgow.

STEWART, CHARLES.

1884 *The Killin Collection of Gaelic Songs, with Music and Translations*. Edinburgh.

THOMSON, DERICK.

1955–8 'Scottish Gaelic Folk-poetry ante 1650'. *Scottish Gaelic Studies* 8: 1–17.

1963–5 'A disputed reading in Cumha Ghriogair Mhic Ghriogair'. *Scottish Gaelic Studies* 10: 68–70.

1974 *Introduction to Gaelic Poetry*. New York.

1983 *Companion to Gaelic Scotland*. Oxford.

TOCHER. School of Scottish Studies, Edinburgh, 1971– .

TOLMIE, FRANCES.

1911 'One Hundred and Five Songs of Occupation from the Western Isles of Scotland'. *Journal of the Folk-Song Society* 16.

n.d. Papers in the National Library of Scotland, NLS 14904: 27 and 14907: 17

TURNER, PATRICK. SEE MAC AN TUAIRNEIR, PARUIG.

WATSON, W. J.

[1918] 1932 *Bardachd Ghàidhlig: Gaelic Poetry 1550–1900*. Second Ed. Inverness.

1939 'Place-Names of Perthshire: The Lyon Basin'. *Transactions of the Gaelic Society of Inverness* 35: 277–96.

‘A Bhean Úd Thall!’
Macallaí Idirghaelacha i bhFilíocht Bhéil na mBan

ANGELA BOURKE

ABSTRACT. Drawing on John MacInnes’s writings on the *òrain-luaidh* and what he calls the ‘panegyric code’ in Gaelic poetry, this essay argues that the *òrain-luaidh* of Scotland and a number of genres of women’s oral poetry in Irish derive from a single oral-formulaic tradition that seems to have belonged particularly to women, and to have been dominated by women’s concerns until responsibility for the waulking of cloth passed to men in the migrant Gaelic-speaking communities of eastern Canada. The Irish texts quoted are best exemplified by the *caoineadh*, or lament for the dead, but also include joke laments, lullabies, work songs, and religious poetry. They share numerous themes and formulas, along with important features of diction, metre and composition, not only with waulking songs recorded in twentieth-century Scotland, but also with the *luinneagan* composed by Màiri nighean Alasdair Ruaidh (Mary MacLeod) in the seventeenth century.

Is minic ina chuid aistí ar fhilíocht bhéil na Gàidhlig a dhéanann Iain Mac Aonghuis iniúchadh ar mhianach dúchasach na filíochta sin. ‘The central strand of the Gaelic tradition is found in the *òrain-luaidh*’, a deir sé, ag áiteamh gur sa mhúnla a dtugtaí *luinneag* air sa 17ú agus san 18ú haois, agus atá beo i gcónaí ag fonnadóirí an 21ú haois, atá dlúth agus inneach an traidisiúin (MacInnes 2006: 250). Is é a thuigeann sé leis an téarma *òrain-luaidh* anseo, an cineál amhráin a chum Màiri nighean Alasdair Ruaidh sa 17ú haois, le loinneog siollaí i ndiaidh gach véarsa mar ‘*Hó lail oho / Hóireann ó*’ (Watson 1965: 2 & *passim*), chomh maith leis na hamhráin a chualathas ag grúpaí ban sa 20ú haois in Inse Gall, agus éadach á ramhrú acu lena lámha, agus a bhfuil athchóiriú déanta go minic air ó shin ag ceoltóirí na mórmheán cumarsáide. ‘The fundamental lyrical urge of Gaelic poetry’ a thug Iain Mac Aonghuis i 1966 ar mheon na filíochta seo, atá lán d’íomhánna coincréideacha agus de mhothúcháin íogaire daonna:

> I suggest that this lyricism is inseparable from the mode in which experience is apprehended and articulated, and that the mode is in turn created by the conditions of the choral refrain functioning in a sort of dramatic opposition to the words. (MacInnes 2006: 228)

In amhráin luaidh na hAlban, tugann fonnadóir aonair amach loinneog rithimiúil i dtosach—an ‘choral refrain’, le siollaí foirmleacha, rithimiúla, seachas focail sothuigthe—agus freagraíonn an chuid eile dá bhfuil i láthair gach líne uaithi ina dhiaidh sin leis an loinneog chéanna: comhcheol mar ‘*Éileadh ’s na hùraibh o ho, a hu o ho*’ (Shaw 1977: 208), a chothaíonn comhobair agus comhthuiscint na mban.

I gCeanada, i measc na nGael a díbríodh go hAlbain Nua agus go Talamh an Éisc, briseadh an ceangal idir na mná agus ramhrú an éadaigh, agus fágadh an chuid is mó den luadh, idir obair agus amhránaíocht, faoi na fir (Bennett 1989: 154–56, 188–237; MacLellan 2000: 16; agus na fadcheirníní *Gaelic Tradition in Cape Breton,* 1978, agus *A Tribute to the North Shore Gaelic Singers,* 1986).[1] Is cosúil gur thit ceisteanna na mban amach as na hamhráin luaidh i gCeanada dá reir sin, ach sna cinn atá againn as Albain, is léir gurb é a bhí iontu cuid mhaith, dioscúrsa

[1] Is cosúil nárbh acmhainn do na mná dul as baile i gCeanada chomh héasca is a dhéanadh siad in Albain sa tírdhreach fuar nua ar thug an file Iain MacGillEathain ‘An Choille Ghruamach’ air (MacLean & Dorgan: 10).

príobháideach, atá lán le tagairtí do shaol corpartha agus sóisialta na mban. Tugann scríbhinní Iain Mhic Aonghuis tríd síos aitheantas ar leith do ról na mban sa chineál 'loinneogach' seo filíochta. Mná, a deir sé, a chum agus a chleachtaigh í, agus is trí shúile ban a fheictear an saol inti (MacInnes 2006: 305 & *passim*).

Tá an rud céanna i gceist i dtaobh na caointeoireachta in Éirinn, chomh maith le roinnt aicmí eile filíochta a shamhlaítear le mná is le cailíní: cuimhnímid ar na suantraithe agus na hamhráin saothair, agus ar na hamhráin bheannaithe (Ó Madagáin 1985: 196–214; Partridge 1983). In ómós do Iain, mar sin, ba mhaith liom roinnt leathanach a chaitheamh le cuid de na cosúlachtaí idir filíocht loinneogach na mban i nGaeilge na hÉireann agus i nGàidhlig na hAlban. Dar liom (i) go mba cheart an fhilíocht seo ar fad a áireamh in éineacht mar dhá chuid den aon oidhreacht ársa amháin, ó thaobh friotail, ábhair agus modh na cumadóireachta de, agus (ii) go mbíodh an fhilíocht loinneogach sa dá thír ag freastal ar chuid mhaith de na riachtanaisí céanna i saol na mban agus i saol an phobail go dtí le déanaí.[2]

Filíocht na Caointeoireachta

Is minic a thagraíonn aistí Iain Mhic Aonghuis do théama an bháis agus téamaí caointeoireachta sna *hòrain-luaidh*, ach ní dhéanann sé aon chomparáid fhoirmeálta idir iad agus caointe na hÉireann (MacInnes 2006: 28; 228; 243; 283). Ní léir ar théacsanna foilsithe na caointeoireachta, áfach, gur traidisiún loinneogach ainteafanúil a bhí inti sin freisin. Ó chuir Osborn Bergin 'Caoineadh Airt Uí Laoghaire' in eagar ag deireadh an 19ú haois (Bergin 1896), tá béim curtha ag scoláirí agus criticeoirí ha hÉireann ar chruthaitheacht 'liteartha' an chumadóra, beag beann ar an traidisiún as ar fáisceadh í, cé go n-aithnítear a leithéid a bheith ann (Bourke 1997).

Tá a fhios againn gur bhain náire as cuimse le 'gol mná aonair' ar shochraid, go mba léiriú nó láithriú beo é an caoineadh, agus go mba chuid lárnach den láithriú sin loinneog an bhróin. Cuireann scríbhneoirí agus seanchaithe síos ar an nglór gol a chloistí os cionn an mharbháin, agus mná d'aon ghuth ag tabhairt freagra loinneogach ar fhilíocht aonair na mná caointe (m.sh. Hall 1841: i, 226; Ó Madagáin 1982). Leithéid '*Och, och agus ochón ó*!', nó '*A bhó bhó go deo*!', a bhíodh ag na mná seo, agus na basa á mbualadh acu, gach uair a chríochnaíodh an príomhchaointeoir dreas filíochta. Cosúil le loinneog na n-amhrán luaidh, siollaí foirmleacha a bhíodh sa ghlór gol, seachas focail sothuigthe.

Foirmlí traidisiúnta is bunús don chuid is mó d'fhilíocht na caointeoireachta freisin, mar a léirigh Rachel Bromwich os cionn 60 bliain ó shin (Bromwich 1948). D'aithin Seán Ó Tuama an traidisiún foirmleach ina eagrán scolártha, *Caoineadh Airt Uí Laoghaire*, ach dúirt, 'is fíor gur tur linn an guth traidisiúnta i gcomórtas leis an nguth [pearsanta]', agus:

> Is minic mar sin, *i gan fhios di féin*, a bhain Eibhlín Dhubh leas speisialta as na téamaí dúchais caointeoireachta: d'fhuaigh sí go healaíonta i bpatrún a cuid véarsaiochta iad. Uaireanta eile, áfach, le déine a paisiúin, d'athbheoigh sí na sean-*clichés* ó bhonn. (Ó Tuama 1961: 29 [uaimse an bhéim])

Ba é Seán Ó Coileáin, a raibh staidéar iarchéime déanta aige le hAlbert Lord in Ollscoil Harvard, a chuir léargas teoiriciúil idirnáisiúnta i bhfeidhm ar an gceist seo, nuair a shamhlaigh sé modh cumadóireachta leis an gcaoineadh de réir theoiric Lord: gurb é a fhoghlaimíonn file óg i dtraidisiún béil, ó aimsir Homer aniar, stór foirmlí a fhanann ina c[h]uimhne mar a bheadh foclóir, chomh maith le modh cumadóireachta a fheidhmíonn mar a dhéanann an ghramadach agus teanga á foghlaim, agus a chuireann ar a c[h]umas téamaí dúchais a fhuáil go healaíonta i bpatrún na véarsaíochta (Lord 1960; Ó Coileáin 1978, 1988). Feicimid na móitífeanna céanna agus na foirmlí céanna cainte á múnlú agus á malartú, agus á gcur in oiriúint dá chéile ó thaobh ríme agus céille,

---

[2] D'fhéadfaí i bhfad níos mó samplaí a sholáthar den fhriotal a bhfuil trácht air thíos; beidh a thuilleadh comparáidí le fáil, nach féidir a thabhairt anseo de cheal spáis, ach na tagairtí a leanúint.

sna caointe a cumadh san 18ú agus sa 19ú haois in Éirinn ar Shéamas Mac Coitir (1720), ar an Athair Nioclás Mac Síthigh (1766), ar Art Ó Laoghaire (1773), agus ar Dhiarmaid mac Eoghain Mhic Chárthaigh (c. 1850) (Bourke &rl 2002: 1365–88).

An 'Panegyric Code' agus Modh na Cumadóireachta

Leanann foirmlí na caointeoireachta an réimse tagairtí do shaol na n-uasal – fiach agus foghlaeracht; fleadh agus féasta; éadaí galánta; claidheamh cinn airgid agus ginealach ársa – a dtugann Iain Mac Aonghuis an 'Panegyric Code' uirthi. Agus é ag trácht ar Mhàiri nighean Alasdair Ruaidh, is léir gur mar fhile ag feidhmiú taobh istigh de thraidisiún foirmleach béil a thuigeann sé í:

> [A]ll her bardic panegyrics consist of complicated permutations of the same commonplaces. It will also be clear that they do not follow any particular order. The poetess will reintroduce the subject's descent, generosity (especially to men of art), personal beauty, and so on, several times, producing a densely woven texture of imagery in which every phrase, indeed almost every word, is significant (MacInnes 2006: 275).

Nuair a chuirimid friotal Mhàiri nighean Alasdair i gcomparáid le friotal na caointeoireachta, is léir ní amháin gur filíocht fhoirmleach bhéil iad ar aon, ach gur leis an traidisiún foirmleach ársa céanna a bhaineann siad. Seo Màiri:

> Nam biodh agamsa fìon
> Gum b'ait leam a dhìol
> Air slàinte do thighinn
> Gu d' chàirdean 's gu d' thìr;
> Mhic àrmuinn mo ghaoil,
> B'e m'àrdan 's mo phrìs
> Alach mo Rìgh thogbhail. (Watson 1965: 60, 732–38)

Ó thaobh struchtúir agus meoin, tá na línte sin comhthreomhar leis na cinn seo ag Eibhlín Dubh Ní Chonaill:

> Tá a fhios ag Íosa Criost
> Ná beidh caidhp ar bhathas mo chinn,
> Ná léine chnis lem thaoibh,
> Ná bróg ar thrácht mo bhoinn,
> Ná trioscán ar fuaid mo thí,
> Ná srian leis an láir ndoinn,
> Ná caithfidh mé le dlí,
> 'S go raghad anonn thar toinn
> Ag comhra leis an rí.... (Ó Tuama 1961: 43, 315–23)

In *Caoineadh Airt Uí Laoghaire*, tugtar le tuiscint go raibh beirt bhan ag caoineadh, ach gan bheith buíoch dá chéile: Eibhlín Dubh Ní Chonaill, bean Airt, agus deirfiúr leis, a tháinig as Corcaigh ar chloisteáil scéala a bháis. Beidh solúbthacht na bhfoirmlí traidisiúnta an-soiléir ach dreas a deirtear a chum Eibhlín (le rím ar an bhfuaim 'é' nó 'ao', agus siolla neamhaiceanta ina dhiaidh) a chur i gcomparáid le dreas an-chosúil leis a leagtar ar an deirfiúr, le rím ar 'ú', móide siolla neamhaiceanta:

> *Eibhlín:*
> M'fhada-chreach léan-ghoirt
> Na rabhas-sa taobh leat
> Nuair lámhadh an piléar leat,

Go ngeobhainn é im thaobh deas
Nó i mbinn mo léine,
Is go léigfinn cead slé' leat
A mharcaigh na ré-ghlac.

An Deirfiúr:
Mo chreach ghéarchúiseach
Ná rabhas ar do chúlaibh
Nuair lámhadh an púdar,
Go ngeobhainn é im chom dheas
Nó i mbinn mo ghúna
Is go léigfinn cead siúil leat
A mharcaigh na súl nglas
Ós tú b'fhearr léigean chucu. (Ó Tuama 1961: 37–38)

Is léir gur de réir na chéad líne, agus go háirithe de réir an aicinn deiridh, a mhúnlaíonn an file an chuid den dreas filíochta a leanann, ach go ligeann a taithí ar na foirmlí agus solúbthacht na bhfoirmlí féin di sin a dhéanamh *ex tempore* (Ó Coileáin 1988: 101). Feicimid an mheadaracht agus an friotal faoi smacht ag an túslíne ar an mbealach céanna i 'Marbhrann' Mhàiri nighean Alasdair. Tosaíonn dreas amháin le seilg na gé, agus an ceann ina dhiaidh le seilg an fhia:

Bu tù sealgair a' gheoidh,
Làmh gun dearmad gun leòn
Air am bu shuarach an t-òr
Thoirt a bhuannachd a' cheoil,
Is gun d'fhuair thu na's leoir is na chaitheadh tu.

Bu tù sealgair an fhéidh
Leis an deargta na béin;
Bhiodh coin earbsach air éill
Aig an Albannach threun;
Càite am faca mi féin
Aon duine fo'n ghréin
A dhèanadh riut euchd flathasach? (Watson 1965: 26)

Is minic scairt bhróin, mar a bhíonn sa chaoineadh, mar thúslíne filíochta ag Máiri nighean Alasdair leis an bhfeidhm chéanna: 'Mo bheud is mo chràdh', sa dán thuas, nó 'Is goirt an naidheachd 's gur cruaidh' (Watson 1965: 68). San amhrán 'Pòsadh Mhic Leoid', baineann sí úsáid as túslíne filíochta a thugann teideal don aiste seo: 'A bhean ud thall!'. Líne í atá le cloisteáil go flúirseach le trí chéad bliain, ní amháin in amhráin luaidh na hAlban, ach i gcaointe agus i bhfilíocht eile na mban ar fud na hÉireann[3]:

A bhean ud thall
A chòir an uisge,

A Trondairnis 's ann
Thàinig thusa:

'S e sin a dh'fhàg
Thu an diugh gun trusgan.

---

3 Féach, mar shampla, an suantraí a thosaíonn 'A bhean úd thíos ar bhruach an tsrutháin' nó 'A bhean úd thall ar lic an átha / Seoithín seó, seoithín seó' (Shields 1993: 75–76; Bourke &rl 2002: 1424–25), agus an bailéad idirnáisiúnta (Child 10), 'A bhean údaí thall', atá pléite ag Hugh Shields (Shields 1972; 1993: 68) agus ag Alan Bruford (Bruford 1973).

Agus tugtar freagra uirthi:

> Air do làimh
> A chaile bhusdubh,
>
> Chan ’eil mi
> Gun òr gun usgar.
>
> Tha mo ghùn dubh
> Ur nam’ chiste,
>
> Is mo sgóid-bhràghad,
> Chan fhaigh thusa ì! (Watson 1965: 8)

Tá an túslíne chéanna tugtha mar theideal ar amhrán luaidh (‘’Mhic Iarla nam bratach bàna’) ar *Waulking Songs from Barra* (1972):

> A bhean ud thall a rinne an gàire (x 3)
> Nach truagh leat piuthar gan bhràthair….

– línte is féidir a shamhlú mar thaobh amháin de choimhlint idir deirfiúr agus bean chéile os cionn chorp fir. Cloisimid a leithéid in an-chuid amhrán caointeacha i dtraidisiún na hÉireann:

> O’s a bhean úd thall atá ag déanamh gáire,
> Nárb é fada go rabh agat fios m’ábhair,
> Do cheann (a) cromtha ’s do chroí cráite
> Is do dhá lámh teanntaithe fa mhac mo mháthara. (Bourke, &rl 2002: 1389)

Ligfeadh línte mar seo don bhean chaointe smacht a chur ar a lucht éisteachta, chomh maith le dul i gcoimhlint le mná eile:

> A ghiolla úd thall a bhfuil casóg bhán ort,
> Más duine ag imeacht thú, nár casa Dia slán thú! (Ó Concheanainn 1978: 7)

Agus tá leagan eile den túsline chéanna i rannscéal faoi thórramh bréige a chuir Caitlín Ní Úrdail, cailín scoile as Doire an Chairn, Eadargóil, Co. Chorcaí, chuig eagarthóir *An Lóchrann* i 1911. Tá coimhlint i gceist arís anseo idir deirfiúr agus bean a dearthár, agus móitíf an-ársa i gcaint na mná pósta:

> A bhean úd thíos go bhfuil an síoda ort.
> Do chos ar do leathghlúin agat agus tú ag deargadh do phíopa,
> Ná tiocfá aníos agus t’fhear a chaoineadh?

‘Ó,’ arsan bhean thíos:

> Gheobhad-sa fear mara bhfuilim críona,
> Agus deartháir ní bhfaghair-se go bráth ná choidhche.[4] (Bourke, &rl 2002: 1393–95)

Is minic comórtas idir bailte agus pobail á leiriú sna véarsaí seo, cosúil leis an díspeagadh ar Throndairnis thuas atá leagtha ar Mhàiri nighean Alasadair. Seo rannscéal as Ciarraí a d’fhoilsigh An Seabhac ar *An Lóchrann* i 1908, agus an litriú caighdeánaithe beagán:

> Do cailleadh seanduine timpeall Ínse agus tháinig iníon leis go tigh an choirp. Bhí sí pósta in Ínse. Bhí bean mhic ag an seanduine leis, agus ó Ínse ab ea í. Dúirt iníon an tseanduine nuair a tháinig sí isteach os a chionn:

---

[4] Féach freisin Ó Concheanainn 1978: 7; Ó Muireadhaigh 1977: 31–32, 73; Ó Duilearga 1939: 235–36; Tierney 1939: 236–38; Ó Súilleabháin 1940: 24–30.

Mo ghrá thú is mo thaisce,
Is ba mhór le rá thú tamall,
Nuair a bátaí muc id chuid bainne,
Idir dhá Chéadaoin an earraigh,
Nuair a bhíodh muintir Ínse dealbh.

Dúirt bean an mhic á freagairt:

Léan ort agus lagar!
A sraoile bhuí 's a chaile,
Is ná cuir bréag go deo ar mhairbh,
Is go mórmhór ar t'athair,
Mar níorbh mhuc é ach banbh,
Is níor leis féin an bainne,
Ach é a bhailiú ar fud na mbailte. (Bourke & rl 2002: 1397)

Dar le Walter Ong, is í an choimhlint a thugann aclaíocht don litríocht bhéil ar fud an domhain agus ó aois go haois, ní amháin ó thaobh ábhair, ach ó thaobh foirme (Ong 1982: 43–45; Cf. Ó Madagáin 1985, 182–84). Is ealaín í nach fiú do dhuine a chleachtadh ina aonar, más féidir féin é, agus luíonn sé le réasún gur mar chomórtas is fuinniúla a mhaireann sí.

Tuigtear in *Caoineadh Airt Uí Laoghaire* gur thug deirfiúr Airt faoi Eibhlín le tagairt do mhná eile a bhí aige, nó a d'fhéadfadh a bheith aige:

Mo chara is mo stór tu!
Is mó bean chumtha chórach
Ó Chorcaigh na seolta
Go Droichead na Tóime,
Do thabharfadh macha mór bó dhuit
Agus dorn buí-óir duit,
Ná raghadh a chodladh ina seomra
Oíche do thórraimh.

Ach go bhfreagraíonn Eibhlín le bród collaí í:

A dhaoine na n-ae istigh,
'Bhfuil aon bhean in Éirinn,
Ó luí na gréine,
A shínfeadh a taobh leis,
Do bhéarfadh trí lao dho,
Ná raghadh le craobhacha
I ndiaidh Airt Uí Laoghaire
Atá anso traochta
Ó mhaidin inné agam? (Ó Tuama 1961: 36–37)

Tá an líne thuas 'Is mó bean chumtha chórach' agus a leanann ina dhiaidh, ar aon déanamh le dreas a leagtar ar mháthair Dhiarmaid Mhic Chárthaigh, a cailleadh thart ar 1850:

Mo ghrá is mo thaisce thú,
Is dá mbeadh agam teachtaire
Nó coisí meanmnach
A raghadh cois Mainge siar,
Is mó bean bhreá mhascalach
Agus marcach breá ceannasach
Lena n-iallaití dearga
Agus a mbéalbhachaí airgid,

Ag trá agus ag tarrac ort,
Do bhainfeadh tine chreasa amach
Ag fágáil na cathrach. (Bourke 2002: 1385)

– agus leis na cinn seo ó Mhàiri nighean Alasdair:

Is iomadh bodach
Leathann ceòsach

Agus cailleach
Rògach leòmach

Thigeadh a nall
A cùirt Dhomhnaill,

Dh’innseadh gun do
Thriall am mòd air:

Gun do ghlais na
Gaill e an seòmar. (Watson 1965: 10)

Chuir Margaret Fay Shaw nóta leis an amhrán Uimhir 85 aici, ‘Alasdair Òig Mhic ’ic Neacail’, a deir sí a bhí coitianta go maith in Uidhist a Deas: ‘Mr Angus Matheson has drawn my attention to *Éigse: A Journal of Irish Studies*, Vol. II, pp. 2–3, where an Irish keen collected by Professor Séamus Ó Duilearga has a resemblance (Shaw 1977: 220–1).[5]

‘Blúire do Shean-Chaoine’ atá ar an téacs a chuir Ó Duilearga i gcló: naoi líne dhéag filíochta agus scéilín mínithe ag dul leo mar údar, a thóg sé ar Edifón ó Phádraig Ó Dubhghaill (78), Inis Díomáin, Co. an Chláir, i Meán Fómhair na bliana 1930, móide aguisín cheithre líne a fuair sé ina dhiaidh sin (Ó Duilearga 1940). Bean óg a chaoineann fear a phós bean eile i ngeall ar spré, agus a fuair bás ina dhiaidh sin. Léiríonn na línte tosaigh an liriciúlacht a bhíonn faoi chaibidil ag Iain Mac Aonghuis. Tá an litriú agus an phoncaíocht caighdeánaithe beagán agam:

Faighim boladh an *thyme* agus an *thyme* go mór ort:
Boladh ismín dearg na móna,
Boladh an úill a chaith bliain i mo chófra ort,
Agus blas na meala ar do theanga sa chónra,
Agus mo léan géar tú ag teacht um thráthnóna!

Is mór mór go mb’fhearr leat iníon an Tiarna Paoraigh,
Ó is mó a luadhadh spré léi.
Má bhí sé aicise de bharr spré orm,
Bhí sé agamsa de bharr léinn uirthi.
Ó, a dhuine uasail, ghlacfainn do léine,
Agus ní ar tuaifeal a d’fhuálfainn féin í,
Ach na greamanna socra míne,
Agus iad a chur le hais a chéile.

Sna línte deiridh atá an chosúlacht le ‘Alasdair Òig Mhic ’ic Neacail’:

Is trua gan mac agamsa leatsa,

[5] Bhí cineál fóraim ar bun sna huimhreacha luatha de *Éigse*, i 1939 agus 1940, agus comhfhreagróirí éagsúla ag soláthar téacsanna d’fhilíocht na caointeoireachta do Ghearóid Ó Murchú mar eagarthóir. Bhí aiste ghearr ag Angus Matheson féin in *Éigse* II, uimhir 1, agus nóta ann freisin ag John Lorne Campbell (1906–96), a phós Margaret Fay Shaw i 1935.

> Mac ina bhráthair, mac ina shagart,
> Cúigear faoi chumhdaigh ag an mbaile,
> Triúr ar scoil Béarla agus Laidne,
> Mac mo mhuirne faoi bhúcla mo chreasa,
> Agus tá súil agam le hÍosa ná déanfar mo mhalairt!

Is é atá san amhrán luaidh, agus leannán na mná óige báite, is cosúil:

> Alasdair Òig, mhic 'ic Neacail,
> B'fheàrr liom fhìn gum beirinn mac dhut,
> Dhà no trì dhiubh, sia no seachd dhiubh,
> Cóigear no sianar no seachdnar;
> Bheirinn cìoch is glùn dhaibh an asgaidh,
> Bheirinn ciùird a làimh gach fear dhiubh;
> Fear 'na dhiùca, fear 'na chaiptin,
> Fear 'na dhròbhair mór air martaibh.
> Fear air a' luing mhóir a' Sasunn,
> Fear 'na cheannard air sluagh feachdach. (Shaw 1977:220)

Ach ní hé an taobh dearfa amháin den ghrá a léirionn an cineál seo filíochta. Bíonn éad agus foréigean i gceist i línte le Màiri:

> Bhean thug uamsa mo roghainn,
> Is gun taghainn thar cheud e.
>
> Ach nam bithinn 'na fianuis,
> Gum biodh spìonadh air bhréidean. (Watson 1965: 50)

– agus macallaí orthu in amhrán luaidh:

> Chuala mi gun d'rinn e réiteach...
> Nan cluininn gum b'fhìor an sgeula,
> Dhòirtinn fuil is ghearrainn féithean
> 'S bheirinn sic a cinn o chéile. (Campbell & Collinson 1977: 66–67)

– agus sa cheann eile seo, a chasann foirmle an fhoréigin ar ais ar an gcainteoir féin:

> Nan cluininn té eile luaidh riut
> Spìonainn bun is bàrr mo chuailein,
> Gu falbhadh m'fheòil 'na ceò uaine. (Campbell & Collinson 1977: 146–47)

Agus céard faoin amhrán éadach as Conamara?:

> Go mbristear do chosa, do chosa,
> Go mbristear do chosa, a bhean Pháidín!
> Go mbristear do chosa, do chosa
> Go mbristear do chosa 's do chnámha!

Mar chlabhsúr, féachaimis nóiméad ar amhráin na Páise in Éirinn, a léiríonn Muire mar bhean chaointe ar an sean-nós. Is iontu a fheicimid loinneog na caointeoireachta i gcló, mar go bhfuil foirm sheasta aici sna hamhráin seo, mar atá sna hamhráin luaidh:

> 'Cé hí siúd siar a bhfuil a gruaig le fána?
> *Im ó chona agus imóchon ó!*
> 'Cé bheadh ann mara mbeadh mo mháthair?'
> *Im ó chona agus imóchon ó!* (Partridge [Bourke] 1983: 168)

Nó:

'Cé'n fear breá sin ar chrann na Páise?'
Óchón is Óchon ó!
'An é nach n-aithníonn tú do mhac, a Mháithrín?'
Óchón is Óchon ó! (Partridge [Bourke] 1983: 170)

Tá cosúlacht ag an leagan amach seo, ceist agus freagra, le móitíf na foraire i scéalta na Sean-Ghaeilge: beirt ag imirt fichille, mar shampla, agus radharc amach ar an bhfuinneog ag duine acu; déanann sise/seisean cur síos don duine ar a aghaidh ar na laochra a fheiceann sí/sé ag teacht, agus insíonn an duine sin cé hiad. Teicníc éifeachtach, drámatúil scéalaíochta é seo, a bhfuil macalla de ag Máirí nighean Alasdair freisin:

An cluin thu, 'Mhàiri
So na ceil orm:

Ciodh ì an long ud
Seach an eirthir?

Don-faighneachd ort!
Cuime an ceilinn?

Ciodh ì tha sud ach
Long mo leinibh? (Watson 1965: 3–4, 11–18)

Tá modh agus teicníc na cumadóireachta béil le tuiscint as na samplaí seo ar fad thuas: friotal agus leaganacha cainte a stiúrann an file trí acmhainní an traidisiúin, cuma más ag moladh taoisigh mhairbh nó leannáin bheo atá sí, ag maslú mná eile, ag magadh faoi dhaoine, nó ag caoineadh a cáis féin. Le hÉirinn a shamhlaítear na mná caointe, Muire ina measc, agus le hAlbain na hamhráin luaidh, ach níl aon amhras ach go bhfuil gaol gairid idir an dá thraidisiún, agus caithfidh sé gur timpist staire, nach bhfuil faisnéis againn fúithi, is cúis leis an tost leataobhach sa mhéid a mhaireann den dá thraidisiún.

Foinsí

Bennett, Margaret.

1989 *The Last Stronghold: Scottish Gaelic Traditions of Newfoundland.* Edinburgh.

Bergin, Osborn.

1896 Caoineadh Airt Uí Laoghaire. *Irisleabhar na Gaedhilge / The Gaelic Journal* VII: 18–23.

Bourke, Angela [= Partridge, Angela].

1988 'Working and Weeping: Women's Oral Poetry in Irish and Scottish Gaelic'. UCD Women's Studies Working Papers 7. Dublin.

1993 'More in Anger than in Sorrow: Irish Women's Lament Poetry'. Joan N. Radner (ed.), *Feminist Messages: Coding in Women's Folk Culture.* Chicago: 160–182.

1997 'Performing, not Writing: The Reception of an Irish Woman's Lament'. Yopie Prins and Maeera Schreiber (eds), *Dwelling in Possibility: Women Poets and Critics on Poetry.* Ithaca, New York: 132–46.

BOURKE, ANGELA, SIOBHÁN KILFEATHER, MARIA LUDDY, MARGARET MAC CURTAIN, GERARDINE MEANEY, MÁIRIN NÍ DHONNCHADHA, MARY O'DOWD AND CLAIR WILLS (EDS).

2002 *The Field Day Anthology of Irish Writing.* Vols. 4 & 5: *Irish Women's Writing and Traditions*. Cork.

BROMWICH, RACHEL.

1948 'The Keen for Art O'Leary, its Background and its Place in the Tradition of Gaelic Keening'. *Éigse* 5: 236–52.

BRUFORD, ALAN.

1973 'The Sea-Divided Gaels: Some Relationships between Scottish Gaelic, Irish and English Traditional Song'. *Éigse Cheol Tíre / Irish Folk Music Studies* 1: 4–27.

CAMPBELL, JOHN LORNE, AND FRANCIS COLLINSON.

1969, 1977, 1981 *Hebridean Folksongs* (3 vols). Oxford.

HALL, SAMUEL CARTER AND ANNA MARIA HALL.

1841 *Ireland: Its Scenery, Character &c.* Vol. 1. London.

LORD, ALBERT B.

1960 *The Singer of Tales*. Cambridge, Massachusetts.

MACINNES, JOHN.

[1978] 2006 'The Panegyric Code in Gaelic Poetry and its Historical Background'. Michael Newton (ed.), *Dùthchas nan Gàidheal: Selected Essays of John MacInnes*. Edinburgh.

MACLEAN, MALCOLM AND THEO DORGAN (EDS).

2002 *An Leabhar Mòr, The Great Book of Gaelic*. Edinburgh.

MACLELLAN, LAUCHIE.

2000 *Brìgh an Òrain: A Story in Every Song: The Songs and Tales of Lauchie MacLellan*. John Shaw (ed.). Montreal.

Ó COILEÁIN, SEÁN.

1978 'Oral or Literary?: Some Strands in the Argument'. *Studia Hibernica* 17 & 18: 7–35.

1988 'The Irish Lament: An Oral Genre'. *Studia Hibernica* 24: 97–117.

Ó CONCHEANAINN, TOMÁS.

1978 *Nua-Dhuanaire* III. Baile Átha Cliath.

Ó DUILEARGA, SÉAMUS.

1939 'Seán do Búrc'. *Éigse* I (4) 235–6.

1940 'Blúire do Shean-Chaoine'. *Éigse* II/1: 2–3.

Ó MADAGÁIN, BREANDÁN.

1982 'Irish Vocal Music of Lament and Syllabic Poetry'. Robert O'Driscoll (ed.), *The Celtic Consciousness.* Portlaoise and Edinburgh: 311-331.

1985 'Functions of Irish Song in the Ninteenth Century'. *Béaloideas* 53: 130–216.

Ó MUIREADHAIGH, LORCÁN.
[1927] 1977 *Amhráin Chúige Uladh*: Atheagrán le Colm Ó Baoill. Baile Átha Cliath.

Ó SÚILLEABHÁIN, SEÁN.
1940 'An Bhean do Thogh a Driotháir'. *Éigse* 2/1: 24–30.

Ó TUAMA, SEÁN.
1961 *Caoineadh Airt Uí Laoghaire.* Baile Átha Cliath.

ONG, WALTER J.
1982 *Orality and Literacy.* London and New York.

PARTRIDGE, ANGELA [= BOURKE, ANGELA].
1980 'Wild Men and Wailing Women'. *Éigse* 28: 25–37.
1983 *Caoineadh na dTrí Muire: Téama na Páise i bhFilíocht Bhéil na Gaeilge.* Baile Átha Cliath.

RADNER, JOAN N. (ED.).
1993 *Feminist Messages: Coding in Women's Folk Culture.* Chicago.

SHAW, MARGARET FAY.
[1955] 1977 *Folksongs and Folklore of South Uist*, 2nd edition. Oxford.

SHIELDS, HUGH.
1972 'Old British Ballads in Ireland'. *Folk-Life: Journal of the Society for Folk Life Studies* 10: 68–103.
1993 *Narrative Singing in Ireland: Lays, Ballads, Come-All-Yes and Other Songs.* Dublin.

TIERNEY, MICHAEL.
1939 'An Ancient Motif in the Lament for Seán do Búrc'. *Éigse* I/4: 236–8.

WATSON, JAMES CARMICHAEL (ED.).
[1934] 1965 *Gaelic Songs of Mary MacLeod.* Edinburgh.

FOINSÍ FUAIME

[1972] 1993 *Scottish Tradition 3: Waulking Songs from Barra.* Greentrax CDTRAX9003. Edinburgh.

1978 *The Music of Cape Breton 1: Gaelic Tradition in Cape Breton.* Topic 12TS354. London.

[1986] 1996 *A Tribute to the North Shore Gaelic Singers: Songs from Cape Breton Island.* B&R Heritage Enterprises BRCD0005. Halifax, N.S.

‘and yes I said yes I will Yes’

AONGHUS PADRAIG CAIMBEUL

ABSTRACT. These thoughts were inspired by the following riddle:[1]

> A young man asked a maiden, as she was at an open window, when she would go a walk with him; and he got the answer that follows: “When I shall have lifted the linen (or net), lowered the glass, and put the dead to bury the living.”
>
> He, thereupon, giving up hope, sailed to foreign parts; and, returning at the end of three years, he heard she was married to another, but was not at all happy. This grieved him, and, on going to see her, he got the solution of her statement, thus: “As soon as I would have lifted the linen off the table, shut the window, and smoored the fire; and that did not long delay me, though you were impatient.”

Tha naidheachd bheag air a bhith ag obair orm riamh bhon a chuala mi an toiseach i. Riamh bhon a leubh mi i an toiseach. Oir cha do leubh mi rud riamh gun a chluinntinn. Agus nuair a chaidh iarraidh orm rudeigin a sgrìobhadh airson Iain, b’e seo an naidheachd a ghairm orm.

’S e naidheachd a th’ ann a fhuair mi on leabhar iongantach sin aig an Sgitheanach Alasdair MacNeacail, ‘Toimhseachain agus Dubh-Fhacail’ (‘Gaelic Riddles and Enigmas’), a chaidh fhoillseachadh le MacLabhrainn ’s a Mhic ann an 1938. Agus tha an sgeulachd a dol mar seo:

Dh’fhaighnich gille do nighinn, agus i aig uinneig fhosgailte, c’uine a rachadh i leis air chuairt; agus fhuair e am freagairt a leanas:–

> *An uair a thogas mi an lìon,*
> *A leagas mi a’ ghlainne,*
> *Agus a chuireas mi am marbh a thiodhlaiceadh a’ bheò.*

Thug esan an sin suas a dhòchas, sheòl e thairis, agus air dha tilleadh an ceann trì bliadhna, chuala e gu robh i pòsda aig fear eile, ach nach robh i idir toilichte : chuir seo smuairean air, agus chaidh e a choimhead oirre, agus fhuair e fuasgladh air na facail mar seo:–

> *Cho luath agus a thogainn an t-anart de’n bhòrd,*
> *A dhùininn an uinneag,*
> *Agus a smàlainn an teinne :*
> *agus cha do chùm sin fada mise, ged bha thusa mi-fhoidhidneach.”*

Nise, aig aon ìre chan eil sìon a dh’fhiosam carson a tha mo chridhe ’s mo mhac-meanmna a’ ceangal na sgeòil seo ri Iain, ach tha mi dol a chosg nam briathran a tha romham a’ meòrachadh air carson a tha mi smaoineachadh a tha sin a’ tachairt.

Oir tha an Dubh-Fhacal a thog MacNeacail agus a thug e dhuinn dhen ghnè as fhèarr a th’ ann: tha e sìmplidh, tha e domhainn, agus tha e a’ dèanamh an rud iongantach sin a tha an sgeulachd as fhèarr daonnan a’ dèanamh: ag obrachadh gu sìmplidh aig àrd-ìre aig dà dhiofar ìre. Tha i a’ fighe, mar gum bitheadh, a’ cholainn ris an spiorad – an *duality* sin eile mun do sgrìobh Sigmund Freud, an strì eadar Eros agus Thanatos. Neo ’s dòcha mar a chuireadh Naomh Pòl e, eadar an fheòil agus an t-anam, eadar an lagh agus an gràs, eadar an lagh agus an spiorad, eadar am math agus am peacadh (Ròmanaich 7).

Dh’fhaodadh tu ràdh gu bheil gach sgeulachd ’san t-saoghal mun a seo: mun chogadh eadar math agus olc, neo co-dhiù mun taghadh eadar beatha agus bàs. Leopold Bloom ann an *Ulysses*

[1] Alexander Nicolson, *Gaelic Riddles and Enigmas [Toimhseachain agus Dubh-Fhacail]*. Glasgow (1938): 92-3.

anns an t-saoghal iomadh-fhillteachd a tha ga chuartachadh (agus ga chruthachadh), le Molly aig a cheann thall a ghairm "and yes I said yes I will Yes." Nach e an aon cheist a bh' aig Somhairle MacGill-Eain anns An Roghainn? Nach ann mu dheidhinn sin a tha Cinderella, agus Cath nan Eun, agus fiù 's gach rann beag a tha againn:

Tha mi sgìth 's mi leam fhìn,
    H-uile là a' buain an rainich;
Tha mi sgìth 's mi leam fhìn,
    H-uile là nam ònar.

Nach ann mun a sin a' sgrìobh Camus agus Sartre cuideachd: *alienation* is aonarachd? Gu bheil sinn, aig a' cheann thall leinn fhèin 'san t-saoghal. Neo a bheil?

THE SOLITUDE OF ALEXANDER SELKIRK

I am monarch of all I survey,
My right there is none to dispute,
From the center all round to the sea,
I am lord of the fowl and the brute.
O Solitude! where are the charms
That sages have seen in thy face?
Better dwell in the midst of alarms
Than reign in this horrible place.

I am out of humanity's reach,
I must finish my journey alone,
Never hear the sweet music of speech, –
I start at the sound of my own.
The beasts that roam over the plain
My form with indifference see;
They are so unacquainted with man,
Their tameness is shocking to me.

Society, Friendship, and Love,
Divinely bestow'd upon man,
Oh, had I the wings of a dove,
How soon would I taste you again!
My sorrows I then might assuage
In the ways of religion and truth,
Might learn from the wisdom of age,
And be cheer'd by the sallies of youth.

Ye winds that have made me your sport,
Convey to this desolate shore
Some cordial endearing report
Of a land I shall visit no more!
My friends – do they now and then send
A wish or a thought after me?
Oh, tell me I yet have a friend,
Though a friend I am never to see.

How fleet is a glance of the mind!
Compared with the speed of its flight,
The tempest itself lags behind,
And the swift-wing'd arrows of light.

When I think of my own native land,
In a moment I seem to be there;
But alas! recollection at hand
Soon hurries me back to despair.

But the seafowl is gone to her nest,
The beast is laid down in his lair,
Even here is a season of rest,
And I to my cabin repair.
There's mercy in every place,
And mercy, encouraging thought!
Gives even affliction a grace,
And reconciles man to his lot.

WILLIAM COWPER.

Gealach fhann bhuidhe air fàire,
Cridhe 'n fhuinn gun phlosgadh gàire,
Aonguidheachd a' dèanamh tàire
Air uinneagan òir an cuan snàgach.

SOMHAIRLE MACGILL-EAIN.

Tha an sgeulachd bheag a dh'fhàg Alasdair MacNeacail againn, saoilidh mise, mar nàdar de *archetype* anns an t-seagh anns an do cleachd Carl Jung am facal sin. Bha Jung dhen bheachd gun robh còig mic-samhail ann (ma chuireas mi mar sin e) aig bun gnothaich, a bha riochdachadh neo a samhlachadh: Fèin, Faileas, an *Anima*, an *Animus* agus am *Persona*. Bha an *Anima* aig Jung a' còmhdachadh na h-ìomhaigh bhoireann anns an fhirionnach, agus an *Animus* a' còmhdachadh an ìomhaigh fhirionn anns a' bhoireannach. B'e am *Persona* an ìomhaigh neo an t-aodannan a tha sinn a' sealltain dhan t-saoghal mhòr; am Fèin meadhan ar *psyche*, agus am Faileas, an taobh eile dhe ar n-*ego*, nach eil sinn ro bhuailteach aideachadh.

Nach eil iad sin uile (agus fada bharrachd) a nochdadh anns an sgeul bheag Ghàidhlig againn? Tha gille ann, agus nighean. Tha esan ag iarraidh, agus e a' smaoineachadh gu bheil na tha e ag iarraidh gu math soilleir. Agus tha ise ga thuigsinn agus ga fhreagairt chan ann gu dìreach, mar gum bitheadh, ach le bàrdachd, le faileas. Agus tha esan a' toirt mìneachadh eile às a briathran. Agus a' falbh. Nam biodh an *Anima* aige ag obrachadh ceart, saoil am biodh e air falbh? Neo nam biodh an *Animus* aice-se (*Animus* sòisealta a bharrachd air *Animus* gnè) air ghleus, am biodh i air freagairt eadar-dhealaichte a thoirt dha?

Agus thug e suas a dhòchas. An e Fèin, neo Faileas, neo am Persona a thrèig e? Agus dh'fhalbh e. Agus cha b' ann dìreach sìos an rathad, dhachaigh. Neo fiù's dhan ath bhaile. Ach sheòl e. A-null thairis. Smaoinich fhèin air na tha na trì faclan sin a' còmhdachadh – "sheòl e thairis". Gu taobh thall an t-saoghail, cho fad 's a tha sear bho siar. Seòlaidh mise null gu dùthaich chaomh mu rùin; A Pheigi, a ghràidh, 's tu dh'fhàg mi buileach gun sunnd, 's mi seòladh an-dràst' thar sàil dh'Aistràilia null; Suidheadh fear-innse gach uisge / Làimh ri m' chluais-sa, / 's cumadh e shùil gu biorach / An cridhe an fhuaraidh….

Ged tha mi tuigsinn cuideachd gur e slighe-ceangail a bharrachd air slighe-gàrraidh a bh' anns na cuantan. Oir thìll an gille an ceann trì bliadhna, agus cò nach tilleadh? Nach robh a' chridhe air las agus na theine leis an nighinn a dh'fhàg e. An do chual' e ceart? An do thuig e i gu ceart? Saoil nach robh i a' ciallachadh rudeigin eile? Saoil an robh i ga ionndrainn? Ciamar a bha, 's an robh cuideigin eile còmhla rithe? An robh i fhathast cho bòidheach 's a bha i, 's nam faiceadh tu an gàire a dhèanadh i, fiù's air an rathad air ais às an eaglais! Bha aodann ga thathaich a h-oidhche 's a latha – timcheall Cape Horn, deas air na h-Innseachan, tuath air New Zealand…. 'S cha robh an obair a' dol robh mhath an seo co-dhiù, ’s am factoraidh an Chicago air dùnadh sìos, ’s chuala e gun robh bàta fàgail oidhche Shatharna….

Agus chual’ e gun robh i pòsda. Chan eil iongnadh gun do chual’, oir b’e sin a’ chiad cheist a dh’fhaignich e air a thilleadh. Ciamar a bha Mòr? Oir nuair thig Latha na Cruinne, ’s e Mòr Ros a dh’iarrainn. ’S bha i pòsda, ma-tha. Agus stad am fear a dh’inns dha tiotan ’s rinn e gluasad beag. Le a làmhan. Neo ’s dòcha le a shùilean, ’s dh’inns sin dha gun robh dòchas fhathast ann.

Cha robh i idir toilichte. Agus saoil ciamar a chaidh a dh’fhaighneachd dhi, anns na làithean follaiseach fosgailte ud mus tàinig na teacstaichean. Mar a b’ fheudar dha smaoineachadh mu dheidhinn. Saoil an tachradh e leatha gun fhiosd’ a-muigh air an t-sliabh? Aig an tobar? Anns an eaglais? Air an t-sràid? An rachadh e ann an solas geal an latha neo an èaladh e a-null anns an dorchadas, ann an ciaradh an fheasgair? Dè an diofar.

Oir tha an sgeulachd ga chuir cho soilleir: “Agus chaidh e a choimhead oirre”. Gun eagal, neo làn-eagal, ach gu follaiseach. Agus fhuair e fuasgladh air na facail mar seo: “Nam biodh tu air éisteachd ceart rium – nam biodh tu air mo bhàrdachd a thuigsinn – bhiodh sinn an seo còmhla.”

Ach cha do dh’éist, agus cha do thuig. Chuala esan rudeigin eile, mar a chuala sinn uile rudeigin eile. Mar a chuala sinn briathran air choireigin ’san sgoil mu Alexander the Great agus Mary Queen of Scots agus Walter Raleigh agus shaoil sinn gun robh iad a’ bruidhinn mu rudeigin nach buineadh dhuinn, neo a bhuineadh. Mar a chuala sinn Iain Sheonaidh ’sa bhaile a’ bruidhinn mu Dhaorghlas agus nach do thuig sinn cò air a bha e a-mach. Mar a chaidh a h-uile facal an lùib a chèile gus an robh iad nan dubh-fhacail: Keats agus Donnchadh Bàn, *Introibo ad altare Dei, Ad Deum, qui laetificat juventutem meam*. Thuig sinn iad mar aon rud gus an tug cuideigin eile mìneachadh eile dha na faclan, ’s gu mìorbhaileach nuair a thìll sinn cha robh e fhathast ro anmoch neo ro fhadalach.

Saoilidh mi cuideachd gu bheil snàthlainn bheag eile ann an sgeulachd a’ ghille agus an nighinn a tha air leth cudromach – agus ’s e sin sgeulachd tìm. Oir, beag ann am faclan agus a tha an sgeul (chan eil innte ach 126 facal) tha i a’ còmhdachadh nam bliadhnachan. (Anns an dol seachad – nach àraidh ann an lìnn *flash-fiction* is *twitter* gu bheil sinn cha mhòr anns an t-saoghal dealantach sin le giorrad na sgeòil Gàidhlig seo?) Ach a thaobh tìm, tha an sgeul a’ tachairt thairis trì bliadhna: agus tha na thachair anns na bliadhnachan sin (anns an do phòs ise fear eile – agus saoil an robh clann aice? agus far an deach esan a sheòladh gu taobh thall an t-saoghail) uile a’ crochadh air neo air a mheas neo air a thomhas a-rèir na thachair anns a’ chiad seantans, air a’ chiad latha, trì bliadhna air ais.

Oir saoilidh mi nach deach latha seachad on latha sin nach do smaoinich ise air-san agus nach do smaoinich esan oirre-se. Bha an còrr dhem beatha air a thomhas a-rèir na rinn iad (na thuig iad) bhon latha ud a dh’fhaighnich esan a’ cheist, agus a fhreagair ise. O, nach i a bha miannachadh “and yes I said yes I will Yes” a ràdh. A ghlaodh a-mach aig àird a claiginn. Tha mi an dòchas. Ged a chaidh e gu taobh thall an t-saoghail, bha an aisling a bha e a’ sireadh aig an taigh: chan eil gach leug aig bonn an tobair neo aig ceann thall na prosbaig.

Agus tha seo (tha mi an dòchas) gam thoirt gu cuspair ar gnothaich, oir saoilidh mi gur e an aon chonaltradh eadar fiosrachadh agus ciall, neo eadar *narrative* agus mìneachadh a tha air a bhith a tachairt ann am beatha agus ann an obair Iain MhicAonghuis. Tha fhios gu bheil sin follaiseach anns an aiste ionmholta sin aige ‘The Panegyric Code in Gaelic Poetry and its Historical Background’ a thug e do Chomunn Gàidhlig Inbhir Nis ann an 1978, far a bheil e dèanamh oidhirp iuchair an dorais a lorg, ged a dh’fhaodadh e bhith a cheart cho iomchaidh a ràdh gur ann ’na sheasamh aig an uinneig a bha e, a’ coimhead a-steach, neo a’ coimhead a-mach.

Oir ged a thuirt am fear eile gun robh bùird is tàirnean air an uinneig troimh ‘m faca e an Àird an Iar, cha b’e an aon fhear a ghabh thuca le gilb neo òrd-ladhrach airson am fuasgladh.

Tha obair Iain MhicAonghuis air sealladh na h-ighne a thoirt dhòmhsa, on taobh a-staigh, agus cuideachd air sealladh a’ bhalaich, on taobh a-muigh. Oir sheas (agus shuidh) Iain a-staigh agus chual’ e na sgeulachdan agus chlàr e iad agus chuimhnich e iad, le am blas, agus sheas e cuideachd le iongnadh taobh a-muigh na h-uinneige feuchainn ri greimeachadh air na bha an tè a bha a-staigh ag ràdha. Iad a' seinn dha (*Nighneag a' chùil duinn, nach fhan thu?*), a' gabhail sgeulachd dha (*Mar a ghoid Aonghas MacSilidh fion Fear a' Choire*), tàlaidhean (*H-othan othan agus ò*), rannan...

Miann mnatha, mac,
Miann fir, feachd,
Miann eich, aonach,
Miann coin, sneachd,
Miann bà, braon,
Miann caorach, teas,
Miann goibhre, gaoth,
Air leathad caoin, cas.....

Agus iad uile air an gabhail chan ann le *abstractions* ach le daoine ann an da-rìreabh: ann am bothain, ann an teantaichean, ann an taighean-tughaidh, ann an taighean-geala, ann am *bungalows*, am Peairt, an Uibhist, an Leòdhas, Nan Eachainn Fhioinnlaigh, Dunnchadh mac Dhòmhnaill 'ic Dhunnchaidh, Dòmhnall Chaluim Bhàin is coitheanail mòr nan Gàidheal....chan eil iongnadh gun do thionndaidh an fheadhainn againn a bha ri far-chluais gu Iain agus gun do dh'fhaighnich sinn dha – "Dè thuirt i?" Agus mo mhìle taing dha airson innse dhuinn, cho math 's a b' urrainn dha, ged a dh'fhalbh sinne an uair sin a dhèanamh sgeulachd eile dheth.

Oir tha seo cuideachd anns an dubh-fhacal aig MacNeacail agus ann an obair-beatha Iain: gu bheil trianaid ann. Anns an sgeul, tha an nighean agus an gille ann, gun teagamh, ach cuideachd tha thusa ann, ag èisteachd, neo a' faicinn: agus tha sin, gu sìmplidh, a' toirt dhuinn bunait phrionnsabalach eile gur e conaltradh neo coluadar – gur e aonta – a tha ann an còmhradh sam bith. Gur e dàimh-aontachd a tha ann am beatha, oir mur a tuig sinn càch-a-chèile idir, nach bidh sinn ach sgaraichte, briste. Cha d' fhuair mise riamh Iain MacAonghuis – mar sgoilear agus mar dhuine – ach 'na fhear a bha a' toirt spèis dhan dara beachd (dhan treas beachd), oir bha sealladh an t-seanachaidh (agus an fhear neo an tè a bha ag èisteachd ris) a cheart cho luachmhor 's a bha sealladh an sgoileir (agus *vice-versa*). Chan eil rud sam bith aon-fhìllteach.

'S e spiorad shaorsa a tha sin, saoilidh mi, agus a dol leis an fhiosrachadh a thug Dòmhnall Nèillidh dhomh uaireigin mun dòigh a bhiodh na cèilidhean a' dol an Uibhist: aig deireadh na h-oidhche b' aonta (deamocrataiceach) a bh'ann dè a sheasadh.

Siud an t-eilean a' dol à sealladh mar a chuir an sàr-bhàrd e, a tha 'na cho-sgrìobhaiche an seo cuideachd. Ach cha b'e siud m'eilean-sa: chaidh e 'san fodha o chionn fhada, a' chuid mhòr dheth, fo dheireas is ainneart; 's na chaidh fodha annam fhèin dheth, 'na ghrianan, 's cnoc eighre, tha e a' seòladh na mara anns am bi mi 'na phrìomh chomharra stiùiridh cunnartach, do-sheachanta, gun fhaochadh.

Taing dhut a Dhòmhnaill airson nam briathran, agus do choibhneas dhomh. Agus dhutsa, Iain MhicAonghuis – taing dhut airson blas siùbhlach do Ghàidhlig; airson d'fhiosrachadh agus d'fhoghlaim; do sgeulachdan 's do sheanachasan; d'aislingean 's do bhruadairean ; d'fhìrinn 's do bhreugan; do sgoilearachd agus do mhisneachd. Taing airson furtachd a thoirt dhomh aig Mòd Pheairt.

Nach math gun do thog thu lìon, gun do leag thu glainne, agus gun do smàl thu teine; agus a cheart cho cìnnteach gun do sgaoil thu lìon, gun do thog thu glainne, agus gun do las thu teine. Uile aig an aon àm. Chan eil iongnadh gun do sgrìobh Joyce *Finnegan's Wake* an uair sin, oir gun Ghàidhlig dè eile a chanadh e....

‘Tha Feum Air Cabhaig’ The Initiative of the Folklore Institute of Scotland

HUGH CHEAPE

‘There is a need for haste’ formed the editorial message in *An Gàidheal* in May 1947, more pithily expressive in Gaelic, calling for the urgent collection of the oral tradition of Gaelic Scotland. Shortly thereafter, The Folklore Institute of Scotland (FIOS) was formed with the stated object of recording song and story and the oral cultural heritage of the country.[1] Just over four years later, The School of Scottish Studies was established with the same broad aim, symbolising the outcome of a process of scholarly argument that had emerged in the 1930s in the context of ‘folkloristics’ espoused by European nation-states. This essay examines the emergence of FIOS to rediscover some of the arguments adduced for the founding of the School of Scottish Studies.[2]

‘Tha feum air cabhaig’ was the title and conclusion of a long editorial by the Rev. Thomas Murchison in *An Gàidheal*, the magazine of An Comunn Gàidhealach. He concluded with an oratorical flourish: ‘Tha cus de’n ùine air ruith cheana, agus tha gach latha ag cur ri ar call. Dèanamaid cabhaig anns a’ chùis.’[3] John Lorne Campbell was one of the names behind this initiative and, significantly in the light of his efforts, was elected President of FIOS at its meeting in Glasgow in September 1947. He had been campaigning for the support and salvaging of Scottish Gaelic and for the recognition of the extraordinary legacy of the language – its literature, its oral tradition and the many facets of the language itself. In developing his arguments, he drew on his personal experience of collecting stories and songs in Barra, Uist and Nova Scotia since 1933, and on the example of the Irish Folklore Commission. He and others placed this cause in a wider context by recalling the work of collectors of the oral tradition since the late eighteenth century, principally the initiative of his namesake, John Francis Campbell of Islay, who had collected nearly 800 stories between 1859 and 1870, and worked according to criteria which marked the emergence of a ‘scientific’ methodology (Campbell 1949: 9).

An able and energetic writer, John Lorne Campbell appealed for national recognition of the value of Scottish Gaelic in the face of rapid cultural attrition and official indifference. His particularist argument for a *vox populi* before an apparently hostile government had been honed with the Sea League, founded by him and Compton Mackenzie in Barra in 1933, which drew inspiration from the activities of the nineteenth-century Land League and from the fishery policies of Norway, Iceland and the Færoes.[4] The context of what seemed to Campbell a lonely campaign

---

[1] The acronym FIOS – a Gaelic word *(fios)* meaning ‘knowledge’, ‘information’ or ‘understanding’ – provided a useful means of representing or symbolising the cause for which the name was adopted. While these initial letters did not supply an appropriate phrase or title in Gaelic, and because not all would recognise *fios*, the symbolic force of *fios* might be muted outside the Gaelic world. *Comunn Beul-Aithris na h-Albann* was adopted as the title in Gaelic, but offered no comparable acronym. The letters FIOS in attenuated form were designed into a circlet of interlace to form a badge or logo placed centrally on the letterhead under the organisation’s names.

[2] This essay is offered to Dr John MacInnes as reprise of past conversations about the contribution of Dr John Lorne Campbell – Fear Chanaigh – to the establishment of the School of Scottish Studies. It is based principally on the papers of FIOS, catalogued under CH2/2/2 Folklore Correspondence in Canna House under the care of the National Trust for Scotland and represents work in progress.

[3] *An Gàidheal* XLII/8 (An Ceitein 1947): 93–94. ‘Too much time has passed already, and every day adds to our loss. Let us make haste in the matter.’

[4] An extensive archive for the Sea League is held with the Campbell Collections in Canna House under the stewardship of the National Trust for Scotland.

was one of the confused politics and coalition governments of the inter-war years, a drift towards centralisation and standardisation, and massive economic insecurity. This was a perplexed age for the economically marginalized Highlands and Islands, under the pressure of far-reaching economic changes, suffering what can now be defined as the trauma of generations of emigration from the region, and witnessing a dramatic fall in the numbers of speakers of the language. The forty-year-old John Lorne Campbell, working outside university circles and by then ensconced in the Island of Canna (see Perman 2010), began to formulate the intellectual and ideological concerns behind economic disadvantage and language loss, and developed a rhetoric that suffuses the surviving documentation of FIOS.

Cultural attrition, as perceived, was being transformed into a political cause, as had also happened in Ireland. A slowly-growing Home Rule movement in Scotland provided a platform from which the likes of Christopher Murray Grieve, among others, urged the salvaging of a distinctive Scottish culture.[5] Although the cause concerned the spoken word, however, no demagogue emerged to punch home the message on public platforms on behalf of the Gaelic language. The message of FIOS was a powerful one, but it seems that, in the political atmosphere of the time and immediate post-war years, the protagonists were largely both receivers and deliverers of a message which failed to become a popular cause. The rhetoric employed the idiom of the twentieth century, using words such as 'struggle' and 'survival', but arguably the liberal humanist edge of such language was blunted in a war-weary Europe in 1947. Intellectual cut-and-thrust were eloquently and fluently delivered – but on paper, as the archives of FIOS and the pages of *An Gaidheal* and contemporary newspapers illustrate. If this was the wordplay of scholars and gentlemen, Campbell was a natural leader. Quietly spoken but of austere and rigorous views, Campbell's favoured medium was the written word, and the opening shots of a new campaign for Scottish Gaelic were fired in print.

A well-crafted review of the 'Journal of the Folklore of Ireland Society', *Béaloideas* Volume 15, was printed in *An Gaidheal* in April 1947. The author, 'A M' (probably Angus Matheson), celebrated the achievements of the Irish Folklore Commission, and deftly described the *seanchas* or 'reminiscences of the old people'. He drew attention to the selection of Scottish stories published in the volume, and briskly countered criticism of the Commission collecting in Scotland, with Calum Maclean having been sent from Dublin in 1945 and 1946 (Maclean 1975: vii–x). He pointed up the contemporary absence of financial backing or any support whatsoever in Scotland for the collecting of oral tradition, and concluded on notes of irony and elegy: 'It is not the fact that Calum Maclean has recorded these old songs and tales for all time that will make them vanish from the Isles, but the passing on of the old people in whose retentive minds they were stored and the like of whom will not be seen again.'

A long letter from John Lorne Campbell under the heading 'Folklore' appeared in the next issue of *An Gaidheal* (May 1947), in a regular column headed 'Eadar Sinn Fhèin'. Campbell wrote to 'express agreement' with A M's remarks, and went on to provide a concise summary of the contemporary situation which identified shortcomings in resources and attitude, critiqued university expenditure on the natural sciences as opposed to the human sciences in the Highlands and Islands, defended the activities of the Irish Folklore Commission, and laid out a well-reasoned programme of action for the immediate future. He pointed not only to the lack of finance but also to the absence of training for the work of collecting oral tradition – preparation that he rightly regarded as the professional pre-requisite based on his own experience in Barra and Cape Breton in 1937. He referred in detail to the support of the Irish Folklore Commission, whose methods he had indeed

[5] Hugh MacDiarmid as Mr C. M. Grieve was noted as having attended the founding meeting of FIOS in Glasgow on behalf of the 'Dunedin Society', CH2/2/2/5.

adopted in his own collecting and editorial work.[6] He concluded – to counter, as he put it, a popular assumption that this was about 'superstition' – by defining 'Folklore' as 'the whole oral tradition of the Gaelic people – local history, songs, stories, music, place-names. This tradition goes back in Gaeldom to the times of Fionn MacCumhail and the Fiann, 1500 years at least, probably the oldest living tradition in Europe today.'

In conversation with the writer of this essay, Campbell frequently alluded to a verbal exchange with 'the Lecturer in Celtic at a certain Scottish University', in which he had suggested to that member of staff that the university might buy an Ediphone recorder which could be used by 'his best Gaelic students' to record songs and stories at home on vacation in the Islands. 'His reply,' he said, 'was that, if he went before the authorities with such a suggestion, he would only be laughed at.' This brief conversation had a profound influence on John Lorne Campbell. It became clear in the re-telling that the Lecturer in Celtic was James Carmichael Watson, the University was Edinburgh and one of the students in question was from Harris.

There is copious sub-text to the recounting of the exchange which self-evidently was Campbell's own response, not as spontaneous personal riposte to Carmichael Watson (since the conversation had then gone no further) but as reasoned counter-argument developed to persuade officialdom to support FIOS' cause. These were some of the points which suffuse FIOS' communications: beyond the lack of official interest or will was the need to develop a professional and properly funded approach to the work of recording in the face of the relative poverty of output from hobby-collectors and amateurs in the field. A professional approach, as exemplified by the Irish Folklore Commission, would be predicated on the changing technology of mechanical recording, then offering opportunities hitherto unavailable. Another point, which Campbell derived from the teaching he had received at Oxford from Professor John Fraser, was an appreciation of the importance of colloquial Gaelic to an understanding of the language and its literature, with views on the superiority of idiom and even of vocabulary of Outer Isles' Gaelic to book-learnt Gaelic, the lack of recognition of this dichotomy in the academic study and teaching of the language, the failure of scholars with too few exceptions to leave their closets and consult the people, and, perhaps on a more personal level, to remind future scholars that if James Carmichael Watson had had recourse to oral tradition in Harris, he might have been able to improve on his published collection of the *bàrdachd* of Mary MacLeod.[7] It was a matter of personal frustration for Campbell that there was so little interest in Scotland in the production of oral recording; he would say that it was very hard to rouse anyone to take an interest in the subject, and that scholars and the universities were 'blatantly uninterested and reprehensibly negligent'.[8] This seemed to have become a personal campaign, to an extent that he wrote in 1951:

> … for a time I considered my researches in the field were finished for good. However with the encouragement of Professor Delargy of the Irish Folklore Commission, who very kindly sent Mr Seumas Ennis of the Commission at their

[6] Campbell had also adopted their editorial principles: 'In writing down these stories, whether from the speaker's own dictation …. or from Ediphone records, I have deliberately reproduced the dialects of the speakers. This is in accordance with the method used by contemporary Irish collectors of oral Gaelic literature, for example by most of the contributors to *Béaloideas* (the Journal of the Irish Folklore Society). In my opinion, any attempt to force oral Gaelic literature into the artificial mould of the standardised literary spelling and grammatical forms is a mistake, as it not only actually produces a false impression of the real language of the stories, but also obscures many interesting grammatical points' (Campbell 1939: 6); see also Campbell 1938.

[7] *An Gàidheal* XLII/8 (An Ceitein 1947): 103–105; see MacInnes 1966: 3–25 for the neglect of music and current traditions in the editing of the record of Màiri nighean Alasdair Ruaidh.

[8] Personal letter from John Lorne Campbell, 10 November 1994. This is also explored in Cheape 2013: 97–98.

expense to transcribe the tunes on my old Ediphone folksong records in the winter of 1946–1947, I took up the work again.[9]

John Lorne Campbell *(l.)* and the Rev. Thomas Murchison *(r.)* with South Uist seanchaidh and storyteller Duncan MacDonald *(photo: Margaret Fay Shaw)*

If John Lorne Campbell spoke to an anglophone world – the world of the status quo and of authority – the editor of *An Gaidheal*, the Rev. Thomas Murchison, sent a compelling message to the Gaelic world in his editorial in the same May 1947 number of the magazine. Other writers in Gaelic, notably Iain M. MacLeòid, a retired headmaster from Beauly, sustained a written campaign which probably drew strength from the contemporary upsurge of support for Home Rule. MacLeòid's article 'Dìmeas na Gàidhlige' pointed to the reluctance of Gaels to use their mother-tongue in the face of a numerically and socially dominant English – 'Beurla chruaidh Shasainn' – and appealed *inter alia* for Gaelic-medium education on an equal footing with English (MacLeòid 1947: 86–7). Thomas Murchison had previously devoted his interest and time to the politics of the crofting cause, and he brought the skills of political argument to the cause of language. By 1939, he had begun active committee work with An Comunn Gàidhealach, taking on the editorship of *An Gàidheal* for twelve years between 1946 and 1958 (MacCalmain 2011: 207–12). Aware of a wider intellectual context, he reminded Gaels of the change in attitude in most of Europe towards the legacy of literature, languages and oral tradition, and of how this change had originated in Sweden and Ireland. His 1947 editorial commended Swedish scholarship, naming Dr Nils Holmer and Professor Carl Hjalmar Borgstrøm for their work in Argyll and Barra respectively.

Murchison wrote movingly of the recent deaths of three tradition-bearers in the Outer Isles, Seonaidh Caimbeul of South Uist and, in Eriskay, of Dugald MacMillan and Gillespic MacIsaac, regretting that more had not been put on paper or on record of what they and others had to tell – 'gach fear dhiubh ag giùlan leis gu sàmhchair na h-uaighe ionmhas prìseil de litreachas-aithris.'[10] Mention had already been made in *An Gaidheal* of the collecting work of Calum Maclean and the Irish Folklore Commission, and a letter from the Commission's Archivist, Seán Ó Suilleabháin, to a third party in Newcastle, was included almost verbatim in the text of Murchison's editorial. Ó Súilleabháin's letter – which can be read either as a wake-up call or as moral blackmail – stated the Commission's preference that the people of Scotland would undertake this recording work but, since this was not being done, the Commission had initiated it: *'B'fhearr linn go mór gurab iad muinntir na hAlban iad féin do thógfadh an obair seo idir lámhaibh, ach ní dócha go bhfuil seans air sin i láthair na huaire'.*[11] The Commission further offered to provide technical and practical

[9] CH2/8/12 Report to Leverhulme Trustees, 2; John Lorne Campbell also reported that he had suffered a breakdown in health in 1945–1946.

[10] '... each one of them carrying to the silence of the grave a precious treasure of oral literature'; but see MacAonghuis 1936.

[11] 'We would greatly prefer that the people of Scotland would themselves take this work in hand, but it is not likely that there is a chance of that at the present time.'

help, including the supplying of copies of recordings on microfilm.[12] The Commission's pan-Gaelic vision encompassed the Gaelic of Scotland as well as that of Ireland, and set out a plan to save the folklore of both countries. Murchison then underlined Ó Súilleabháin's message by rehearsing it in Scottish Gaelic, and closed with an appeal for a 'Comunn Beul-oideas na h-Albann' to be created, and for An Comunn Gàidhealach, the Gaelic Society of Inverness and other societies and groups to join in the enterprise (Murchison 1947: 93–94).

On 14 June 1947, Thomas Murchison convened a meeting in Glasgow of 'persons interested in Gaelic folklore' to discuss the urgent need for systematic collecting work. The business for the meeting was prefigured in the pages of *An Gàidheal*, the imperative had been delivered by Thomas Murchison and others, and John Lorne Campbell's 'Folklore' letter supplied the agenda. The meeting agreed unanimously to form a committee under the convenorship of Thomas Murchison to set about establishing a 'Scottish Gaelic Folklore Society' for the collection, preservation and publication of oral lore, with the ultimate and more wide-reaching (and presumably appealing and popularising) aim of establishing a 'Scottish Folklore Institute'. A further meeting was agreed, and the Convenor and Secretary invited representatives from the Scottish Anthropological and Folklore Society and the Saltire Society to a meeting in Glasgow on 9 July 1947.[13] The discussion was widened to encompass the formation of one organisation for 'the whole field of Scottish folk culture', and those attending agreed to enlarge the Committee by co-opting interested persons and representatives of cultural organisations.

An enlarged Committee met in the Saltire Club in Wellington Street, Glasgow, on Saturday morning, 20 September 1947. Thirty-one people attended, a notable list of names representing the cultural organisations of the day; in addition, letters of support were received from other individuals and organisations. A special guest at the meeting was Professor Seumas Ó Duilearga, Director of the Irish Folklore Commission and recently appointed to the Chair of Irish Folklore in University College Dublin. Added to Seán Ó Suilleabháin's letter, Ó Duilearga's attendance in Glasgow and the Commission's work to date in Raasay, Eigg, Canna, South Uist and Benbecula lent a significant note to the proceedings. A draft Constitution was tabled along with a resolution from the Scottish Anthropological and Folklore Society 'that a Committee be appointed to form the nucleus of a Scottish Institute of Folk-Culture, with a view to co-ordinating the activities of all interested and authoritative bodies'.[14] The ensuing debate, *more Scotico*, revealed divisions and the difficulty of forming a national group devoted to the cause of Gaelic. The meeting finally resolved 'that those present do now constitute themselves the Folklore Institute of Scotland', and it was minuted additionally that 'the initials of this title form the Gaelic word "FIOS", meaning "knowledge". It was also agreed that in the Gaelic name of the Institute the older form of the genitive case of "Alba" be used, namely, "Albann".'[15] A draft constitution was approved, and office-bearers were appointed with twenty-four nominations for a proposed Council of seven.

[12] It was the practice of the Irish Folklore Commission that all Ediphone wax-cylinder recordings be transcribed and the pages bound into volumes, leaving the wax cylinders available for re-use. The Main Manuscripts or core collection of the Irish Folklore Commission amounts to 1,735 volumes of orally-collected material (Almqvist 1979: 5).

[13] See www.therai.org.uk/archives-and-manuscripts and papers in Edinburgh University Library Special Collections for the Scottish Anthropological and Folklore Society, founded in 1934 and wound up in the early 1960s.

[14] The resolution, tabled by Cyril Aldred of the Royal Scottish Museum, appealed for all interested bodies to combine forces for folklore collection and the establishment of folk museums. Mr C. M. Grieve opposed the resolution with the view that learned but moribund societies were merely 'trying to horn in on the work of others after they had proved themselves utterly incapable of doing the work themselves'. Alexander Nicolson returned to the founding imperative of the initiative: 'the Gaelic aspect of the matter was being obscured, and he urged that we should get to work in the Gaelic field without further delay and that steps be taken to ensure that the Gaelic interest should not be further obscured in constituting the Institute.'

[15] Folklore Institute of Scotland. Minutes of Meeting held on 20 September 1947, CH2/2/2.

Possibly only ten of these were Gaelic speakers, and it was agreed to hold a postal ballot. As it happened, the seven elected were all from among the Gaelic nominees.

The onward progress of FIOS then evidently proceeded according to the individual effort and input of John Lorne Campbell and Thomas Murchison, who effectively shared all the secretarial work between them, thereby producing the detailed record that has survived. The development of the Institute had apparently been handicapped by the failure of the Honorary Secretary to attend to the administration and he had had to be asked to resign. References to this issue in FIOS documents suggest that the zeal and practical application needed to carry forward the cause was not more widely shared. Thomas Murchison acted as Interim Secretary until April 1948, when Ian M. Campbell, Lecturer in Comparative Philology in Glasgow University, was appointed. Campbell, who had studied Old and Middle Irish with Professor John Fraser at Oxford and was a great-great-grandson of 'Cruachan Beann' author Patrick MacIntyre, met with the approval of the Council.[16] In due course, Derick Thomson became Secretary of FIOS.

The finances of FIOS never prospered as its instigators had hoped. After five years, the balance sheet stood at under £300. Membership had barely topped fifty, and brought in under £70 per annum, although income had been boosted at the start by a small number of life memberships which rose to ten. Subscriptions included some from overseas as well as grants from organisations such as An Comunn Gàidhealach, the Gaelic League of Scotland, and the Saltire Society.[17] The cryptic comment recorded in July 1949 encapsulated the problem of FIOS: 'These funds are now almost exhausted.' The lack of funds struck at the heart of the initiative, since professional fieldworkers could not be paid or recording machinery purchased. No money was available even to pay for a brochure to advertise the aims and methods of FIOS. The fortunes of FIOS were entirely wrapped up in the efforts of a few individuals, their families and friends, some of whom were probably less motivated personally to take action to support FIOS as a political cause in the face of what were described as 'difficulties and discouragements'.

On the other hand, positive progress was reported in terms of fieldwork, which John Lorne Campbell put in the context of his own work since 1937 and of a group of ten individuals consisting of his wife, Margaret Fay Shaw, and a number of his friends in Barra and South Uist, including members of the 'Barra Folklore Committee'.[18] International relations were healthy thanks to Campbell's personally-sustained links with France, the USA, Canada and Ireland, with Seumas Ó Duilearga's offer to FIOS of all the material from their full-time collector in the Hebrides for publication in any journal founded by the Institute. The Constitution of FIOS had declared that 'The Institute shall as soon as possible establish a periodical (Scottish Folklore Journal), which shall be published once a year and preferably twice a year, in which shall be published some of the material collected and also matters of more general interest which may further the objects of the Institute'. The printing of a 'Folk-Song Journal' was reported as imminent in July 1949, and was to have been dedicated to a collection of waulking songs from Barra and Cape Breton, to be followed by 'Folklore of a Uist Township' by Margaret Fay Shaw. Although FIOS never produced a journal under its own imprint, John Lorne Campbell's efforts and input from others such as Annie Johnson in Barra led to the production, for FIOS, of a set of five 12-inch discs of songs recorded in Barra in 1938, together with a booklet, by the Linguaphone Institute in London. Campbell's comment on these was:

[16] *An Gaidheal* Leabhar XLIII Earrann 7 (An Giblein 1948), 86.

[17] CH2/2/2 Folklore 1952-1953.

[18] The FIOS Bulletin No. 1 lists the fieldworkers as: The President [John Lorne Campbell], Margaret Fay Shaw, Annie Johnston, Barra, John MacPherson, Barra, J. MacCormick, Eriskay, Rev. A. MacKellaig, Bornish, John MacLean, Mallaig School, Rev. D. MacKellaig, Roy Bridge, Donald Sinclair, Barra, and Calum Johnston, Edinburgh.

> Such songs are amongst the greatest of our traditional songs, but owing to their length and the intricacy of their airs they are never heard nowadays on concert platforms or on the radio. They are representative of the ancient pentatonic modal folk-music of the Hebrides that is one of the most interesting survivals of our times.[19]

A robust résumé of 'Gaelic Folk-Songs' by John Lorne Campbell appeared in *The Scotsman* on 17 September 1949. He opened in stringent style on the subject of a 'controversy that raged in the correspondence columns of *The Scotsman* a year ago' concerning the treatment of Gaelic folk-songs by Marjorie Kennedy Fraser, and concluded trenchantly that 'the arrangements she published have no scientific value and the notion that she has exhausted the subject has done great harm'. He listed the work of other collectors – Frances Tolmie, Lucy Broadwood, Amy Murray, Margaret Fay Shaw, Calum Maclean, the Linguistic Survey of Scotland, and 'the writer and other collaborators working under the aegis of the Folklore Institute of Scotland' – and compared their results to the work of collectors in England, Ireland and Hungary, such as Bartók, Kodály, and the Irish Folklore Commission. He urged that international interest and technical advances with 'portable mechanical means of recording on tape, wire or discs' made the 'endowment of a body in Scotland similar to the Irish Folklore Commission' an imperative, and called for the co-operation of the universities, the BBC and the Scottish Education Department. He concluded in rhetorical style but in a mood of seeming desperation:

> The expense of the work puts it beyond the means of amateurs and unendowed bodies. Its dignity and intrinsic merit and significance for the cultural life of Scotland demand that it be recognised as an important object of research and adequately carried out. For folk-music is the basis of all national music, and how can Scottish music flourish at the top, if its roots are neglected? (Campbell 1949: 9)

The constantly reiterated appeal by FIOS for a properly funded organisation supported by the universities was also prefigured in its Constitution, with the undertaking to appoint necessary staff such as Director of Research, Librarian or Archivist, Editor, and one or more 'Field Secretaries' or Collectors, ideally as full-time salaried appointments. None of this was achieved, and in August 1951 the situation was spelt out starkly and in a tone of frustration in the bulletin of FIOS. The author – probably Thomas Murchison – declared:

> Until the Institute receives a wider measure of public recognition and support, the burden of its work – administrative as well as field work – will continue to fall upon a small number, and if they grow weary in this particular enterprise the whole thing may just fade out. This explanation of the situation should help to meet the criticism sometimes made (by people who have not raised a finger to help) that the Institute has so little to show for its five years of existence.

The same bulletin countered the criticism that FIOS was only interested in the Gaelic areas of the country by declaring that all Scotland was its field of operation, but that the situation of Gaelic was more precarious. It further claimed, tendentiously, that 'Gaelic folklore is by far the most considerable, the most coherent, and the most ancient body of folklore in Scotland'.[20]

By this time, however, the pessimistic report and counter-claims published by FIOS had been overtaken by events. Edinburgh University's Dialect and Folklore Survey, set up in 1949, was recast in 1950 as the 'Linguistic Survey of Scotland'; and the following year saw the establishment of the School of Scottish Studies.[21] John Lorne Campbell endowed the nascent School with copies

[19] CH2/2/2/5 Folklore Institute of Scotland, Bulletin No. 1 (July 1949): 4.

[20] CH2/2/2/5 Folklore Institute of Scotland, Bulletin No. 2 (August 1951), 4.

[21] Edinburgh University Library. Papers of Professor David Abercrombie. GEN 1045 Papers, Minutes *etc.* relating to the Linguistic Survey of Scotland; see, *inter alia*, 'Report on a Sampling Survey of Scottish Dialects' (August–

of many of his recordings, and composed a ten-page 'Report to the School of Scottish Studies' on the methodology and output of FIOS.[22]

At the Annual General Meeting of FIOS in Glasgow in December 1952, John Lorne Campbell presented his president's report, reiterating the need for financial support of the ongoing recording and collecting work, and his conviction that FIOS should be headed by a professional scholar and associated with the Celtic Department of one of the universities. His call for the cataloguing of existing collections such as the Carmichael and Henderson Papers, by then in Edinburgh and Glasgow Universities respectively, indicated that his own interests were moving on. The report included what is clearly a valedictory note:

> I believe the struggle to preserve our folklore and popularise it in its authentic form is well worth while. In these five years I have not been unconscious of opposition – partly from those interests which would like our tradition to disappear entirely, partly from others who only want them to survive in a sentimentalised form; but I think this could, and should, be overcome ...[23]

John Lorne Campbell declined to stand for re-election as president, and Angus Matheson of Glasgow University's Department of Celtic took up the honour. The Council of FIOS passed a resolution effectively putting the organisation on hold, and the existing administration and scholarly assets of FIOS were lodged in the Glasgow University Celtic Department.

The development to national status of the School of Scottish Studies has tended to overshadow the work of its precursor, FIOS. It is debatable how much the former owes to the latter for its coming into being, and how much weight should be given to the apparently crucial intervention in Scotland of the Irish Folklore Commission.[24] Prejudice against the Irish Folklore Commission's role in recording in Scotland is detectable in a reported comment: 'Fàgaibh sin againne; nì sinn fhèin e'.[25] The papers of FIOS, however, are unequivocal in their appreciation of the Commission's support, referring frequently to the Commission and its methodology, to Seumas Ó Duilearga's advocacy, and to the work of the Commission through the agency of Calum Maclean. The reception by Ó Duilearga of *Òrain Ghàidhlig le Seonaidh Caimbeul* (1936) and *Sia Sgeulachdan* (1939) was, according to John Lorne Campbell, crucial in the Commission's decision to send Maclean to conduct fieldwork in Scotland.[26]

Campbell's own summation of FIOS was that it was intended as a 'ginger-group' to pressurise academics and politicians. FIOS's formulation of a cause and ideology, supported by Ó Duilearga's

---

September 1949) by J. C. Catford, page 13: 'However, if one is pressed for time, as I was in the South West, one should be aware of the clerical tendency to prolong interviews with anecdotes and sometimes inaccurate information about the local dialect.'

[22] CH2/2/2 Folklore Correspondence 1951–1952; this document is couched in terms that might be seen as offering a 'founding charter' for the School.

[23] CH2/2/2/5 President's Address at the AGM of FIOS, December 1952.

[24] See Briody 2007, for a view of the central role of Seumas Ó Duilearga in the founding of the School of Scottish Studies.

[25] 'Leave that to us; we'll do it!' *An Gaidheal* XLII/10 (An t-Iuchar 1947): 126, an intriguing and strongly partisan letter headed 'Eadar Sinn Fhèin / Beul-aithris' and signed 'Calum MacGilleathain'. The strongest advocacy of the Irish Folklore Commission together with the Gaelic Society of Inverness, and a side-swipe at John Lorne Campbell as *'tarcuiseach'* (*i.e.* showing contempt), suggests that the writer of the letter was not Calum I. Maclean of Raasay but may have been the Rev. Malcolm Maclean of Scarp. I am grateful to Dr John MacInnes for this suggestion.

[26] CH2/2/2 Folklore Correspondence. Letter (part only) from Ó Duilearga to J. L. Campbell, 1936 (?), urging Campbell to come to Ireland to join him and Professor Carl von Sydow and to initiate a process of co-operation: 'I am convinced that active co-operation can only be accomplished through personal contact. I don't believe in letter-writing.' See also Briody 2007 and Bringéus 2009.

activities and utterances, might well have contributed to this outcome, but at the cost of FIOS's continuing existence and a measure of disappointment for those who formed it and worked for it. Given John Lorne Campbell's personal input into FIOS, the expression of disappointment might be taken as largely his own pique and a reflection of an ambivalence about his own status as an 'independent scholar'. Though there might have been no official disavowal of FIOS, the organization seems to have been ignored. In retrospect this seems disingenuous; a closer study of the friendship between one of the principal architects of the 'Linguistic Survey of Scotland', Professor Angus McIntosh, and John Lorne Campbell, whom he had met in Barra in the 1930s, will probably reveal more about the dynamics of the development of the School and of the views of those who had created FIOS.

Once Edinburgh University had taken up the challenge of fieldwork recording, it seemed to disassociate itself from FIOS and its efforts. Professor McIntosh, writing in *The Scotsman* about the work of the Linguistic Survey in October 1951, presented the new initiative as very much their own, and did so in positive and optimistic terms:

> An academic interest in the great wealth of dialect and other folk material still available for collection and study has been slow to develop. Scholarship has till recently been more preoccupied with the evidence provided by books and manuscripts than with that which can be obtained by exploring the knowledge of everyday people. …. But the tide has turned and there is now a growing awareness of what can be learnt from material so acquired and it is a precious heritage, fast disappearing, with a very great significance both in a general cultural way and from a narrow academic standpoint (McIntosh 1951).

ACKNOWLEDGEMENTS

I wish to thank Kate Mavor, Chief Executive of the National Trust for Scotland, and her staff for access to the Campbell of Canna Papers, and in particular to thank Magdalena Sagarzazu, Archivist Canna House, and Ian Riches, NTS Archivist, for their continuing support. I am indebted to my colleague, Professor Norman MacDonald, for sharing references to Fear Chanaigh with such enthusiasm. I am very grateful to Dr Virginia Blankenhorn for her guidance in completing this study, and to Dr John MacInnes for his generous and patient answering of questions and supplying of information over so many years. *Is mise a tha fada, fada nur comain.*

SOURCES

ALMQVIST, BO.

1979 *The Irish Folklore Commission. Achievement and Legacy.* Baile Átha Cliath: An Coláiste Ollscoile, Comhairle Bhéaloideas Éireann.

AN GÀIDHEAL.

1947–49 *The Gael. The Official Magazine of An Comunn Gàidhealach*: XLII–XLIV.

BRINGÉUS, NILS-ARVID.

2009 *Carl Wilhelm von Sydow: A Swedish Pioneer in Folklore*. Helsinki.

BRIODY, MICHEÁL.

2007 *The Irish Folklore Commission 1935–1970: History, Ideology, Methodology.* Helsinki.

CAMPBELL, JOHN LORNE.

1938 'A visit to Cape Breton'. *Scots Magazine,* September 1938: 423–432 and October 1938: 17–27.

1939 *Sia Sgeulachdan a chruinnich 's a dheasaich Iain Latharna Caimbeul ann am Barraidh 's an Uidhist a Deas*. Dùn-éideann.

1949 'Gaelic Folk-songs: Work of the Collectors'. *The Scotsman*, 17 September 1949.

CHEAPE, HUGH.

2013 '"Cuir siud sa' Ghàidhlig": Toradh na h-obrach aig Fear Chanaigh'. Bob Chambers (ed.), *The Carrying Stream Flows On: Celebrating the Diamond Jubilee of the School of Scottish Studies.* Kershader, South Lochs, Isle of Lewis: 95–117.

MAC AONGHUIS, IAIN.

1936 *Òrain Ghàidhlig le Seonaidh Caimbeul*. Dùn Phàrlain.

MACINNES, JOHN.

1966 'Gaelic Songs of Mary MacLeod'. *Scottish Gaelic Studies* XI/1: 3–25.

MACLEAN, CALUM I.

1975 *The Highlands.* Inverness.

MACLEOID, IAIN N.

1947 'Dìmeas na Gàidhlig'. *An Gàidheal* XLII/7 (An Giblein 1947): 86–87.

MCINTOSH, ANGUS.

1951 'Scottish Dialect Studies: Collecting Information for the Linguistic Survey'. *The Scotsman,* 5 October 1951.

MAC CALMAIN, TÒMAS M.

2011 *Mo Là Gu Seo. Eachdraidh mo Bheatha le Tòmas M. MacCalmain.* Dòmhnall E. Meek (deas.). Dùn-éideann.

MURCHISON, REV. T. M.

1947 'Tha feum air cabhaig. Na seanchaidhean a' falbh oirnn'. *An Gàidheal* XLII /8: 93–94.

PERMAN, RAY.

2010 *The Man Who Gave Away His Island.* Edinburgh.

Clan Chief, Clan Embarrassment: The Seventeenth-Century Campbells

EDWARD J. COWAN

It is a pleasure to be invited to contribute to this collection honouring John MacInnes, a man whose friendship and knowledge I have long been privileged to enjoy. One discussion to which we have frequently returned concerns Gilleasbuig Gruamach, a designation first conferred on Archibald Campbell seventh Earl of Argyll, though I am convinced that in Gaelic tradition 'the Grim' is frequently applied to the eighth earl as well and perhaps the ninth, all of whom were potentially disastrous for the well-being of their clan. The name Gilleasbuig, the English version of which is Archibald, was not uncommon in the House of Loch Awe. It can be traced as far back as the mid-thirteenth-century and it was conferred on the second, fourth and fifth earls of Argyll, as well as the first and second dukes. The following discussion explores the reciprocal relationships between Campbell chiefs and their kindreds during the particularly fraught era of the three Gilleasbuigs each of whom, disastrously for their clan, defied their Stewart kings, until a fourth, the tenth earl, became first Duke of Argyll in 1703.

Professor Willie Gillies has convincingly challenged the view that the Campbells somehow became less Gaelic the more deeply they were involved in national politics. If anything, their role on the larger stage enhanced their reputations. Bardic verse celebrated the activities of Sliochd Diarmaid chiefs from the battle of Flodden to the time of John second Duke of Argyll, who died in 1743, while Campbell poetry continued to be composed into the nineteenth century (Gillies 1978: 261). Although it is true that much anti-Campbell poesy appeared, particularly in the seventeenth-century, we are left with a lingering suspicion that a residual pride in Campbell achievement survived in Gaeldom, that Gaels rejoiced in the Gaelic-ness of the Campbells while deploring many of their more outrageous actions. Their incredible success as a clan was a source of envy as much as despair on the part of their enemies, who fell far short of their achievements.

A recent account indicates how troubled and vexatious the career of Gilleasbuig Gruamach, seventh earl, actually was (Campbell 2002: 91–197). Just nine years old when his father died in 1584, he was taken into the protection of the eighteen-year-old James VI, while his affairs, and hence those of the clan at large, were assigned to six Campbell trustees. His minority was seen by some of his powerful kinsmen as an opportunity for personal aggrandizement. Matters came to a head when Black Duncan of Glenorchy, in alliance with the Earl of Huntly, orchestrated a conspiracy in which Campbell of Cawdor and James Stewart, Earl of Moray, were murdered. Also targeted was Gilleasbuig, who believed, with some reason, that his uncle, Glenorchy, was attempting to replace him as chief. The ensuing chaos set the great harp of the Highlands ajangling, setting off wide reverberations in the Lowlands as well (Cowan 1986).

In the aftermath, Clan Campbell came close to the fragmentation that had bedeviled such clans as the Macdonalds and the Macleods. Argyll was reprimanded by the privy council for failing to keep good order among 'all persons of the surname of Campbell' (RPC: v, 190). The main threat to his person reposed in his own kindred; Archibald's legendary grimness was clan inspired. Fortunately, wiser heads prevailed thanks to the efforts of Campbell of Loudon, chief of the 'English Campbells' (Cowan 1986: 292–3) and John, Earl of Mar, who secured an obligation in 1595 between Argyll and Glenorchy. 'Evil disposed persons' had orchestrated coldness between the two but Argyll swore never to act deceitfully towards his kinsman. In the event of 'misreports', he was to give two weeks notice of a meeting in the Lowlands to investigate them. Glenorchy agreed to 'behave kindly' to his chief, refusing to believe any derogatory reports without consulting him.

Confidence in such agreements was shaken as other details emerged, most worryingly of plots against young Argyll inspired by other Campbell kin. Comital confidence was again shattered when the earl, seeking vengeance upon Huntly, was defeated at the battle of Glenlivat; 'Argyll, *puer*, gratt' (Calderwood 1844: V, 350).

Argyll received several commissions to hunt down MacGregors, largely ignored until 1602 when new harsh methods, reinforced by the Crown, generated disgust and alarm throughout the Gàidhealtachd, compounded when, shortly after James moved south to London, he granted him a commission of fire and sword against Macdonalds, Macleans, MacLeods and Clanranald, colourfully described as 'an infamous byke of lawless limmers' (HMC, iv, Argyll MSS: App. 489). Acquisition of the lands of these clans was the incentive to intensify MacGregor hunting until only twelve remained alive. Hundreds of people from Dumbarton to Dornoch were fined for sheltering MacGregors. Argyll was accused of pursuing personal agendas with reference to the western clans. There can be little doubt that he did more to blacken the name of Clan Campbell than any of his predecessors, bequeathing much pent-up trouble to his successors. Gilleasbuig was engaged in nothing short of MacGregor genocide. That James approved such a policy was reflected in his admission that, 'We wilbe spairing to dispose upon ony pairt of these Yllis, and unwilling to *extermine, yea skairse to transplant the inhabitants of the same, bot upon a just caus*' [my italics] (RPC viii: 745–6). It seems that in the view of the king the clan as a whole was as culpable as the chief for the atrocities of which they were accused.[1]

As the climax to a succession of woes, Argyll, in 1617, became, according to Sir Thomas Urquhart of Cromarty, 'the most obstinate and rigid papist that ever was upon the earth' (Millar 1912: 86), decamping to Spain and further seriously threatening clan fortunes.

Once again the heir was a minor, Archibald, Lord Lorne, the future marquess. The situation demanded swift action, as represented by the earliest surviving correspondence to run in Lorne's name, but masterminded by his uncle, Campbell of Lundy, of the Angus Campbells (Cowan 1981), as well as Glenorchy and Lawers. Lorne's letter to the heads of the name, written in response to royal demands, indicated that if they did not take action the entire clan was threatened with total destruction:

> I think or now ye ar advertised of the cours my lord and father hes takin, quherby he has so kindled his majesties wrath aganes him and his hous, that it sall not mis presentlie to be indangered, if not altidder ruined (unless) all instrumental means by the wisdom and mediatioun of good freindis be speciallie used for the mitigation of his majesties heiche displeasure. And because natur and dewtie doe boeth concur to astrict me to succor both my father and the hous of my expectatioun, were it the derrest blood of my bodie (Innes 1859: 246)

He entreated all recipients of the letter to appear at Edinburgh on 15 December 1617 to give their best counsel as to how to satisfy the king 'and the approaching danger to my father and his house spedilie prevented'. Lorne must have been gratified by the largest assembly of the name ever seen in the capital, when Lundy and other Campbells were appointed to manage the earldom. Even more impressive perhaps was a gathering at Inveraray a month later, when it was agreed that the 1592 conspiracy had threatened the 'prejuduce, hurte, damnage and losse' of the 'haill kyn and freindis of the name of Campbell', and the feuds were solemnly quenched (Innes: 243–5; Cowan 1986: 280–1). Thus, in an impressive example of clan cohesion, securing the chiefship and the succession of its future occupant, the present danger was averted.

[1] The Crown's dealings with the MacGregors and other clans are exceedingly complex. I have attempted to discuss these developments, unsatisfactorily I fear and with considerable overlap, in at least three articles: Cowan 1979, 1986 and 2006.

Gilleasbuig died in London having made one last visit, overlooked by recent authorities, to his homeland in 1634 (Stevenson 1980: 49–50; Campbell 2002), when he was almost entirely shunned by his kindred. His purpose was to sort out an acrimonious dispute between Lorne and his half-brother, Lord James, about the possession of Kintyre. Campbells were never short of disputes, least of all with their own kind. But Lorne had the right idea about such disagreements when he advised Glenorchy and Glenlyon to keep their quarrel with one another out of the courts, 'to lat the business be rewlait be the mediatioune of freindis for boith your weilles' (Cowan 1986: 279). Clan internalisation of contentious issues and avoidance of Edinburgh lawyers would benefit Campbell cohesion.

In 1638 Lorne became eighth Earl of Argyll and leader of the Covenanting Revolution. It is doubtful if his followers shared his deep presbyterianism. In the course of the civil wars, Campbells became the targets of royalist troops, clan hatred and a Catholic crusade; they endured overwhelming defeats and hundreds of dead and wounded at the hands of Montrose and Alistair Mac Colla; their estates suffered devastation. Argyll's own military reputation was not enhanced by his habit of retreating from conflict, leaving his kindred to perish at Inveraray, Inverlochy and Kilsyth. He is often reputed a politician of extreme deviousness, characterized by a strabismus which gave rise to his designation as 'gley'd eye'd Archibald'. He was also a ruthless negotiator and a completely unforgiving enemy. He placed himself at the head of the Covenanting movement out of religious conviction and genuine concern for the survival of the Scottish kirk, and because he wished to contain the revolutionary fervor of some of the covenanters, notably the ministers. He believed that 'popular furies would never have end if not overawed by their superiors'. He hoped for an accommodation with Charles I as a covenanted king, but as the monarch's actions became more extreme, so too Argyll's radicalism. There is no doubt that he actually discussed the possible deposition of Charles, yet he was revolted by the execution of the king. He must have realized that the arguments justifying the removal of a king could also apply to a clan chief (Cowan 1994).

There is some truth in the view that he manipulated support for the Covenant to his own advantage in pursuing clan agendas, but he also suffered greatly in the same cause at the hands of his enemies. At the end of his life, Argyll admitted that all of his plans and schemes went awry. Whatever he attempted had unforeseen consequences, such as his attempted accommodations with Charles II, Cromwell and Monck. His career is an example to historians of the inconsistencies in the lifetimes of individuals whose decisions may be made for reasons of policy, pragmatism, pique or prejudice in circumstances that are far beyond their personal control. Awaiting execution in 1661, he memorably described himself as 'a distracted man, a distracted subject, of a distracted time wherein I lived'.

At the Restoration he hastened south to greet Charles II, but was promptly shipped back to Edinburgh for trial as a traitor. When found guilty, his titles and lands were automatically forfeited, and once again the mighty Clan Campbell feared for its future. Following the execution, Argyll's heir, Archibald Lord Lorne and his 'freinds' wrote, pledging their loyalty to their 'dear father', Charles II, just as all previous Campbells had been faithful to their monarchs ever since the time of 'that great rebel Somerled', in whose overthrow they assisted. The 'inbred loyalty of their house' had been consistent from the reign of Robert Bruce to that of James VI, who described the Campbells as 'the soundest and most loyall family to the croun of Scotland that ever he knew'. Campbells had always been active in suppressing the 'many horrid insurrections and rebellions of Islanders, and remote mountanous men that have been broken, destroyed and overthrowen by our Cheiffs and ther friends'. No chiefs, cousins or cadets had ever been charged with disloyalty or disobedience,

> but by the contrar they have alwayes been most willing, to sett themselves for bearing doun the insollencie of the remote rebellious lawless men, which is much occasioned by the remoteness and distance of these places quher we live, far from the lawes and Justice, the horror of rocks, woods and mountains contributing much unto

> this. Let the most ancient of men be consulted, and all the progress of the history of this Nation considered and all that we have said shall be found to be certain and unanswerable.

If the king would consider their track-record 'then it shall be no greif to your Majestie, nor offence of heart, that yow have not rooted out so loyall and so ancient a family, who in most backslyding tymes have still retained our loyaltie and integrity' (*Letters*: 45–50).

Thus the Campbells sought to avoid their extirpation. It is noteworthy that recent conflicts with the Macdonalds, as represented by Alistair mac Colla during the Montrose wars, were made to resonate with the idea that Clan Donald, personified by Somerled, had been rebels as long as the Campbells had been royalists. The references to remoteness and justice remind the king that his forebears could not have ruled the Gàidhealtachd without Campbell assistance. Finally Charles had not yet outlawed the whole clan and hopefully he would not do so.

Argyll had taken the precaution of encouraging his eldest son and heir to cultivate more promising links with monarchy than his own personal history permitted. Father on one side and son on the other was a long-standing ploy of the Scottish nobility, and while Argyll cultivated the Cromwellians, his son supported the royalists. The stratagem paid off. The new earl, thirty-four year-old Archibald, ninth of Argyll, succeeded his father, regaining his titles (but not the marquessate) and most of the comital lands in 1663. The king issued an Act of Indemnity which specified a long list of Campbells who were exempted and heavily fined. Throughout his lifetime he had to fight off the malicious intentions of some of the most skulduggerous politicians to disgrace the pages of Scottish history, while the Campbell estates were drowning in debt. He is notable for having survived a trepanning operation as a young man, and he also has the distinction of having received two death sentences, both for leasing-making, in 1662 and 1681. The latter followed his taking of the Test Oath, in good faith, in so far as it was 'consistent with itself and the protestant religion'. On that occasion he was undoubtedly the victim of a plot, but he managed to escape from Edinburgh Castle, thus avoiding beheading until 1685 when he led the Scottish wing of Monmouth's rebellion (Willcock 1907).

There is at Inveraray the transcript of a document from the Breadalbane Charter Chest, apparently commissioned by John Campbell of Glenorchy, recently raised to the peerage as first Earl of Breadalbane, and drawn up by Sir James Dalrymple, Viscount Stair, an associate of Argyll when both were exiled to the Netherlands and author of the famous *Institutions of the Law of Scotland* (AT, c. 1686).[2] The memorandum opposes planned legislation concerning the abolition or prescription of the surname Campbell after the forfeiture and execution of Argyll. It considers whether there was any provision in Scots Law for outlawing the Campbell name due to the crimes of the chief or other prominent Campbells; second whether it was in the interest of king and kingdom to procure the proposed abolition of the surname; and third a consideration of the precedents for such abolition. It categorically states:

> Ther is no standing law declaring or inacting that upon the rebellione of the chief of the clan or any pairt of the clan that the rest shall be obleidged to quite ther name and the Surname to be abolished . . . But the clans in Scotland being septs or tribes of people generally haveing lands lyeing together, and sometimes without lands or fixed residence, the Chief of these Clans had by our ancient custome a despotick power or influence upon his clane or name which in severall exigencies in the more ancient and ruder times was of great use and subserviencie to the Monarchie. These Cheiftanes

[2] At time of writing I have been unable to establish whether the original document survives in the Breadalbane Collection at NAS. I have consulted the Argyll Transcripts at Inveraray Castle, a copy of which is held in the former Scottish History Department at the University of Glasgow. I first consulted the Argyll Muniments around 1970 since when all my call numbers are hopelessly out of date. I understand that the Muniments are currently being re-organised and will soon be available for public access.

> being alwayes in capacitie and readines with ther clans for the publict service and thereafter when civilitie, lawes and good maners were more introduced the law did obleidge in many caices the cheiff for the faults of his clan, bot by the ancient policie of this Kingdome the clan had never power to restrain or coerce their cheiff and by noe law or custome was ever a clan in Scotland made lyable or obnoxious for the crymes of ther chief or of particular persones of the clan, wherin the rest were not involved.

Herein it was clearly forgotten that the Campbells had coerced, if not Gilleasbuig Gruamach, then his office, in 1617. Later in the document there is mention of the MacGregors who, of course, were held as culpable as their chief to the point of near destruction, a liability which brought the Campbells great riches. Stair's second argument against proscription was that 'the name is universallie scattered through the Kingdome and more of that surname in the Lowlands than the Highlands, haveing no dependence by holding or uther tyes to ther cheiff, nor no communicatione amongst themselves, bot the bulk of that name, nather by speech, garb or inclination, doeth affect the highland methode or custome of a clan, bot are as polyte regular and descreit persones as any surname of the Kingdom'. He must however have been aware that in the past Campbells, like other clans, could and did claim that anyone sharing the name, irrespective of residence, from Angus to Ayrshire, were members of the clan whose chief they were expected to acknowledge.

Stair then asserts that even when people have taken, or been forced to use, another name, they are still known to be descendants of their original clan. Abolition of the name Campbell would only be practical where the Lowland Campbells were concerned, 'which are not properlie a clan or in hazard to raise or rune together for ther cheiff or with the clan'. Yet bearers of the name might be resentful if it was abolished and so enraged as to 'follow the resentments of the cheiff'. Also there were Campbells who did not claim to be descended from the main family and did not own Argyll as their chief. It was not just, that these should be obliged 'to abandon the names of ther Inogenitors upon a suspitione of ane inbred disloyaltie affecting the blood of severall families'.

> As to the comons of the name of Campbell it is not so considerable and for the heretors they are generallie in the Lowlands disentangled from the Clan, and the heretors of the highlands doe generallie holde of the familie of Argyle with sever (stringent) clausses of personall services and attendances. And if these heretors shall be allowed to continew to braith in a frier ayre and have the honor to hold immidiatlie of his Majestie they wold quicklie perceave the advantage of ther change and turne ill favorable not onlie to the rebellious practices of the Earl of Argyle bot even to any motion that might restore the familie.

On his third point, concerning precedents for abolishing clans and surnames for the chief's crimes, he cites the Comyns, the Ruthvens, the MacLeods of Lewis and the MacGregors, only to state that the evidence for the Comyns is inconclusive. The others are not discussed, as the document concludes very abruptly.

Stair was possessed of one of the greatest legal minds that Scotland ever produced, but it has to be wondered if his third point defeated him, for the MacGregor name was clearly proscribed. His paper seems to argue that the clan has no status in Scots law, and he minimizes the reciprocal relationship between clansmen and chief. While these matters require further consideration, Stair writes as if he wishes to abrogate clans altogether, writing them out of history, in anticipation of the abolition of heritable jurisdictions in 1747. Three years before the first Jacobite Rising, in his mind, the clans were already redundant.

ABBREVIATIONS

AT	Argyll Transcripts, Inverary Castle. Copies in Scottish History Department, University of Glasgow.
HMC	Historical Manuscripts Commission.
Letters	*Letters to the Argyll Family*. Maitland Club, Edinburgh (1839).
RPC	Register of the Privy Council of Scotland, 1st Series. J. H. Burton *et al.* (eds). 14 vols. Edinburgh (1877–1898).

SOURCES

CALDERWOOD, DAVID.

1844 *History of the Kirk of Scotland*, 6 vols. Edinburgh.

CAMPBELL, ALISTAIR.

2002 *A History of Clan Campbell, Vol. 2: From Flodden to the Restoration*. Edinburgh.

COWAN, EDWARD J.

1979 'Clanship, Kinship and the Campbell Acquisition of Islay'. *Scottish Historical Review* LVIII: 132–57.

1981 'The Angus Campbells and the Origin of the Campbell-Ogilvie Feud'. *Scottish Studies* 25: 25–38.

1986 'Fishers in Drumlie Waters: Clanship and Campbell Expansion in the Time of Gilleasbuig Gruamach'. *Transactions of the Gaelic Society of Inverness* LIV: 269–312.

1994 'The political ideas of a covenanting leader: Archibald Campbell, Marquis of Argyll, 1607–1661'. Roger A. Mason (ed.), *Scots and Britons: Scottish Political Thought and the Union of 1603*. Cambridge: 241–61.

2006 'Highland and Lowland, Gael and non-Gael: West Dunbartonshire from the Thirteenth to the Eighteenth Centuries'. Ian Brown (ed.), *Changing Identities, Ancient Roots: The History of West Dunbartonshire from Earliest Times*. Edinburgh.

GILLIES, WILLIAM.

1978 'Some Aspects of Campbell History'. *Transactions of the Gaelic Society of Inverness* L: 256–95.

INNES, COSMO (ED.).

1859 *The Book of the Thanes of Cawdor*. Spalding Club, Aberdeen.

MILLAR, JOHN HEPBURN.

1912 *Scottish Prose of the Seventeenth and Eighteenth Centuries*. Glasgow.

STEVENSON, DAVID.

1980 *Alasdair Mac-Colla and the Highland Problem in the Seventeenth Century.* Edinburgh.

WILLCOCK, JOHN.

1907 *A Scots Earl in Covenanting Times: Being Life and Times of Archibald, 9th Earl of Argyll (1629–1685).* Edinburgh.

Air do Dheagh Shlàinte Iain Mhic Aonghuis

AILEAN DÒMHNALLACH

Urlar

Siubhal

Dithis

Taorludh Breabach agus Crunludh Singilte

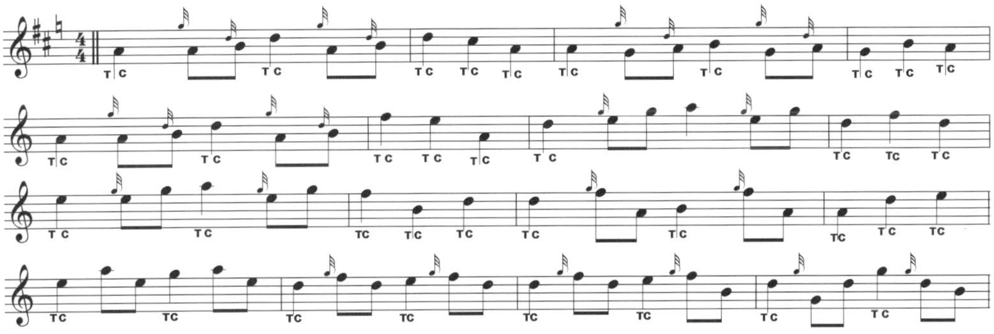

1: Taorludh Dubailte 2: Crunludh Dubailte 3: Crunludh a mach

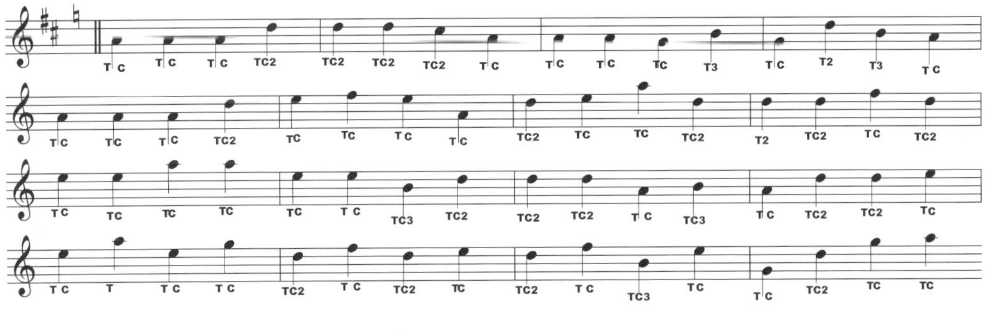

Giorrachaidhean

Taorludh (T) Crunludh (C) Crunludh a mach (C2)

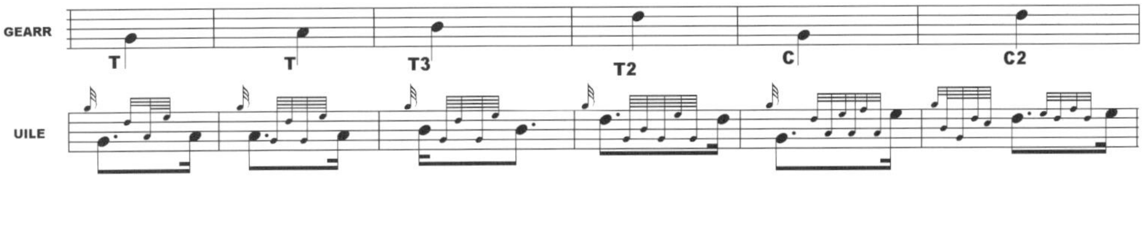

The School of Scottish Studies and Language Policy and Planning for Gaelic

ROBERT DUNBAR

The School of Scottish Studies (the 'School') was inaugurated on 31 January 1951 as a semi-autonomous institution within the University of Edinburgh, with the broad aim of studying 'Scottish traditional life in its European setting, on lines similar to those developed in several Scandinavian institutes and, more recently, in Ireland and Wales' (Kerr, n.d.: 1). The principal activities of the School have been described as the recording, documentation and study of oral traditions (e.g. tales, legends, proverbs, custom and belief), traditional song and instrumental music, material culture, and place-names, covering the whole of Scotland and including Gaelic and Scots-speaking districts (ibid).

The School's holdings comprise a sound archive of over 30,000 items, including song and verse, instrumental music, oral narrative, custom and belief, traditional knowledge, material culture and contemporary ethnology in Scots, Gaelic and English, a film/video archive of about 320 items, including craft processes, customs, storytelling and song performances, a photographic archive of over 50,000 images, including those taken on fieldwork, and a manuscript collection which includes original manuscripts and copies of those held elsewhere, the Scottish Place-name Survey and the Gaelic and Scots Linguistic Surveys, project papers, and fieldwork notes (Ranft and Richmond 2012: 6). The School has benefited from the work of a number of outstanding collector-scholars, many of whom were Gaelic-speakers focusing on the Gaelic tradition, including the first collector in the school, Calum Maclean (1915–1960; see Wiseman 2010 and MacGilleathain 2011), James Ross (1923–1971), Morag MacLeod, Donald Archie MacDonald (1929–1999), Alan Bruford (1927–1995), Eric Cregeen (1921–1983), and, of course, John MacInnes (see, generally, M. Mackay 2013).

The cultural importance of the Archives is obvious, but relationships between the Archives, and in particular the activities of its staff over the years, to language planning for Gaelic are not immediately so; indeed, that there may be such a relationship might have surprised at least some of the School's collectors, who may not have considered language planning to have been part of their remit. Nevertheless, in this paper, I shall explore the ways in which not only the School and its collectors, but also their precedessors, were indeed engaged in a kind of language planning, among many other things. I shall also explore how the legacy of these efforts, in the form of the Archives, is now contributing to language planning for Gaelic, and how it may continue to do so in the future.

As Margaret Mackay has noted, 'the collecting of material relating to Scotland's oral and material culture, its songs, narratives, customs, beliefs and ways of life, has been carried out for many centuries' (M. Mackay 2013: 1), although as she also notes, it was not until the founding of the School that this activity 'became firmly fixed within an institutional framework' (*ibid:* 2). Thus, in some respects, the work of the School builds on the efforts of earlier collectors who relied on somewhat different media for the preservation of the traditions which they recorded. Until the twentieth century, this material was found in manuscripts, books and similar text-based media.

The older Gaelic tradition of Scotland and Ireland is preserved to some extent in a considerable number of manuscripts dating from the twelfth century onwards, most of which have an Irish provenance (McLeod and Bateman 2007: xxx–xxxi). There appears to have been only very limited collecting of material in vernacular Scottish Gaelic circulating in the oral tradition until the eighteenth century, when a number of collectors began taking down poetry and song (Thomson 1954: 5); the collection of most other genres had to wait until about the middle of the mid-nineteenth century. For example, in the 1750s, both the Rev. Donald MacNicol (1735–1802) and Jerome Stone (1727–1756) were collecting material, including songs and poetry (Henderson 1908–11; Mackinnon 1887–88). Perhaps the two most important manuscript collections of this period were those made by the Rev. Ewen MacDiarmid (d. 1801) (Thomson 1992) and the Rev. James MacLagan (1728–1805) (Thomson 1993–94), although the manuscript collections of Dr Hector Maclean (1704–83) of Grulin, Mull (Ó Baoill 2001), and, a little later, of Rev. Dr. Alexander Irvine (1773–1824; see Hogg 2011) are also important.

The printing press allowed for the much wider circulation of the Gaelic material which was being collected, and beginning with the publication in 1751 of *Ais-eiridh na sean chánoin Albannaich; no, An nuadh oranaiche Gaidhealach* by Alexander MacDonald ('Alasdair Mac Mhaighstir Alasdair', c. 1695–c. 1770), Gaels began seizing on the opportunities which print provided. *Comh-chruinneachidh Orannaigh Gaidhealach*, the 'Eigg Collection', published in 1776 by Ranald MacDonald ('Raghnall Dubh', c. 1728–c. 1808), the son of Alasdair mac Mhaighstir Alasdair, was the first of many important anthologies of Gaelic poetry drawn at least in part from the oral tradition. From about the middle of the nineteenth century, the range of Gaelic material which was being collected and published began to expand. Between 1859 and 1862, for example, John Francis Campbell of Islay ('Iain Òg Ìle' 1821–85) (see Thompson 1984–86; National Library of Scotland 1985; Shaw 2007), in collaboration with some exceptional fieldworkers, amassed a huge collection of Gaelic tales, some of which were published in four volumes in 1860 and 1862 as *Popular Tales of the West Highlands*. Alexander Carmichael (1832–1912) collected a wide variety of material, some of which was published in five volumes of *Carmina Gadelica* (from 1900 onwards (Stiùbhart 2008). The Rev. John Gregorson Campbell (1836–91) was also an extremely important collector, not only of folktales, but also of belief legends, Fenian material, and clan lore (see Black 2005), as was Fr Allan MacDonald (1859–1905) (see Hutchison 2010).

The development in the twentieth century of sound recording technology created new possibilities for collectors, and one of the earliest to seize upon these was Marjory Kennedy-Fraser (1857–1930) (Ahlander 2011: xvii–xviii). Perhaps the most important of these early collectors was John Lorne Campbell, 'Fear Chanaidh' (1906–1996), who by the 1930s was already compiling a large collection of sound recordings (Perman 2010). Campbell's recording activities led to a number of important publications (for example, Campbell 1939, 1961, 1962, 1972, 1973, 1990), and now some of the material he collected is being digitised and made available through the *Tobar an Dualchais* project.

A variety of motives have propelled collectors of Gaelic oral tradition – both individual and institutional – in their work; however, from the eighteenth century through to the present, there have been significant continuities, some of which are relevant to this discussion. To some extent, the work of collectors of Gaelic oral tradition mirrored contemporary initiatives – although John MacInnes has pointed out that there were other very particular agendas at work in eighteenth century Gaelic Scotland (MacInnes 1976: 244), something which is true of later periods as well. Certainly, the pioneering work of John Francis Campbell on Gaelic oral narrative owed much to George Dasent and to Norwegian and German antecedents – notably, the Grimms – (Dorson 1968:393–4); and both the establishment and early activities of the School of Scottish Studies were inspired to a considerable degree by developments in Ireland (M. Mackay 2013), and in particular the creation of the Irish Folklore Commission, the creation of which was itself informed by developments in Scandinavia (Briody 2008). Concerns about the fragility of the oral tradition – the impact of modernity on traditional, rural-based peasant folk cultures, and the necessity of recording it for posterity before it disappeared – rather than more particular concerns about the fragility of the languages themselves lay behind much of this activity. However, in the Gaelic context, those more particular concerns were frequently also deeply and intimately involved.

Linguistic concerns are evident in Alexander MacDonald's groundbreaking 1751 collection, as its very title, *Ais-eiridh na sean chánoin Albannaich*, 'The Resurrection of the the Old Scottish

Language', reveals. As Peter Mackay notes, MacDonald 'engages in celebration, advertisement and rapprochement' (P. Mackay 2013: 117). Rapprochement was certainly a priority – the book was published only five years after Culloden, and as John MacInnes has noted, MacDonald 'is obviously attempting to heal the wounds that still smarted in Scotland from the effects of the late Rising' (MacInnes 1976: 245). With regard to 'advertisement', Mackay notes that MacDonald is attempting 'in part to advertise the merits of Gaelic literature, and in part to highlight the 'Scottishness' of that literature', but that he also 'presents his collection of poems as entertainment for those who can read Gaelic, and a possible encouragement for those who cannot to learn' (P. Mackay 2013: 117). Purely linguistic concerns, and indeed an awareness of the precariousness of the Gaelic language itself, were a key part of the agenda of MacDonald's son, Ranald, in his publication in 1776 of the Eigg Collection. Indeed, Ranald MacDonald begins his preface by noting that '[t]he Gaelic language, *now struggling for existence in a narrow corner*, was once the mother tongue of the principal states of Europe' (emphasis added) (MacDhomhnuill 1776: v). He then stakes its claim as the original language of Scotland, and provides what is in essence a sociolinguistic analysis of the reasons for its decline:

> The intrinsic excellence of the language itself, added to that love of ancient customs so prevalent among mankind, and so conspicuous among the Caledonians, might seem, at first view, to give immortality to the Gaelic tongue: But many political causes, which it is not my present purpose to enumerate, concurred to introduce the English language into this country and to render it fashionable at Court.—From this date, we date the decay of the Gaelic language. The English, which paved the way to honour and preferment, was naturally cultivated with care; while the Gaelic, the knowledge or study of which could not then be attended with any emolument, and the speaking of which became even unpolite, was as naturally neglected, and often treated with contempt. The influence of these causes became the more obvious, and operated the more powerfully, the nearer they approached to our times; so that the very remembrance of a language which had once been general over almost all Europe, was in danger of being entirely obliterated. (*ibid:* v–vi)

The work of collecting and publishing Gaelic literature is clearly conceived by Ranald MacDonald as being part of a greater effort to defend the language. Referring implicitly to James MacPherson – and it is clear that Ranald was also, like many of his contemporary Gaels, responding to the Ossianic Controversy and engaged in a defence of MacPherson (see MacInnes 1976) – and others engaged in the publication of Gaelic literuare at about this time, he continues:

> At this critical period a fortunate event happened. Some individuals, animated with the love of their native language, regretted the danger to which they saw it exposed. Compositions of great merit in the language were known to exist. Inquiry was made after these, with a view to publish them, and this was esteemed the best method of preserving the language itself. (ibid: vi–vii).

He concludes his argument as follows: 'The Editor, moved by these considerations [i.e. the Ossianic Controversy], *and desirous to preserve his mother tongue*, has bestowed much labour and expence, during the course of two years, in collecting the poems now offered to the public.' Collecting and publishing of Gaelic oral literature is, then, to no small degree part of a language maintenance project.

The intertwined fates of Gaelic oral literature and the language itself, the importance of maintaining both, and the role that collecting such material played in both initiatives, remained a theme in subsequent periods. And while Gaelic language maintenance and revitalisation, and Gaelic language policy more generally, were not matters which were explicitly recognised as forming part of the mission or activities of the School of Scottish Studies, it is important to remember that these matters did form part of the context which led to the establishment of the School. Gaelic language maintenance and revitalisation were of great concern to John Lorne Campbell, Derick Thomson, and the Rev. T. M. Murchison, whose Folklore Institute of Scotland, formed in 1947, played an important role in the inspiring the creation of the School (M. Mackay 2013: 5). As early as 1936, the desirability of a survey of Scottish dialects was being discussed, and shortly after his appointment in 1948 to the Chair of English Language and General Linguistics at the University of Edinburgh, Angus McIntosh (1914–2005) – who enjoyed a close relationship with John Lorne Campbell – established the Linguistic Surveys of Scotland (Scots and Gaelic) (M. Mackay 2013: 3, 6–7). McIntosh also played a central role in the establishment of the School, and it is clear that the linguistic surveys and the collecting of oral traditions were conceived of as complementary initiatives, each designed to preserve a record of Scotland's linguistic diversity and cultural richness in the face of the homogenising and anglifying influences of twentieth century Britain. Clearly, linguistic considerations, and an awareness of the sociolinguistic and demographic threats which confronted the Gaelic language, continued to inform the work of collectors.

The relationship between the motives and activities of collectors of Gaelic oral tradition on the one hand and language planning become clearer, and the potential inherent in this relationship become even more evident, when the nature of language planning, and in particular language planning for minoritised languages, is considered. Language planning is a relatively young academic discipline, and in the 1960s and 1970s, it was considered to have involved two aspects: corpus planning and status planning. 'Corpus planning' involves modifying the language itself, such as 'coining new terms, reforming spelling, and adopting new script[1] . . . in short, to the creation of new forms,[2] the modification of old ones,[3] or the selection from alternative forms in spoken or written code (Cooper 1989: 31). Corpus planning also often involves the development of dictionaries and grammars, and even of a written literature.

Material collected from an oral tradition constitutes a potentially extremely rich foundation upon which corpus planning activities can be based, something which is particularly true with respect to minority languages. Joshua Fishman, still the most prominent theorist of minority language maintenance and revitalisation (or 'reversing language shift', 'RLS'), has developed a well-known eight stage model, the 'Graded Intergenerational Disruption Scale', or 'GIDS', which both allows an assessment of the degree to which a minority language is threatened and provides a guide as to strategies which should be deployed to improve the situation of such languages (Fishman 1991: 81–121). Stage 8 on the GIDS, which is indicative of the stage at which the most threatened languages are situated, occurs when most remaining users of the minority language are isolated older people having few opportunities to use their language. At this stage, Fishman argues that these users are 'individuals who are well recognized as informants by folklorists and by linguists', and the priority is to save 'the last few remnants' of the language as spoken:

> Such preservative efforts are certainly extremely worthwhile because they help both professional and amateur 'collectors' to piece together and restore folksongs, proverbs and folktales, formulaic expressions (greetings, apologies, benedictions, maledictions, etc.) and, from the foregoing, subsequently, to assemble partial phonologies, grammars and lexicons, piece by piece until a reasonable whole is once more at hand....(Fishman 1991: 88)

Quite apart from the cultural and literary value of such material, it represents the foundation on which subsequent language maintenance strategies – most crucially the acquisition of the language by a broader range of people – can be built; indeed, the use of archival resources in the development

---

[1] Sometimes referred to as 'graphization': Hornberger 2006: 29.

[2] Sometimes referred to as 'renovation': *ibid.*

[3] Sometimes referred to as 'modernisation': *ibid.*

of reference and learning materials has frequently been highlighted by theorists and practicitioners of minority language maintenance and revitalisation (see Hinton 2001a: 419–23). The recordings made in 1948 by the Irish Folklore Commission of some of the last remaining native speakers of Manx is an excellent example of this sort of project, and these recordings have been a very important resource in the contemporary renewal of Manx (see Manx National Heritage 2004).

Alexander MacDonald, 'Alasdair mac Mhaighstir Alasdair', was certainly consciously engaged in corpus planning in his 1751 collection. For example, he provided in his preface a summary of the orthographic conventions he uses 'for the more easy perusal of this work to those who are not expert in reading the language, though perhaps their mother tongue'. He also provided details on his editorial principles, noting that 'no pains have been spared to render the language as plain and intelligible as reasonably can be expected' (Mac-Dhonuill 1751: ix–x). His son Ranald followed his preface with a page-and-a-half section entitled 'Instructions for reading the Gaelic Language', which focused mostly on orthographic matters; thus, he, too, was engaged in corpus planning. Both the Linguistic Survey of Scotland and the School of Scottish Studies Archives provide a huge source of material of relevance to future corpus planning activities in support of Gaelic. Contained within the archives is a wealth of terminology, idioms, placenames and so forth that could be used to enrich contemporary Gaelic language use and inform the development of appropriate terminology and styles for a range of domains. Indeed, Dr Gary West of Celtic and Scottish Studies at the University of Edinburgh has recently noted that the Scottish Government is committed to increased promotion of both the Gaelic and Scots languages, and that the Archives 'are a rich and unique source for both' (Ranft and Richmond 2012: 34).

The second aspect of language planning,'Status planning', deals with the modification of the functions which a particular language is meant to serve (or, to put it another way, modifications in the domains[4] in which a language is used). It therefore relates to the social and political position of the language (Cooper 1989, 32–3). Status planning has often played a significant part in the decline in minority languages: the designation of a particular language as the 'official' one usually meant the exclusion of other languages from those domains, so-called 'high' domains, which are perceived as socially important and most closely associated with institutions of power and influence. Status planning for minority languages such as Gaelic often involves initiatives aimed at introducing or reintroducing their use in such domains. As the name implies, status planning also relates more generally to enhancing the prestige of a language. It is in respect of this aspect of status planning that the collection of oral traditions is of most relevance and importance: the act of collecting, and of preserving, and then of disseminating such traditions can send an important signal about the value which is attached to the language and its related culture. This was well understood by Alasdair mac Mhaighstir Alasdair. As noted earlier, his 1751 collection was meant as a possible encouragement for those who could not speak Gaelic to learn it – essentially, he had in mind a form of status planning that would lead to an increase in the prestige of the language, resulting in increased acquisition which, as we shall see, is a further area of language planning activity. His more general goals of 'celebration, advertisement and rapprochement', and in particular his desire to demonstrate that Gaelic and its literature were 'cultivated' and 'refined' (P. Mackay 2013: 117) – a desire which was shared by many later editors of Gaelic material, particularly those of the latter part of the nineteenth century (see, for example, Linkletter 2011) – had as their purpose the enhancement of the reputation of the language and its speakers in the wider Scottish context, and this clearly was an exercise in status planning.

[4] Domains are the contexts in which language is used, and they are defined by three dimensions: the location in which discourse is taking place, the participants in the discourse, and the topic of the discourse. Examples would include the home, the church, the school and the workplace. See Fishman, Cooper, and Ma 1971; Spolsky 2004: 39-56.

In recent years, reference has sometimes been made, in the context of language planning for minority languages, to an additional type of language planning, 'use (or usage) planning' (see, for example, Welsh Language Board, n.d.). In fact, use planning subsumes many aspects of what status planning is concerned with: the encouragement of the practical use of the language in a greater number of domains. However, it is not only concerned with the introduction or reintroduction of the language in so-called 'higher' domains, but also with the protection of the language, and even its reintroduction, in more intimate, informal domains such as the home, the community, and in a variety of local institutions which, though less prestigious and powerful in a broad societal sense, are nonetheless important in terms of actual patterns of daily language use. The contribution which collections such as the Archives make to this aspect of language planning is not as obvious, but there are nonetheless potential indirect links. As noted in the discussion of corpus planning, such collections provide terminology, idioms and styles which may be used to support the introduction or reintroduction of a minority language into a wide variety of domains. As one of many examples, the alleged lack of relevant material for use in early years child-care and pre-school education has been highlighted by researchers (Stephen *et al.* 2010: 31–2). The Gaelic oral tradition has a wealth of such material, much of which is contained in collections such as those of the Archives, which could be deployed by parents and other caregivers, including those working in the pre-school and primary school sectors, through, for example, the development of teaching materials and aides, supported where necessary by training.

'Acquisition planning' is another important area of language planning, added to corpus and status planning by Robert Cooper (Cooper 1989: 33–4). It concerns planning for the increase in the number of users – speakers, writers, listeners or readers – of the language. Obviously, schools and other formal educational institutions are important settings for acquisition planning, but a language is first acquired in the home and local community, and language skills are enhanced by other institutions than educational ones, particularly the media. Acquisition planning, therefore, also involves planning activities outside of the educational system. Acquisition planning is of particular importance to minority languages, as they tend to suffer ongoing losses in numbers of users, often due in part to their exclusion from the education system.

Collections of oral tradition such as those of the School Archives are important in acquisition planning for a variety of reasons. As we have already seen, they are a valuable source of terminology, idioms, placenames and of registers, as well as of dialects, all of which can be extremely useful in the development of language acquisition programmes. As a source of literature, history and cultural information, they also have a huge potential in broader educational programming, something to which we shall return momentarily. Gaelic revitalisation efforts in Nova Scotia provide a good example of how archival material, and in particular digitised sound archives made available through the world wide web, are being deployed in other, non-school based language acquisition initiatives. Modelled on the 'master-apprentice' programmes developed by Leanne Hinton and others (see, for example, Hinton 2001b),'Bun is Bàrr' is an initiative in which a younger Gaelic learner who has reached a reasonable level of fluency works intensively on a one-to-one basis with a native speaker in order to develop high levels of proficiency in spoken Gaelic. Web-based resources, all drawing on sound recordings made by field workers, are used regularly in these sessions, with the tutor explaining and contextualising the material, and drawing on it as a means of enriching language skills and cultural knowledge. Also notable is the 'Stòras a' Bhaile' programme, held annually at the Nova Scotia Highland Village Museum, which uses a variety of sound recordings in intensive instructional programmes designed to further develop the language skills of participants, and also to impart cultural skills associated with traditional Gaelic culture as it is found in Nova Scotia (Watson 2010). The potential for the use of the School Archives in a variety of language acquisition initiatives, both school-based and community- and locally-based, is very considerable.

One final aspect of the contribution which collections such as the School Archives can make to language planning for Gaelic relates to the cultural value of the contents of the recorded material. Joshua Fishman has emphasised the importance to any language maintenance initiative of supporting a cultural identity associated with and based in the language (Fishman 1991: 5–6, 28), and he argues that traditional forms of cultural expression and traditional aspects of the culture associated with the language are crucial in such identity maintenance efforts. Mark Fettes also emphasises the importance of broader cultural considerations in language maintenance efforts, arguing that 'confronting, marginalizing, and dismantling' dominant discourses transmitted through the majority language and culture which tend to contribute to the linguistic and cultural dislocation of minority language communities is an essential step in any language maintenance effort, but is not by itself sufficient. Communities commited to language renewal must also develop and transmit 'a web of stories attuned to local experience':

> The local language has to be used to meet its speakers' need for concepts and stories that make sense of the world *in their terms*. So storytelling is crucial, in the broad sense used here. Traditional myths and historical accounts; stories about people's relationship with the land and with nature; contemporary tales of despair and hope, love and death; poetry, songs, poems, and so on. Every good story is another reason to cherish the language, another branch on the fire to keep it burning (Fettes 1997: online).

John Shaw has made much the same point. His argument is not that material based in the traditional oral culture of the Gaels is the only cultural content that should be deployed in a language maintenance effort – far from it, as he welcomes and stresses the importance of the language and culture expanding 'into new forms, institutions and sectors' – but that the fostering of a distinctive cultural identity that is based in the language is crucial, and that 'the traditional content which has been maintained in Gaelic communities over generations' (the sort of material which exists in abundance in the School Archives) is also an important component in the mix, and also needs to be nurtured and developed. Thus, apart from any 'instrumental' value that the wealth of material in the School Archives may have in Gaelic language maintenance – for example, as a source for corpus planning and as a tool in language acquisition planning – it clearly has an intrinsic value, not only in a broader sense but in terms of Gaelic language maintenance. As a result, the current generation of Gaelic language planners should be grateful for the efforts of the collectors and preservers of the School of Scottish Studies Archives.

SOURCES

AHLANDER, PER.

2011 *A Life of Song: Marjory Kennedy-Fraser*. South Lochs, Isle of Lewis.

BLACK, RONALD (ED.).

2005 *The Gaelic Otherworld*. Edinburgh.

BRIODY, MÍCHEÁL.

2008 *The Irish Folklore Commission 1935–1970: History, ideology, methodology*. Helsinki.

CAMPBELL, JOHN LORNE (ED.).

1939 *Sia Sgialachdan a chruinnich agus a dheasaidh Iain Latharna Caimbeul ann am Barraigh 's an Uidhist a Deas*. Dùn-éideann.

[1961] 1997 *Stories from South Uist, told by Angus MacLellan.* Edinburgh.

1962 *The furrow behind me. The autobiography of a Hebridean crofter, told by Angus MacLellan, translated by John Lorne Campbell.* Edinburgh.

1972 *Saoghal an Treobhaiche, le Aonghus Mac 'ill Fhialain ('Aonghus Beag'); air a recòrdadh's air a sgrìobhadh le Fear Chanaidh.* Inbhirnis.

1973 *Tales from Barra, told by the Coddy (John MacPherson, Northbay, Barra, 1876–1955)*. Edinburgh.

1990 *Songs Remembered in Exile: Traditional Gaelic songs from Nova Scotia recorded in Cape Breton and Antigonish in 1937 with an account of the causes of Highland emigration, 1790–1830*. Aberdeen.

COOPER, ROBERT L.

1989 *Language Planning and Social Change*. Cambridge.

DELARGY, J. H.

1960 'Three Men of Islay'. *Scottish Studies* 4: 126–33.

DORSON, RICHARD.

1968 *The British Folklorists: A History*. London.

FETTES, MARK.

1997 'Stabilizing What? An Ecological Approach to Language Renewal'. Jon Reyhner (ed.), *Teaching Indigenous Languages*. Flagstaff, AZ: Northern Arizona University: http://jan.ucc.nau.edu/~jar/TIL_25.html

FISHMAN, JOSHUA A.

1991 *Reversing Language Shift: Theoretical and Empirical Foundations of Assistance to Threatened Languages*. Clevedon.

FISHMAN, JOSHUA A., ROBERT L. COOPER AND ROXANA MA.

1971 *Bilingualism in the Barrio*. Bloomington, IN.

HENDERSON, REV. GEORGE.

1908–11 'Lamh-Sgrìobhainnean Mhic-Neacail'. *Transactions of the Gaelic Society of Inverness* 27: 340–409.

HINTON, LEANNE.

2001a 'The Use of Linguistic Archives in Language Revitalization'. Leanne Hinton and Ken Hale (eds), *The Green Book of Language Revitalization in Practice*. San Diego: 419–23.

2001b 'The Master-Apprentice Language Learning Program'. Leanne Hinton and Ken Hale (eds), *The Green Book of Language Revitalization in Practice*. San Diego: 217–226.

HOGG, ULRIKE.

2011 'The life and papers of the Rev. Dr. Alexander Irvine'. *Scottish Gaelic Studies* 28: 97–174.

HORNBERGER, NANCY H.

2006 'Frameworks and Models in Language Policy and Planning'. Thomas Ricento (ed.), *An Introduction to Language Policy: Theory and Method.* Blackwell Publishing, Oxford: 24–41.

HUTCHINSON, ROGER.

2010 *Father Allan: The Life and Legacy of a Hebridean Priest*. Edinburgh.

KERR, ROBERT.

n.d. 'The School of Scottish Studies'. https://scholarworks.iu.edu/dspace/bitstream/handle/2022/1044/Archivist_6_3_kerr.pdf? sequence=1

LINKLETTER, MICHAEL.

2011 'Bhiodh e maslach mearachdan a chur an clò: A. Maclean Sinclair the Editor'. *Scottish Gaelic Studies* 28: 211–225.

MACDHOMHNUILL, RAONUILL.

1776 *Comh-chruinneachidh Orannaigh Gaidhealach, le Raonuill MacDhomhnuill, Anns 'n Eilean Eige* [the 'Eigg Collection']. Duneidiunn.

MAC-DHONUILL, ALASTAIR [ALEXANDER MACDONALD].

1751 *Ais-eiridh na sean chánoin Albannaich; no, An nuadh oranaiche Gaidhealach.* Dùn-éideann.

MACGHILLEATHAIN, CAILEAN.

2011 'A' beothachadh na cuimhne aosda', Calum Iain MacGhilleathain (1915–1960): Bho Alba gu Èirinn.' *Béaloideas* 79: 1–21.

MACINNES, JOHN.

1976 'The cultural background to the eighteenth century collections of Gaelic poetry'. *Papers Presented to Kenneth Jackson by some of his Pupils and Colleagues in June 1976*. Edinburgh: 242–52.

MACKAY, MARGARET A.

2013 'The First Sixty Years of the School of Scottish Studies: An Overview'. Bob Chambers (ed.), *The Carrying Stream Flows On: Celebrating the Diamond Jubilee of the School of Scottish Studies*. Kershader, Isle of Lewis: 2–33.

MACKAY, PETER.

2013 'The Gaelic Tradition'. Gerard Carruthers and Liam McIlvanney (eds), *The Cambridge Companion to Scottish Literature*. Cambridge.

MACKINNON, DONALD.

1887-88 'Collection of Ossianic Ballads by Jerome Stone'. *Transactions of the Gaelic Society of Inverness* 14: 314-69.

MCLEOD, WILSON AND MEG BATEMAN (EDS).

2007 *Duanaire na Sracaire / Songbook of the Pillagers: Anthology of Medieval Gaelic Poetry*. Edinburgh.

MANX NATIONAL HERITAGE.

2004 *Skeealyn Vannin – Stories of Mann. The complete collection of Manx Language archive recordings made by the Irish Folklore Commission in 1948.* Douglas.

NATIONAL LIBRARY OF SCOTLAND.

1985 *Lamplighter and Story-Teller: John Francis Campbell of Islay 1821–1885.* Edinburgh.

Ó BAOILL, COLM.

2001 *Maclean Manuscripts in Nova Scotia: a catalogue of the Gaelic verse collections MG15G/2/1 and MG15G/2/2 in the Public Archives of Nova Scotia.* Aberdeen.

PERMAN, RAY.

2010 *The Man Who Gave Away His Island: A Life of John Lorne Campbell of Canna*. Edinburgh.

RANFT, RICHARD, AND LESLEY RICHMOND.

2012 'Review of the School of Scottish Studies Archives, University of Edinburgh'. Internal administrative document, University of Edinburgh.

SHAW, JOHN.

2007 'The Collectors: John Francis Campbell and Alexander Carmichael'. Susan Manning (ed.), *The Edinburgh History of Scottish Literature, Volume Two: Enlightenment, Britain and Empire (1707–1918)*. Edinburgh.

SPOLSKY, BERNARD.

2004 *Language Policy*. Cambridge.

STEPHEN, CHRISTINE, JOANNA MCPAKE, WILSON MCLEOD, IRENE POLLOCK, AND TESSA CARROLL.

2010 *Review of Gaelic Medium Early Education and Childcare*. Edinburgh: Scottish Government Social Research.

STIÙBHART, DOMHNALL UILLEAM (ED.).

2008 *The Life and Legacy of Alexander Carmichael*. Port of Ness, Isle of Lewis.

THOMPSON, FRANK G.

1984–86 'John Francis Campbell'. *Transactions of the Gaelic Society of Inverness* 54: 1–57.

THOMSON, DERICK S.

1954 'The Gaelic Oral Tradition'. *The Proceedings of the Scottish Anthropological and Folklore Society* 5:1, 1–17.

1992 *The MacDiarmid MS Anthology: Poems and Songs mainly anonymous from the collection dated 1770*. D. S. Thomson (ed.). Edinburgh.

1993–94 'The McLagan MSS in Glasgow University Library: A Survey'. *Transactions of the Gaelic Society of Inverness* 58: 406–24

WATSON, SEUMAS.

2010 'Trì Chearcallan Ceangailte: A' Leasachadh Thobraichean airson Ùr-nuadhachadh na Gàidhlig an Albainn Nodha'. Unpublished presentation at the Soillse Residential Research Conference, 1–2 September 2010, Sàbhal Mòr Ostaig, Isle of Skye.

WELSH LANGUAGE BOARD.

n.d. *The Welsh Language: a Vision and a Mission for 2000–2005*. Cardiff.

WISEMAN, ANDREW.

2010 'Fear Beag a' Chridhe Mhòir: The Life and Legacy of Calum Iain Maclean (1915–1960)'. Kenneth E. Nilsen (ed.), *Rannsachadh na Gàidhlig 5: Fifth Scottish Gaelic Research Conference, St. Francis Xavier University, Antigonish, Nova Scotia, July 21–24, 2008*. Sydney, N.S.: 280–298.

'The Disembowelled Horse'
A Place-Name Tale From Gaelic Oral Tradition

IAN A. FRASER

The recording of traditional information by the School of Scottish Studies, at least in the Gaelic-speaking area, was at its height in the 1960s and 1970s. This was the period when funds for field collection were relatively available, while there were still many native bearers of tradition who were willing to impart important amounts of precious material. Nevertheless, it was becoming increasingly obvious that the Gaelic mainland was losing its native speakers rapidly and that collection there should be a priority. Their dispersed populations, from Kintyre to Sutherland, meant that the costs associated with fieldwork were rising, as these areas lacked the concentrated populations found in the Western Isles. A special effort was called for to overcome the difficulties.

My own work, from 1965 onwards, concentrated on the collection of traditional place-name material from the whole Gaelic-speaking area, but it was to some extent targeted at mainland areas which were on the brink of losing traditional onomastic material.[1] The collection of these place-names used Ordnance Survey maps at 6-inch (1:10,560), or 1:10,000 scale, depending on their availability, and the informant was recorded on reel-to-reel tape, with a numbered key identifying individual place-names. This provided a pronunciation record as well as a physical location.[2]

There were, naturally, instances where the tape recorder was absent, and the map unavailable. Such situations generally involved casual conversations with informants, which remained un-noted. These were often family occasions, when stories were told in an informal setting. In pre-television days, there were frequent occasions when 'ceilidhing' produced some significant stories which evaded the formal process of recording, and were seldom repeated in circumstances when recording was possible. In families such as my own, when at work around the land, it was common for conversation to include traditional stories, old sayings, lines of verse, obsolete words and expressions. My late uncle, John Fraser, a native of Gairloch in Ross-shire, was tenant of the large hill-farm of Carnoch, at the head of Loch Sunart, in North Argyll. Although he employed local men when the demands of the farming year required it, he often recruited shepherds from the Gairloch area. His love of *seann rabhdaireachd* – 'old gossip' as he called it – meant that he was very much aware of traditional practices, mostly in connection with livestock and with the wild animals and birds in his immediate environment.

In the winter of 1959–60, I worked on Carnoch as general handyman, driver, wool-packer, and the many other jobs required on the farm. One very cold evening, when we were penning cattle in the byre, Uncle John produced an unusual expression: *'Fuar an nochd a bhith an Allt Leacachain mu thuath!'*('Cold tonight it would be in Allt Leacachain in the north!'). When I asked for an explanation, he told the following story.

A young woman of a prosperous family was travelling on horseback from Strathgarve to Lochbroom in Ross-shire. She was heavy with child, and was accompanied by a young groom, on foot, who led the horse. It was winter, and as they reached the highest point of the route, the *Dìridh Mór*, 'the great ascent', it began to snow heavily. Eventually, the horse began to founder, and to make matters worse, the woman went into labour. The groom, finding no habitable shelter, led the

[1] See, for example, Ian A. Fraser, 'The place-names of a deserted island: Eilean nan Ròn', *Scottish Studies* 22, (1978), 83–90.

[2] Ian A. Fraser, 'Recording place-names from oral tradition,' *Scottish Literary Journal*, Supplement No. 10 (1980), 19–24.

horse onto the bank of a burn. Here, he killed the horse, removed the stomach and its contents, placed the girl inside the still-warm space, and delivered the child. By morning, the storm had cleared, and the groom was able to escort the woman and child to her destination.

This was not the end of the story. The young man left Lochbroom to seek his fortune in Glasgow. Many years later, he fell on hard times, and was very much down on his luck. One cold winter evening, as he trudged along a street, he heard a woman's voice call out from a big house, '*Fuar an nochd a bhi an Allt Leacachain mu thuath!*' The young woman whose life he had saved had recognised him. She welcomed him into her household, and employed him for many years. That, as they say, is how I remember my uncle's version of the story.

The location of the incident with the disembowelled horse lies a few miles east of the junction of the modern A835 and A832 roads. *Allt Leacachain* (O.S. grid ref. NH 232762)[3] crosses the A835 on the west side of *An Dìridh Mór*. The name means 'burn of the place of flagstones'. It is certainly in a stretch of bleak terrain, overlooked by *Meall Leacachain* (618 metres) to the north-east, and *Meall Breac* (532 metres) to the south.

The Tale Archive in the School of Scottish Studies produced two further examples of the 'disembowelled horse' story. Both of these were recorded by John MacInnes.

The first of these concerned the incident related by my uncle, but with several variations. According to John's informant, Alick Maclean of Ullapool, the character involved in this rescue was one Ruairidh Mór, a well-known cattle-thief who resided at Braemore, at the head of Strath Mór in Lochbroom.[4] The recording, dated 1960, contains several stories about Ruairidh Mór, including one where he is riding towards *An Díridh Mór* in winter, when he encounters a woman who is about to give birth. He kills his own horse, empties its stomach, and the woman's baby is delivered in the still-warm cavity. Ruairidh then brings the woman back to his house in Braemore. Many years later, Ruairidh's cattle-thieving exploits result in his arrest by the authorities, and he is taken to Edinburgh for trial. While being escorted through the city (presumably with gyves upon his wrists) on a cold evening, he hears a woman's voice call from a house above, *'Fuar an nochd a bhi an Leathad Leacachain mu thuath!'* 'Cold tonight it would be in Leathad Leacachain in the north!' The woman, now revealed to be the wife of a sea captain, eventually arranges for Ruairidh's release.

The place-name *Leathad Leacachain,* 'the hill-slope of Leacachain', refers to the lower slopes of *Meall Leacachain*, beside the stream already mentioned.

The other incident, which was recorded by John MacInnes from an Argyll informant in 1963, is very different in character.[5] The rescuer here is a soldier whose duty it was to pursue and kill the Glencoe MacDonalds after the infamous massacre of Glencoe in 1692. In bitterly cold weather, he finds a MacDonald woman carrying a small child. To save them both, he kills his horse, and having disembowelled it, shelters them in the horse's stomach. She turns out to be a daughter of MacIain of Glencoe, and so has to flee the district.[6] Many years later, the soldier, now impoverished, enters an inn in the south and, asking for food, is served by a youth who enquires his background. On hearing that the soldier was one of those who persecuted his family, he runs for his weapons and is about to kill the man, when his mother intervenes, having recognised her protector of old. A bargain is then struck. The soldier instructs the lad in the use of the sword, and together they eventually return to Glencoe to claim the mother's inheritance.

While these tales are in their own way formulaic, I feel that the *Allt Leacachain* incident is very likely to have a basis in fact. In any case, the story was obviously current in oral tradition up to the

[3] See Ordnance Survey 1:50,000 map sheet 20 (2002 edition).

[4] Scottish Studies tape SA1960/189A.

[5] Scottish Studies tape SA1963/78B.

[6] The MacIains of Glencoe were a sept of the MacDonalds of Glencoe, and were among the principal victims of the massacre.

middle of the last century. It is coincidental that my uncle John recounted it to me at about the same time that John MacInnes was recording Alick Maclean’s version on tape. In both cases, the rescuer is in turn aided by the rescued woman when he is in straitened circumstances, and when he least expects help.

It must be every fieldworker’s regret that the tales, expressions and snippets of traditional lore were frequently ignored in our early years, particularly by those of us who were exposed to such influences by our elders. How often have we thought, ‘I wish I could remember what old So-and-so told me.’ It is therefore a tribute to such ethnologists as John MacInnes that these ethnological varia were recorded with such care, reflecting, as they do, a rich oral culture which has virtually vanished in our own lifetimes.

Acknowledgements

I am most grateful to Mrs Cathie Scott for searching the Scottish Tale Archive, and to Caroline Milligan for invaluable technical assistance.

'Cacmhor an Comann na Goill'

WILLIAM GILLIES

Introduction

This poem has not been edited before, but is of interest at several levels. I offer it to John MacInnes as one who has had a longstanding interest in the Highland-Lowland cultural interface, and more particularly as one who has written perceptively about the way Gaels perceive their Lowland neighbours, a perspective that can be obscured by the plethora of writings on the way the Lowlanders perceive the Gaels (MacInnes 1989).

The poem in question occurs in the Book of the Dean of Lismore (hereafter BDL), which was compiled in Fortingall, in eastern Perthshire, between 1512 and 1542.[1] It is ascribed to Duncan MacGregor, the Dean's brother and coadjutor in the enterprise which is somehow reflected in BDL. With these credentials it offers a potentially intimate insight into the mind-set of the Dean's literary circle, bearing in mind that Fortingall was at a meeting-point of Highland and Lowland culture in the early sixteenth century (MacGregor 2007: 37–8).

Cultural stereotyping and the stigmatising of racial or linguistic neighbours are pretty much ubiquitous human practices, and the Highland-Lowland divide has its own share of such manifestations. There are some well-known examples of anti-Gaelic sentiments in Late Medieval Scots literature, including the caricature of the Gaelic bard in Richard Holland's *Buke of the Howlat* and the anonymous picture of the Highlander created by God from 'ane horss turd in Argylle'.[2] The traffic is not all one-way, of course. When William Dunbar castigates Walter Kennedy for his Gaelic origins and traits we know that it is part of a *jeu parti*, in which Kennedy will have his turn to satirise Dunbar's Lowland ways; a one-handed flyting would not be much fun for anyone (Meier 2008: xcviii–cxvii and 88–179). Moreover, Dr MacInnes has published in the article just mentioned some rhymes from more recent times which show the contempt of Gaelic-speakers for the 'Lowland carles' (MacInnes 1989: 94–5, 100). It is useful, even so, to find this early sixteenth-century example, if only to counter-balance the Middle Scots anti-Gaelic items so frequently quoted.[3] The terms of the Gaelic poem are pretty explicit, though the same can be said of Gaelic satire in general, and no less truly of the Scots flyting tradition. We should doubtless recall that BDL also contains scorching assaults on members of the Church and of the female gender (Gillies 1978:31–5 and 1983:71–6).

The burden of Duncan's complaint is that the Lowlanders are *cacmhor* ('full of shit'). Was this meant literally, or in the modified way that 'shit'-words are often used nowadays, both in Gaelic ('is iomadh *cousin* caca a th'agam', etc.) and in English? We may recall that Sir Duncan Campbell's poem *Créad dá ndearnadh Domhnall Donn?* ('What is Donald Donn made of?') identifies different sorts of dung or ordure, along with other unsavoury ingredients, in a fanciful analysis of Domhnall Donn's physical make-up (Gillies 1983:76–82). Again, bodily functions and malfunctions are part of the rhetoric of Gaelic satire, one procedure of which is to bestialise its victims (McCaughey 1989: 109–19). However, a more literal interpretation may be suggested by the fact that some other

[1] National Library of Scotland Gaelic MS 72.1.37, p. 28.

[2] For the 'bard owt of Irland' in the *Buke of the Howlat*, see R. Watson 1995: 25; for the poem 'God and Sanct Petir was gangand be the way', see *id.* 143–4.

[3] M. Pía Coira remarks on an absence of anti-Lowland sentiment on the part of Gaels before the seventeenth century (Coira 2008: 149). This is certainly true of the 'official' poetry; but the present poem reminds us that what remains of that poetry is not the whole story.

texts of the time use allegations of insanitary habits as a mark of the backwardness and barbarity of racial neighbours. A well-known account of the native Irish in Elizabethan times, contained in John Derricke's *Image of Ireland* (published in 1581) contains an illustration of an Irish chieftain's feasting hall, complete with poet and harper, and also shows two men exposing their posteriors over by a wall, with the following legends attached to each: (1) *Aspice, spectator, sic me docuere parentes* ('Behold, viewer, this is how my parents taught me'), and (2) *Me quoque maiores omnes, virtute carentes* ('All my forbears too, lacking (any) decency'). Although it has been suggested that they are buffoons, part of the entertainment, the legends may rather suggest simply that they are about to defecate without going outside (Breatnach 1997: 124–6 and Plate III). A slightly later example of this canard, this time from within the Gaelic-speaking world, is found in a well-known poem against the bardic poets, *A lucht chumas bréag san dán* ('All you who make up falsehood in verse'), attributed in the O'Conor Don's Book to 'An Pearsún Riabhach' (Simms 2010: 43). Here we find the following accusation:

> An fear do-ní istigh a [chac]
>   's nach beireann amach a [mhúin],
> adéarthaoi re giolla an tuill,
>   'Biaidh Banbha Chuinn aige súd.'[4]

For the present poem, it seems likeliest that both literal and dyslogistic levels are equally in play: as we shall see, the Lowlanders both shit without shame or discrimination and are 'shitty' in that they are devoid of manners and liberality.

Duncan MacGregor is credited with four other poems amongst those preserved in BDL. They are scattered throughout the MS as we have it. They are as follows. (1) *Marthain uaim go Eóin* (p. 7), a single quatrain of compliment to a friend;[5] (2) *Féicheamhoin sibh, a chlann cuil* (p. 64), a moralising quatrain (Gillies 2008:218); (3) *Aithris fhréimhe ruanaidh Eóin* (p. 208), a substantial praise-poem addressed to the chief of the MacGregors (W. J. Watson 1937: 212–17); and (4) *Mairg bean nach bí ag aon-sagart* (p. 223), a substantial satirical poem on the sexual excesses of the clergy (Quiggin 1937: 80–1). Of these, *Aithris fhréimhe* shows some evidence of literary and historical learning, though it is not metrically or linguistically strict; *Féicheamhoin sibh* is more linguistically polished, but brief; *Mairg bean*, like *Cacmhor an comann*, has some neat touches, but is not meant to be a formally high-level production. As for the present poem, as well as being metrically and linguistically unambitious, it contains a couple of vernacular touches which are probably to be attributed to the poet: see Notes on 2*c* and 2*d*. Overall, the evidence of language and metre suggests that the author intended it as an upper-register Early Modern poem, like the rest of his compositions, but possibly with a couthy dimension.[6]

The imperfect legibility of this part of the MS, together with the novelty of the subject-matter, leaves some uncertainty over certain readings, but I hope enough has been correctly decoded to give a fair sense of what the poet intended. As in other recent editions of BDL poems, I have given first the MS text as we find it in BDL; then a 'Dean's version', indicating what the Dean of Lismore may have understood as he read the poem in BDL, rendered in Gaelic spelling; and finally an edited version, in the fairly correct Early Modern orthography that the linguistic and metrical aims of the poet seem to demand.

---

[4] ('The man who defecates indoors and doesn't take his urine outside, you (poets) would say to the lad with the (arse-)hole, "Conn's Ireland shall be his".'). The poem is edited in O'Rahilly, *Measgra Dánta* I, no. 13, ll. 33–36. The words in square brackets are omitted in O'Rahilly's edition.

[5] For a transcription (not wholly accurate) of the verse see Quiggin 1937: 95. For the identification of Eóin as John Campbell of Lawers see MacGregor 2007: 56 and Coira 2008: 154–6.

[6] Compare *Och is mise an giolla (*or *gille?) mór*, in Gillies 1978: 41–5.

The MS Version

Duncha mak kowle voyl Gi m*ir*zin sai i*n* dr[…

Cakkor in comyn*n* ny^{t} gyle donny^{t} dy*n* clynn dan*n*e ny^{t} rai^{t}
Ne weit fey prap rayn rai ~~d~~ gin chaky^{t} fai^{t} hai na fa vi[..
Cakkit y^{t} geny^{t} sy^{t} goil gy^{t} hunty^{t} ny*n* sloy fane sacht
Er chawni^{t} an*n*e gaggit fa chaid cakkit said ir vith is [..
Ran*n*an*is* er gy^{t} gow zane glory mnai^{t} sin don gy*n* smacht
ma^{t} ry*n*nit forrin ny*n* doyl^{t} ne ry*n*nit bonn a*is* in va[.]t[..
trow na^{t} dalyt i*n* gud said myr zalit said i*n* cac
ona^{t} churrin ^{said} in bree an*n*e rannach ran i*m* be i*n* cak
lan lass lan*is* cak bar be in nymit ny*n* gawle […] C[..

'The Dean's Version'

Donncha(dh) mac Dhu(bhgh)a(i)ll Mhao(i)l[7]

Cac(mh)or an comunn na Goill   daoine don c(h)loinn dána ria(mh)
Ní bhíd faoi p(h)rap rén rádh   gan chacadh fá sháth na fá bhi[adh]
Cacaid ag aonach 's ag ól   go h-ionta(dh) nan sló(gh) fán seach
Air cheann an gcacaid fá chéad   cacaid séad air mhith is [air mhath]
Rannan is air gach guth dhán glór   mná 's an dtón gan smacht
Má roinnid foireann nan dtoll ní roinnid bonn as an bha[c]
Trua(gh) nach dáilid an gcuid séad   mar dháilid séad an cac
Ó nach c<h>uireann séad an brí(gh)   éan rann 'ach rann am bí an cac
lán leas leana(i)s cac barr   bí(dh) an n-a(dh)mad nan Gall [cac].

Cac.

Edited version

Donnchadh mac Dhubhghaill Mhaoil

1	*Cacmhor an comann na Goill,*	The Lowlanders are a shitty crowd,
	daoine don chloinn dána a-ria[mh];	men of the impudent tribe (as) ever;
	ní bhíd faoi phrapadh ré rádh	they're never known to hesitate
	gan chacadh fá sháth nó biadh.	from shitting at meal-time or food.
2	*Cacaid ag aonach 's ag ól,*	They shit at an assembly and when drinking,
	go h-ionntódh na slógh má seach;	till every company in turn is repelled;
	tar cheann a gcacaid fó chéad	for all they shit, a hundred times,
	cacaid séad ar mhith 's ar mhath.	they shit upon peasantry and nobility.
3	*Ránán ar gach guth dhá nglór,*	Every word of their speech is a roar,
	[fir is] mná 's a dtón gan smacht;	men and women with arses out of control,
	má roinnid foireann na dtoll	if the (arse-)hole squad are dealing (?)
	ní roinnid bonn as an bhac.	they don't deal (?) a *bonn* from the *bac*.

[7] For the comment which follows Duncan's name in MS see Notes.

4 *Truagh nach dáilid a gcuid séad*	Sad that they don't distribute their wealth
mar dháilid séad a [gcuid] cac;	in the way they distribute their shit;
ó nach cuireann séad i mbrígh	since they don't think it of importance
aon rann seach rainn i mbí a gcac,	whatever airt their shit is in,
lén leas leanais cac [go] barr:	shit adheres to their haunches to the top:
bídh a n-adhmad na nGall cac!	shit is always in the make-up of the Lowlanders.

NOTES

Ascription

To the right of the author's name another hand has added some additional words, which are not easy to understand. It looks at first sight as though MS *Gi mirzin sai* (or perhaps rather *Gi minzin sai*) is a present-tense verb (*go m...eann sé* or *go mb...eann sé* or similar), which could constitute a comment on Donnchadh by another of the Dean's associates, or even by Donnchadh himself, rather as the second scribal hand has added *An Ridire Maith* 'the Good Knight' after the name of Duncan Campbell above the poem *Mairg ón deachaidh a léim lúidh* (Gillies 1981: 277). However, the lines immediately before the present poem in BDL are the final lines of Donnchadh Mór Ó Dálaigh's poem on the *dreén* ('wren', ScG *dreathan*), and the added words here may constitute a comment on the preceding poem (note that the last legible letters are a new word beginning with *dr...*), either on its content or on the fact that the first part of the wren poem has been separated from the last part by an early dislocation, so that it now appears at the foot of p. 11 of the MS (see Ó Cuív 1977: 13–18).

Verse 1

1a: *cac(mh)or* MS, cf. Mod ScG *lìonar* for *lìonmhar*, etc., or the elimination of the *-f-* of the future after verb-stems ending in consonants.

1b: I am by no means sure that my reconstruction has captured the meaning of this line. For *donny'* = *duine* (rather than *daoine*), cf. *zonna* (= *dhuine*) Quiggin, *Poems*, LXXV 9*a*, and *eundon* (= *éanduine*) id., XXXVI 3c beside *eandvnni* 4a.

Although MS *-ai-* stands sometimes for *ia* in conventional spelling, *a/á* or *ea/éa* would be more normal; compare Gillies, '*"Créad fá seachnainn-sa suirghe?"*', 219, notes 5 and 6, for some not untypical statistics.

1c: MS *prap* stands for *prapadh* with the modern Perthshire Gaelic apocope of *-adh* in nouns and verbal nouns. The longer form is needed to rhyme with *cacadh*. I take the phrase to mean, literally, that the *Goill* 'are not under an eye's blink' before they relieve themselves.

1c: *rén rádh* (Dean's text): The scribe seems to have understood *rádh* as agreeing with 'they' (literally 'they are not to be said'); but this should have been *ré n-a rádh* in Classical Gaelic, which may suggest reading *ré rádh* and linking it with *prapadh* (literally 'an eye's-blink to be said').

1d: *fá sháth ná fá bhi[adh]* MS, but this is hypermetric; one can eliminate either *ná* or (as above) *fá*.

Verse 2

2a: If the conjoining of 'fair' (noun) and 'drinking' (verbal noun) is deemed uncomfortable, we could omit '*'s*'; but *ól* can mean 'drinking bout, carousal' as well as 'drinking'.

2b: For *ionntódh* see *Dictionary of the Irish Language* [hereafter DIL]), s.v. *intód* and compare the much commoner *tintód* (Modern ScG *tionndadh*). I assume it means 'turning away, repulsion' here.

Another possibility might be to read *iongnadh* 'astonishment', but this is usually *eny*[1] in B (e.g. Quiggin XLIV, 1*a* and 18*d*).

2bd: The rhyme between *seach* and *math* is unusually loose. For *math* rather than *maith* see W. J. Watson 1937: xxxii and Glossary, s.v. *math*.

2c: Here, as elsewhere, BDL's *er* (for *air*) represents earlier *t(h)ar* 'despite, against' (cf. ScG *air cho beag* 'however small', etc.). It has to be said that *ceann* is more usually *kenn* or similar in BDL. I have also considered *ar chaomhna*, for which see DIL, s.v. *cáemna* '(protection), entertainment, cheer'. If this were correct, the phrase would mean 'when being entertained, receiving hospitality' (with *air* < *ar*).

2cd: The necessary rhyme between *chéad* and the 3 pl. pronoun which is usually *siad* prompts the question whether the *é* in *chéad* could have been diphthongised to *ia*. But since this breaking is not an expected feature in the dialects of Perthshire, and since a rhyme between the 3rd plural pronoun and a word in *é* is also needed 4ab, it seems preferable to assume that Duncan used a 3 pl. form *séad* here. Note the similar usage in a poem by Fionnlagh am Bard Ruadh: *giodh oirdheirc a* méad *'s a gcosnamh / ní f(h)earr* éad *'ná ar n-each-ne* (W. J. Watson, XVII, ll. 1315–6, *sic leg.*); compare also Ó Murchú 1989: 357, where the form *éad* is reported beside the more widely recurrent *ád*. Because it is used here in both the occurrences where rhyme can be checked, I have generalised *séad* throughout the poem, surmising that its use was a deliberate stylistic matter. (For Duncan's use of the form *iad* elsewhere, compare Quiggin LXIX 8*b*, *eaid* = *iad*.) I have also noted one example of *éad : éag* in a putatively Irish poem (a dialogue between Mac Liag and Mac Coise): see Quiggin XXXVI, 3cd; but this could be a local Scotticism not original to the poem.

2d: The phrase *mith agus math* 'lowly and gentle folk' is found only in Mod. ScG, so far as I am aware; similarly with the adjectival use of *mith* found in *mith-òrain* 'folksongs'. DIL gives *mith* beside *meith* as a gen. sing. of *meth* 'wasting, decay, failure, etc.', and gives examples of its being used attributively, e.g. *bliadain meith* (M 118.6), *athig mith* (M 118.8–14). I suspect that an adjective *mith* was abstracted from such usages and then substantivised as 'peasant, churl'. The jingling possibility of *mith agus ma(i)th* may have helped. So may the existence of *mid-* 'middling, sub-optimal', and perhaps also that of the EIr *(fer) midba(d)* 'small-holder' and its derivative *midbaid* 'dependents' (DIL M 131.18–25).

Verse 3

3a: Dwelly gives *rànan* (and *ràn* etc. is common in ScG); for the formation cf. *langan*, *nuallan*. By an interesting coincidence, the Irish bard in Holland's *Buke of the Howlat* is pictured as making his entry with a *rane rocht* (glossed as 'rough rant' by R. Watson 1995: 25). I am unclear whether DIL's 2 *rann* and *rannán*, which apparently refer to some sort of noise, are to be connected.

3b: The supplied *[fir is]* is a guess. The unexplained and unnecessary *-is* of *rananis* in MS 3a may suggest textual corruption: perhaps an earlier writing of the poem had omitted the beginning of 3b and the missing words were supplied above the line, whence they were partially restored to the text, but in the wrong place.

3cd: *roinnid* can mean either 'distributes (money, gifts, food)' or 'deals out (cards or similar)'; see DIL R 13.56–8 for its use with 'suppressed object'. This variability makes it hard to be sure what the couplet means; perhaps the ambiguity was intended. (1) If *foireann na dtoll* is the subject of the verb, it must mean 'the people with the (arse-)holes', or 'the Ass-holes' in contemporary American parlance; cf. *giolla an tuill* in the verse quoted above from *A lucht chumas bréag san dán*. (2) If the subject is 'they', carrying on from the previous verbs, then *foireann na dtoll* will be the object of the verb and could refer to 'the holed pieces' of a chess-set or similar game. On assumption (1), the relevant meanings of *bonn* and *bac* are open to various interpretations; on assumption (2) they could be technical terms of some form of gaming (see next note).

3d: *bonn as an bhac*: rhyme and alliteration enable us to pinpoint the forms involved in this difficult phrase, whose general meaning is nevertheless clear. If we are dealing with a board game (assumption 2 above), then *bonn* most probably has the primary meaning 'coin', and is to be translated in the present context 'counter' or 'piece', while *bac* could perhaps refer to the 'angle' or 'corner', of a playing-board where unused or forfeited pieces are stored or held by one player. On another tack, I sense that there is some uncertainty about the meaning of 'back' in 'backgammon' (< *ba(c)k* + *gamen*), and wonder if there could be a connection here. (Cf. also Scottish National Dictionary, s.v. *back* (vb.) 2 (5) 'wager'.) If, on the other hand, a board-game is not being specifically referred to (i.e. assumption 1 above), *bonn* may have the meaning '*sou*', i.e. the smallest coin, perhaps in an extended meaning 'the slightest iota'; and *bac* may mean 'stack, pile' or similar. The phrase could then simply mean that the *Goill* are exceptionally mean. I note the expression *bun-bac* 'portion of horizon, part of roof next to wall', plural *bunnacha-bac* (or similar), in Dwelly, but cannot see any way of relating these entries to the present context.

Verse 4

4ab: On *séad : séad* see note on 2cd.

4b: This line is hypometric; either add *gcuid* as above or perhaps replace *mar* with *amhail.*

4c: For *cuir i mbrígh* 'deem important', compare *ní chuirfeadh siad sin i mbrígh* (W. J. Watson, XXVII 8d); *díoth carad ná cuir i mbrígh* (Mac Cionnaith no. 26, 7b).

4d: MS *rann [se]ach rann* looks to contain an example of the ScG idiom seen in *fear seach fear* 'one or the other, either one' etc., corresponding roughly to the Early Gaelic usage of *fer sech aroile* etc. Has the initial *s-* of *seach* been omitted by scribal error, or does it represent *sheach*? I have no other evidence for the lenition of *seach,* though other prepositions certainly undergo it in ScG (e.g. *thar* for *tar*, *throimh* for *troimh*), and a parallel exists in the reduction of *feuch an* 'to see whether' to *ach an.*

A further question arises in regard to the syntax of the proposed sentence. While I have taken MS *ane* as representing *éan* 'any', it is worth asking whether it should rather be taken as *an* = interrogative particle + copula.

4ef: I assume, for reasons of sense and rhetoric, that this verse is the *corránach* variety of the metre, rather than half of another verse. Cf. the BDL poem *Námha dhomh an dán* (Mac Cárthaigh and Uhlich 2012: 317–45), whose final verse contains two extra couplets, making a build-up to a final 'punch-line'.

4e: I take it that *leanais*, where *leanaidh* continues Early Gaelic *glenaid* 'sticks to' as well as *lenaid* 'follows', means literally 'has cloven to' = 'is inseparable from'. For the meaning, cf. *lean an aiste chéadna oirn* (W. J. Watson XXIV, 7d, translated there 'the same nature has adhered to me'), and, in more recent Gaelic, *An uair bha dùil gun leanadh sinn / se 'n dealachadh a b'fheudar* in the Lewis song *On dh'fhàg thu mi 's mulad orm.*

leas: The meaning 'buttock, thigh' (i.e. 3 *les* in DIL; cf. W. J. Watson XXX 8c), seems inherently more likely than 'courtyard' (i.e. 2 *les* in DIL), though the latter certainly suggests a picture of sorts.

The line is a syllable short. Textually and in terms of sense, the simplest emendation is to add *go* as above, though other prepositions are also found with *barr.*

4f: I believe *adhmad* (with ScG /d/ > /t/) is the most natural interpretation of the MS spelling *ymit* as it stands (though **eymyt* would have been more clear-cut); other possibilities worth considering include *imirt* 'practice' (with /rt/ > /t/) and *imeacht* 'proceeding' or perhaps, more concretely, 'stepping' (with /xt/ > /t/ as in ScG *giorrad*, *liuthad*, etc.). Whereas 'make-up, constitution' is the most obvious translation of *adhmad* in an Early Modern context, note also Mac Cionnaith no. 108, 17b, glossed *cineadh* ('race').

Sources

BREATNACH, PÁDRAIG.

1997 *Téamaí Taighde NuaGhaeilge*. Maynooth.

COIRA, M. PÍA.

2008 'The Earl of Argyll and the *Goill:* The "Flodden Poem" revisited'. *Scottish Gaelic Studies* 24:137–68.

DICTIONARY OF THE IRISH LANGUAGE (DIL)

1913–76 Dublin.

GILLIES, WILLIAM.

1978 'The Gaelic poems of Sir Duncan Campbell of Glenorchy (I)'. *Scottish Gaelic Studies* 13/1: 18–45.

1981 'The Gaelic poems of Sir Duncan Campbell of Glenorchy (II)'. *Scottish Gaelic Studies* 13/2: 263–88.

1983 'The Gaelic poems of Sir Duncan Campbell of Glenorchy (III)'. *Scottish Gaelic Studies* 14/1: 59–82.

2008 '*"Créad fá seachnainn-sa suirghe?"*'. *Scottish Gaelic Studies* 24: 215–44.

MAC CÁRTHAIGH, E. AND J. UHLICH (EDS).

2012 *Féilscríbhinn do Chathal Ó Háinle*. Indreabhán.

MAC CIONNAITH, LAMBERT.

1938 *Dioghluim Dána*. Dublin.

MACGREGOR, MARTIN.

2007 'The view from Fortingall: The worlds of the *Book of the Dean of Lismore*'. *Scottish Gaelic Studies* 22:35–86.

MACINNES, JOHN.

1989 'The Gaelic perception of the Lowlands'. William Gillies (ed.), *Gaelic and Scotland / Alba agus a' Ghàidhlig*. Edinburgh: 89–100.

MCCAUGHEY, TERENCE.

1989 'Bards, beasts and men'. Donncha Ó Corráin, Liam Breatnach and Kim McCone (eds), *Saints, Sages and Story-tellers: Celtic Studies in Honour of Professor James Carney*. Maynooth: 102–21.

MEIER, NICOLE (ED.).

2008 *The Poems of Walter Kennedy*. Woodbridge.

NATIONAL LIBRARY OF SCOTLAND.

Gaelic MS 72.1.37.

Ó CUÍV, BRIAN.

1977 'Donnchadh Mór's poem on the wren'. *Éigse* 17/1: 13–18.

Ó MURCHÚ, MÁIRTÍN.

1989 *East Perthshire Gaelic*. Dublin.

O'RAHILLY, THOMAS F.

1927 *Measgra Dánta I.* Dublin and Cork.

QUIGGIN, E. C.

1937 *Poems from the Book of the Dean of Lismore.* Cambridge.

SIMMS, KATHARINE.

2010 'The selection of poems for inclusion in the Book of the O'Conor Don'. P. Ó Macháin (ed.), *The Book of the O'Conor Don: Essays on an Irish Manuscript.* Dublin: 32–60.

WATSON, RODERICK (ED.).

1995 *The Poetry of Scotland.* Edinburgh.

WATSON, WILLIAM J.

1937 *Scottish Verse from the Book of the Dean of Lismore.* Edinburgh.

Grafting Culture: On the Development and Diffusion of the Strathspey in Scottish Music

WILLIAM LAMB

In his article, 'Gaelic Song and the Dance', Dr John MacInnes speculates that an early dance-song tradition may lie behind some forms of Gaelic labour song and instrumental music. He proposes that the modern Gaelic term for dancing, *dannsa* (< Fr *dance*), could have overtaken an earlier word, *luinneag* (2006: 262). Today, *luinneag* tends to mean a 'ditty'. However, in the recent past, *luinneag* was used to denote 'choral songs with vocal refrains' (*ibid*), such as those found in the waulking and dance-song traditions. MacInnes suggests that *dannsa* might have displaced *luinneag* at some point to mean the dance act in a general sense, with *luinneag* continuing in a more limited context (262). This is an attractive argument, and it offers a sound retort to the claim that the Gaels did not dance before their contact with Norman traditions because they lacked a word for 'dancing'. It also raises the question, could aspects of an older Gaelic dance-song tradition be lurking in ostensibly modern musical forms? MacInnes (2006: 254) proposes that tune types such as the strathspey, jig and reel might be older than they seem: 'perhaps *ceòl-beag*[1] borrowed initially from vocal music, whatever influences subsequently modified its genres' (*ibid.*). This is plausible: instrumental dance music traditions the world over are known to have developed from earlier dance-song (Sachs 1937: 181). Here, as in many of his articles, MacInnes signposts uncharted territory in Scottish ethnology and hands over a road map.

I recently strove to contribute to this particular map by investigating the origins of the strathspey (Lamb 2013). The evidence led me to believe that, before it gained a separate designation, the 'strathspey' was simply the style in which Gaels tended to sing and play for dancing. Going back further, I speculated that its ultimate origins might lie in an earlier form of Gaelic movement-song. If this is true, it is clear that the modern tune type has evolved away from its vocal roots. How could this have happened? What socio-cultural milieu could have produced the strathspey, as we know it today? Furthermore, why was it named thus? In the following article, I will provide a preliminary response to these questions and suggest that the strathspey, as a type of instrumental dance music, is an artefact of historical intercultural contact between Gaelic and Anglo society. As I write, however, I am conscious that my basic premise might seem controversial to some readers. Accordingly, it will be useful to discuss some of the reasons for proposing that the strathspey evolved from song before proceeding.

The Origins of the Strathspey: An Overview

The strathspey is typically understood to be an eighteenth-century variety of fiddle music instigated by two well-known musical families native to the Spey valley region, the Browns and the Cummings (see Newte 1791: 163–165; Collinson 1966: 206; Bruford 1994: 74; Doherty 1999; Newton 2009: 253). Campbell (1798: 20) describes it as being 'peculiar to the great tract of country through which the river Spey runs'. However, evidence suggests that it was more widely distributed.[2] Dance master Francis Peacock (1727–1807), who worked with students from across the *Gaidhealtachd*, writes that the strathspey 'is, in many parts of the Highlands preferred to the common Reel' (1805: 89–90). Peacock's statement is supported by evidence from an early collection of Gaelic music (McDonald: 1995), which contains traditional melodies described as

[1] That is, instrumental dance music (lit. 'small music').

[2] See Gibson (1998: 110–115) for additional information on this point, from the perspective of bagpiping.

strathspeys from the North Highlands (*e.g.* Sutherland), Perthshire and the Western Isles. Of course, a distinctive form of dance-music could have diffused across the Highlands and Islands over time. Nevertheless, the defining quality of the strathspey, 'a dotted quaver-semiquaver rhythm and the inversion of this, the "Scotch-snap"' (Collinson 2012: see Figure 1), is widely represented in the Gaelic labour song and dance-song genres. As Emmerson states, '[I]t is not possible to claim that the rhythm is peculiar to the district of Strathspey, for it has an obviously ancient hold on the vocal dance music of the Gael' (1972: 173).[3] Although we have yet to reach a consensus on the age of Gaelic dance-song, labour song is no doubt older than the eighteenth century.[4] Hence, if a 'strathspey' is merely its characteristic rhythm,[5] then there was nothing to diffuse; the rhythm was already present in Gaelic culture. On the other hand, the testimonies of Newte and Campbell give us reason to believe that the Spey river valley spawned something. To better understand its nature, we must first interrogate our terminology, for 'strathspey' means too many things.

Figure 1: Dotted rhythms and 'Scots snaps' in the strathspey: the first two bars of 'Let's to the Ard' (Bremner: 62)

It is useful to distinguish between the strathspey as a 'rhythmic meme' closely associated with Scottish Gaelic movement song, the strathspey as a conventionalised form of instrumental dance music, the 'slow strathspey' – a later, more refined version (Bruford 1994: 74) – and the strathspey as a type of dance.[6] Here, we will concern ourselves with the first two forms only. By making these distinctions, we avoid circularity and introduce an important diachronic dimension. Given the highly developed and archaic Gaelic song tradition – and remembering that instrumental dance music tends to develop from dance-song (Sachs 1937: 181) – we can be certain that Gaelic song imbued a rhythmic substrate (i.e. the meme) upon a later instrumental tradition as opposed to the converse. Unless we are prepared to believe that the Gaelic movement song tradition is a relatively modern development, and that it was conditioned by fiddle music, we must accept that the meme existed in Gaelic culture long before it was recognised in Strathspey. In other words, the strathspey must have evolved from Gaelic song. However, what is its cultural provenance, exactly? Herein lies a paradox, for the Spey valley region was on the boundary between two cultures in 1749,[7] when

---

[3] Keith Norman MacDonald was thinking along similar lines when he said: 'there is very strong evidence to show that much of our strathspey music was taken originally from the Gaelic' (see Lamb 2012: 135). In the prefact to Angus Cumming's collection of strathspeys – the first by a native of the area – it says: 'THAT species of musical composition called a REEL, and particularly the STRATHSPEY REEL, is the CATCH, the brisk and lively SONG, of the natives of Caledonia' (see Alburger 2007: 254) [emphasis in original].

[4] William Matheson contends that most of the waulking songs are from the seventeenth century, although the genre itself 'must have existed from a much earlier period' (in Collinson 1966: 70f). One lullaby featuring the rhythmic meme, '*Griogal Cridhe*', is thought to date from 1570. See Lamb 2013 for other examples.

[5] In musical terms, for instance, there is no structural difference between the strathspey and the common reel.

[6] These distinctions are somewhat artificial, but necessary for our analysis. Properly, in earlier times in Scotland, music and dance were a unified notion; they were a semantic fusion from our modern standpoint (Lamb 2013: 71). See Flett for information on the strathspey as dance.

[7] It first appears as a form of dance in the Menzies ms (1749). Two items occur in volume III of *The Caledonian Pocket Companion* (Oswald 1743–59) named 'A New Strathspey Reel'. This volume might have

the strathspey first entered into the written record. In fact, there is good reason to believe that the strathspey *qua* tune type is a product of that very contact.

Grafting and Diffusing Culture in Eighteenth Century Strathspey

Contact between ethnic groups often precipitates swift and dramatic changes in a region's musical culture (Nettl 2005: 282). When that contact results in certain aspects of one culture's traditions becoming superimposed upon those of another, it is called a culture graft (Sachs 1962: 212). This is a useful way of understanding the strathspey. Sachs (*ibid.*) provides an example of culture graft from the Orang Kubu culture of Sumatra, whose instruments are Malay. Contact with the Malay people led to the type of music associated with these instruments being grafted upon the Kubu's native song traditions. A similar phenomenon appears to have occurred in early modern times in Strathspey. In this case, musical change was catalysed by the appearance of an Italian instrument, the modern violin.

It is difficult to say when the modern violin arrived in Scotland (Collinson 1966: 203), but it was certainly present by the late seventeenth century.[8] As in the Lowlands, we can assume that it was introduced to the Spey valley region via the gentry, who had a keen interest in classical music, European culture, and social dance (Johnson 1972: 101; Emmerson 1972: 78). Violin players are recorded in Elgin, at Thunderton House – from 1710 – and Nairn, at Kilravock Castle (Johnson 1972: 28). Hugh Rose, the laird of Kilravock, was host to Charles Edward Stuart two days before Culloden and purportedly entertained him on the violin (*ibid*). The title 'Castle Grant' turns up in the Bodlein Manuscript (Young 1740), a collection of Scottish country dances with music and figures (Emmerson 1971: 224–5), indicating that this baronial home in the heart of Strathspey was a musical one, at least in an appreciative capacity. Corroborating the information above, Emmerson (1972: 78) depicts the landed families of Strathspey and northern Perthshire[9] as the movers and shakers of Scottish social dancing in the eighteenth century.[10] Thus, we know that the social élite of the Spey valley region had an interest in classical and Scottish dance music, and could well have introduced the violin to the area, either directly or via their contacts.

As in the case of the Orang Kubu, aspects of repertoire and technique followed the new instrument and influenced native Gaelic culture (Dunlay and Greenberg 1996: 4, 11; Newton: 2009: 253[11]).[12] By the time that that the first arrangements of anonymous strathspeys appear in Bremner (1757), we see multiple parts, the full violin compass and bass arrangements. Clearly, these are not transcriptions of pre-literate musical performances. Beyond a collection having a superficial badge

---

appeared in 1745 (see Alburger 1996: 45), but, as no date occurs in the front matter of the collection, we cannot be certain.

[8] The first evidence for its use in Scottish folk music – or any kind of music in Scotland for that matter – is a tutor from 1680, *Lessones for ye violin*, in which Scots melodies are presented as practice pieces or warm-ups for the more difficult classical arrangements (Johnson 1972: 17, 101).

[9] It appears that the 'strathspey' was known in Perthshire as well. As mentioned, Patrick McDonald's collection (1784) features tunes described as strathspeys in the Perthshire section. Additionally, the title of McGlashan's 1786 collection, *A Collection of Reels Consisting Chiefly of Strathspeys, Athole Reels...* indicates that the strathspey might have been known in northern Perthshire as the 'Athole reel' (see Alburger 1996: 67).

[10] Keith Sanger has reached the same conclusion after archival research on these families' histories.

[11] Newton (2009: 253) maintains that this new repertoire and technique provided the impetus for the strathspey. By discriminating between the rhythmic meme and the modern tune type, we can see how the meme existed before European-based influences, but became incorporated within a type of instrumental music, *per se*, only after these influences had become manifested in Highland musical culture.

[12] It might have even become intertwined with pre-existing medieval fiddle traditions (Johnson 1972: 101).

of authenticity, what mattered most to professional musicians, like Bremner, was how well it would be received in the drawing-room (Gelbert, in McAulay 2013: 30), for 'a traditional tune was still regarded as traditional even if it was played on the pianoforte in a well-to-do parlour' (McAulay 2013: 103). Still, Bremner was the first collector to take proper notice of Highland dance music traditions (Collinson 1966: 207; cf Alburger 1996: 53) and we have reason to believe that some of these melodies, at least, were based upon pre-existing dance-songs (see Lamb 2012: 23).[13] Classical sensibilities and the new musical opportunities presented by the violin clearly blended with the native Gaelic dance-song tradition, and Bremner's arrangements might be our first indication of this process.

Regarding how the strathspey *qua* tune type diffused, we must remember that it would have easily taken root in the Highlands because it was so close to what was already present. Apart from new compositions, techniques and ornamentation, little would have been available for diffusion. The tune collectors *cum* professional musicians would have grown aware of the strathspey and, through their publications, helped to legitimise its association with Speyside. We can imagine that Gaelic speakers, for whom the strathspey *qua* rhythmic meme was an autochthonous idiom (see Lamb 2013: 75), would have been amenable, yet inwardly amused, when informed that the strathspey was a new creation. However, because few Highlanders were literate in the eighteenth century, and the *Gàidhealtachd* was almost entirely populated by monoglot Gaelic-speakers (MacKinnon 1991: 63),[14] we have little in the written record to challenge its espoused origin. As ever, history is written by the writers. Certainly, Lowlanders would not have challenged the notion that the strathspey came from Strathspey; they were far too ignorant of the *Gàidhealtachd.* Until the military roads of General Wade became common thoroughfares in the post-Culloden period, the region was a veritable *terra incognita* (Rackwitz 2007: 151). Therefore, a lack of literacy and language barrier, on one hand, and an ignorance of Gaelic culture, on the other, explains why the strathspey *qua* tune type has been conflated with the strathspey *qua* rhythmic meme for so long.

It is difficult to evaluate the level of past intercultural contact between Anglo and Gaelic society in Strathspey. However, a clear indication that contact did occur there in the early to mid-eighteenth century – while it did not, in other parts of the Highlands – comes from a data set well-suited to our needs: the place-names in early Scottish dance music collections. We will examine this presently, and conclude by discussing its implications for the culture graft hypothesis.

Place-names in Scottish Dance Music Titles

From Gore's database, I retrieved every fiddle title place-name that appeared between 1700[15] and 1783 (N=180).[16] A colleague specialising in Scottish toponymy, Dr Jake King, helped to standardise, grid reference and plot the place-names on a digital map. We discarded place-names that we could not locate with confidence.[17]

Table 1: Place-name categories

Dedications to noble personage	54%
Geographical features and settlements	19%
Baronial houses	7%
Other dedications	6%
Transportation (roads and bridges)	4%
Misc	10%

[13] Certainly, this is true of the first collection of 'Old Highland Reels' by a native of Strathspey, Angus Cumming (see Lamb 2013: 73).

[14] MacKinnon indicates that only about 10% of Highlanders were able to speak English in 1800: 300,000 Gaelic-only speakers existed out of a total population of 335,000 (1991: 63).

[15] The year of the first publication in Gore to feature Scottish place-names: Playford's *A Collection of Original Scotch-Tunes (Full of the Highland Humours) for the Violin.*

[16] Three years after Cumming's collection (1780) was published.

[17] Occasionally, with common place-names, it was impossible to determine the intended location.

As Table 1 shows, sixty percent of the place-names are dedicatory. References to noble personages, such as 'Lord Kinnaird' and 'The Dutchess of Argyll', account for 54 percent. Several mentions of baronial houses also occur, such as 'Castle Grant', alluded to previously. Together, references to nobility and their domiciles account for 61 percent of the place-name titles. Therefore, most of the place-names in collections at this time describe the network between the nobility and the professional musicians *cum* music collectors. They indicate those parts of Scotland that were known to Anglo musical society.

Figure 2: Place-names in tune titles 1700–1749

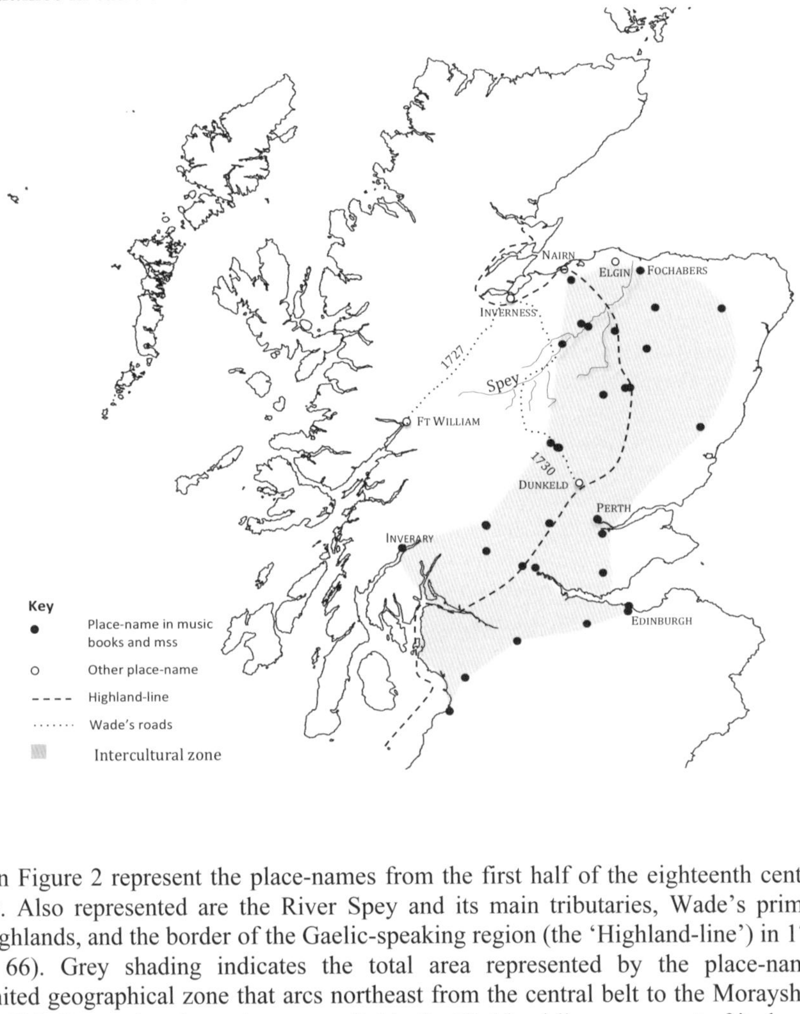

The black dots in Figure 2 represent the place-names from the first half of the eighteenth century (i.e. 1700–1749). Also represented are the River Spey and its main tributaries, Wade's primary roads into the Highlands, and the border of the Gaelic-speaking region (the 'Highland-line') in 1745 (Withers 1984: 66). Grey shading indicates the total area represented by the place-names, comprising a limited geographical zone that arcs northeast from the central belt to the Morayshire-Banffshire coast. This 'intercultural zone' runs parallel to the Highland-line over most of its length, and protrudes roughly fifteen miles into the Gaelic-speaking region at its greatest extent. The strong correlation between the western boundary of the 'musical zone' and the Highland-line indicates that it is, essentially, a linguistic boundary. The language barrier and lack of roads, as mentioned previously, explains why leisured Anglo society and music collectors had yet to acquaint themselves with the region west of Nairn and north of Inverary. Turning to Strathspey, consider the cluster of four points on the Gaelic side of the Highland line and lying within the Spey valley region. This is the densest such cluster on the map and from it, we can gather that Strathspey was a significant intercultural zone even before the conclusion of the Forty-Five. This is unsurprising, given the number of nearby burghs (e.g. Inverness, Nairn, Elgin and Fochabers), which had been at least partly English-speaking since the Middle Ages (Withers 1984: 21): they must have exerted linguistic pressure on the area. In all, it is clear that Speyside was already on the musical map of Scotland in the period preceding the first mention of the strathspey, whereas most of the Highlands were not. Musical intercultural contact is likely to have occurred in Strathspey in the first half of the 1700s, based upon this data.

Figure 3: Place-names in tune titles 1700–1749 with parish boundaries and the Highland-line

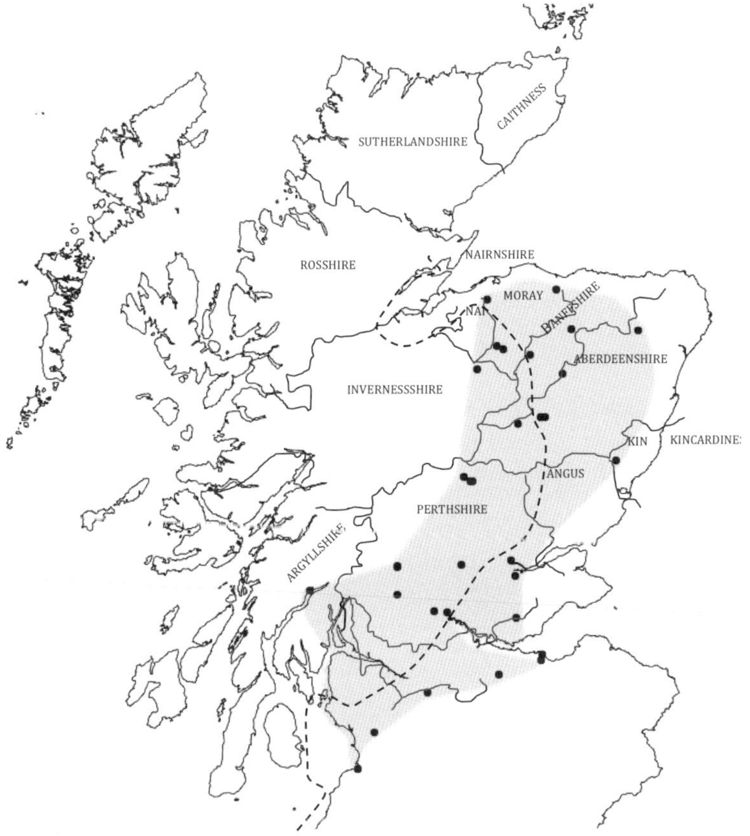

When looking at the same points plotted on a parish map (Figure 3), we find one point each in Inverness-shire and Argyllshire, but none in Ross-shire, Sutherland, Caithness or the Hebrides. It appears that most of the *Gàidhealtachd* in the middle of the eighteenth century was unknown to Anglo musical society. If those areas had been more accessible – and consequently available for intercultural contact – perhaps the strathspey would be better known to us today as the 'Ross-shire Reel', the 'Skye Fling' or the 'Sutherland'.

Figure 4, on the next page, plots the place-names appearing in tune titles between 1750 and 1783. It shows the expansion of the intercultural zone over much of the Highland region and throughout Scotland, in general. Presumably, this expansion was due to the greater mobility afforded by Wade's roads, as well as the growing interest in dance music and music publishing. Although this map includes areas such as Skye ('Isle of Sky', Bremner 1757) and Mull ('Miss Maclean of Duart', Dow 1775), most of Ross-shire, Sutherland and the Hebrides, as far as we can tell, remained obscure to musical collectors and their gentry sponsors.

Figure 4: Place-names in tune titles 1750-1783

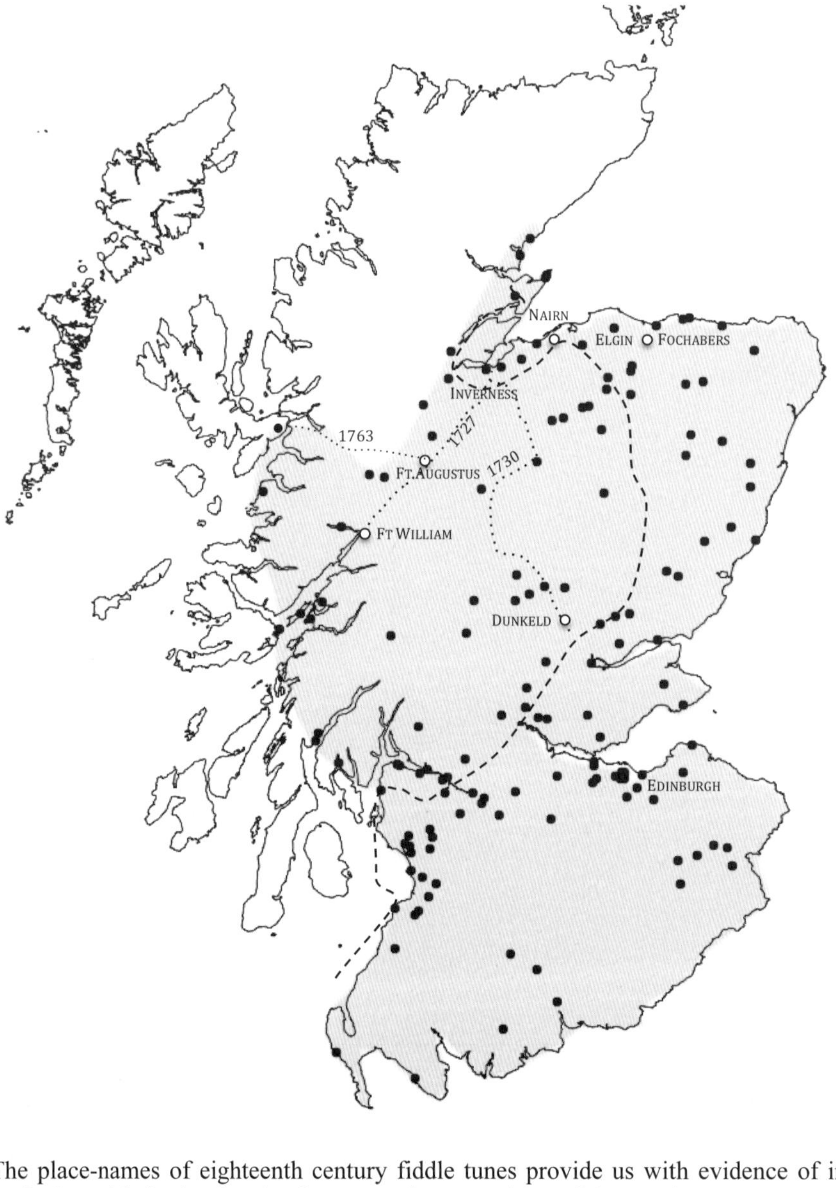

The place-names of eighteenth century fiddle tunes provide us with evidence of intercultural contact in Speyside in the time leading up to the recognition of the strathspey as a type of music or dance. Armed with a knowledge of the roads available and the position of the Highland-line, we get the impression that the Spey valley area was accessible to Anglo musical society. We see the geographical extent of this intercultural contact, as well as its absence over many other parts of the Highlands. While intercultural contact took place in Strathspey in the first half of the eighteenth century, it would not occur with any vigour in the far north of the Highlands for many years. The Lowland *literati* would have accepted the notion that the strathspey rhythm had been devised in Strathspey *prima facie*. Once the strathspey *qua* tune type had been popularised, the new moniker would have swallowed up earlier dance-song airs featuring the rhythmic meme. They would have become 'strathspeys' overnight, as it were. Eventually, many Gaelic speakers would have forgotten their origins in Gaelic song, and outsiders would have never perceived this in the first place. We have all the makings of a folk-etymology.

Conclusions

The strathspey is a paradox. As a type of instrumental music, it shares traits of Gaelic and Anglo culture alike. By conceiving the strathspey as culture graft, rather than monogenetic invention, we can account both for its origins in an earlier tradition of Gaelic movement song and its conventionalisation as a classically influenced variety of instrumental music. Our analysis of the place-names of fiddle tune titles shows that Strathspey was in the right place, and at the right time, as it were, for culture graft to have occurred. Additionally, we see that Wade's roads and the burgeoning interest in Scottish dance music provided the conditions necessary for the musical form to be popularised, and its association with Strathspey reinforced. Key to all of this was the arrival of the European violin.

Although we will never know the exact developmental path taken by the strathspey as it evolved into the tune type that we recognise today, perhaps it resembled the following: Sometime in the latter half of the 17th century, Gaelic-speaking musicians in Strathspey began playing dance-songs[18] on the newly-arrived modern violin. The violin was available to them due to Strathspey's culturally peripheral status and the presence of musically-interested gentry in the area. In instrumentalising their songs, the Gaelic-speaking fiddlers responded to the opportunities afforded by the violin, as well as the classical aesthetic and technique that followed it.[19] Anglo gentry – or dance musicians in their employ – took notice of the resultant tunes and some aspects of Strathspey traditional dance, and the resulting form became popular in haute society as an alternative to the common Reel. The rhythmic meme, to borrow Hans Naumann's term (in Nettl 2005: 331), could be seen as a case of *gehobenes Kulturgut* – a form that travels from a lower to a higher status group. One might say, along the same line, that the modern violin and the classical aesthetic that followed it are a type of *gesunkenes Kulturgut* (*ibid.*) – the adoption of a prestige form by a lower status group. However, the most economical way to regard the strathspey is as culture graft. The term implies the dominance of one culture over another, which I think is accurate in this case. The evolution and diffusion of the strathspey *qua* tune type was a product of the Anglo musical sphere, although its roots are in a form of Gaelic tradition that preceded it and co-existed with it for many years.

Culture graft could have occurred in the Highlands in earlier periods as well. Indeed, Allan MacDonald's thesis could be seen in this light. He maintained that pibroch (*ceòl mòr*), the classical music of the pipes, was once more integrated with song and that modern renditions of pibroch are

[18] Michael Newton (2013) argues that social dances such as the reel, and their associated musical forms, could not have existed amongst the peasantry in the *Gàidhealtachd* prior to the diffusion of a 'package' of French court culture to them via the Gaelic-speaking gentry. Although available space and time preclude a detailed assessment of this viewpoint here, I believe it is reasonable to assume that an earlier dance-song tradition – obscure to us due to the limitations of our record – informed these developments rather than being obliterated by them.

[19] Or, perhaps, it was first 'codified' by classically-trained musicians, who imparted their conceptions of proper aesthetics and technique through their notated representations.

rhythmically bereft due to a break in oral tradition. With Gaelic musical culture so strongly vocal in nature, would it be surprising if all of its instrumental traditions were once based upon, or inextricable from, pre-existing song traditions? Unfortunately, when researching oral cultures, our capacity for diachronic precision is limited. As Sachs says, 'In all probability, the first songs to be instrumentalised are those for which the words have been forgotten' (1937: 181). However, once we have fully traced the intricate web of Gaelic music, we may well find a centre spun of song.

Acknowledgements

My sincere gratitude to Virginia Blankenhorn, Keith Sanger, John Shaw and Gordon Wells for reading a draft of this manuscript and providing useful comments.

Sources

ALBURGER, MARY ANNE.

1996 *Scottish Fiddlers and Their Music*. Edinburgh.

2007 'The fiddle.' John Beech, Owen Hand, Fiona MacDonald, Mark A. Mulhern and Jeremy Weston (eds), *Oral Literature and Performance Culture*. Edinburgh: 238–273.

ANONYMOUS.

1749 The Register of Dances at Castle Menzies. *Atholl Collection*: Sandeman Library, Perth.

BREMNER, ROBERT.

1757 *A Collection of Scots Reels or Country Dances*. Edinburgh.

BRUFORD, ALAN.

1994 'Highland fiddle music.' Derick Thomson (ed.), *The Companion to Gaelic Scotland.* Glasgow: 73–75.

CAMPBELL, ALEXANDER.

1798 *An Introduction to the History of Poetry in Scotland from the Beginning of the Thirteenth Century Down to the Present Time*. Edinburgh.

COLLINSON, FRANCIS M.

1966 *The Traditional and National Music of Scotland.* London.

2012 *Strathspey*. Oxford Music Online <www.oxfordmusiconline.com> [accessed 7 May 2013].

CUMMING, ANGUS.

1780 *A Collection of Strathspey, or Old Highland Reels: By Angus Cumming at Grantown in Strathspey*. Edinburgh.

DOHERTY, LIZ.

1999 'Strathspey.' Fintan Vallely (ed.), *The Companion to Irish Traditional Music*. Cork: 385–386.

DOW, DANIEL.

1775 *37 New Reels and Strathspeys for the Violin, Harpsichord, Pianoforte, or German Flute, composed. by [D.D.].* Edinburgh.

DUNLAY, KATE AND DAVID GREENBERG.

1996 *Traditional Celtic Violin Music of Cape Breton.* Toronto.

EMMERSON, GEORGE SINCLAIR.

1971 *Rantin' Pipe and Tremblin' String: A History of Scottish Dance Music.* London.

1972 *A Social History of Scottish Dance: Ane Celestial Recreatioun.* London.

FLETT, J. F., AND T. M. FLETT.

1964 *Traditional Dancing in Scotland.* London.

GELBART, MATTHEW.

2007 *The Invention of "Folk Music" and "Art Music": Emerging Categories from Ossian to Wagner.* Cambridge.

GIBSON, JOHN G.

1998 *Traditional Gaelic Bagpiping, 1745 to 1945.* Edinburgh.

GORE, CHARLES.

2013 The Scottish Music Index: The 18th and 19th Century Printed Collections. www.scottishmusicindex.org/ [Accessed 7 May 2013].

JOHNSON, DAVID.

1972 *Music and Society in Lowland Scotland in the Eighteenth Century.* 2nd ed. London.

LAMB, WILLIAM.

2012 (ed.) *Keith Norman MacDonald's Puirt-à-Beul: The Vocal Dance Music of the Scottish Gaels.* Skye.

2013 'Reeling in the strathspey: The origins of Scotland's national music.' *Scottish Studies* 36: 66–102.

MACDONALD, ALLAN.

1995 The Relationship between Pibroch and Gaelic Song: Its Implications on the Performance Style of the Pibroch Urlar. Unpublished MLitt Thesis, School of Scottish Studies, University of Edinburgh: Edinburgh.

MACINNES, JOHN.

[1996] 2006 'Gaelic song and the dance.' Michael Newton (ed.), *Dùthchas nan Gàidheal: Selected Essays of John MacInnes.* Edinburgh: 248–264.

MACKINNON, KENNETH.

1991 *Gaelic: A Past and Future Prospect.* Edinburgh.

MCAULAY, KAREN.

2013 *Our Ancient National Airs: Scottish Song Collecting from the Enlightenment to the Romantic Era.* Farnham.

McDONALD, PATRICK.

[1784] 2000 *A Collection of Highland Vocal Airs*. Broadford.

McGLASHAN, ALEXANDER.

1786 *A Collection of Reels Consisting Chiefly of Strathspeys, Athole Reels, &c.* Vol. 3. Edinburgh.

NAUMANN, HANS.

1921 *Primitive Gemeinschaftskultur*. Jena.

NETTL, BRUNO.

[1983] 2005 *The Study of Ethnomusicology: Thirty-one Issues and Concepts*. Urbana.

NEWTE, THOMAS [WILLIAM THOMSON].

1791 *Prospects and Observations; On a Tour in England and Scotland: Natural, Œconomical, and Literary. By Thomas Newte, Esq*. London: G. G. J. and J. Robinson.

NEWTON, MICHAEL.

2009 *Warriors of the Word: The World of the Scottish Highlanders*. Edinburgh.

2013 '"Dannsair air ùrlar-déile thu": Gaelic evidence about dance from the mid-17th to late-18th century Highlands.' *International Review of Scottish Studies* 38: 49–78.

OSWALD, JAMES.

1743–1759 *The Caledonian Pocket Companion*. 12 vols. London.

PEACOCK, FRANCIS.

1805 *Sketches Relative to the History and Theory, but More Especially to the Practice of Dancing: Intended as Hints to the Young Teachers of the Art of Dancing*. Aberdeen.

RACKWITZ, MARTIN.

2007 *Travels to Terra Incognita: The Scottish Highlands and Hebrides in Early Modern Travellers' Accounts, c. 1600 to 1800*. Münster.

SACHS, CURT.

1937 *World History of the Dance*. New York.

1962 *The Wellsprings of Music,* ed. Jaap Kunst. The Hague.

WITHERS, CHARLES.

1984 *Gaelic in Scotland 1698–1981: The Geographical History of a Language*. Edinburgh.

YOUNG, DAVID.

1740 A Collection of the Newest Country Dances Performed in Scotland written at Edinburgh by D. A. Young. Oxford (Bodlein Library).

The Legendary History of Alasdair MacColla As Received from Dugald Macdougall of Crubasdale, Kintyre, in 1825

EMILY LYLE

This legendary history is found among the papers of Andrew Crawfurd held in the Central Library in Paisley. It is written on six folios measuring 30 x 18 cm which are bound into the eighth volume of a set entitled 'Lochwinyoch Matters'.[1] I have not come upon any explanation for the presence of this Kintyre document in the Crawfurd collection (which mainly consists of Renfrewshire and Ayrshire materials) and I have not identified the handwriting. The text exhibits a number of revisions and appears to be the actual record as freely taken down from the teller, Dugald Macdougall. The transcriber was perhaps translating as he went, for it seems not improbable that the history was being delivered orally in the Gaelic language, of which isolated words occur in the record.

Although it is an English-language text, and so is at a remove from the culture to which the hero and his narrative primarily belong, it has a high degree of interest as a heroic biography. John MacInnes, when writing about 'Clan Sagas and Historical Legends' in the context of Gaelic traditional lore, mentions the occurrence of this genre in a wide range of cultures, and remarks, quoting his own family tradition (Newton 2006: 60):

> Probably the nearest to a full heroic biography is to be found in the cycle of stories about Alasdair mac Colla. His birth was attended by the proper manifestations. 'The night that Alasdair mac Colla was born, the swords leapt out of their scabbards, the shields clanged together on the wall, the mares cast their foals and the midwife said: "Truly this will be a great hero." '

It is a pleasure to be able to present in Dr MacInnes's honour a previously unpublished traditional narrative that recounts episodes from Alasdair's life from the time of the portents at his birth up to his last words. It is a well-structured whole, and has a special interest since it seems to be the fullest life-story that has been recorded from tradition, although there are many accounts of Alasdair and many more incidents are known than the ones included in it.

The text of the history is given below. The transcriber used small dashes in place of full stops and sometimes also in place of commas; usage has been normalised here, and capitalisation has been added at the first word of a sentence. There is some paragraphing in the manuscript, but additional paragraph divisions have been introduced for the sake of clarity. Superscript letters have been lowered. Expansion of abbreviations is indicated by underlining, and insertion by carat marks. Presumed missing letters are indicated by <>. Deletions are struck through, and illegible deletions are indicated by ~~xxx~~. Words underlined in the manuscript are shown in italics.

[1] On this manuscript, see Lyle 1975: xvi–xvii. The relevant item was marked 97 by Crawfurd, who numbered its pages from 1 to 12. His page numbering is given here with the text. The page numbers within the volume appear in pencil in my hand and are 123–34. A legend entitled 'The Origin of the Macalister's of Loup', written in the same hand as the history, follows it on the last folio.

NOTES OF THE HISTORY OF ALEXANDER MACCOLLA, TAKEN FROM THE RECITATION OF DUGALD MACDOUGALL TENANT CRUBASDALE 1825

Alexander Son of Col. Macdonald was born in Colonsa about the beginning ^or near^ of the 17th Century and at his birth, the same as at Glendower's the

> 'Frame and the foundation of <th>e earth,
> Shook like a Coward'.[2]

The Cows calved, every Sword sprung out of its scabbard, and pregnant women were delivered of their Children. From the moment of his birth the father entertained a deep jealousy of his Son's future Genius, and to prevent all umbrage some of his friends procured a nurse who fled with young Alexander to Clachaig a small farm in Killean parish Kintyre.[3] He was a straggling indolent boy running about without shoes or Stocking as ragged a little devil as was in the whole parish.

Nothing remarkable happened (at least there is no traditionary account) during his stay with the *Saor beag* or little Wright at Clachaig except ^that^ being frequently employed by the Wright ^in^ defending his Kail-Garden from his neighbour's Cattle and particularly ^from^ a very strong Bull that paid a daily Visit to it, Alister being tired of this Bull and being of a mischievous nature got hold of it and took out the *duirn fhuar* an Action only [p. 2] performed by heroes, that is he wrenched off the four feet from the knees without any instrument.[4] He took the feet home to his Master ^or host^ and told him the Bull should no more trouble him as he had given him his feet in pledg<e> thereof, producing them at the sam<e> time as George Buchanan did the hand of the fellow that went to rob him.[5]

As he grew in years he often breathed ^a wish^ of recovering the lands in Kintyre which the Campbell's wrested from Macdonald of the Isles and in order to perfect himself in war and the use of arms he went along with Campbell of Auchnanbreck who was an Officer under General Munro in the Scottish Army that went to quell the Irish insurgents in 1643.[6] Auchnambreck appears to have

---

[2] Shakespeare, *Henry IV Part 1*, III.1.15–17. Glendower, addressing Hotspur, says: 'and at my birth/ The frame and huge foundation of the earth/ Shaked like a coward.'

[3] Crubasdale, where Macdougall was a tenant, is in Killean parish, and this history is the only known account to mention fostering in Kintyre. According to the history told by John Gillespie of Port Charlotte, Islay, Alasdair was fostered by Donnacha nan Curachd at Aoradh in Islay (Maclagan MS, p. 3174).

[4] Cf. the bull episode in John Gillespie's history (Maclagan MS, p. 3175), and in a recording by Donald Archie MacDonald from Michael MacIntyre of Gerinish, South Uist (SA1968.147.A+B1). Matheson, commenting on the account he publishes of Alasdair subduing and slaughtering an uncontrollable cow (1958: 14–15, 89 n. 7), refers to Laoide 1914: 54, and says that, according to a Rathlin tradition, Alasdair 'twisted the feet off a bull i.e. the feat known as *a' toirt a mach an dòrn bhuar*.'

[5] The story occurs in chapbooks. A nobleman agreed with the king that they would play a trick on George Buchanan, the king's fool, and test his courage. They sent him for a bag of money and arranged for a fellow armed with sword and pistol to rob him on the way back. George managed to get the better of the supposed robber, and he cut off his right hand and carried it to the king. The anecdote ends (Anonymous [1809]: 7):

> No sooner did he come before him, but they asked him, saying, Well George did you meet any body to trouble you by the way? No, said he, but a fellow who was going to take the money from me; but I made him give his hand he would not do the like again. You did, says the fellow's master. Yes I did, says George, let the work bear witness, throwing down the fellow's hand on the table before them all.

[6] A document dated 19 September 1642 proves that Alasdair was under the command of Sir Duncan Campbell of Auchinbreck, colonel of Argyll's regiment in Ireland (Stevenson 1994: 89–91, 159–60).

received notice of Alisters aforesaid wish and probably having heard the phenomena that took place at his birth together with the many predictions of his ^future^ greatness by the diviners and pretenders to second sight and seeing the determined boldness with which he rushe'd into every danger under his own eye, he looked upon Alister as alike dangerous both to his life and interes<t>.

Consequently he ordered a large dinner to be prepared, to which he invited a number of his brother Officers [p. 3] and Friends among whom was Alister. The guests as they arrived ^were to^ deliver~~ed~~ their arms to the host before entering into the banquetting room who accordingly claimed them, but Alister overhearing one of the Servants sing ^some^ verses of a song from which he learned that his life was aimed at,[7] refused to deliver up his Sword, affirming that it was in the second best hand in Ireland already. The host enquired who had the first. It is here said he catching the Sword with his right hand. An altercation immediately took ^place^ between Alister & Auchnambreck which caused Alister to leave him and go to his ~~Old~~ Friend and namesake the Earl of Antrim.

About this time the Marquis of Montrose intending to engage against the Covenanters consulted an old wizard as to his future ~~fate~~ ^success^. The wizard recommended him to procure Alister as one on whom the fates smiled propitiously and with whom he could not fail of success, telling him at the same time of his difference with Auchnambreck and the deadly hatred he bore to ~~all~~ the Campbell's. Montrose immediately wrote to ~~Alister at~~ ^the Earl of^ Antrim to send over Alister with a few men to assist ^him^ against the Covenanters. Alister received 500 men from Antrim and embarked with them for Kintyre.[8]

He intended to land at Saddale ^and spend the night with his brother in Law Mac Kay of Ugidale^,[9] but the Wind not permitting he proceeded to Carridle where he landed during [the] night. Alister went to Carridle house expecting to receive entertainment for the night [p. 4] thinking they were not aware of his coming against the Campbells in an ~~hostyle~~ hostile manner. He availed himself of a peep in at the Window before entering, where he saw young Carridle flourishing his sword and preparing ^his armour^ to join Argyle against Montrose. His Mother Mrs Campbell chid him for his vanity asking him what could he do with a Sword being so young. He answered had I Alister Mac Colla here I would empale it into him to the hilt. Alister did not choose to trust himself ~~to so~~ to such an host, but spent the night along with his men.

Mac Kay of Ugadale ^his Friend^ and a ~~few~~ ^number of^ others perhaps four in number^ from whom the Campbells had taken lands went along with Alister to join Montrose against Argyle. They fell in with Monstrose a short time previous to the battle of Inverlochy. Alister with his men was engaged at Inverlochy where Alister was almost overcome by an officer of Argyle's Army ^called the Laird of Lawers.^[10] Mac Kay his brother in Law seeing him thus ~~nearly beat said "he never before ^that^ thought he would yield to any xxx alive"~~ ^exhausted asked the reason^. Alister answerd ~~xxx~~ that ^it was^ thirst that made him so <we>ak and desired MacKay to encounter the Convenanter till he would find a drink, but ~~when~~ ^as^ Alister returned, Mac Kay fell [p. 5]

---

[7] In other accounts, Alasdair learns of the plan to kill him through intercepting a letter (Matheson 1958: 20–23; Campbell 1898: 212–13; John Gillespie's history, Maclagan MS, pp. 3175–80).

[8] The two landings, which took place on 7 and 8 July 1644, were actually in Morvern and Ardnamurchan (Stevenson 1994: 110, 260), but the landing was said to be in Kintyre in another traditional account (Matheson 1958: 22–23).

[9] Mackay of Ugadale (or Ardnacross) was married to Alasdair's sister, Jean (Stevenson 1994: 55).

[10] The two royalist victories of Inverlochy (2 February 1645) and Auldearn (9 May 1645) sometimes became fused in tradition (Stevenson 1994: 190), and Macdougall's history ascribes events at Auldearn to Inverlochy. Sir Mungo Campbell of Lawers was killed at the battle of Auldearn (Stevenson 1994: 182–84; cf. Matheson 1958: 32–35).

breathless on the field.[11] Alister ~~on~~ seeing his friend thus lifeless rushed with fury on the Officer and in a few moments he laid him at his feet. He looked not on him after he fell but rushed sweepingly on Sacrificing to the Manes of Mac Kay.[12] The field of battle was on the side of a hill and was so keenly contested that Montrose expended all his Amunition. Alister advised him to roll down stones upon the enemy with which the hill was covered. They did so and in a few moments they beat back Argyle's ^men^ into a small ~~river~~ ^glen^ that was behind them, that they lay so thick in the ~~river~~ ^glen^ that they served as a bridge to pass over. Argyle's men fled ~~and~~. ^Next morning^ some of Alister's ^men^ seeing young Carridale riding hard along a hill told him that he ought to pursue him. Alister said if it was not for the Bitch that bore him and the Whore that gave him suck he would ~~put~~ ^join^ the needle to the Coulter, meaning he would kill him, as there were eighteen lairds of the Campbell's fell that day.[13] ^Argyle lost 1500 men at Inverlochy.^

Alister was with Monstrose during the whole of the war till ^after^ the battle of Kilsyth, where the auxiliares of Monstrose were loaded with spoils and returned to their homes. For an account of such ^& the demolishing of Churches & robbery of arms from Glasgow^ see the Scottish histories.

[p. 6] In the predictions ^by his Stepmother, his own Mother['s] midwife^[14] respecting Alister it was prophesyed that when he arrived at the mill of Gocumgo ^near Inverary^ if the machinery went deisiuil ~~xx~~ south with the sun the<n> he would continue to prosper but if the mill went tual or the reverse of the above then his success was at an end.[15] The old highland mills were more apt to turn wrong than those of our days because the water wheel was placed horizontally not perpendicular. On Alisters return to Argyllshire he having probably been in quest of some of the Campbells he ~~happend to to come through Knapdale where he~~ met with the aforesaid Mill which when he first viewed it was going the wrong way which caused a damp to fall on his spirits notwithstanding of the boldness which he ~~always~~ inherited from his forebearers.

---

[11] A variant tradition says that MacKay lost his life after he gave his sword to Alasdair when Alasdair's was broken (Stevenson 1994: 189–90).

[12] According to Campbell 1885: 226, the MacKay who was killed at Auldearn was Alasdair's nephew, Iver Mor MacKay, and Alasdair 'was so much distressed at his fate that it made him pursue the fugitives at Auldearn with an impetuosity equal to the pitch of madness'.

[13] A letter by an Irish officer under MacColla's command written shortly after the Battle of Inverlochy reports: 'There *Aghenbracke* was killed, with 16 or 17 of the chief Lords of *Campbell*; … four others of the name of *Campbell* taken prisoners [including] the young Laird *Carrindel*, …' (Carte 1759: 1.76; cf. Stevenson 1994: 158–60). Archibald Campbell of Carradale or Glencarradale was among those killed at Inverlochy, and his eldest son, Archibald, who was taken prisoner, can be equated with the young man who is said in the Macdougall history to have been allowed to escape with his life (Stevenson 1994: 161, 196). Alasdair is quoting a proverbial saying given in Nicolson (2011: 5) as: 'A' cur na snàthaid air a' choltar. – Putting the needle on the coulter.'

[14] 'Stepmother' appears to be used in the sense of 'foster-mother'. The passage indicates that the midwife who told Alasdair's fortune was the same person as the nurse who fled with him to Kintyre and raised him there.

[15] The place of omen, Gocumgo or Gocamgo, is strongly attached to Alasdair's legend (Matheson 1958: 12–15, 52–55, 66–69; Campbell 1885: 221–2; Campbell 1898: 232–34; Anonymous 1874: 369–71; Stevenson 1994: 219–220). It is by Ederline at the south end of Loch Awe (NM86980204) and occurs on Roy's map (1747–55) as *Cochkumgoe*. Only Macdougall's history and an account taken down from John MacDonald of Brae Lochaber (Calum Maclean Project, 20 January 1951) indicate that the omen was given by the mill-wheel, with turning to the left or being idle portending bad fortune.

Yet Alister ~~left Knapdale and~~ proceeded to try his fortunes against Campbell of Skipness to the Castle of which he laid siege for the space of six weeks[16] but an old woman having told him notwithstanding of his cutting off the water from the Castle that they had sufficie[n]t quantity of all things necessary for many months Alister having no canon to batter he was forced to forbear [and] proceed down to Kintyre but he did not go far when he got intelligence that an army under the Command of General Lesly was coming to Kintyre by the west side thereof [p. 7] thereof.

Alister ~~crossed~~ being on the east side crossed the moor to engage Leslie. ~~and proceeded up the Country to meet him. Leslie had placed his men in Ambuscade in the Woods of Largie~~. They encamped for the night in Arnad[17] moor where one ~~of them~~ Clark went to see his family that was ~~only~~ a short distance from the Army. On his return he saw an apparition ~~following him with a [sword] and making as if he attack~~ before [him] ^and pursued him with his^ sword ^to^ run him through.[18] At last ~~the Apparition~~ ^he^ made ^a^ desperate effort, but the stroke made no impression on ~~Clark~~ [the] apparition, ~~and~~ which gave a hideous shreik and Vanished. Clark as he drew nigh the army heard a mighty noise as if every one's sword was turned against his fellow but when he came to them he found them all locked fast in the Arms of Morpheus.

The next morning Alister proceeded with his men to meet Leslie. When they came to Killean Alister went in to take a dram[19] but his men pressed forward. ^Two of Alister's men were on the advance and Leslie came upon them going round a hill. They could not fly, and were necissetatd to tell how far distant Mac Colla was, and it [was] upon their information that Leslie placed the Ambuscade.^ Leslie had placed his men in Ambuscade in the Woods of Largie, and the moment Alisters men were opposite them they fired the large and small guns upon them at once.[20] They were not able to bear the shock, but immediately wheeled and fled to Largie house. ^They thought to have been secure ~~there~~ with the walls of a great garden there because Macdonald of Largy was near.^ Leslie followed them closely and directed his ~~guns~~ ^cannons^ against ^the^ walls ~~of the ^that^ surrounding the Castle as they~~ were in the ~~Court~~. They were soon driven out of the place and fled down the Country towards [p. 8] Dunaverty. Alister ~~thus~~ seeing ^thus^ his men fly and knowing it to arise partly from his own neglect was cut to the heart and an old fellow a Macalister ^of Loup^ reproached him severely for his misconduct. Alister proposed to MacAlister that they ^should^ collect their ^men^ and try them once more but Macalister ^replied^ they would not assist him any more seeing he had acted so unworthily, and ^said he^ repented of doing so much for him already. Alister replied ~~that~~ perhaps I may escape, but your Old neck will be in a few days stretchd upon Cnoc-na-muc, the common pasture of Campbellton ^which was accordingly fulfilled

---

[16] Skipness Castle was besieged by the royalist forces in 1646, and was relieved by the Campbells, probably in May (Stevenson 1994: 221–22).

[17] Although the word has been read as Arnad, the letters between 'A' and 'd' are uncertain. The name has not been identified but the context would place the moor with this name near or at Rhunahaorine (NR707484), of which the final element is *Aoireann*, 'ferry, headland or landing-place'. If Arnad were emended to Aorin or something similar, it could denote the moor by the headland.

[18] The transcriber wrongly thought at first that the apparition, not Clark, had the sword.

[19] Cf. Matheson 1958: 78–81; Campbell 1898: 237.

[20] Cf. Matheson 1958: 78–81. Leslie's troops killed sixty to eighty royalists in this Battle of Rhunahaorine fought on 24 May 1647 (Stevenson 1994: 232).

~~afterwards~~^.[21] Alister about 14 miles from Campbelton at Beal~~l~~acha gaichan took a small boat and went off to Ireland[22] since he could not prevail upon the Army to give ^battle^ to Leslie.

~~The Kintyre~~ Alisters people fled before Leslie under the command of Macdonald of Penny-land & Sanda and arrived at Dunavarty a large steep rock ^about 10 miles from Campbelton^ in the South end of Kintyre on three sides of ~~it~~ ^which^ is a large plain and the sea dashing on the back of it. Leslie surrounded the Dun but could make nothing of it. An old woman discovered to Leslie the leaden pipe that conducted the water to the beseiged, which Leslie cut and deprived them of Water.[23] Argyle and Lesly proposed conditions of peace to the besieged that they should deliver their arms and their lives would be spared ^and liberty^. The besieged for sometime disagreed some of whom were for giving battle. The Commanding officer who was a big bellied and heavy person was sure to fall himself in the engagement if they began. He and some others were willing to surrender. [p. 9] The latter at last prevailed upon the rest they being wearied with fatigue and in want of necessarys of life and so they deliver<d> their arms.

Argyle at the same time promised that their lives would be spared shortly after which a few vessels appeared to be making for the Dun whom the besieged at last recognised to be Alisters father from Islay with a supply of men ^he^ not knowing but Alister was on the Dun. The Piper of the besieged took up his bagpipe and played the well known march of Colla nan run, Seachain an dun, Glacadh and Dun, 'S tha mis an laimh etc. Loving Col, shun the Dun the Dun is taken & I am in hand etc. which Coll immediately understood and sailed off back to Islay. The besiegers did not understand the tune but by ~~the~~ Colls putting about and sailing away, and they orderd the fingers to be cut off the Piper.[24]

Some of the besieged having concealed some arms an Irishman having a gun and seeing Campbell of Skipness walking on the shore he shot him[25] which so incensed Argyle and Lesly that they determined from that time to massacre the whole of them which was accordingly done shortly afterward. ^About 100 Macdougall's that had never shaved were among them.^[26] Argyle having

[21] Hector MacAlister of Loup, Alasdair's father-in-law, was hanged there shortly after the massacre at Dunaverty (Stevenson 1994: 220; Campbell 1885: 225–6).

[22] The place where Alasdair found the boat to take him to Ireland is named Bealach a' Ghaochain in Matheson (1958: 82–83). A reference by Charles M. Robertson in the Robertson Collection in the National Library of Scotland (MS370, p. 37) identifies it as: '*Bealach a' Ghaothachainn* thro' which road ascends from shoreside at Stac a Chr[ochaire]'. This point (NR68074073) is on the east coast of Kintyre half a kilometre north of Muasdale.

[23] A preliminary attack on the castle left the source of the drinking water in the hands of the besiegers. Leslie was besieging Dunaverty by 31 May 1647 and the massacre occurred in early June (Stevenson 1994: 236).

[24] In a study of the story of the piper's warning, Ronald Black argued that references to Dunaverty arose through confusion with Dunnyveg and tentatively concluded that this tune was played at Dunnyveg in 1615 as a warning to Coll that Sir John Campbell of Calder still held the castle (1976: 232, 234). In Matheson (1958: 18–19), the story is set at Dunstaffnage and, in this case as in the Macdougall history, the song is identified by the opening words: '*A Cholla mo ruin, seachain an Dùn, tha mise an làimh*, etc.' ('Dear Coll, avoid the castle, I am a prisoner etc.').

[25] Although Major Matthew MacDonald, captain of Skipness, was killed in the preliminary attack on Dunaverty, there was a tradition that he was treacherously shot when returning from a negotiation with the garrison (Campbell 1898: 239; Stevenson 1994: 236), which connects indirectly with this shooting episode set after the surrender.

[26] Stevenson notes (1994: 237) that 'the only list to survive naming some of the dead includes forty-nine MacDougalls among ninety names, the others named evidently being their tenants and followers'. The motif of the killing of lads so young that they had never shaved is attached elsewhere to the flight after the Battle of Rhunahaorine (Matheson 1958: 80–81).

previous to the massacre departed ~~to get to~~ for Inveraray that he might not be present because he had given his promise that their lives would be spared. At the time of the massacre Lesly's [p. 10] men came so close to the Besieged with their cannon and other arms that it is reported that one of ~~of~~ the Besieged after boith his legs were carried off killed eighteen of Leslys men by a sword he had concealed. Their bones are still to be seen and from their appearance the men must have been above the ordinary size. Alisters father was pursued and apprehended at Islay brought prisoner to Dunstaffnage and beheaded.

Alister himself skulked for a long time in Ireland on account of a Large reward being offered to any person who might apprehend him. At last being weary of life he met with two weavers[27] who began to interrogate him. He immediately told who he was and willingly became their prisoner. They having a poney with them bound Alister and put him upon the poney but they did not proceed far when they were overtaken by a gentleman who examined the weavers respecting the person they had bound on the pony. He judging him to be alister from his appearance and finding him to be Alister he said he was his prisoner. The weavers disputed with him for some time as to whom alister belonged as prisoner. At length the dispute being referred to Alister himself he said that the time allotted him by his maker was spent which had it been otherwise he would not be made prisoner by their superior.[28] The [p. 11] Gentleman immediately run him through<h> and thus obscurely ended the life of one at whose birth nature trembled, concerning whom many things were predicted, and who performed ^single^ feats of bravery against the Campbell's ^scarcely ever equalled but^ of which tradition itself has ceased to speak.

ACKNOWLEDGEMENTS

I am grateful to Paisley Central Library for permission to print this document, and would like to thank David Weir and Pamela Logue for their help. It has been a pleasure to be able to consult with Jacob King about the place names in this traditional history, and I am most grateful to him for supplying the place-name information that appears in notes 15, 17 and 22. I would like to offer my warm thanks also to Morag MacLeod, Caroline Milligan, John Shaw and Andrew Wiseman for their assistance.

SOURCES

Manuscripts

CRAWFURD, ANDREW.

c. 1840 *Lochwinyoch Matters*, Volume 8. Paisley Central Library 941.41 REN-9 ARC 677 (formerly PC 2846).

[27] The mention of weavers here ties in with the tradition alluded to by Matheson (1958: 23) that Alasdair was killed by the son of a weaver whom he had killed when leaving Ireland as a blood-offering to ensure the success of his enterprise (Campbell 1898: 215–17; Matheson 1958: 22–23).

[28] Cf. the Lewis version of Alasdair's last words from Donald Morrison (1787–1834) in Macdonald 1975: 101. Alasdair was probably killed in cold blood by Major Nicholas Purdon after the Battle of Knocknanuss which was fought on 12 November 1647 (Stevenson 1994: 252–53).

GILLESPIE, JOHN.

Eachdraidh Alasdair Mac Colla (The history of Alexander, the son of Coll [Ciotach]). Maclagan MSS, pp. 3174–83. School of Scottish Studies Archives, University of Edinburgh.

ROBERTSON, CHARLES M.

[Notebook on Argyll Place-Names.] National Library of Scotland MS 370.

Sound Recordings

SCHOOL OF SCOTTISH STUDIES ARCHIVES.

SA1968.147. University of Edinburgh.

Electronic Sources

CALUM MACLEAN ONLINE CATALOGUE.

University of Edinburgh: http://www.celtscot.ed.ac.uk/calum-maclean/.

ROY'S MILITARY SURVEY OF SCOTLAND.

1747–1755 National Library of Scotland: http://maps.nls.uk/roy/.

Printed Sources

ANONYMOUS.

[1809] *The Witty and Entertaining Exploits of George Buchanan who was commonly called the King's fool*. Edinburgh.

ANONYMOUS (AN TEACHDAIRE GAIDHEALACH).

1874 Alasdair Mac Cholla. *An Gaidheal* 3: 369–72.

BLACK, RONALD.

1976 Colla Ciotach. *Transactions of the Gaelic Society of Inverness* 48: 201–43.

CAMPBELL, ARCHIBALD.

1885 *Records of Argyll: Legends, Traditions, and Recollections of Argyllshire Highlanders*. Edinburgh and London.

CAMPBELL, JOHN DOUGLAS SUTHERLAND.

1898 *Adventures in Legend: Being the last Heroic Legends of the Western Highlands*. Westminster.

CARTE, THOMAS, (ED.).

1759 A Collection of Original Letters and Papers, concerning the affairs of England, from the year 1641 to 1660, found among the Duke of Ormonde's papers. 2 vols. Dublin.

LAOIDE, SEOSAMH, WITH EOIN MHAC NÉILL AND NIALL MAC MHUIREADHAIGH.

1914 *Alasdair Mac Colla*. Dublin.

LYLE, EMILY, (ED.).

1975 *Andrew Crawfurd's Collection of Ballads and Songs*. Volume 1. Edinburgh

MACDONALD, NORMAN, (ED.).

1975 *The Morrison Manuscript: Traditions of the Western Isles by Donald Morrison, Cooper, Stornoway*. Stornoway.

MATHESON, ANGUS, (ED.).

1958 Traditions of Alasdair Mac Colla [drawn from John Francis Campbell's collection of historical tales: National Library of Scotland MSS 50.2.18, 19, 20]. *The Transactions of the Gaelic Society of Glasgow* 5: 9–93.

NEWTON, MICHAEL, (ED.).

2006 *Dùthchas nan Gàidheal: Selected Essays of John MacInnes*. Edinburgh.

NICOLSON, ALEXANDER, (ED.).

2011 *A Collection of Gaelic Proverbs and Familiar Phrases*. 3rd Edition (reprint). Edinburgh.

STEVENSON, DAVID.

1994 *Highland Warrior: Alasdair MacColla and the Civil Wars*. Edinburgh. (First published 1980.)

Coire agus Coin-Shìdh am Beàrnaraigh

DÒMHNALL MAC AMHLAIDH

ABSTRACT: A re-telling and short discussion of the popular story 'The Tale of the Cauldron' as told by the author's grand-uncle in Bernera, Lewis – a story in which the protagonist is pursued by fairy dogs. This is followed by a place-name story, which the author heard from Iain Mac Coinnich (Iain Dhòmhnaill a' Phìobair), also of Bernera, concerning *Creag 'Ille Chaluim Ghlais*, a fairy dwelling-place which was – according to the storyteller – the last place in which fairy dogs were ever seen.

I

Fhuair mi an sgeul-sa bho bhràthair mo sheanmhar, Dànaidh Ruadh – Dànaidh Choinnich Iain mhic Dhòmhnaill Mhic Choinnich (1876–1954) – a bha a' fuireach air ceann-a-deas Chirceaboist, air lota 15, far an robh e air a thighinn à Bòstadh còmhla ris an teaghlach an 1878 nuair a chaidh baile Chirceabost a chur air ais fo shluagh an dèidh a bhith timcheall air trì fichead bliadhna bàn. Mar a chì sinn, 's ann am Bòstadh a tha an sgeul air a suidheachadh. Bha an t-àite glè bheò an cuimhne an fheadhainn a thàinig às agus bhiodh iad tric a' tighinn air.

Fhuair mi an sgeul an 1946 no1947. Bha mi air a bhith leughadh stuth mu dheidhinn shìdhean is shìdhichean, ach bha e uamhasach doirbh càil sam bith fhaighinn anns a' chomharsnachd. Bha mi staigh a' cèilidh an taigh Dhànaidh aon fheasgar agus dh'fhaighnich mi dheth an robh fhios aigesan air gin de sheanchas dhen t-seòrsa, agus an toiseach thuirt e nach robh idir. Ach an ceann greis thuirt e, 'An cuala tu a-riamh *Sgeul a' Choire*?' Thuirt mi nach cuala a-riamh agus thòisich e ag innse na sgeòil mar a leanas:

> *'S e Taigh na Lic ann am Bòstadh taigh as seana a tha an Leòdhas air fad. Muinntir an taighe sean – an fheadhainn a bha a' fuireach ann anns an t-sean-aimsir – cha robh mòran dhan t-saoghal aca – ach dìreach na bheireadh iad far talamh is creig. Cha robh mòran air an seilbh – ach bha aon rud aca, bha coire aca. Agus 'ach-uile feasgar, an ciaradh an fheasgair, thigeadh neach as a' bhrugh air tòir a' choire. Mus tugaist seachad an coire dh'fheumadh an duine a bha an urra ris aig an am cantainn,*
>
> *Dleasaidh coire cnàimh,*
> *'s a chur slàn gu theach.*
>
> *Agus nan deidheadh sin a chantainn bhiodh an coire air ais an tac an teine anns a' mhadainn agus cnàimh math feòladh ann.*
>
> *Am feasgar a bha an seo bha muinntir an taighe amuigh a' cosnadh bidh – ag iasgach creige 's mar sin – 's bha iad anmoch gun thighinn dhachaidh. Cha robh duine air fhàgail astaigh ach aon nighean a bha an sàs ag ullachadh air an coinneamh. Thàinig a' bhan-sìdh oirre gun fhios dhith, 's ghabh i a leithid de mhìothapadh roimhpe 's nach tàinig cuimhne sam bith air facail a' choire a ghràdha: 'Dleasaidh coire cnàimh, 's a chur slàn gu theach.' Is rug a' bhan-sìdh air a' choire is leum i air falbh leis às a sealladh.*
>
> *Nuair a thill muinntir an taighe dhachaigh, dh'aidich i mar a thachair – ged nach robh sin farast dhith. Cha robh iad idir air an dòigh! An dèidh mòran còmhraidh is àraich, ghabh iad comhairle agus 's e a' bhinn a thug iad a-mach 'an tè a chaill an coire gur h-ì a dh'fheumadh a dhol air a thòir.' Cha robh ise idir saorsainneil mun sean, leis na bha oirre dh'eagal roimh luchd an t-sìdh. Ach bha fhios aice gum*

feumadh i e dhèanamh, is nach [robh] dol às aice. Agus bho dheireadh, dh'ullaich i i-fhèin agus rinn i air a' bhrugh. Nuair a ràinig i an doras stad i agus sheall i asteach. Bha an coire an sin an tac an teine ach cha robh duine ri fhacinn a-staigh ach bodach liath is brat mu uachdair na shuidhe ri taobh an teine agus cuideigin nach dèanadh i a-mach an dorchadas uachdair a bhrugh. Chaidh i a-steach air a corra-bid cho fiata 's a b' urrainn dhith agus rug i air a' choire gus a thoirt leatha agus rinn i air an doras. Nuair a bha i ga thogail gus a chur air a gualainn rinn e gliong ris an ursainn, agus dhùisg am bodach. Thilg e dheth am brat is dh'èibh e àrd a chinn,

> *A' bhean bhalbh ud 's a' bhean bhalbh,*
> *a thàinig à Tìr nam Marbh,*
> *thug i 'n coire leatha 'na crubh;*
> *fosgail an Dubh is leig an Dearg!*

Agus leig am fear a bha an uachdair a' bhrugh cù mòr dubh agus cù mòr dearg a bha air thaod aige an sean ma sgaoil a-mach as a dèidh.

Dh'fhabh i na ruith cho luath 's a dhèanadh a casan dhith nuair a chuala i na coin as a dèidh. Rinn i air an allta is chaidh i a null air a' smaoineachadh nach fhaodadh iad a leantainn. Ach chaidh iad timcheall agus fhuair iad a null air an staran agus cha b'fhada gus an robh iad air a sàilibh a rithist. A' dìreadh suas Cnoc a' Choilich thug iad iuchair an dà bhon-duibh aisde. Ach chum i oirre suas an leathad cho luath 's a ghabhadh dhith, is na coin ga dian ruith. Dìreach nuair a bha i a' faireachdainn teas an analach air cùl a calpannan, dh'èirich ciad ghathan na grèine os cionn a' chnuic an ear. Mhothaich i an sean nach robh i cluinntinn fuaim nan con agus nuair a thug i sùil air a gualainn chunnaic i iad nan deann mar fhaileasan a'dèanamh air a' bhrugh!

Rinn i an taigh dheth leis a' choire, is chàirich i e air ais air an teinntean Ach bha na bha am broinn a' choire air dòrtadh buileach as air an t-slighe dhachaidh. Is cha tàinig duine as a' bhrugh air a thòir a riamh bhon latha ud.

Bha lorg aig mòran am Beàrnaraigh air an sgeul aig an am a thog mise i. Ach is e glè bheag aig an robh fios iomlan oirre: mar bu trice b'e an leth-rann *'Dleasaidh coire cnàimh /'s a chur slàn gu theach'* na bha air chuimhne aca, ged a thigeadh corra-rud thuca nuair a chuireadh tu 'nan cuimhne e, mar an loidhne *'Fosgail an Dubh is leig an Dearg'*. Cuideachd, chaidh riochd Beurla dhen sgeul à Beàrnaraigh a chur an clò toiseach an 20mh linn: 'Fairies borrow Pot' le 'Anon from Bernera, Lewis'.[1]

A rèir coltais bha eòlas air 'Sgeul a' Choire' an diofar cheàrnaidhean dhen Ghàidhealtachd – gach ceàrnaidh a' cur a blas fhèin oirre gu ìre le ainmnean ionadail is le tionntaidhean sònraichte. Tha eiseamplair againn an sgrìobhadh co-dhiù cho tràth ri 1859 a thog Eachann Mac GillEathain bho Alasdair Dòmhnallach am Barraigh.[2] 'S ann air eilean Shanntraigh, a deas air Barraigh, a tha an sgeul sa air a suidheachadh, agus tha i anbarrach coltach 'na riochd ri sgeul a thog Dòmhnall Eardsaidh Dòmhnallach bho Chalum Johnston a Barraigh an 1966, faisg air ceud bliadhna as deidh sin.[3] Anns an riochd sin dhen sgeul, 's e fear an taighe a chaidh fhàgail an urra ris a' choire agus a ghabh a leithid a dh'fheagal ron bhean-shìdh 's gu deach na facail mu dhlighe a' choire tur às inntinn.

[1] *Celtic Review* V (1908-9): 155-6.

[2] *West Highland Tales* II: 52-54.

[3] Tasglann Sgoil Eòlais na h-Alba, SA 1966/16.A1.

Chaidh leabhar fon ainm *The Tale of the Cauldron* a chur an clò an 1929 le Calum MacLeòid an Dùn Dè leis an sgeul ann an Gàidhlig agus am Beurla. Bha an teacsa air a cur air dòigh le J. G. MacAoidh, agus, cuideachd, bha an sgeul air a riochdachadh an sia deug de dhealbhan briagha (ach caran mì-fhreagarrach 'nan còmhdadh!) le Gordon Browne R.I. 'S ann gu soilleir do chlann sgoile a bha an leabhar – àite anns am faigheadh iad gach cuid cothrom air leughadh ionnsachadh agus air beagan fiosrachaidh fhaotainn mu'n dualchas. Tha fhios gur e seo aon dòigh anns am faodadh an riochd-sa dhen sgeul a bhith air leudachadh, ach chan eil lorg againn air co-mheud sgoil a fhuair an leabhar no cò iad (cha robh e an sgoil Bheàrnaraigh, no san àite idir, le m' fhiosrachadh-sa). Tha iomadh ceist mun ghnothaich air am bu mhath leinn fuasgladh fhaighinn, ach tha sinn ro ghann de eiseamplairean 's de cho-theacsa riatanach gus tighinn gu codhùnadh cothromach sam bith mun deidhinn aig an ìre-sa.

II

Fhuair mi an aon iomradh eile a tha agam air cù-sìdh am Beàrnaraigh, tiomcheall air meadhan nan 1950an, bho Iain Dhòmhnaill a' Phìobair: Iain MacCoinnich (1877–1962) a bha a' fuireach air lota Druim a' Ghàrraidh – lota 5 an Tàcleit – a' chiad lota an iar air cnoc Chleitir. Bhitheadh e glè thric ag obair tiomcheall an taighe nuair a bhithinn a' dol seachad air an t-slighe a-null gu mullach a' bhaile a chèilidh air càirdean, 's bhitheadh e an còmhnaidh a' stad a' còmhradh. Bha mi aig an àm sin air tòiseachadh a' gabhail ùidh ann an sean ainmean àiteachan anns an eilean, agus dh'fhaighnich mi dha mu chreag mhòr a bha a tuath oirrn, eadar sinn agus ceann-a-deas Loch Bharabhat, 'An e siod "Creag 'Ille Chaluim Ghlais"?'

''S e,' thuirt e, 'Siod agad i.'

'Agus cò,' dh'fhaighnich mi dha, 'a bh'ann "Gille Calum Glas"?'

Rinn e sgal gàire is thuirt e, 'Chan eil duine beò an diugh aig eil fhios air sean!' Stad e greiseag, is an uair sin thug e sùil air oir orm is thuirt e, 'Tha fhios agad gum biodh iad ag radha gun robh na sìthichean uair a' fuireach anns a' chreig sin?' Thuirt mi nach cuala mi sean a-riamh. 'O, bha,' thuirt e, 'is 's e sean an t-àite bho dheireadh anns am facas an cù-sìdh!' Is dh'innis e dhomh an sgeul a leanas:

> *An latha bha seo bha muinntir mullach a' bhaile dripeil an sàs anns an arbhar a bha am fàs aca air na raointean air an leathad an ear sìos gu ceann a deas Loch Bharabhat. Bha an foghar air bhith fliuch, is mar a bha coltas bagarrach air a' mhadainn bha iad a-muigh glè thràth. Nuair a bha iad trang a' cur na h-uibhir de dhìon air cùisean mus tigeadh an ath dhìle 's ann a chualas an guth caol binn a bha seo èigheach 'Golabhsaigh! Golabhsaigh! Golabhsaigh!' Agus an ceann greis chunnaic iad cù mòr riabhach is aitheamh de shlabhraidh ceangailte ris a ruith le sinnteagan mòra, fada sìos seachad orra. Chaidh e a-null mu cheann an loch dìreach gu Creag 'Ille Chaluim Ghlais agus nuair a ràinig e i dh'fhosgail doras anns a' chreig. Ruith e a-steach agus dhùin a' chreag anns a dhèidh. An sin chualas na h-iollaichean aige, is e faigheann a laiseadh bhon a dh'fhalbh e gun chead air an t-siabhan. Is chan fhacas sealladh air a' chù-sìdh a riamh bhon latha sean.*

Cha robh eòlas aig daoine air an t-seanchas sin cho tric 's a bha aca air seanchas a' choire-shìdh, agus anns a' chumantas cha robh air chuimhne aca ach ainm a' choin. Ach bha a choltas gu dòcha gun robh uair a bha dà mheur dhen t-seanchas san àite, oir bha dà riochd aca de ainm a'choin: 'Golabhsaigh' mar a thog mise e agus, na bu trice, 'Trolabhsaigh', gu sònraichte aig a' chuid a b' aosda. Cha robh fuasgladh sam bith aca air a' cheist a tha sin a' togail. Is chan eil agam-sa na's motha. 'S dòcha gu bheil aig Iain MacAonghais...?

Yeatsian Shades
In Ó Direáin and Macgill-Eain

CAOIMHÍN MAC GIOLLA LÉITH

I say farewell to English verse,
to those I found in English nets:
my Lorca holding out his arms
to love the beauty of his bullets,
Pasternak who outlived Stalin
and died because of lesser beasts;
to all the poets I have loved
from Wyatt to Robert Browning;
to Father Hopkins in his crowded grave
and to our bugbear Mr. Yeats
who forced us into exile
on islands of bad verse. (Hartnett 1984: 61)

Michael Hartnett's grandiloquent valediction 'A Farewell to English', first delivered from the stage of the Peacock Theatre in Dublin in 1974, announced the thirty-three year-old poet's decision to cease publishing in his native English, the language in which he had already earned a considerable reputation, in order to devote himself henceforth to poetry in Irish. His insistence that to do so he must turn his back on the canon of English verse was not without precedent. It echoed the advice offered in his well-known poem *Fill Arís* ('Return Again') by a poet of the preceding generation, Seán Ó Ríordáin, the leading innovator in an unexpected renaissance of Irish Gaelic poetry during the 1940s:

...bain ded mheabhair
Srathair shibhialtacht an Bhéarla,
Shelley, Keats is Shakespeare.
Nigh d'anam is nigh
Do theanga chuaigh ceangailte i gcomhréiribh
'Bhí bunoiscionn le d'éirim. (Ó Ríordáin 2011: 154)

...Unshackle your mind
Of its civil English tackling,
Shelley, Keats and Shakespeare.
Wash your mind and wash your tongue
That was spancelled in a syntax
Putting you out of step with yourself.

Fill Arís is implicitly addressed in the first instance to the poet himself and by extension to all Irish writers and to the Irish people in general. Such purist rhetoric was understandably discomfiting to some otherwise sympathetic Irish poets writing in English. Seamus Heaney's response to the poem's argument, for instance, was one of characteristically gentle dissent in a lecture from 1983, in which he provides the no less characteristic translation just quoted (Heaney 1983: 18–21). What is notable in the litany from Hartnett's isolationist manifesto, however, in which even European masters encountered in English guise must be ruefully abjured, is its singling out of W.B. Yeats for particular reproach. While a resentment of Yeats's stifling influence, actual or imagined, was not unheard of among Hartnett's peers, the antidote he opts for, of abandoning English forthwith, is extreme. (It was also short-lived, lasting little more than a decade, after which he proceeded to publish in both languages.) Besides, the prevailing view of Yeats among Gaelic poets of the generation before Hartnett, in Scotland as well as Ireland, was far from negative, and his precedent was generally seen as enabling rather than disabling. Máirtín Ó Direáin, the other leading light of Irish Gaelic poetry in the 1940s, acknowledged a significant debt to Yeats on more than one occasion, as did his Scottish contemporary Somhairle MacGill-Eain, author of a fine elegy, *Aig Uaigh Yeats* / 'At Yeats's Grave', though the latter also expressed some telling, not to say typical reservations about Yeats's character. Despite significant divergences in sensibility between the two Gaelic poets (the similarities between Ó Direáin and Ruaraidh MacThómais, for example, are more obvious) the shadows cast on their work by this eminent precursor may serve to point up some intriguing parallels and overlaps.

As it happens, both poets have left us comparable pithy summations in verse of their long-term commitments. MacGill-Eain's comprises section XII of *Dàin do Eimhir*:

Do cheathrar dan tug mi luaidh
do cheathrar seirbheis caochladh buaidh –
an t-adhbhar mòr agus a' bhardachd
an t-Eilean álainn 's an nighean ruadh.

Four there are to whom I gave love,
to four a service of varying effect:
the great cause and poetry,
the lovely island and the red-haired girl. (MacGill-Eain 2011: 107)

Ó Direáin's apologia, *Ionracas* ('Integrity'), on the other hand, was famously prompted by a stinging remark made by Ó Ríordáin on Irish national radio, and is given here in full:

Dúirt file mór tráth
Go mba oileán is grá mná
Ábhar is fáth mo dháin;
Is fíor a chan mo bhráthair.

Coinneod féin an t-oileán
Seal eile i mo dhán,
Toisc a ionraice atá
Cloch, carraig is trá. (Ó Direáin 2010: 114)

A great poet once said
That the island and love of a woman
were my poem's only grounds;
My brother spoke true.

I will keep the island
a while longer in my poem,
Because of the integrity
of rock, stone and strand.[1]

It is difficult to imagine what residual influence, pernicious or otherwise, distant echoes of the early Yeats might have had on the less resourceful of Hartnett's generation by the 1970s. That said, the epitome of Hartnett's 'islands of bad verse' is surely Yeats's 'Lake Isle of Inisfree', and the sheer popularity of lines such as 'I will arise and go now, and go to Inisfree.... And I shall have some peace there, for peace comes dropping slow...' allowed them to resound across language

[1] All translations from Irish are by the writer, unless otherwise indicated.

lines, a generation earlier, in Ó Direáin's early *Faoiseamh a Gheobhadsa*, written shortly after Yeats's death in 1939.

Faoiseamh a gheobhadsa
Seal beag gairid
I measc mo dhaoine
Ar oileán mara,
Ag siúl cois cladaigh
Maidin is tráthnóna
Ó Luan go Satharn
Thiar ag baile. (Ó Direáin 2010: 27)

I will find peace
For a short while
Among my people
On an island in the sea,
Walking by the shore
Morning and evening
Monday to Saturday
At home in the West.

The crucial distinction signaled here by the phrase *'mo dhaoine'*, which is similarly deployed elsewhere by Ó Direáin, as well as the end-line *'Thiar ag baile'* ('At home in the West'), which closes both stanzas of this poem, is that for him, unlike Yeats, this is a return as much as an escape, however temporary, from the city life he was reluctantly enduring, having abandoned his native Aran at the age of eighteen. (Ó Ríordáin's rhetorical injunction to 'return again' to the South-West Kerry Gaeltacht was not so conveniently sanctioned by biography.) This romantic vision of an island idyll did not, however, remain untroubled or unquestioned. Seamus Deane's contention that 'Yeats began his career by inventing an Ireland amenable to his imagination…[and] ended by finding an Ireland recalcitrant to it' (Deane 1985: 38) is dramatically rendered in microcosm and telescoped into a few short years as Ó Direáin registers with dismay the rapid changes in Aran life through the 1940s. The succession of serene, picture-postcard images of traditional labour on the western seaboard presented in a lyric like *An tEarrach Thiar* ('Spring in the West') contrasts with the bleak account of such backbreaking activities provided, for instance, in the short stories written during these same years by Ó Direáin's contemporary Máirtín Ó Cadhain. Yet Ó Direáin soon conceded that such consoling memories and sentimentalizing images of traditional life could not withstand the reality of a rising tide of emigration. *Árainn 1947* ('Aran 1947') echoes the formal structure of both *Faoiseamh a Gheobhadsa* and *An tEarrach Thiar* in its use of a repeated end-line as binding agent. But in place of the fond affirmations in the closing lines of each stanza of *An tEarrach Thiar* (*Binn an fhuaim /San Earrach thiar,…Niamhrach an radharc /San Earrach thiar,* etc.: 'Sweet the sound/ In Spring out west'…'Brilliant the view / In Spring out west' etc.), we find a weary negation, as the various sounds of community are silenced one by one with the line: *…an tráth seo thiar níor chualas* ('…this time out west I did not hear.') The earlier poem's strong emphasis on the visual is reflected in its almost painterly attention to colour, light and shade (*Is an fheamainn dhearg / Ag lonrú / I dtaitneamh gréine /Ar dhuirling bhán,* 'And the red seaweed/ Glistening / In the shining sun / On a white shore.') This contrasts with the subjugation of sight to sound in *Árainn 1947*, whose accumulating references to (the absence of) *'feadail'* ('whistling'), *'amhrán'* ('song'), *'uaill mhaíte'* ('boastful roar'), and *'liú'* ('joyful shout') – *i.e.* loud sounds heard at some physical remove, and mostly at night – amplify the poem's sense of distance and disembodiment. The death knell in the closing couplet, which provides the poem's coda, is an ironic inversion of the opening lines of Yeats's 'Byzantium', as Ó Direáin despondently acknowledges that his narrow, windswept island is no longer a country for young men.

Ní don óige feasta
An sceirdoileán cúng úd. (Ó Direáin 2010: 74)

The myth-deflating poem of disenchanted return to a native isle was of course not unknown among Ó Direáin's Scottish Gaelic contemporaries, though they tend to strike a more sardonic note. Iain Mac a' Ghobhainn's familiar *A' Dol Dhachaidh* ('Going Home') is a case in point. MacGill-Eain's less familiar 'Road to the Isles' is another, and while there were more than enough mawkish Scottish predecessors to gall him – the poem's overt target is Marjory Kennedy-Fraser – Yeats's 'Inisfree' also springs, once more, to mind:

Thèid mi thun nan Eileanan
is ataidh mi lem bhaothalachd
mu bhruthan sìth an Canaigh 's Eige,
mu ghusgal ròn an Èirisgeidh,
mu chlàrsaichean 's mu Eilean Bharraigh...

I will go to the Isles
and inflate with my vapidity
about fairy mounds in Canna and Eigg,
about the wailing of seas in Eriskay,
about 'clarsachs' and the Isle of Barra... (MacGill-Eain 2011: 14–15)

Turning from *'an t-Eilean álainn'* to *'an nighean ruadh'*, and from *'oileán'* to *'grá mná'*, much might be said about the Yeatsian echoes of regret and recrimination in certain poems addressed to unnamed women by both Ó Direáin and MacGill-Eain, and the affinity is explicitly acknowledged by the latter:

Thug Yeats dà fhichead bliadhna'
gu tric 's cruaidh a' fiachainn
ri annas aon aodainn
chur an caoine bhriathran.

Thug mise còrr 's dà bhliadhna
am faoine a' cheart fhiachainn,
agus thàrrla dhòmhsa
searbhachd, bròn is iargain.

Yeats spent forty years
struggling repeatedly and doggedly
to set down in skilled words
the rarity of one face.

I gave in excess of two years
to the same futile attempt,
and what has befallen me is
bitterness, sorrow and woe. (MacGill-Eain 2011: 50–51)

Of course there is no comparison between the sustained intensity of MacGill-Eain's *Dàin do Eimhir*, on the one hand, and Ó Direáin's intermittent lyrics on unhappy encounters or soured relationships with women, on the other. Nevertheless, the Irish poet was equally capable of *'searbhachd, bròn is iargain'*. After all, implicit in the declaration of renewed commitment to his beloved island in *Ionracas*, on account of its inherent integrity, is the suggestion that the object of his *'grá mná'* may not be similarly favoured because she cannot be similarly characterized. As the title of the poem *Do Mhnaoi ar bith mar Í* ('To any Woman Like Her') suggests, and various later poems confirm, Ó Direáin found it all too easy to extrapolate from the behaviour of individual women who had somehow offended him and generalize his distrust, disdain, or, in the extreme case of the epochal long poem *Ár Ré Dhearóil* ('Our Wretched Era'), outright disgust. The image of the embittered, misogynistic barfly in *Blianta an Chogaidh* ('The War Years') can by no means be taken as a self-portrait. Yet it gains in poignancy by being presented, in a poem governed from its opening line by the first person plural (*'Ní sinne na daoine céanna a...'* 'We are not the same people who....'), as simply an extreme manifestation of a general attitude with which the poet is complicit.

Thuig fear amháin na mná
Is é a thuig a gcluain thar barr,
An bhantracht go léir a thuig,
I gcrot aon mhná nach raibh dílis. (Ó Direáin 2010: 114)

One man understood women,
He knew their guiles so well,
All womenfolk he understood
In the form of one unfaithful woman.

Ó Direáin and MacGill-Eain's common commitment to a poetry of public conscience, as well as private hurt, is also indebted to Yeats, as signaled most obviously in the title of the former's poem *Éire Ina bhFuil Romhainn*, lifted straight from Yeats's 'To Ireland in the Coming Times'. Despite their varying degrees of indignation at social injustice, all three poets were prone to 'daring sympathies with power', as Wordsworth put it in a rather different context. MacGill-Eain's heartfelt socialism can sometimes sit awkwardly with his reverence for the traditional hierarchies of the old Gaelic order. Similarly, Ó Direáin's strong sense of social injustice and natural empathy with the marginalized or oppressed is complicated by a fascination with the figure of the *Übermensch* – he offers his own '*an t-osfhear', nó an sárfhear, nó an tréanfhear*' as translations of Nietzche's term. This is especially evident in the long poem *Ó Mórna,* which most critics number among his finest achievements. His affinity with the Yeats who enjoined his peers to 'Sing the peasantry, and then / Hard-riding country gentlemen /...Sing the lords and ladies gay / That were beaten into the clay / Through seven heroic centuries...' ('Under Ben Bulben') is overtly acknowledged in *An Dá Aicme* ('The Two Classes'), in which he also invokes Nicola Alexandrovich Berdyaev (1874–1948), the erstwhile Marxist revolutionary who later spoke out against the oppression of the Bolshevik regime and ended life as a Christian mystic in exile in Paris:

Thuig Yéats is dhearbhaigh
Gurbh iad scoth an dá aicme
A chothaigh aithinne is lasair.

Berdyaev níor dhearmad
An sách is an folamh
A chur ar dhá cheann na meá... (Ó Direáin 2010: 196)

Yeats understood and declared
That it was the best of the two classes
Who guarded the embers and the flame.

Berdyaev did not forget
to put the well-fed and the starving
at both ends of the scale...

Despite his unease with aspects of Yeats's politics, it is clear from remarks such as the following that Ó Direáin was reluctant to condemn the older poet outright (the phrase '*más maith leat'* is disingenuous, but hardly disarming):

> *Bhí Yeats é féin ag suirí le faisisteachas, más maith leat, nuair a tháinig na Léinteacha Gorma anseo agus Eoin O'Duffy. Bhí Yeats agus is dóigh go raibh filí riamh anall, ag smaoineamh ar rudaí mar sin. B'fhéidir gur thúsaigh sé in aimsir na pátrúntachta, na taoisigh, níl a fhios agam.* (Ó Direáin 2002: 131)
>
> Yeats was flirting with fascism, if you like, when the Blue Shirts came here and Eoin O'Duffy. Yeats and, I think, poets since the beginning of time, have thought about such things. Maybe it began in the age of patronage and chieftains, I don't know.

Like Yeats, Ó Direáin and MacGill-Eain assembled personal pantheons of exemplary forebears. Ó Direáin composed poems in honour of various figures whose virtues and values he felt were sorely missing from the Ireland of his day ('Yet they were of a different kind / The names that stilled your childish play...', as Yeats put it in 'September 1913'). These include the nineteenth-century Archbishop John MacHale, the writers John Millington Synge and Seán O'Casey, and above all, the leaders of the 1916 Rising, Pádraig Pearse and James Connolly, whose imagined conversation famously forms the basis of Yeats's 'The Rose Tree'. The last-mentioned of these provides a particularly intriguing point of comparison with MacGill-Eain.

In *Dàin do Eimhir* XVIII, subtitled *Ùrnaigh*, MacGill-Eain's roll-call of heroes of the left comprises the English soldier-poet John Cornford, the Bulgarian trade-unionist and communist leader Georgi Mikhailovich Dimitrov, and the Scotsman James Connolly. Connolly is invoked in an explicitly Irish context in Part V of *An Cuilithionn* ('*Tha Ó Conghaile in Èirinn / ag èirigh thar àmhghair...*'/ 'Connolly is in Ireland / rising above agony...') alongside Lenin, Liebknecht and John MacLean. In Part VI of the same poem, he appears again as a crucial player in the history of Irish rebellion ('*S mise Clio na h-Èireann /...'s mise Chlio mhòr uallach, / óir chunnaic mi Ó Conghaile 's am Pearsach, / Wolfe Tone, MacGearailt agus Emmet.* ('I am the Clio of Ireland/ ...I am the Clio of great spirit, / for I have seen Connolly and Pearse, / Wolfe Tone, Fitzgerald and Emmet.'). Here the grouping of Tone, Fitzgerald and Emmet is borrowed directly from Yeats's 'September 1913'. In Part VII MacGill-Eain's pantheon of visionaries, again including Connolly, is further augmented by the addition of the eighteenth-century Haitian revolutionary Toussaint l'Ouverture, as well as the respective authors of *Das Kapital* and *Utopia.*

Finally, Connolly is the subject of the late poem *Àrd-Mhusaeum na h-Èireann* ('The National Museum of Ireland') in which the poet is transfixed by the 'rusty red spot of blood/ rather dirty on the shirt/ that was once on the hero/ who is dearest to me of them all' (*spot meirgeach ruadh na fala/ 's i caran salach air an lèinidh/ a bha aon uair air a' churaidh/ as docha liumsa dhiubh uile*). This poem closes with the image of the wounded Connolly being tied to a chair to be shot:

> *...ann an Àrd-Phost-Oifis Èirinn*
> *'s e ag ullachadh na h-ìobairt*
> *a chuir suas e fhèin air sheithear*
> *as naoimhe na 'n Lia Fàil*
> *th'air Cnoc na Teamhrach an Èirinn.*
>
> *Tha an curaidh mòr fhathast*
> *'na shuidhe air an t-sèithear,*
> *a' cur a' chatha sa Phost-Oifis*
> *'s a glanadh shràidean an Dùn Èideann.*
>
> ...In the General Post Office
> while he was preparing the sacrifice
> that put himself up on a chair
> that is holier than the Lia Fáil
> that is on the hill of Tara in Ireland.

The great hero is still
sitting on the chair,
fighting the battle in the Post Office
and cleaning streets in Edinburgh. (MacGill-Eain 2011: 270–271)

Though the details of Connolly's execution are well-known, the specific genesis of this arresting image, which reaches rhetorically back into a common Gaelic mythological past in order to draw together the struggle for social justice and self-determination in modern Ireland and Scotland alike, is particularly intriguing, as the following two stanzas attest:

Aig bánadh an lá ghil am bliadhna nan Sia-Deug,
tràighte, faoin-lag, cràdhte, fo chreuchdaibh,
ceangailte go dlùth ri cathair nam pian dhut –
seadh, tilgeil t'anam an làthair Mhic Dhè uat,

nan abradh neach riut madainn an là ud
gum biodh daoine an-dràsta air feadh do thìre
bhiodh bochd is nochd; gun an dùil ri aon rud
ach an-shòdh is call, is iad beò an dèirce.

When the pale day dawned in 1916
weak and dazed, with tormenting wounds,
tightly bound to the chair you would be executed in,
having cast your soul from you before God's Son,

if anyone could have told you on that morning
that men and women today throughout your land
would be poverty-stricken and naked, with no aspiration
beyond misery and deprivation, living as beggars! (MacGill-Eain 2011: 442–443)

While the editors of the 2011 volume of MacGill-Eain's collected poems present this as an unpublished early poem by MacGill-Eain, it is in fact a faithful, though abruptly truncated translation of the first two stanzas of a longer poem by Máirtín Ó Direáin, titled *Séamus Ó Conghaile,* the first four stanzas of which are as follows:

Le bánú an lae ghil i mbliain a sé déag,
Tnáite, faonlag, cráite ag créachtaí,
Ceangailte go dlúth de chathaoir na bpian duit
Is ea teilgeadh t'anam i láthair Mhic Dé uait.

Dá n-abraíodh neach leat maidin an lae úd,
Go mbeadh daoine an tráth seo ar fud do thíre
Bheadh bocht is nocht; gan a gcoinne le haon rud
Ach anró is call, is iad beo ar dhéirce.

Déarfá féin leis gurbh éitheach a fhís duit
Go mbeadh fuíoll gach fuíll arís ag Gaelaibh
Is só is sonas i ndán do gach aon díobh,
De thortha d'íobartha is íobairt gach laoich dhíbh.

Ach is trua le n-aithris an scéal atá amhlaidh.
Fiche bliain is cúig ó thit tú go calma;
Fir mhóra láidre is a ndroim le balla
Is ocras is fuacht ar bhean is ar leanbh… (Ó Direáin 2010: 33)

...You would tell him that to you his vision was false,
That Gaels would again have wealth aplenty
That comfort and joy would be everyone's lot,
Because of the sacrifice made by all you heroes.

But, sad to relate, this is not so
Twenty five years since you fell bravely;
Big, strong men with their backs to the wall
And hunger and cold among women and children...

Written in 1941, two years after the death of W.B. Yeats, this is by no means one of Máirtín Ó Direáin's most accomplished poems, and was not included in his *Dánta 1939–1979* (Ó Direáin 1980). That said, it is not difficult to see why this elegy for a Scotsman, whose contribution to Irish history Yeats himself had been forced to reassess a generation earlier, should have attracted the attention of Ó Direáin's great contemporary, Somhairle MacGill-Eain.

Sources

DEANE, SEAMUS.

1985 *Celtic Revivals.* London & Boston.

HARTNETT, MICHAEL.

1984 *Collected Poems,* Vol. 1. Dublin/Manchester.

HEANEY, SEAMUS.

1983 'Forked Tongues Céilís and Incubators'. *Fortnight:* 197.

MACGILL-EAIN, SOMHAIRLE (MACLEAN, SORLEY).

2011 *Caoir Gheal Leumraich / White Leaping Flame.* Christopher Whyte and Emma Dymock (eds). Edinburgh.

Ó DIREÁIN, MÁIRTÍN.

1980 *Máirtín Ó Direáin: Dánta 1939–1979.* Baile Átha Cliath.
2002 *Ón Ulán Ramhar Siar.* Eoghan Ó hAnluain (eag.). Baile Átha Cliath.
2010 *Máirtín Ó Direáin: Na Dánta.* Indreabhán.

Ó RÍORDÁIN, SEÁN.

2011 *Seán Ó Ríordáin: Na Dánta.* Indreabhán.

An t-Each-Uisge

RAGHNALL MACILLEDHUIBH

ABSTRACT. Traditional descriptions of the Gaelic water-horse display intriguing similarities to the mysterious 'Pictish Beast' or 'Swimming Elephant', the most ubiquitous yet least recognisable creature of our symbol-stones, which is dateable to *c.* AD 700. This paper sets out a typology of water-horse stories and attempts to show that they can be dated to that period. It then considers whether the iconography of the Beast, the 'head-lappet' in particular, can be explained in terms of the ethnography of the water-horse, whose principal attribute is its cap or magic bridle. The Torrs Pony-Cap, Adomnán's river-monster and the 'kelpie' of Lowland tradition are taken into account, and it is suggested in conclusion that the water-horse and kelpie are Gaelic and Anglo-Norman reflexes of a leading Pictish deity, the guardian of their otherworld.

Ann am beul-aithris Ghàidhlig na h-Alba, tha barrachd air innse mun each-uisge na mu chreutair neo-thalmhaidh sam bith eile. (Ann an Éirinn tha am prìomh àite seo aig a' bhan-shìth.) Tha sgeulachdan mun each-uisge a' tighinn á gach ceàrnaidh den Ghaidhealtachd, ach faodar a ràdh gu bheil iad uile a' gabhail aon de na trì cruthan seo:

Each-uisge agus tuathanach. Tha tuathanach a' treabhadh le each nach aithne dha / ga chleachdadh ceangailte le earball ri eich eile son luchdan a ghiùlan. Chan fhaod e treabhadh as déidh dol sìos na gréine / feumaidh e buarach no srian a chumail air an each, neo *far* an eich, neo uisge a thaomadh air. Nì e dearmad air seo. Tha an t-each ga thoirt leis a-staigh do loch / tha e a' leum far a mhuin le bhith a' sìneadh a-mach a chasan a' dol tro gheata neo tro bhealach a' ghàraidh / tha e a' gearradh dheth a mheur, a tha a' leantainn ris an each / tha na h-eich eile air an slaodadh a-staigh dhan loch. Tha sgamhain/grùthain/mionaich a' nochdadh ('s a' toirt ainm dhan àite).

Each-uisge agus boireannach. Tha fear òg maiseach a' nochdadh, a' cur a chinn an uchd a' bhoireannaich, agus a' dol a chadal. Tha i a' lorg shligean/gainmhich/planndrais-uisge 'na ghruaig. Tha i a' gearradh toll anns an dreas aice neo ga thoirt dhith, neo a' cur ploc fo cheann an duine, agus a' teicheadh. Tha esan ga toirt air falbh (air Di-Dòmhnaich) á meadhan sluaigh. Tha a sgamhan/grùthan/mionach a' nochdadh san loch ('s a' toirt ainm dhan àite).

Each-uisge agus clann. Tha àireamh na cloinne air a toirt seachad. (Se Di-Dòmhnaich a th' ann.) Tha iad uile a' dol air each nach aithne dhaibh, a tha a' sìneadh a dhroma gus rùm a dheanamh dhaibh. Tha e gan toirt leis a-staigh do loch. Tha aon den chloinn agus duilleagan Bìobaill aige / a' tighinn far an eich leis an earball / a' gearradh dheth a mheur, a tha a' leantainn ris an each. Tha sgamhain/grùthain/mionaich na cloinne a' nochdadh ('s a' toirt ainm dhan àite).

Mar as trice chan eil dad anns na sgeulachdan mu choltas an eich-uisge, ach tha a' bheàrn seo air a lìonadh dhuinn le sgrìobhadairean mar Iain Griogarach Caimbeul (1834–91). Thuirt esan (Black 2005: 109):

> In shape and colour it resembled an ordinary horse, and was often mistaken for one . . . The cow-shackle round its neck, or a cap on its head, completely subdued it, and as long as either of these was kept on it, it could be as safely employed in farm labour as any other horse. In Skye it was said to have a sharp bill (*gob biorach*), or, as others describe it, a narrow brown slippery snout. Accounts are uniform that it had a long flowing tail and mane. In colour it was sometimes grey, sometimes black, and

sometimes black with a white spot on its forehead. This variation arose, some say, from the water-horse being of any colour like other horses, and others say from its having the power of changing its colour as well as its shape . . . However much benefit the farmer might at first derive from securing one with the cap or cow-shackle, he was ultimately involved by it in ruinous loss.

Tha seo 'na dhealbh-pinn cho math 's a ghabhas den chreutair neònach ris an canar a' Bhiast Chruithneach, an t-Ailbhean air an t-Snàmh, no an t-Each/Damh Cruithneach. Se a' Bhiast (mar a chanas mise ris) an creutair as cumanta a chithear snaidhte sna clachan Cruithneach a tha sgapte air feadh ear-thuath na h-Alba. Tha airceòlaichean agus eachdraichean ealain air a bhith deasbaireachd mu deidhinn fad còrr agus ceud bliadhna. Dé seòrsa creutair a th' innte? Co ás a thàinig i? Oir bha na Cruithnich air leth math air snaidheadh, agus aithnichear na creutairean eile air fad aca anns a' bhad – an tarbh a tha an-diugh 'na shamhla do Shabhal Mór Ostaig, mar eisimpleir.

Is gann a bhios a' Bhiast ag atharrachadh ga brith dé cho tric 's a tha i air a snaidheadh. 'S i air a faicinn daonnan on dara taobh, tha i a' fiaradh mar gun robh i a' leum no a' snàmh, tha earball fada agus spògan cruinne aice, tha rudeigin crom mar mhuing a' tighinn o mhullach a cinn 's a' leantainn le druim, tha i a' coimhead sìos, agus tha gob fada caol, dlùth dh'a broilleach, a' toirt coltas tunnaige dh'a ceann.

Tarbh Cheann Bhuirgh, samhla Sabhal Mór Ostaig, a tha gu follaiseach 'na tharbh © Taigh-Tasgaidh Bhreatainn

Am faod e bhith, ma-thà, gur e a' Bhiast an t-each-uisge? Chan eil 'dearbhadh' ann, ach cha mhotha tha 'dearbhadh' ann air nì sam bith, cha mhór, mu ealain nan Cruithneach. Se tha a dhìth ach gun gabh a shealltainn gu bheil na sgeulachdan mun each-uisge cho sean ri clachan nan Cruithneach, agus gun gabh *iconography* – dealbhsgrìobhainn – na Béiste, an *head-lappet* gu sònraichte, a mhìneachadh a réir *ethnography* – sluaghsgrìobhainn – an eich-uisge.

Tha a' Bhiast suaicheanta cheana air clachan 'Clas I', an fheadhainn a chaidh a shnaidheadh eadar AD 650 agus 750. Ann am pàipear a thug i aig Còmhdhail Eadar-Nàiseanta na Ceiltis ann an Dùn Éideann ann an 1995, rinn mo nighean Catrìona a-mach bho fhianais ealain-eachdraidheil gun do nochd a' Bhiast eadar AD 650 agus 680 (Black *et al.* 1999: 497, cf. Curle 1939–40: 75). Thuirt cuid a sgoilearan aig an àm gun robh na deatachan seo ro thràth; ach mar as tràithe na deatachan, sann as motha an dùbhlan dhuinne. Gu h-iongantach, sann aig dìreach an aon àm, timcheall air AD 670, a sgrìobh Eònan 'Beatha Chaluim Chille', anns a bheil e a' cumail a-mach gun do thachair an naomh ri 'biast uisge' ann an abhainn Nis, faisg air ceannabhaile rìgh nan Cruithneach. (Bhiodh seo timcheall air ceud bliadhna roimhe, mu AD 570.) Mharbh a' bhiast aon duine agus chuir i eagal a bheatha air companach an naoimh, Luighne mac Min, a bha a' snàmh a-null a dh'fhaighinn curach a bh' air an taobh eile. Thog Calum Cille a làmh, rinn e comharradh na croise, agus dh'òrdaich e dhan bhéist gun a dhol nas fhaide, gun beantainn ri Luighne, agus tilleadh an rathad a thàinig i, rud a rinn i 'cho luath 's gun saoileadh tu gun robh i ga slaodadh le ròpannan' (Adomnán 1995: 175–76).

Chum ealainichean Cruithneach orra a' snaidheadh na Béiste fad dhà na thrì cheud bliadhna eile, gu timcheall air AD 900, mun àm a chaidh an sgeul 'Fled Bricrend' a sgrìobhadh. Tha 'Fled Bricrend' ag innse mar a fhuair Cú Chulainn an dà each-carbaid aige. Thachair e air an Liath Macha ri taobh Linne Léith ann an Sliabh Fuaid. Nuair thàinig an t-each ás an loch dh'èalaidh Cú Chulainn ga ionnsaigh 's chuir e a dhà làimh mu amhaich. Lean iad orra a' carachd uile thimcheall na h-Éireann gus an tàinig an Liath Macha an oidhche sin 'na each carbaid aige gu Eamhain Macha.

Lorg e an Dubhshaoileann san dòigh cheudna ann an Loch Duib Sainglend (Henderson 1899: 38–41). Bheirear fanear gur ann liath (glas) agus dubh a bha na h-eich seo, dathan nan each-uisge.

Clach 'Clas I' á Mìgeil, Siorrachd Pheairt
© Alba Aosmhor

Bha an t-Oll. Bo Almqvist a' creidsinn (1991: 117, 119) gun robh na bun-stòireannan mun each-uisge làn leasaichte ro *c.* 1000, oir dh'imrich iad a-mach dha na h-eileanan far an robh Seann Lochlannais ga bruidhinn. Tha 'Each-uisge agus tuathanach' a' nochdadh anns an *Landnámabók* san treas linn deug, agus dh'aidich an sgoilear Finnur Jónsson (nach robh, mar bu thrice, deònach gabhail ris gun robh buaidh sam bith aig na Gaidhil air dualchas Inis Tile) gun robh e coltach gun tàinig e á Alba no Éirinn (Almqvist 1991: 118; cf. Strömbäck 1970: 245–46, 251).

Ma tha e fìor gur ann on Bhreatnais/Chuimris/Chruithnis *ceffyl-pol*, *celpow* 'each-puill, each-aibhne' a thàinig am facal Albais *kelpie*, mar a chuir mi fhìn air adhart (MacilleDhuibh 1999; Black 2005: 372), buinidh am facal do linn nan Cruithneach. Tha coltas na h-aoise air an sgaradh eadar creutair Gaidhealach a tha a chòmhnaidh ann an uisge sèimh agus creutair Gallda a tha a chòmhnaidh ann an uisge ruith (Stewart 1885: 40–41; Mackenzie 1935: 237, 238; Black 2005: 115). Agus gabhaidh a leigeil fhaicinn gun robh làraichean coisrigte ann an dùthaich nan Cruithneach do thrì, co-dhiù, de na ceithir naoimh Éireannach aig a bheil eich-uisge a' nochdadh anns na beathannan aca – Brèanainn, Féichín, Maedhóg agus Ruadhan (Watson 1926: 274, 321–22, 327; MacNickle 1934: 218–19; Ó hÓgáin 1990: 252; Black 2000: 46–48).

Each-uisge? A' Bhiast bho chloich eile ann am Mìgeil
© Alba Aosmhor

Uile gu léir, ma-thà, ged nach deach agam air a nochdadh gu bheil na sgeulachdan mun each-uisge nas sine na Biast nan clachan (ach faic shìos mu Cheap-Pònaidh nan Torran), lorg sinn rudeigin nas inntinniche fhéin: fianais gun do nochd an t-each-*aibhne* 's a' Bhiast còmhla mun bhliadhna 670, 's gun robh an t-each-*uisge* ann mun do sguir na Cruithnich a shnaidheadh na Béiste mun bhliadhna 900.

Tha tighinn oirnn tionndadh a-nis gu nitheòlas, no *material culture*, an eich-uisge – an t-srian 's an còrr – agus faighneachd dé a' chiall a tha e deanamh fa chomhair na Béiste. Tha dealbh-pinn math dheth aig Eachann MacDhughaill á Cola (1929–30: 127–28).

> Bha na Gàidheil ag creidsinn gu'n gabhadh an t-each-uisge ceannsachadh, is a chur an gréim anns a' chrann no an ceann oibreach sam bith eile a bhiodhte a' dèanamh. Am bitheantas, ged thà, is ann ri obair treabhaidh a bhiodhte 'ga chur. Bha dòigh no dhà gus an ceannsal so a chur air. Dheante e le fìor neart thar a' chumantais anns an fhear a ghabhadh air féin a laimhseachadh, agus mar an ceudna le cumhachdan eile as eugmhais neart bodhaig. De na dòighean mu dheireadh so, is e srian shònraichte, no buarach na boine, air am bitheanta sgeul. An uair a gheibhte a' bhuarach gu

sònraichte m'a cheann no m'a amhaich bha e cho còir ri each sam bith eile. A thaobh cuid a choltais dheth, cha robh a' bheag de eadar-dhealachadh eadar e féin is each nàdurra an fhuinn. Gun teagamh, bha a chomas aig an each-uisge a chruth is a dhath atharrachadh, oir, mar a thugas fa-near, rachadh e an riochd an duine féin. Ach eadhon 'na chruth féin, mar each, dh'aithnicheadh an t-sùil eòlach e seach each an fhuinn. Am bitheantas is ann dorcha a bhiodh e anns an dath, ged a bhiodh e air uairean is fiamh glas dheth. Bha earball is muing fhada dhosrach air, a shròn fada, sleamhuin, is air uairean ball geal 'na aodann.

An uair a gheibhte a làn-cheannsachadh is a chur gu feum, cha robh obair a rachadh a chur m'a choinneamh ro throm leis. Leathan 'gam biodh an t-achadh ris an seolte e an ám a chur anns a' chrann sa mhaduinn, is e glé bheag dheth a bhiodh glas an ám an fheasgair. A dh'aindeoin sin uile, ged thà, direach mar chuideachadh nan sithichean féin, cha bhiodh obair an eich-uisge gu a bheag de bhuaidh dhàsan a chuireadh an cuing e. Luath no mall, dheante dearmad a thaobh-eigin an ám a laimhseachadh: dheante diochuimhne air an t-srian sheunaidh, no a' bhuarach, a chumail an ceangal gu diongmhalta air, agus an uair sin dh'éireadh an dosgainn sgriosail a bhiodh eu-comasach a casg do'n fhear a bu treise.

Theagamh gur e gach crann, gach each eile a bhiodh an cuing leis, is eadhon an duine no na daoine a bhiodh 'na fhochair a tharruing leis do'n loch a dheanadh e; agus de na beothaibh a bheireadh e leis, a chaoidh tuille chan fhaicte dhiubh ach na sgamhain. Thigeadh a' chuid sin de am buill-cuirp, eich is daoine, gu tir am measg cobhair is ruaim an locha an ath latha.

Na'n tachradh gu'm faigheadh fear le neart bodhaig lamh-an-uachdar air an each-uisge, is a mharbhadh, cha bhiodh air fhàgail air an lom air am biodh a' chòmhrag ach silteach streamhain de rud sleamhuin, tiacte, mar gu'm biodh muir-tiac no sùil éisg. Tha aon iomradh mar so air each-uisge a bhi air a mharbhadh, agus an uair a chaidh crioch air an iomairt is a sgaoil an ceathach a thog i, cha robh r'a fhaicinn ach sgonnan phloc far an do thuit an t-each marbh fo 'n fhuar-bhuille a rinn an gnothach air mu dheireadh thall.

Seo ma-tà na h-aon fheartan mu'n cuala sinn roimhe – an t-srian sheunaidh no a' bhuarach mu cheann no mu amhaich, an cruth-atharrachadh, an dath dorcha no glas, an t-earball fada, a' mhuing dhosrach, am ball geal 'na aodann, an t-sròn fhada shleamhainn. Ach tha rud eil' ann cho math: ma mharbhar an t-each-uisge théid e 'na shilidh neo 'na phluic. Tha seo aig a' Chaimbeulach cuideachd. Nuair chaidh each-uisge Ratharsair a mharbhadh, ars esan (Black 2005: 112), 'the monster proved to be merely grey turves (*pluic ghlas*), or, as others say, a soft mass (*sgling*) like jellyfish (*muir-tiachd*)'. Chithinn seo mar innleachd gu mìneachadh ma tha a leithid de nì ann ri each-uisge 's ma ghabhas a mharbhadh, ciamar nach deach corp eich-uisge a lorg riamh – ach gu bheil an 'sgling' ud ri fhaotainn air na monaidhean . . . (Campbell 1890: 204).

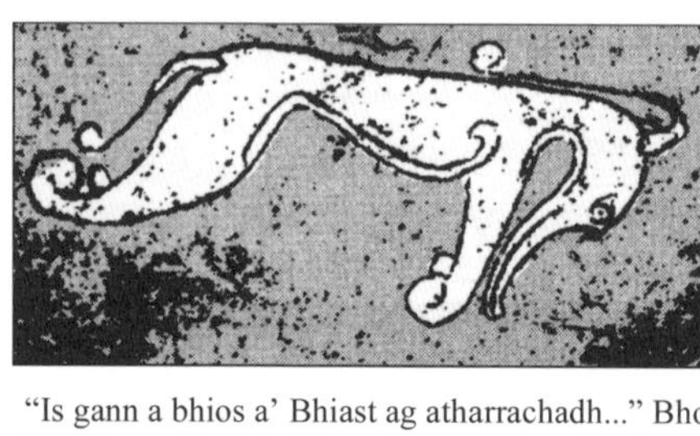

"Is gann a bhios a' Bhiast ag atharrachadh..." Bho Chlach Ghoillspidh (shuas, © Alba Aosmhor) agus bho Chlach Thulaich Dhiarmaid (shìos, © Pinkfoot Press)

Se an *head-lappet* prìomh fheart na Béiste; se an t-srian prìomh fheart an eich-uisge. Tha dealbh-sgrìobhainn na Béiste a' sealltainn gu soilleir 's gu cunbhalach nach eil an *lappet* 'na phàirt dh'a bodhaig ach 'na sheòrsa de churrac fada air a ceann. Tha e a' siubhal fada air ais ri druim far am bu chòir dhan mhuing a bhith (feumaidh gur e an t-srian a chuir ás dhan mhuing). A réir a' Chaimbeulaich 's an Dùghallaich sann leis an t-sréin a tha an tuathanach a' gabhail smachd air, ach saoilidh mi gu bheil iad ceàrr. Tha an t-srian air an each-uisge cheana nuair thig e ás an loch, agus sann le bhith ga toirt dheth a tha an tuathanach a' gabhail smachd air (Stewart 1823: 147–57; Polson 1926: 82), a cheart choltach ri cochall na maighdinn-mhara a tha an tuathanach a' cur air an fhardoras an uair a phòsas e i (Campbell 1960: 116–19; Black 2005: 108). Mar their Alastair MacBheathain, 'the horse is ready caparisoned' (Macbain 1887–88: 248).

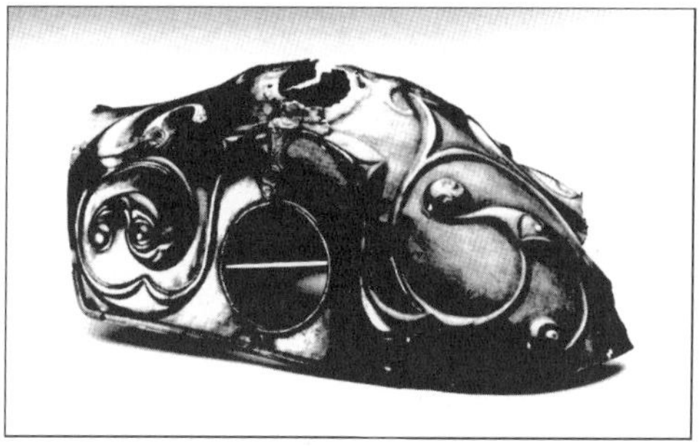

Srian eich-uisge bho Linn an Iarainn? Ceap-Pònaidh nan Torran
© Taighean-Tasgaidh Nàiseanta na h-Alba

Tha briathrachas na sréine dà-fhillte no trì-fhillte. Ann an Gàidhlig cluinnidh sinn mun t-sréin 's mun bhuaraich. Mar as trice se tha ann am buarach ach rud leis a bheil casan-deiridh na bà air an ceangal aig àm bleoghainn. Ann am Beurla cluinnidh sinn mu *bridle*, *shackle*, neo, aig a' Chaimbeulach a-mhàin, *cap* (Black 2005: 109, 111). Feumaidh gun tug e *cap* bho fhacal mar 'chopan' (*the boss of a bridle*, Dwelly 1977: 252). Sann ann an Alba a lorgadh an aon cheap-pònaidh a th' againn bho Linn Iarainn Taobh Siar na Roinn Eòrpa, ás na Torran ann an Siorrachd Chille Chùbaid, bhon treas linn ro Chrìost (Calder 1989: 97–99). Ma ghabhar ris gum buin an *Torrs Pony-Cap* air dhòigh air choreigin do sheanchas an eich-uisge, tha e a' cur toiseach na sgeòil againn mìle bliadhna ron chiad Bhéist Chruithnich.

Tha fianais ann, gun teagamh, gum faodte an t-srian fhaicinn mar nì sìmplidh draoidheach seach mar shreath amallach de dh'iallan 's de bhucaill, no de mhurain 's de shnaoimeannan. Cha robh anns an 't-sréin draoidhich' a bh' aig Griogar Willox mun bhliadhna 1830 ach pìos pràise mu'n tuirt fear a chunnaic 's a tharraing e 'it has not the most distant resemblance to any part of a bridle' (Lauder 1881: 5; McGregor 1994: 12). Tha sìmplidheachd den t-seòrsa seo feumail ann am buidseachd, ann an creideamh, 's ann an seanchas, mar chithear san sgeulachd 'Each-Uisge Pholl nan Craobhan', anns an robh 'srian loinnireach' an eich 'air a cheann' agus chan ann air a shròin (MacDougall 1910: 308–15). "Cha'n 'eil 'san t-sréin aon chuid sparrag (*bit*) no smeachan (*chin-strap*)," tha cailleach dhubh Allnaig a' cur an céill do dh'Iain Beag; "agus, uime sin, an uair a gheibh thu dlùth gu leòir, bheir thu leum a dh' ionnsaidh na sréine, agus spìonaidh tu dheth i. An sin bithidh an t-each dubh fo do smachd, agu nì e ni air bith is toil leat, cho fad is a chumas tu an t-srian uaith. Bi cùramach mu 'n t-sréin, air neo is ann duitse is miosa e." Agus chaidh leis, oir "le cruaidh leum fhuair e greim air an t-sréin loinnirich, spìon e bhàrr an eich i, agus rug e air a bhad-mullaich air (*he caught him by the forelock*)".

Air an làimh eile tha sgeulachd aig Alastair Stiùbhart mu shrian draoidheach nach eil air a slaodadh far eich chrosta idir, ach air a faotainn le dròbhair air bruach lochain (Stewart 1885: 44):

> As he sat on a stone by the side of the lake he saw something glittering in the moonlight, which, on taking it up, he found to be a horse-bridle. Dòmhnull Mòr carried the bridle home with him, and was surprised next morning to find that the bit and buckles were of pure silver, and the reins of a soft and beautifully speckled sort of leather, such as he had never seen before. What astonished him most was, that on touching the silver bit it felt so hot as to be unbearable. He was very much frightened as well as astonished, and now wished that he had let it lie where he found it. It was only when a 'wise woman' was sent for from a neighbouring glen that the truth became known. She declared it to be a water-horse's bridle, the bit of deep down,

> subterranean silver still retaining part of the heat which belonged to it in its primeval molten state. The reins, she said, were the skin of *Buarach-Baoibh*, a sort of magical serpents, dreadfully poisonous, that frequent such rivers and lakes as are inhabited by the kelpy and water-horse.

Tha a' bhuarach-bhaoibh 'na seòrsa de *lamprey* neo de dh'easgann dealain (Black 2005: 118), ach tha barail na cailliche gar tilleadh chun na buaraich, 's a' toirt ceist eile gu bàrr: on as ann de dh'airgead a bha an sparrag agus na bucaill seo, nach fhaodadh e bhith gum biodh currac airgid ann uaireannan cuideachd, coltach ris a' churrac umha bh' air pònaidh nan Torran?

Se an currac, neo an copan, an dara nì as fheàrr, as déidh a' ghuib, a nì an ceangal eadar a' Bhiast 's an t-each-uisge. Nuair sgrìobh an Caimbeulach 'the cow-shackle round its neck, or a cap on its head, completely subdued it' (Black 2005: 109) feumaidh gun robh dealbh 'na cheann de dhà rud seach aon, dà stuth seach aon, 's nam b'e a' bhuarach pàirtean boga na sréine, b'e an *cap* na pàirtean cruaidhe – bucaill, sparrag, currac sam bith.

Griogar Willox agus an t-srian a ghoid e, masa fìor, bho each-uisge (Sir Thomas Dick Lauder, *Legendary Tales of the Highlands*, 1841)

A-nise, ma tha a' Bhiast 'na h-each-uisge, nach bu chòir casan eich a bhith aice mar anns na sgeulachdan? Chaidh a coltachadh ri creutairean mara mar a' phèileag (Hicks 1993a: 49–50; Hicks 1993b: 199), ach chanainn fhìn gu bheil a casan leathach-shlighe eadar cruidhean eich agus spògan ròin, agus co-dhiù bha cruth-atharrachadh 'na phàirt de nàdar an eich-uisge. Tha ar beul-aithris gu léir a' déiligeadh ri cruth an eich-uisge air tìr seach anns an uisge, ach tha e coltach gur e snàmh a bh' air inntinn an luchd-ealain a bhiodh a' snaidheadh na Béiste. Tha seo gar stiùireadh chun a' cho-dhùnaidh gu bheil a' Bhiast a' riochdachadh an eich-uisge sa chiad dhreuchd aige, se sin, mar bhandia nan aibhnichean 's mar fhreiceadan air an t-saoghal eile.

Ann an seanchas na Gàidhlig, tha an t-each-uisge 'na gheàrd air lochain mhòintich a tha 'nan dorsan dhan t-saoghal eile. Tha e 'na chreutair eagallach ach tha e comasach air a dhol 'na riochd taitneach. Ma tha dàimh aige ris a' Bhéist, tha sin a' deanamh dà rud dheth, neo trì: Cruithneach, dia, neo (nas miosa fhéin) dia Cruithneach. Ann an seanchas na Beurla, tha an *kelpie* 'na fhreiceadan air aibhnichean 's tha ainm, masa fìor, 'na fhacal Cruithneach. Tha sin ga cheangal ris a' chreutair a thachair (a réir Eònain) ri Calum Cille. Tha an t-ainm a' ciallachadh an dearbh rud, cha mhór, ri 'each-uisge'. Tha gu leór an-seo gu toirt oirnn a chreidsinn gun robh a' Bhiast air a meas 'na creutair aibhne seach locha.

Tha leasachadh na Béiste, mar sin, 'na cheist chruinneòlais. Bha na Cruithnich agus luchd na Beurla a' fuireach ri taobh nan aibhnichean móra. Sann annta a lorgadh iad na diathannan aca. B' iad na Gaidhil a thuinich an talamh àrd, ach (mar a thachras le gach sluagh a tha a' dol ás) bha na Cruithnich mu dheireadh ri fhaotainn àrd anns na monaidhean iad fhéin. Mar sin, ann an seanchas nan Gaidheal bha suaicheantas nan Cruithneach ceangailte ri lochain mhòintich. Sann sa chruth sin a nochd e ann an Éirinn mu AD 900.

Aig na Gaidhil 's aig luchd na Beurla bha an t-each-uisge 's an *kelpie* 'nan nàmhaid. Aig na Cruithnich bha a' Bhiast 'na caraid. Chan eil dad a choltas bagairteach mu deidhinn, 's gu dearbh bha taobh eile ri pearsantachd an eich-uisge fhéin, air na chuir MacDhughaill a chorrag (1929–30: 125–26):

> Tha aon bheachd a dh'fhaodamaid meomhrachadh air; agus is e sin ged a bhiodh clann is cailean òga air an toirt do'n loch, nach 'eil mi ro chinnteach gu'n robhas anns an t-seann aimsir ag creidsinn gu'n robhtar 'gam marbhadh no 'gam bàthadh. Bha còmhnuidhean dhaoine, is saoghal dha féin anns an doimhne fo'n chuan is fo lochan tire ... mur robh anns an each-uisge ach teachdaire gu sluagh a thoirt air falbh do'n tir àluinn so, bhiodh e coltach gu leor gu'm fàgadh iadsan 'nan déidh am ball-cuirp sin – an sgamhan – air nach biodh iad a nis ag cur an corr feuma.

Agus uaireannan ann an 'Each-uisge agus boireannach' tha an sgeulaiche a' cumail a-mach gu bheil uisge an loch a' dol dearg, ach a réir Nèill MhicGille Sheathanaich (1938: 18) chan e fuil na maighdinn a th' ann idir: "An uair a thill an creutair neo-chneasda so air ais do'n Loch ás an d'thàinig e, 's a mhothaich na h-uile-bheistean eile gu'n robh e an comunn neach talmhaidh, ghleac iad cho searbh is gu'n robh uisge an locha dearg le am fuil." Bha cho math dha 'caileag bhrèagha' a ràdh an àite 'neach talmhaidh'.

Tha seo gar toirt gu leantainneachd creidimh. Tha a' Bhiast nas bitheanta air na clachan na creutair sam bith eile, agus chithinn-s' i mar phrìomh dhia (neo spiorad) nan Cruithneach. Mar sin tha an sgeul aig Eònan, a tha a' cur na Béiste san aon dealbh ri comharradh na Croise, 'na shamhla. Ma thogar a' cheist an uair sin car son a tha a' Bhiast a' nochdadh air na h-aon chlachan 'Clas II' (*c.* AD 750–850) ris a' Chrois, tha i furasta a freagairt on eòlas a th' againn air làithean tràtha na Crìostaidheachd: cha deach cur ás dhan Bhéist, chaidh gabhail rithe mar shuaicheantas nan Cruithneach, mar spiorad, 's mar aingeal dìona air an t-saoghal ud eile fon uisge.

TÙSAN

ADOMNÁN OF IONA.

1995 *Life of St Columba*. Richard Sharpe (ed.). London.

ALMQVIST, BO.

1991 'Waterhorse Legends'. *Béaloideas* 59: 107–20.

BLACK, RONALD [= MACILLEDHUIBH, RAGHNALL].

2000 'Scottish Fairs and Fair-Names'. *Scottish Studies* 33: 1–75.

2005 *The Gaelic Otherworld: John Gregorson Campbell's Superstitions of the Highlands & Islands of Scotland and Witchcraft & Second Sight in the Highlands & Islands*. Edinburgh.

BLACK, RONALD, WILLIAM GILLIES AND ROIBEARD Ó MAOLALAIGH (EDS).

1999 *Celtic Connections: Proceedings of the 10th International Congress of Celtic Studies*, vol. 1. Edinburgh.

CALDER, JENNI (ED.).

1989 *The Wealth of a Nation in the National Museums of Scotland.* Edinburgh.

CAMPBELL, J. F.

1890 *Popular Tales of the West Highlands*, 2nd edition, vol. 2. Paisley.

1960 *More West Highland Tales,* vol. 2. Edinburgh.

CURLE, CECIL L.

1939-40 'The Chronology of the Early Christian Monuments of Scotland'. *Proceedings of the Society of Antiquaries of Scotland* 74: 60–116.

DWELLY, EDWARD.

1977 *The Illustrated Gaelic-English Dictionary*, 9th edition. Glasgow.

HENDERSON, GEORGE (ED.).

1899 *Fled Bricrend: The Feast of Bricriu.* London.

HICKS, CAROLA.

1993a *Animals in Early Medieval Art.* Edinburgh.

1993b 'The Pictish Class I Animals'. R. Michael Spearman and John Higgitt (eds), *The Age of Migrating Ideas: Early Medieval Art in Northern Britain and Ireland.* Edinburgh: 196–202..

LAUDER, SIR THOMAS DICK.

1881 *Tales of the Highlands.* London.

MACBAIN, ALEXANDER.

1887-88 'Highland Superstition'. *Transactions of the Gaelic Society of Inverness* 14: 232–72.

MACDHUGHAILL, EACHANN M.

1929-30 'Beachdachadh mu Ainmhidhean na Gaidhealtachd. Earann II.' *Transactions of the Gaelic Society of Inverness* 35: 98–144.

MACDOUGALL, REV. JAMES.

1910 *Folk Tales and Fairy Lore*. Edinburgh.

MACGILLE SHEATHANAICH, NIALL.

1938 'Diura'. Eoghan Mac a Phi (deas.), *Am Measg nam Bodach.* Glaschu: 17–24.

MCGREGOR, RICHARD E.

1994 *Gregor Willox the Warlock.* Aberdeen.

MACILLEDHUIBH, RAGHNALL [= BLACK, RONALD].

1999 'Kelpie the Lowland Water-Horse'. *West Highland Free Press*, 21 May.

MACKENZIE, DONALD A.

1935 *Scottish Folk-Lore and Folk Life.* London.

[MACNICKLE], SISTER MARY DONATUS.

1934 *Beasts and Birds in the Lives of the Early Irish Saints.* Philadelphia.

Ó HÓGÁIN, DÁITHÍ.

1990 *Myth, Legend & Romance: An Encyclopædia of the Irish Folk Tradition.* London.

POLSON, ALEXANDER.

1926 *Our Highland Folklore Heritage*. Dingwall.

STEWART, REV. ALEXANDER.

1885 *'Twixt Ben Nevis and Glencoe.* Edinburgh.

STEWART, W. GRANT.

1823 *The Popular Superstitions and Festive Amusements of the Highlanders of Scotland.* Edinburgh.

STRÖMBÄCK, DAG.

1970 'Some Notes on the Nix in Older Nordic Tradition'. Jerome Mandel and Bruce A. Rosenberg (eds), *Medieval Literature and Folklore Studies: Essays in Honor of Francis Lee Utley.* New Brunswick: 245–56.

WATSON, WILLIAM J.

1926 *The History of the Celtic Place-Names of Scotland.* Edinburgh.

An Axle and Two Wheels: Material Culture and Memory in a Sutherland Emigrant Family of the Nineteenth Century

MARGARET A. MACKAY

In June 1831 a Mackay family group from Sutherland departed from Scotland on the ship *Cleopatra*, heading for a district of Upper Canada (later known as Canada West and the present-day province of Ontario), where others from their area had settled in the previous years. There are aspects of their story which may offer useful insights for the ethnologist. I have a personal as well as a professional interest in it, for these were my own Mackay forebears. And it is for personal as well as professional reasons that I offer this paper as a gesture of warm respect and gratitude to Dr John MacInnes, friend and colleague, for he too has Sutherland in his family history, and his work for the School of Scottish Studies took him there for field work and recording sessions on many occasions in the course of his long career.

The senior members of the family who took ship from the port of Cromarty were John Mackay (1785–1869) and Christena Munro (1788–1867). They had a family of nine children in total, born between 1807 and 1827, and all but one accompanied them to Canada that year, a daughter joining them the following year with her husband and two small children. The youngest of the children, Alexander, was in his fourth year in 1831. He is likely the oldest of the men in the centre of a Mackay family photograph taken on New Year's Day 1909. He died later that year.

Gaelic had faded from use among my older Mackay relations well before I knew any of them, but I did experience a hint of the tradition of naming the generations through the *sloinneadh* or pedigree, though in this instance in the reverse order, at a family reunion. An elderly relative, a descendant of another of the emigrant children of Christena and John, was having difficulty in placing my sister Alison and me, in spite of promptings by one of our older cousins. At last a smile of understanding spread over her face and she declared, 'Oh yes, you're Uncle Sandy's Willie's boy's girls!' We are indeed the daughters of Eoin, son of William, and grandson of Alexander.[1] William, our grandfather, is in the back row of the family photograph, wearing a top hat. He was by this time an ordained minister of the Presbyterian Church in Canada.

The custom of holding an annual family picnic appears to have started in 1904, following the celebration of the golden wedding anniversary of Alexander and his wife Jane Sutherland in 1903.

[1] In Gaelic my *sloinneadh* would be 'Mairead nic Eoin (1916–1993) 'ic Uilleam (1871–1952) 'ic Alasdair (1827–1909) 'ic Iain (1785–1869)'.

In later years, as family members came to be scattered across the North American continent and beyond, this gathering became a less frequent occurrence, but notable, well-attended ones took place in 1967, the centenary of Canadian Confederation in 1867, when relatives from Scotland took part, and in 1981, the 150th anniversary of the arrival of our ancestors in Canada.

These occasions quite naturally provided a focus for rehearsing features of the family saga, and in the 1930s, to mark the centenary of the family's arrival in Canada, it was decided to produce a booklet containing the by-then extensive family trees of the descendants of John Mackay and Christena Munro to which people who had known the emigrants and their children could contribute memories, their first-hand experiences as well as inherited lore. *From Highland Croft to Canadian Homestead 1831–1936* became a family history bible for the various branches of the family, and copies are treasured and consulted to this day. It is the source of much of the factual material here.

There is also, however, a real Bible in family hands, the Gaelic translation of 1803, given to John and Christena by their minister the Reverend Hector Allen before they left and inscribed as follows:

> *Do' Ian MacAoidh agus do a' thearlach, na h'uile maith! agus le deadh dhochus gu'm be an leabhran beannicht so, a treorachadh an ceum, agus a toirst comhfhurtachd dhoibh anns an tir a rhoghainn iad mar aite comhnuidh.*
>
> To John Mackay and family with best wishes in the earnest hope that this blessed book may be their guide and solace in the land of their adoption.

John's family home had been in the township of Torroble, near Lairg, where his father, John Mackay 'Catechist', was born in 1755 and lived with his wife Betsy Matheson and four children, of whom John was the eldest. The family's holding is today located at 92 Torroble. But before emigrating, he lived and farmed at Culrain in the parish of Kincardine, Ross-shire. His wife, with whom he first made acquaintance, it was said, at a communion season (a welcome occasion for meeting and courting), was a daughter of John Munro, tacksman of Balblair in the parish of Creich near Bonar Bridge.

Hector Allen was the author of the account of the parish of Kincardine which was published in volume 14 of the *New Statistical Account of Scotland* (1834–45). Allen's account refers to the fact that Alexander Ross, who served as a schoolmaster in the parish from 1822 to 1829, was ordained in the latter year to the 'Gaelic and English congregation at Dundas in Upper Canada', not far from present-day Toronto. It may well have been from earlier emigrants like Ross, and settlers who had preceded the Mackays to their exact destination two years earlier, that advice was received on what to expect in the new country, and what to bring with them for the journey and thereafter.

The *NSA* entry provides a picture of life in the parish around the time of the Mackays' departure. The following year, 1832, was to bring the Great Reform Act and also an outbreak of the dreaded disease of cholera. The years since publication of the *Old Statistical Account* in the 1790s had seen improvements in agriculture, communication, and housing. There were eight schools in the parish, a parochial library and a reading club; and a savings bank had recently been established in Tain. The district offered positive opportunities for development. On the other hand, the introduction of sheep had been 'turning whole straths ... into sheep-walks', and problems were arising because of non-resident proprietors. There had been agricultural depression in the 1820s, and evictions from the Novar lands at Culrain were no doubt creating an air of unease and uncertainty.[2]

[2] *New Statistical Account of Scotland,* Vol. XIV: Parish of Kincardine, Ross and Cromarty. Edinburgh: 403–433.

The Mackays took ship in June 1831 at the port of Cromarty in the Black Isle. The ship was the *Cleopatra,* commanded by Captain Morris – names embedded in family legend. She and another ship, the *Salamis*, seem to have replaced two other vessels, the *Clio* and the *Corsair,* which receive enthusiastic descriptions in advertisements in the *Inverness Courier* earlier that spring. They were swift, copper-bottomed, with airy tween-decks. But they failed to arrive to take the would-be emigrants from the north of Scotland to North America. Instead came – but not very swiftly – a vessel for which no such favourable account was given. The *Cleopatra* was expected to sail on June 1, but it was not until June 8 that the local agent, William Allan & Son, announced that she was hourly expected to arrive at Cromarty.

> NOTICE TO PASSENGERS FOR QUEBEC.
>
> THE FINE A. I. SHIP SALAMIS, Capt. Royal, is now at CROMARTY, and will positively Sail on the 25th inst., direct for QUEBEC. Passengers must therefore be on board a few days previous.
>
> The CLEOPATRA, Capt. Morris, may be expected at Cromarty about 25 h, and will Sail on the 1st June.
>
> These Vessels are in place of the CORSAIR and CLIO, formerly advertised, but could not be got ready in sufficient time. Experienced Surgeons are engaged for both.
>
> Agents, John Mowat, Jun., Cromarty; John Fraser, Dornoch; and William Gordon, Pittentrail, Rogart.
>
> Leith, 13th May, 1831.
>
> The Brig ZEALOUS, Capt. Bell, is also fitting out, and will call at Cromarty if required.

The sailing of the *Cleopatra* in 1831 was described in the *Inverness Courier* by the Cromarty-born folklorist, geologist and journalist Hugh Miller (1802–1856):

> *The* Cleopatra *as she swept past the town of Cromarty was greeted with three cheers by crowds of the inhabitants and the emigrants returned the salute but mingled with the dash of the waves and the murmur of the breeze their faint huzzas seemed rather sounds of wailing and lamentation than of a congratulatory farewell.*

Miller's words are now inscribed on a monument erected at the shore there in 2002 to mark the 200th anniversary of his birth, and to commemorate thirty-nine emigrant ships known to have sailed from its harbour in the 1830s and 1840s. Their names are listed from A (*Ami*) to Z (*Zephyr*) on a stone designed and carved by Richard Kindersley.

> NOTICE TO PASSENGERS
> *FOR AMERICA.*
>
> THE Ship CLEOPATRA is hourly expected at Cromarty, and will be despatched for Quebec direct, within three days of her arrival. The CORSAIR for Pictou and Quebec, and ROVER for Pictou, may [illegible] expected to Sail in all next week; and another suitable [illegible] for Pictou and Quebec is also fitting out, which [illegible] Sail between the 15th and 20th inst.
>
> For Passage apply to John Mowat, jun. Cromarty; John Fraser, Dornoch; and William Gordon, Pittentrail, Rogart.
>
> WILLIAM ALLAN & SON.
>
> Cromarty, 8th June, 1831.

One major feature of the emigration story of the Mackays, as it came down through the generations, is the length of time it took for them to reach their destination. In this period, the normal trans-Atlantic voyage in the summer months took between four and six weeks. But their journey, according to family tradition, took over twice the maximum – thirteen weeks and three days. Fortunately, they had been in a position to take with them on board more provisions than they expected to need themselves. The ship was becalmed and finally the passengers had to help the debilitated sailors bring the vessel into berth.

I have to admit that, for all my belief in the core veracity of oral sources, I doubted this detail. Could they have survived a crossing of that duration? I decided to put the tradition to the test. With the help of the maritime historian A. W. H. Pearson at the National Maritime Museum at Greenwich and consultation of *Lloyd's List* and the *Quebec Gazette*, I was able to ascertain that the *Cleopatra,* a brig of 267 tons built at Whitby in 1817 and owned by Dickens & Co of London, arrived at

Quebec on 8 September 1831. The family tale, one of endurance and fortitude, was thereby confirmed and the process of oral transmission vindicated.

From Quebec in Lower Canada they had to make their way by river boat up the St Lawrence River into Lake Ontario. Their goal was a township called Zorra in Upper Canada, now Ontario, where a community of emigrants from Sutherland had already been established. Zorra was surveyed in 1820 and organised as a municipality in 1822, and two Mackay brothers were amongst the earliest settlers, encouraging others to join them, amongst whom were a group who had arrived in 1829. My Mackays should have disembarked at the Lake Ontario port of Hamilton and travelled north from there into the interior. But before reaching Hamilton, on the quayside at York (now Toronto), they heard people speaking of a township called Thorah and mistook this for Zorra, an easy error for Gaelic-speakers to make. They let the boat go on before realising their mistake, but before setting off for Thorah, which was located to the north and east of York. Their trek through the bush to join the others in Zorra was thus extended by many miles.

In the 1970s, I was undertaking fieldwork among the descendants of emigrants who left the island of Tiree at a similar period, and this research happened to take me to the township of Thorah. When people there heard my surname, I was at once told the story of a Mackay family from Sutherland who had done exactly the same thing but had realised their mistake too late. They had journeyed all the way to Thorah and, unable to face the lengthy trek across country west to Zorra, decided to stay where they were, sole Sutherland settlers with a surname that was rare in a community of families from Mull, Tiree and other parts of Argyll. Once again an oral tradition was confirmed, in this case by the chance discovery of a parallel family experience.

As well as extra provisions for the journey, John and Christena Mackay took with them on board the *Cleopatra* an axle and two wheels. In over thirty years of taking an interest in, and conducting focused research on, emigrant traditions, culture transfer and adaptation, often using family histories as a tool, I have never found an instance parallel to this, though I have gathered references to many other items taken from Scotland to Canada. A drinking horn, a shoemaker's lasts, a hay knife, a *slabhraidh* (pot chain or hook), garden seeds, a spinning wheel carefully transported in a feather tick – these and other items are referred to in family traditions I have examined and, in some cases, are lovingly preserved by descendants of the emigrants.

This detail in the family story tells us not only about needs in the New World but also about features of the 'Old Country' (a usage which I often heard from another family member, my maternal grandmother, who emigrated from Badenoch immediately after the First World War). An axle and two wheels could be described as relatively modern technology in the 1830s. There were parts of Sutherland and Ross-shire where a creel on the back, a highland pony with a pack-saddle, a slide-car or travois, or a sledge would have been the only means of moving items any distance, this determined by the terrain and the presence or absence of roads (Fenton 1984a).

Four-wheeled wagons and two-wheeled carts, the latter often known as a 'Scotch' or 'Leith' cart, were making an appearance by the end of the 18th century where the provision of roads allowed. Correspondence between estate officials in the Sutherland Papers in the National Library of Scotland in 1828 reports that

> Wherever Roads have been introduced there is an immediate and evident Change in the habits and manners of the people. The Smallest lotter Considers his establishment incomplete unless he has a Cart and many when their lots are not Sufficient to Support both deprive themselves of the luxury of a Cow to be able to Keep a Horse.[3]

The cart in question may have been the type known in Scots as a 'tumbler', a light box-cart with a pair of wheels and axle that revolved together (Fenton 1984b: 128). Wagons or wains were noted in the *OSA* (1790s) in parishes around the Dornoch Firth and into Ross, the Black Isle and

[3] National Library of Scotland, Sutherland Estate Papers, Dep. 313/1471, G. Gunn to J. Loch, 12 May 1828.

Moray on farms influenced by agricultural improvement, and 'oxen wains' were in use in the parishes of Kiltearn, Kincardine (Nigg) and Avoch.

Though Allen reported that 'the parish is not blessed with the convenience of good roads', there was an exception in the road from the church of Kincardine to Ardgay, and the means of communication were ample as there was a post office at Bonar Bridge and a daily post, the mail coming from Tain in a double-seated gig and arriving every morning at the Balnagown Arms Inn, Ardgay. A Parliamentary Bridge had been erected by Thomas Telford in 1812 to span a narrow part of the Dornoch Firth. John Mackay, who was able to take a generous supply of provisions on the *Cleopatra*, was obviously also able to ensure that he and his family had this potential means of transport at their disposal on arrival. We cannot know if he was advised by correspondence from earlier settlers that such would be useful, or whether it was his own ingenuity which prompted him to take this with him.

Two wheels and an axle would take up considerable room on ship-board, but they provided the basis of a means of transport immediately they reached the other side. A platform, box or other superstructure was constructed, and an ox acquired to draw the cart. By this means they arrived in Zorra. Because theirs is reputed to have been the first ox in the community, and because nicknames or by-names are necessary in order to distinguish families in a place where many have the same surname, they were ever after designated the 'Ox Mackays'.

The Mackays took up land in the township adjacent to Zorra, called East Nissouri, in the county of Oxford. The nearest village is Thamesford and not far away is London, now a major city in Western Ontario. The surveyors were, as one can easily guess, Englishmen, and this may account for the fact that the main centre in Zorra was named on the map as 'Embro' (= Edinburgh) rather than 'Embo', a Sutherland name preferred by the settlers. In time the map name was accepted as correct and it remains Embro to this day.

Written records are scant for the early years. There are details of land transactions in the township papers, and by mid-century an agricultural census detailing the amount of land broken for cultivation, crops, stock and other produce, and a nominal census as well. But we are fortunate in having an eye-witness account of their community provided by journal entries kept by a missionary, the Reverend John Carruthers, who was travelling through the area in the autumn of 1832 conducting services wherever he was welcomed. He preached in the Mackays' locality and noted in his diary, which he published several decades later, that he took his departure from London, crossing a branch of the Thames River, to a township 'not yet much opened from the forest, though the settlers are labouring hard and onward to obtain bread for themselves and families'. On 2 October, a Tuesday, he took a service, describing the scene as follows:

> This was one of the first Presbyterian services in the woods here and the hearts of the people were filled with gladness. The Psalms which were sung reverberated in the forest, filling their souls with joy as they remembered the days of old in their native land, when they associated with those who kept the solemn holy days (Carruthers, 27).

John Mackay may have been helping to lead the singing; he is known to have been a precentor in his local congregation later. The nature of popular piety in Sutherland and Easter Ross provides the backdrop to religious expression in the new homeland, where family worship, Sabbath observance, the communion season lasting from Thursday to Monday, and catechising came to be practised as they had been at home. A local history published in 1900, noted below, includes memories of these. The metrical paraphrase 'O God of Bethel' came to be regarded as a family hymn, and was regularly used at gatherings and funerals.

Carruthers returned at the end of January 1833, by which time a rough log structure had been erected to provide shelter for worship purposes, with benches to seat 200 people but no doors, windows or fire. On Sunday the 27th of that month, he conducted a service. Metrical Psalm 122 and

Paraphrase 61 were sung. He makes no comment on the language used, but he was not a Gaelic-speaker. The following year a Gaelic-speaking minister, Donald MacKenzie (1798–1884), was ordained by the Presbytery of Dingwall in the Synod of Ross, and was inducted into the Zorra charge in 1835.

Glengarry County in eastern Ontario, with its early history arising from the settlement there of Highland Loyalists leaving the USA after the Declaration of Independence, joined by many more directly from the north-west highlands in a series of well-documented waves, and its strong and continuing Highland and Gaelic culture and identity, came to assume an iconic status within the consciousness of Canadians of Highland descent. Glengarry had its famous authors, most notably Charles Gordon, who took the pen-name 'Ralph Connor' for his novels based on the exploits of Glengarry people and whose father had been a minister in Zorra for a time, but others such as Grace Campbell as well. These brought the story of Glengarry to a wide audience in the twentieth century.

In its own way, the smaller district in western Ontario, composed of Zorra and the townships adjacent, gained something of this iconic status, too. It had its heroes, amongst them the tug-of-war team, skilled in a harvest-time sport which became a competitive one as Highland games developed in Scotland, Canada and elsewhere, who brought back the world championship trophy from the Chicago World's Fair of 1893. And while Zorra's authors were not as acclaimed as the Glengarry novelists, they nevertheless put its history on record in works such as William Alexander MacKay's *Pioneer Life in Zorra* of 1899 and W. D. McIntosh's *One Hundred Years in the Zorra Church* of 1930.

The church played an important role in this as in many emigrant Scottish communities, and the Zorra congregation came to be notable for the number of candidates it sent into the ministry as clergymen or missionaries. Another publication by W. A. MacKay documents in sketches the achievements of Zorra men in a range of fields, and exhibits a sense of local pride in its title, *Zorra Boys at Home and Abroad, or, How to Succeed* (1900). Amongst the most notable of these was George Leslie MacKay, the first missionary to be sent abroad by the Presbyterian Church in Canada. His destination was present-day Taiwan, then known as Formosa, where he founded Oxford College (so named because of the donations towards its creation received from his home county in Canada and not for any other pretensions). His wife was a local woman, and he regarded Formosa as his home for the rest of his life. His museum of artefacts relating to the natural and cultural history of Formosa bears witness to his interest in all aspects of life there, as do donations to the collections of the Royal Ontario Museum in Toronto; his publication *From Far Formosa* of 1896 was the first ethnographic study of that island in English and a pioneering work.

Scotland drew some of their descendants back, for study or for permanent settlement. One of these was the Reverend Angus Mackay (1854–1939), a son of John Mackay and Christena Munro's daughter Grace and her husband Donald Mackay. With his wife Annie Mark, from New Pitsligo in Aberdeenshire, he took his family to Scotland in 1905, where he was Free Church minister in Kingussie until his death in 1939. Two of their children were Free Church missionaries, the Reverend John Calvin Mackay in Peru, and Dr Annie Mackay in India, as was a grand-daughter who carried on her aunt's medical work there.

I myself remember Dr Annie and her sister Catherine, when they were very elderly and then resident in Inverness, holding hands and reciting for me in a rhythmical fashion a family chant recalled from their childhood: 'We're Highland-Lowland-Scotch-Canadian-Presbyterian-Grits' – 'Grits' being the Canadian term for supporters of the Liberal Party. Angus Mackay wrote occasional articles in the Free Church magazine *The Monthly Record* based on the life experienced in the early days in Canada by his forebears, and thus supplemented anything the family may have written to relations themselves in taking their story back to Scotland.

There is an extensive literature on the role of objects in focusing memory and triggering oral accounts relating to their making, function or ownership. The Swedish ethnologist Åse Ljungström has provided an analytical model which connects an artefact, a narrator, people in the past and the listener (Ljungström: 81). In this case, arising from a documentation project, the artefact itself was present. But I would argue that the memory of an artefact can operate in a similar way. I must confess that with the help of a cousin, I once scoured the outbuildings on the farm worked by my father's uncle George, called by the name 'Maple Springs' from the stand of maple trees which provided maple syrup and maple sugar for many years, in the hope that we might just find vestiges of that cart made from the axle and two wheels, but to no avail. No doubt it was in use until no longer functional and then disposed of.

But the very memory of those items, reinforced by re-tellings in print or in oral form, has equally acted as a focus of identity, the mere mention serving to unite members of the same family group in an embrace of familiarity. Their physical presence is not required.

In the story of the 'Ox Mackays', oral accounts were over the years captured and transmitted in print, to be spoken about again on appropriate occasions, in the same interplay of written and oral forms of transmission that would have been familiar to our medieval ancestors. In its own way, it shows the contribution which the micro-genre of family lore can make to our understanding of human interaction past and present.

ACKNOWLEDGEMENT

The author acknowledges with gratitude the help of Dr Malcolm Bangor-Jones in the preparation of this article.

SOURCES

ALLEN, HECTOR.

1834-45 *New Statistical Account of Scotland,* XIV: Parish of Kincardine, Ross and Cromarty. Edinburgh.

ANONYMOUS.

n.d. *From Highland Croft to Canadian Homestead 1831–1936.* [Genealogical history of the family of John Mackay and Christena Munro Mackay.] Privately printed.

ASH, MARINELL.

1991 *This Noble Harbour: A History of the Cromarty Firth.* James Macaulay and Margaret A. Mackay (eds.). Invergordon/Edinburgh.

BORLEY, LESTER (ED.)

2002 *Hugh Miller in Context: The Cromarty Years and the Edinburgh Years.* Cromarty.

2003 *Celebrating the Life and Times of Hugh Miller: Scotland in the Early 19th Century – Ethnography and Folklore, Geology and Natural History, Church and Society.* Cromarty.

CARRUTHERS, JOHN.

1861 *Retrospect of Thirty-Six Years Residence in Canada West.* Hamilton, Ontario.

FENTON, ALEXANDER.

1984a 'Wheelless Transport in Northern Scotland'. Alexander Fenton and Geoffrey Stell (eds), *Loads and Roads in Scotland and Beyond.* Edinburgh: 105–123.

1984b 'The Distribution of Carts and Wagons'. Alexander Fenton and Geoffrey Stell (eds), *Loads and Roads in Scotland and Beyond.* Edinburgh: 124–140.

JENKINS, J. GERAINT.

1958–9 'Two-Wheeled Carts.' *Gwerin* 2: 162–175.

LJUNGSTRÖM, ÅSE.

1989–90 'Craft Artefacts: Keys to the Past.' *Folk Life* 28: 75–89.

MACKAY, GEORGE LESLIE.

1986 *From Far Formosa*. New York.

MACKAY, WILLIAM ALEXANDER.

1899 *Pioneer Life in Zorra.* Toronto.

1900 *Zorra Boys at Home and Abroad, or, How to Succeed.* Toronto. [Available as Project Gutenberg Canada ebook 550].

MCINTOSH, W. D.

1930 *One Hundred Years in the Zorra Church.* Toronto.

From Stornoway to 'Mortuary View': A Memoir

COLIN SCOTT MACKENZIE

I was born in Stornoway in 1938 – the year of Munich – in the house where I still live. The world in which I was brought up was a tiny enclave of monoglot, or apparently monoglot, English speakers surrounded by a large rural area whose population still spoke Gaelic – a language of which I was, for much of my childhood and adolescence, largely and woefully ignorant. At the time of my birth, and for the next couple of decades, Stornoway was undergoing one of its periodic lurches away from its Gaelic roots. Those of its denizens who imagined themselves sophisticated tended, often somewhat snootily, to disdain those roots – passing by Gaelic-speaking citizens as it were 'on the other side'.

My parents, however, were of a different sort. They were both university graduates at a time when university attendance was a privilege of the few, and they were well-read and relatively comfortably off. My mother was a fluent and literate Gaelic speaker. She was always supportive of the language, and a life-member of An Comunn Gàidhealach to boot. She had certainly passed her Higher Gaelic at the Nicolson Institute, and may have attended some classes in the language at University in the 20s. Even so, she never spoke Gaelic to either of her children – any more than she did the classical Greek with which she was also familiar.

I am sure she had no positive intention of suppressing Gaelic, but she probably imagined that, if we were interested, we could pick it up as we went along, just as she had done so easily as a child in the early 1900s. Although my grandmother's first language had been Gaelic, my mother's father was born in Inverness to a Highland family which had long since lost its facility with the language. While his work as a chemist taught him an adequate amount of 'Stornoway Gaelic' (he could talk quite fluently in his shop to concerned *cailleachs* – or so it appeared to me), the language was not spoken in my grandparents' home, though they all presumably could converse in it at a pinch. During my mother's childhood, a hundred years ago and more, it was still possible to pick up Gaelic from other children on the streets of Stornoway – something which my mother clearly had done, and which she imagined we also would do as a matter of course. But by the 1940s this was no longer possible – at least not on the street where I lived.

While I always knew that my mother spoke something called 'Gaelic', I had thought of my father, who had been born and raised in Stornoway, as an English speaker, pure and simple. I have, since he passed on, learned that he could actually converse in Gaelic, when necessity arose: born in 1893, he would have needed the language to get by in Stornoway at any level. Even in 1893, however, there would already have been a small nucleus of determined North British monoglot English speakers resident there. I don't know if his father, my paternal grandfather, who died a couple of years before I was born, could speak Gaelic. He was a lawyer and a classicist, and I strongly suspect that he must have had some inkling of the language, having been born and brought up in Stornoway in the 1860s, when the vast majority of the citizenry must have been Gaels. His mother, however, came from Inverness; and though my great-grandfather had been born (1800) and raised in Stornoway, they had spent their married life in South Carolina, before the American Civil War drove them out, and I suspect that the language of their family was English.

My paternal grandmother, who predeceased my grandfather by a month or two, was also of Stornoway parentage, but she had been born and raised in Liverpool. I believe she was very musical and apparently took a lively interest in opera and operetta, but Gaelic songs and traditions never seemed to feature in her repertoire. I reckon she had no Gaelic, and therefore – whatever Grandpa professed – the language would not have been spoken in their home either.

All that said, my father must have gained some facility in Gaelic quite apart from what he would have picked up from other children. He survived the Gallipoli campaign in 1915 with the Left Section of the Ross Mountain Battery, an artillery unit recruited largely from Lewis and, to a lesser degree, from still-Gaelic-speaking Wester Ross, in which Gaelic was the *lingua franca*. Even 'the Londoners' (*i.e.* recruits from anywhere south of the border who were drafted in as casualty replacements) had to acquire more than a word or two of Gaelic just in order to survive. I suspect, however, that my father's grasp of the language never went much beyond basic conversation. As a professional in later life, he was probably able to put at ease the elderly near-monoglot Gaelic speakers whose wills he had been called in to draft, but maybe not much more. He never spoke any kind of Gaelic to me, nor did I ever hear my parents conversing in it, other than using the odd word here and there. Even so, I am quite sure that neither of them felt any animosity whatsoever towards Gaelic – quite the contrary in fact.

None of my immediate pals spoke Gaelic either, though much later on, in middle-age, I found out to my considerable surprise that many acquaintances in my 'townie' peer group were perfectly able to do so – or at, the very least, understood it perfectly.[1] They never spoke the language in my hearing, however. By the 1940s, Gaelic in Stornoway (though not yet in rural districts) had become unfashionable and restricted to home use. It was used when speaking to Grannie, but not much otherwise.

My own awareness of Gaelic came about because we had, when I was small, resident housemaids to help in the house, and occasionally I would encounter my mother talking to them in a language I did not understand. Obviously 'big-ears' was not meant to understand! But I was intrigued. It bothered me, when I found out how widespread this linguistic ability was, that I was unable to join in the fun. Eventually I asked my maternal grandmother if she would teach me Gaelic. Poor Grandma! She was a lovely lady who I knew was fluent and literate in Gaelic and a keen supporter of the language. She, too, was a life member of An Comunn. She had been a teacher in Lochs and Point in the 1880s and '90s, and later had run her own business in Stornoway before WW1. She was up to-date in most things all her life, but she was not aware of how Gaelic even then was sliding into desuetude in the town. She just laughed at me. 'Go and ask the boys on the street to speak to you – you'll soon learn,' she said. She did not believe me when I said I did not know any other children who spoke the language. The new kids on the block no longer spoke it. So although I got all the love and affection I could have possibly hoped for from Grandma, I got no practical help from her in learning Gaelic.

I then asked my father and mother for assistance. Do not misunderstand me – it was not that I had a burning ambition in that connection bothering me day and night: far from it. I did not think about my linguistic disability very often, but every now and again it would surface. My parents took me seriously, and having obviously thought about the matter, asked me if I would go and spend a summer with a family they had identified who would give me a good grounding in the tongue. I would then have been ten or eleven years of age. I simply said I would and waited for the call. And waited. It never came, and I never knew why. Many years later, recalling this episode with my mother, I asked why nothing had transpired. I was told, much to my chagrin, that apparently I had not shown enough enthusiasm, so the idea was not pursued. I thought that was so unfair! I had been taught not to pester for things, and the misunderstanding still rankles. It would have been so easy

[1] These Gaelic 'understanders', if I may call them that, had a pretty good grasp of English and they distinguished easily and accurately between English, Gaelic and even the Stornoway patois which had grown up along the quays during the town's heyday as a herring port. They spoke clearly, and when speaking English could easily be understood wherever they went. That may no longer be the case, as too many of the island monoglot English-speakers of today have a much poorer grasp of English grammar than had their bi-glot ancestors, coupled with what has become a sloppy and almost indecipherable vocal delivery.

then to learn another language while my grey-matter was still sponge-like in its ability to absorb new information.

Still, my lack of any command of Gaelic was, as I said, not a matter which occupied my daily thoughts. It remained, however, in the background as an irritant. I recall being asked, in the qualifying class of the Nicolson Primary, to fill in a form stating what language subjects I would like to take up in the Secondary Department. Out of a hundred or more pupils moving up that year (many of whom, I now realise, would have been at least Gaelic 'understanders'), only two of us – Marco Capaldi, scion of a local restaurant family, was the other – sought to take Gaelic and French. Marco's pragmatic and practical interest was understandable enough, but mine was obviously regarded as an aberration. In the event, neither of our requests was honoured, and Latin and French is what we got.

While Marco and I might have been alone in wanting to do something about our lack of Gaelic at the time, I should say that subsequently *every single* monoglot English-speaking Stornowegian that I have ever spoken to from that period resented the fact that they had gone through school without being taught Gaelic, and bemoaned the fact that the language had not otherwise been passed on to them – not that many of them were sufficiently concerned to do anything about it. We were in the middle of a period of language change which was transforming island society, and there was little or nothing that those most affected could do about it. Parents had increasingly subscribed to the idea that Gaelic ceased to have any value once one sailed out of Stornoway Harbour.

Gaelic-speakers in the town had lost confidence, and the language itself had lost status even within its own community. Even those who wanted to learn found few facilities to help: There were no classes, other than for fluent speakers who wanted to learn how to read and write. There were few teach-yourself books available in the 1940s and '50s, and those that were available, such as *Gaelic Without Groans*, were of limited value. The few bakelite record courses available were very expensive and of little practical use without an easily-accessible milieu in which to practice. Unless one is immersed in it, it is almost impossible to acquire any language to any degree of fluency, and it becomes easy to lose interest. When most people are bilingual and can switch easily between languages, the earnest learner can, alas, often be regarded as an irritant.

At the age of fourteen, I left Stornoway to complete my schooling in Edinburgh. Gaelic was far from my thoughts. However, one of my earliest friends in the city was a big, clever lad from Broadford in Skye, Iain Baird MacInnes, whose grasp of Gaelic was, I found, no better than mine. Stornoway was, obviously, not the only place suffering from language change at the time. During the 1950s, as I found out later, Gaelic was melting away like snow off the proverbial dyke not just in Stornoway but throughout much of the *Gàidhealtachd.* Iain and I would occasionally exchange the few words we had picked up just to demonstrate our difference (and perhaps our superiority); but we both had other fish to fry, and our Gaelic did not progress at all. I fitted in fairly well amongst the English and South American lads who formed a high proportion of my contemporaries at school, and did not worry overmuch about the sore gap in my education.

When I went to Edinburgh University, however, I found that, as a Lewisman, I was generally *expected* to know Gaelic. Although I felt this expectation as an ever-present reproach, I still failed to do much about it. For some reason I came across few Gaelic-speakers in my student peregrinations. At that time there were more than ten thousand students at Edinburgh University. They were spread out all over the place, and unless one went out of one's way to find fellow islanders one did not necessarily meet them. Even when, in the hope of finding some kindred spirits, I one year attended the Highland Society's Annual Ball, I found few actual Gaels at that particular stramash. It had, alas, acquired a reputation for disorderliness, and therefore attracted too many of the wrong sort, most of whom had probably never been north of Queensferry. So while I enjoyed the experience, it was not really my style, and I never bothered to attend the other Highland Society meetings where I might have met more congenial friends. Those in my year whom I knew from Stornoway were usually heads down in pursuit of the 1st Class Honours degrees they largely obtained, and our paths did not cross.

Aware of my linguistic shortcomings, however, I enrolled in a Gaelic evening class being taught in Boroughmuir school by an island teacher. Perhaps an abler scholar might have made something of it, but the acquisition of a language as an adult, when the synapses have closed, is a skill not given to everyone. What I do recall noticing was that the class was full of very old people – at least 30 years of age, some 40 and even older! 'What one earth do these ancients think they are doing?' thought I to myself. 'They'll never live long enough to be able to use an additional language! Why are they bothering?'

Ah well! The arrogance of youth! But I was also beginning to think, 'What on earth am *I* doing?' I was getting nowhere fast, and I still knew nothing about the background of Gaelic, about its literature or traditions. It was for me merely a language like Esperanto or Interlingua or Solresol or whatever – just another means of communication, though one possessed of some fine tunes! I knew much more French, which I could converse in not too badly, if haltingly – and which I have scarcely ever used. In other words, my ignorance was still woeful, and I was about to give up the struggle. That, however, was when I had my Damascene moment.

I had by then acquired a law degree, and the world was my oyster. I regarded myself as having acquired some knowledge of the world – perhaps even some sophistication. Suddenly, however, life started to get complicated. Throughout my undergraduate years I had always shared a flat with other students, and my last flat had been a happy arrangement. The flat was very well-organised and orderly – we had rotas for cleaning (to which we adhered) and some of us even cooked – and we got on very well together. But when a couple of the lads graduated and departed, the rest of us could not afford to keep the flat on and I had, to my dismay, to look for another billet in a hurry, for I still had my apprenticeship to complete and no long summer vac for me! I had friends in various other student flats where I dossed down for a few weeks, but I could not expect to impose upon them for ever.

I was by that time about as far removed from Gaelic as I ever would be. The world beckoned. I was having a good time and enjoying life pretty well. Wine was just starting to become relatively plentiful: a bottle of *Entre Deux Mers* only cost 7/6d and was quite sufficient to bring as a present to a party-thrower. I became used to wearing a dinner jacket – even occasionally a white tie and tails – and I probably thought I was no end of a card. This homeless interlude in the uneven tenor of my ways was no fun.

I had mentioned my predicament to a fellow law apprentice, Ian S. W. Donaldson, and I was delighted when he told me that he was leaving his flat and that there might be a place in it for me in his stead, if his two flatmates agreed. So it eventually came to pass that, after I had spent the first few weeks sleeping on a Li-Lo in front of the sitting-room fireplace, Ian at last departed and I could move into his room. What an eye-opener my new lodgings turned out to be.

To start with, the flat's location was a mystery. Lauriston Terrace it was – no. 3, I think. Everyone in Edinburgh could guide you to Lauriston Place or Lauriston Gardens, but the Terrace was *terra incognita*. Even taxi-drivers were baffled. The flat itself was located at the top of a tenement block at the west end of the vast Royal Infirmary complex. A pedestrian close leading from Lauriston Place is still the only means of access to this building, a fact which probably accounts for its anonymity.

Following the departure of Ian Donaldson, who later followed a successful career as a solicitor, my flat-mates were Jimmy Porter, a music student who was later to become Professor of Music in Aberdeen, and John MacInnes, a young lecturer in the School of Scottish Studies in George Square – the last named being, as I later found out to my considerable surprise, a first cousin of my former school-friend Iain Baird MacInnes. The flat itself was not very prepossessing. Everything about it was well-worn, if not worn-out, and to my eye little housekeeping was being carried on. Any port in a storm, I thought. If it proved too uncomfortable I would have time to make alternative arrangements – which, however, is not to say that I was not properly grateful for the harbour I was being offered. I never met the landlord, and I never saw an electricity or gas bill, but just stumped up my modest share whenever Jimmy – who I *think* was the principal tenant – asked me.

From the window above the kitchen sink we could see across a jumble of back-yards to the rear of a nurses' hostel on Lauriston Gardens, the uncurtained windows of which may have occasionally provided light entertainment as we washed our dishes. Because we tended to approach this task only when the sink was full and we had otherwise run out of crockery, I cannot myself vouch for the truth of 'eyewitness' accounts. I have, however, no trouble remembering the opposite view from our flat's sitting-room windows, overlooking certain workshops connected to the Infirmary, including its mortuary. Shortly after I arrived on the scene we took to calling our flat 'Mortuary View', and the name has stuck for those of us who were there.

While we may not initially have paid much attention to that group of anonymous sheds visible below, a change in hospital management policy brought them into sudden focus. The Royal Infirmary decided to do away with its pianos. Until then, every ward had its own piano. Whether they were originally intended for the use, on the Sabbath, of visiting bands of evangelicals, or for the more secular entertainment of inmates, the ward pianos were seemingly deemed by medical staff to harbour a huge variety of germs and bugs, and they simply had to go in the name of general sanitation. Once that decision had been made, all the hospital's pianos were, one after the other, taken for disposal to the yard outside the mortuary.

While deceased patients and dead pianos both followed the same route up to that point, the transition afforded the latter was anything but discreet and peaceful. Every weekday we awoke at what seemed like 5 a.m. to a dreadful cacophony from down below. There a manic workman performed last rites on the day's keyboard. Once he had vented his wrath, others would join him, with axes and sledgehammers, until, with many jangles and twangs, they had reduced the instrument to its constituent parts. It is no easy thing to destroy a piano in this fashion, and they tended to deal with only one piano per day, so the litany of musical abuse lofted itself skyward for a considerable number of days or weeks. How the other residents of the block stood for this auditory mayhem I do not know. Presumably the nursing staff in the Infirmary did not mind – they would have wakened their patients at first light anyway. I do recall, however, that Jimmy Porter was at the time writing the score for an orchestral piece to be played at the Edinburgh Festival. I often wondered if the dawn chorus helped or hindered him.

Although I had a number of friends in Edinburgh, my summertime move into 'Mortuary View' meant that most of the people I would ordinarily have socialised with were out of town. My seeming lonesome state did not bother me at all – it would only have been temporary anyway – but John immediately ensured that I was included in whatever ploy he and his group had planned, and I was happy to join in. I thus became involved with a crowd of intelligent, well-educated Gaels, mostly from Skye and Uist, who introduced me to a world of Gaelic culture – a world through which I had previously only sleep-walked. I was fascinated and totally hooked. Here at last I was among a body of Gaelic literati and cognoscenti who could supply what my own education had not. Being a friend of John's meant that I was tolerated, even when my lack of Gaelic became painfully obvious. They all knew who I was – they called me *Cailean Òg* ('Young Colin', as I then was) – and took pains to explain whatever it was they were saying, especially when they had said it in Gaelic.

John himself was a natural and gifted teacher – though obviously in my case an unintentional one – but his comments and expositions on our Celtic background and on matters of Gaelic history generally have stuck with me ever since. He recognised the importance of what he was doing in the School of Scottish Studies, and was able to pass on to others and certainly to me the sense of that importance. Through his influence, I began to appreciate that the Gaelic language came in different registers, and that the register employed by my new friends was a high one, as far removed from ordinary conversational Gaelic as street English is from that spoken in most drawing-rooms. John was the first person I heard point out just how important each language is in itself – how every language can present a different and probably untranslatable slant on the world. Gaelic itself is resoundingly different in philosophic approach from English. I recall John explaining to me how in English a swain might pledge eternal troth to his inamorata 'for as long as *he* lived'. In Gaelic, the poet, as in the love-song *Duan a' Chìobair* by Donald Campbell, could say much more pragmatically 'for as long as *you* live, I'll seek no one else'! Is that not a significantly different point of view?

John's circle was wide-ranging. He seemed to know everybody, including even then a large number of our Scottish savants, among whom he was always warmly received. In his company I met Norman McCaig, Sydney Goodsir Smith, Christopher Grieve (Hugh McDiarmaid), and George Mackay Brown. I met Professor Angus Matheson of Glasgow University, and his equally brilliant brother the Rev. William Matheson. All the conversations were brilliant, and albeit that my own participation was negligible, some fifty years on I still remember some of the topics discussed.

As I frequently called at the School of Scottish Studies in John's company, I was there introduced to a whole host of academics from Kenneth Jackson and Hamish Henderson downwards. In particular, John was very supportive of Sorley (Somhairle) MacLean, whose work he felt was not just of Gaelic or Scottish importance but of European stature – higher than that of any English writer or poet of the time. This judgement has been gathering in strength and acceptance ever since. I met Somhairle several times, and particularly recall one dark and stormy winter's night, driving John and some others to Plocton where Somhairle was headmaster. There we were royally entertained in the schoolhouse by the great man himself and his family – including two young daughters who played the *clarsach* delightfully for us – the first time I had ever heard the instrument which was then starting its revival.

In this fashion, I became aware of a whole world of Gaelic culture which was inaccessible to those who spoke only English. To the extent that this situation has now been reversed it is, I firmly believe, thanks in large part to the work of people like John and his colleagues who, over the years, collected a huge amount of stories, songs and oral culture as part of their researches at the School. They were active just at a time when oral tradition was vanishing fast, and the School has done tremendous work in preserving so much for future generations.

After I left Edinburgh, John and I kept in touch. Whenever he came to Lewis we would make contact, and I often acted as his chauffeur when he was carrying out his island researches. He was fascinated by *na Torgairean* – our Gaelic Travellers as they are commonly called in English these days – and he carried out detailed research into their way of life and their languages. He was particularly interested in the Travellers' secret language, the *Beurla Reagairt*, which he told me has nothing, bar a very few borrowings, to do with the language of the Gypsies. Our Travellers are not Romanys – they are seagulls of our own shore; and while there would, of course, have been tinsmiths, probably itinerant, ever since the bronze age, I recall John telling me of the Travellers' own belief that some of them were descended from members of tacksman families who had suffered after the Jacobite Risings, among them Stewarts of Appin or, before then, members of the Clan MacGregor.

Nowadays, the former Hebridean travelling families have all but vanished back to their mainland origins, or have been absorbed into the settled community. At that time, however, several clans still occupied semi-permanent camps on the outskirts of Stornoway, and elsewhere in the islands they kept up the tradition of going on the road in the summer months. I remember going with John to visit Pàdruig Sheonaidh Stiùbhart, a former Traveller who had been allowed to build a permanent home for himself and his family outside the village of Barvas in Lewis. Pàdruig Sheonaidh's house, though built of concrete blocks and stone and wood, was constructed on the 'tent principle' and, as John pointed out to me, while it looked small enough from the outside, once you were inside you could swear you were in a large and commodious tent.

John MacInnes helped me – as he has helped so many – become aware of the vast cultural riches that exist in the Gaelic language. I learned a huge amount from him, possibly through some kind of intellectual osmosis. Although nowadays many more translations of Gaelic literature and lore are available than was the case fifty years ago, I remain convinced that in order to appreciate such translations one must have a reasonable reading knowledge of the original language – and a speaking knowledge, too, if possible. While I am no linguist, my friendship with John so fired my enthusiasm for Gaelic that I kept at it, albeit in fits and starts. My best opportunity for self-improvement came when I went to live for some twelve years in the Northern Isles where, with slightly more free time to myself, I came across two Gaelic speakers, one in each archipelago, who were willing to speak face to face to me for hours at a time. It was thus that I at last managed to acquire the rudiments of conversational Gaelic. I am still anything but fluent, but I can now make myself generally understood, and I am determined to be completely fluent by my 100th birthday. In the meantime, I too have become a life member of An Comunn!

It is now more than fifty years since I heard John lay blame for the destruction of Gaelic on the Education (Scotland) Act of 1872, which required that children throughout the *Gàidhealtachd* be educated in English alone. I had been brought up to believe, along with the majority of my fellow Gaels, that success in the wider world depended upon our willingness to embrace English and that the 1872 Act was a 'good thing'. Almost too late, it is being increasingly realised that those who learned English while retaining their Gaelic had the best of both worlds, as someone who is truly bilingual always has an intellectual advantage. Language and culture are inextricably linked, and there are, after all, many places in the world where languages exist side by side. Maybe there can be a revival – I sincerely hope so – but the fight will be long and hard. In rural Lewis, at least, there is still a glimmer of hope.

Luchd na Gàidhlig and the 'detritus of a nation'

WILSON McLEOD

In his doctoral thesis, with its elegantly straightforward title 'Gaelic Poetry', John MacInnes argued as follows:

> The Gaels in Scotland for most of our history have been a nation....I know of no more adequate term to express the particular sense of identity possessed by the Gaels through the vicissitudes of Scottish history.... During the last two and a half centuries the processes of decline have produced what can only be regarded now as the detritus of a nation (1975: 1; see also MacInnes 1978: 436–7).

A comprehensive analysis of this provocative claim would require an extensive discussion of the nature of 'nations' in the pre-modern era as well as the period since 1789, taking into account the work of scholars such as Anthony Smith and Ernest Gellner (Smith 2004, 2010; Gellner 1983). What constitutes, or constituted, a nation at different stages in history, and to what extent can the Gaels' collective experience and sense of connectedness, and the social, political and economic structures that underpinned them, be framed in 'national' terms? How to interpret MacInnes' term 'detritus', which calls to mind Friedrich Engels's characterisation of the Scottish Gaels, the Bretons and the Basques as 'relics of a nation' and 'ruined fragments of peoples' (Engels 1977 [1848])?

It would also be important to assess the extent to which MacInnes' characterisation of the Gaels as a 'nation' has become adopted and accepted by the Gaelic community, either in modern discourse or at different points in the past. There is certainly evidence of the term 'Gaelic nation' being used, in different ways, by various Gaelic writers and intellectuals. The term appears sporadically in the nineteenth century (e.g. 'Abriensis' 1817) and was used fairly frequently by Ruaraidh Erskine of Marr and other language revivalists of the early and mid-twentieth century (e.g. Erskine 1906: 212; Paterson 1954: 3); in more recent decades there are still occasional sightings (e.g. Buchanan 2002: 271; MacLeod 2006; Watson 2011: 110). Conversely, forms like *an nàisean Gàidhealach/Gàidhlig* seem rarer in Gaelic, although the singer and music scholar Griogair Labhruidh (2012: 100–01) has discussed the cultural decline of 'an nàisean Gàidhealach' from the eighteenth century on, and poet Maoilios Caimbeul has referred to 'nàisean nan Gàidheal' (Caimbeul 2006). So far as I am aware, however, there has been no detailed explication of the concept of the 'Gaelic nation', and in particular how this concept articulates with the more widespread (if controversial) idea that Gaelic is the true language of the Scottish nation, and indeed that Scotland as a whole should be understood as a 'Gaelic nation' (e.g. MacNeacail 1920; Mac a' Ghobhainn [1977] 2000; Paterson 1954: 3).

This article will confine itself to one particular aspect of this problem: the way in which the ethnic identifying label *Gàidheal* has come to be replaced in many contexts by language-centred verbal formulae such as *luchd (na) Gàidhlig* or *muinntir na Gàidhlig*, literally 'the people of the Gaelic language'.[1] Similarly, in modern media usage and in usage arising out of the diverse

[1] These terms are plural and do not have counterpart singular forms such as **neach na Gàidhlig*. Indeed, there are no simple terms that correspond to the English 'Gaelic speaker' or to the 'ethnic' identifier *Gàidheal*; *neach-labhairt na Gàidhlig* is used in some contexts but is unwieldy and not common in ordinary usage. In Irish, the simple noun *cainteoir* equates to 'speaker' (and is well established in the phrase *cainteoir dúchais* 'native speaker'). In Basque the term *Euskaldun* takes the place of an 'ethnic' identifier, although it means simply 'Basque speaker'; with this terminology, it is impossible to be a Basque without a knowledge of the language (Urla 2012: 127–8).

contemporary initiatives that seek to sustain and revitalise Gaelic in Scotland, the language term *Gàidhlig* (technically a noun, but used adjectivally) is far more widely used than the ethnic adjective *Gàidhealach*. This marks a clear shift from the nineteenth century, when *Gàidheal(ach)* tended to predominate, matched in English by the obsolescent term *Highland(er)*. For example, early collections of Gaelic poetry tended to use the term *Gàidhealach* – most obviously in the repetitive titles of the early anthologies (*Comh-chruinneachaidh Òrannaigh Gàidhealach* and the like), causing them to be known now as the Eigg Collection, Gillies Collection, Turner Collection and so on – but by the early twentieth century *Gàidhlig* seems to have become more common, most famously in the title of W. J. Watson's important anthology *Bàrdachd Ghàidhlig* (1918) and the accompanying volume of prose extracts *Rosg Gàidhlig* (Watson 1915).

The term *luchd na Gàidhlig* is attested in a number of Gaelic sources from the late nineteenth and early twentieth centuries, but it tends to appear alongside the term *Gàidheal*, and to be used interchangeably (e.g. 'Seanachaidh' 1901: 38; MacGilleMhoire 1911: [i]). For example, in her 1876 poem to Charles Fraser Mackintosh, MP, 'Soraidh slàn, a Theàrlaich, leat', Màiri Mhòr nan Òran uses the phrase 'dùrachd luchd na Gàidhlig duit', but in an earlier stanza expresses this wish as 'durachd math [*sic*] nan Gàidheal duit' (Nic a' Phearsain 1891: 143–4). Màiri Mhòr is better known for her use of the term 'luchd na Beurla' in her famous song 'Tha Mi Sgìth de Luchd na Beurla' (Nic a' Phearsain 1891: 225–31); this term of hostility to Lowlanders, from which *luchd na Gàidhlig* would appear to represent an extension, is much older, and comes into regular use from the seventeenth century onwards (McLeod 2003; Coira 2012). In the constitution of the Gaelic Society of Inverness, adopted in 1871, the English term used to correspond to 'na Gàidheil' is 'the Gaelic people' (Gaelic Society of Inverness 1872: iv–v), and Màiri Mhòr and other writers of this period may have had this same understanding in mind. In contrast, W. J. Watson used a more language-based formula when he asserted in his inaugural lecture as Professor of Celtic in the University of Edinburgh in 1914 that John Stuart Blackie, the leading campaigner for the establishment of the Chair, 'deserves the lasting gratitude of the Gaelic-speaking people' (Watson 1914: 69).

In contemporary usage a clear semantic divergence has developed between *luchd na Gàidhlig* and *na Gàidheil*, reflecting the important social and sociolinguistic changes of recent decades by which the relationship between the Gaelic language and the geographical communities in the Highlands and Islands where it has traditionally been spoken has become much less straightforward. These processes are multifaceted but have two main aspects. First, traditional Gaelic communities are now less Gaelic in linguistic terms than they were, in that the proportion of the local population who can speak Gaelic has declined, through both the failure of language transmission and the influx of non-Gaelic speakers (e.g. Mac an Tàilleir, Rothach and Armstrong 2010). At the same time, the cultural distinctiveness of Gaelic communities has also diminished, as the lifestyles, social norms and cultural practices of Gaelic speakers in such localities are increasingly aligned with those of English monoglots in Scotland and Britain as a whole (Glaser 2007: 184; MacDonald 1997). Second, and more important, the social demography of Gaelic speaking has changed considerably, with the speech community becoming both more geographically dispersed and socially diverse. The 2011 census showed that almost half (48 percent) of those claiming to be able to speak Gaelic live in Lowland Scotland rather than the Highlands and Islands. The growth of Gaelic education (in schools, colleges and universities and other settings) has generated steadily increasing numbers of people who can and do speak Gaelic, but whose family or 'ethnic' links to Gaelic may be weak or even non-existent. These 'new speakers'[2] of Gaelic – more typically and problematically known as 'learners' (MacCaluim 2007) – often feel reluctant to identify themselves as 'Gaels' (or, in Gaelic, as *Gàidheil*) (MacAulay 1994: 42; McLeod, O'Rourke and Dunmore forthcoming), and many people with stronger family and 'ethnic' links to the language appear unwilling to accept 'new

[2] See O'Rourke & Ramallo (2013) for an explication of the term 'new speaker'.

speakers' as 'Gaels' (Oliver 2004; McEwan-Fujita 2010). Conversely, some individuals with appropriate family or community connections might consider themselves – and be accepted – as 'Gaels' even if they have no meaningful communicative competence in the Gaelic language (Dorian 1981).

Although its definition has never been a matter of focused debate, the term *luchd na Gàidhlig*, in contrast to *Gàidheal*, can be and is used to refer without distinction to everyone with an ability in the Gaelic language, although perhaps it might also be extended to those whose relationship is rather more aspirational, more in the nature of an affinity. Critically, the boundaries of a group defined exclusively by language ability are a great deal more porous and permeable than one defined by ancestry, ethnicity or nationality, so that the term *luchd na Gàidhlig* is perceived by some 'new speakers' as being more 'inclusive' than *Gàidheal* (McLeod, O'Rourke and Dunmore forthcoming). A number of scholars writing on the contemporary sociology of Gaelic in Scotland have pointed to the increasing 'linguicentrism' of Gaelic revitalisation efforts (e.g. Glaser 2007), with Gaelic promotion initiatives becoming increasingly focused on the actual use of the Gaelic language itself, rather than manifestations of 'Gaelic culture' that do not demand Gaelic language ability. The growing use of a group term that defines membership simply in terms of language ability should be understood within this context.

Interestingly, the related terms *coimhearsnachd na Gàidhlig* and *coimhearsnachd Ghàidhlig* have come to develop somewhat divergent semantic significance. The term *coimhearsnachd na Gàidhlig*, now widely used in the context of Gaelic development initiatives, effectively equates to *luchd na Gàidhlig*, i.e. the broad group of Gaelic speakers and users, of whatever origin and wherever they may be found. With a definite article, *a' choimhearsnachd Ghàidhlig*, the meaning is effectively the same. But the indefinite *coimhearsnachd Ghàidhlig* and *coimhearsnachdan Gàidhlig* are, like the English 'a Gaelic community' or 'Gaelic communities', much more likely to refer to 'traditional' Gaelic communities, i.e. geographical areas in which the language has been used for centuries but which now contain large proportions of English monoglots. An interesting illustration of the semantic subtleties is the title of the recent volume *Coimhearsnachd na Gàidhlig An-Diugh/Gaelic Communities Today* (Munro & Mac an Tàilleir 2010) – i.e. 'community' singular in Gaelic, 'communities' plural in English.

To return to MacInnes' classification, then, *luchd na Gàidhlig* can be understood as a term that represents a post-national situation, as the last vestiges of MacInnes' 'detritus' have slowly disappeared. As the only real and relevant marker of distinctiveness becomes the language itself, then an identifier that names the language becomes a necessity.

Sources

'Abriensis'.

1817 Letter to *The Scotsman*. 14 June 1817.

Buchanan, Joni.

2002 'The Gaelic Communities'. Gerry Hassan and Chris Warhurst (eds), *Anatomy of the New Scotland: Power, Influence and Change*. Edinburgh: 270-77.

Caimbeul, Maoilios.

2006 Letter to *The West Highland Free Press*. 3 February 2006.

Coira, M. Pia.

2012 *By Poetic Authority: The Rhetoric of Panegyric in Gaelic Poetry of Scotland to c.1700*. Edinburgh.

Dorian, Nancy.

1981 *Language Death: The Life Cycle of a Scottish Gaelic Dialect*. Philadelphia.

Engels, Friedrich.

[1848] 1977 'The Magyar Struggle'. Karl Marx and Friedrich Engels, *Karl Marx/ Friedrich Engels: Collected Works*, vol. 8: 227–39. London.

Erskine, Ruaraidh, of Marr.

1906 'Agrarian Efficiency'. *Guth na Bliadhna* 3: 206–16.

Gaelic Society of Inverness.

1872 'Coimh-Dhealbhadh'/'Constitution'. *Transactions of the Gaelic Society of Inverness* 1: iv–vi.

Gellner, Ernest.

1983 *Nations and Nationalism*. Oxford.

Glaser, Konstanze.

2007 *Minority Languages and Cultural Identity in Europe: Gaelic and Sorbian Perspectives*. Clevedon.

Labhruidh, Griogair.

2012 '"Seinneam Ceòl air Bàrr Gach Bidean": Gnàthasan Seinn, Ceannsachadh nan Gàidheal agus Òrain Alasdair mhic Mhaighstir Alasdair'. Camille Dressler and Dòmhnall Uilleam Stiùbhart (eds), *Alexander MacDonald: Bard of the Gaelic Enlightenment / Alasdair mac Mhaighstir Alasdair: Bàrd an t-Soillearachaidh Ghàidhealaich*. Kershader, Isle of Lewis: 90–103.

Mac a' Ghobhainn, Seumas.

[1977] 2000 'A' Ghàidhlig — The Scottish Language'. Peter Berresford Ellis, *Scotland Not Only Free But Gaelic — A Tribute to Seumas Mac A' Ghobhainn*. Risnidh Mag Aoidh (ed.). Glasgow.

Mac an Tàilleir, Iain, Gillian Rothach, and Timothy Currie Armstrong

2010 *Barail agus Comas Cànain: Aithisg rannsachaidh airson Bòrd na Gàidhlig*. Inbhir Nis.

MacAulay, Donald.

1994 'Canons, myths and cannon fodder'. *Scotlands* 1: 35–54.

MacCaluim, Alasdair.

2007 *Reversing Language Shift? The Social Identity and Role of Scottish Gaelic Learners*. Belfast.

MACDONALD, SHARON.

1997 *Reimagining Culture: Histories, Identities and the Gaelic Renaissance.* Oxford.

MCEWAN-FUJITA, EMILY.

2010 'Linguistic Ethnography of Gaelic Communities'. Moray Watson and Michelle Macleod (eds), *The Edinburgh Companion to the Gaelic Language.* Edinburgh: 172–217.

MACGILLEMHOIRE, U. U. (TRANS.).

1911 *Iulius Caesar: Dàn-cluiche Shacspeair.* Edinburgh.

MACINNES, JOHN.

1975 Gaelic Poetry. Unpublished doctoral dissertation. University of Edinburgh.

1978 'The Panegyric Code in Gaelic Poetry and its Historical Background'. *Transactions of the Gaelic Society of Inverness* 50: 435–98.

MACLEOD, MURDO.

2006 'Book Review: *Invisible Islands:* Net Loss for Isles on Life Support.' *Scotland on Sunday*, 27 August 2006.

MACNEACAIL, H. C.

1920 'The Scottish Language.' *The Scottish Review* 43/97: 59–68.

MCLEOD, WILSON.

2003 'Language Politics and Ethnolinguistic Consciousness in Scottish Gaelic Poetry.' *Scottish Gaelic Studies* 21: 91–146.

MCLEOD, WILSON, BERNADETTE O'ROURKE AND STUART DUNMORE.

Forthcoming *New Speakers of Gaelic in Edinburgh and Glasgow.* Report for Soillse.

MUNRO, GILLIAN, AND IAIN MAC AN TÀILLEIR (EDS).

2010 *Coimhearsnachd na Gàidhlig An-Diugh / Gaelic Communities Today.* Edinburgh.

NIC A' PHEARSAIN, MÀIRI.

1891 *Dàin agus Òrain Ghàidhlig.* Inverness.

O'ROURKE, BERNADETTE, AND FERNANDO RAMALLO.

2013 'Competing Ideologies of Linguistic Authority amongst "New Speakers" in Contemporary Galicia.' *Language in Society* 42: 287–305.

OLIVER, JAMES.

2004 'Scottish Gaelic Identities: Contexts and Contingencies.' *Scottish Affairs* 51:1–24.

PATERSON, JOHN M.

1954 *Gaelic Made Easy: A guide to Gaelic for Beginners.* Glasgow.

'SEANACHAIDH'

1901 'Diarmaid Donn na Féinne.' *Am Bàrd* 1: 38–40.

SMITH, ANTHONY D.

2004 *The Antiquity of Nations*. Cambridge.

2010 *Nationalism: Theory, Ideology, History*. 2nd edn. Cambridge.

URLA, JACQUELINE.

2012 *Reclaiming Basque: Language, Nation, and Cultural Activism*. Reno, Nevada.

WATSON, MORAY.

2011 *An Introduction to Gaelic Fiction*. Edinburgh.

WATSON, WILLIAM J.

1914 'The Position of Gaelic in Scotland.' *The Celtic Review* 10: 69–84.

WATSON, WILLIAM J. (ED.).

1915 *Rosg Gàidhlig: Specimens of Gaelic Prose*. Inverness.

1918 *Bàrdachd Ghàidhlig: Specimens of Gaelic Poetry 1550–1900*. Inverness.

John Bunyan in the Kilt: The Influence of Bunyan Texts on Religious Expression and Experience in the Scottish Highlands and Islands

DONALD E. MEEK

Dr John MacInnes has contributed greatly to our understanding of many different aspects of Highland and Gaelic culture, including evangelical Protestantism and its impact on Gaelic secular tradition. He has also had much to say about translation, commonly from Gaelic to English, and most frequently in the context of insightful reviews of modern Gaelic verse. In appreciation of John's warm-hearted sharing of insights into both subjects, from which I have benefited immensely, I am delighted to offer him in return a *beannachadh* which combines both the Christian faith and also translation, though, on this occasion, from English to Gaelic. As John is well aware, evangelical Protestantism in its Highland garb was deeply indebted to seventeenth-century English Puritan writers such as Richard Baxter (1615–1691) of Kidderminster, whose *Call to the Unconverted* was translated into Gaelic in 1750, thus establishing a literary genre which has continued, though in diminishing form, well into the twentieth century. In particular, I wish to consider the writings of John Bunyan (1628–1688) of Bedford, whose work is well known in the British Isles, and has been translated into many languages, including Gaelic (Sharrock 1968; Dunan-Page 2010).

Back in my boyhood days in Tiree, I was a regular attender at Gaelic church services, which were held by both the Baptist church and the Church of Scotland in the island. The sermon was always the test of my boyhood stamina. In addition to paying close attention to the fine woodcuts of coal-carrying puffers and other steamships which had been cut into the pews of the most popular church buildings by an earlier generation of homiletic enthusiasts, I used to find some degree of relaxation from doctrinal tedium in the many anecdotes, illustrations and citations with which the best sermons were equipped. Sometimes no source would be given for the anecdote, but occasionally the source would be provided, in order to strengthen the argument. It was not uncommon for the preacher to appeal to a certain John Bunyan, who was apparently one of the greatest storytellers and wisdom figures of all time. On such occasions, the preacher would preface his observations with the phrase, 'Mar a thuirt Iain Buinian...'('As John Bunyan said...'), as if he were appealing to the ultimate authority beyond Scripture. Most frequently, allusion would be made to a book called *Turas a' Chrìosdaidh*, which had a wealth of wonderful characters and spine-chilling encounters. My own favourite character was *Famhair gun Dòchas,* 'Giant without Hope'. The preacher offered no explanation of Bunyan's background or origins, and, in my boyhood innocence, I assumed that Bunyan was a Gaelic-speaking Highlander. Later, as my innocence declined and my literacy increased, I became familiar with Bunyan's role in English as well as Gaelic literature, and gradually the realisation dawned upon me that Bunyan was not a Highlander after all. He was, in fact, an Englishman who had lived in the middle of the seventeenth century. *Turas a' Chrìosdaidh* meant 'The Pilgrim's Progress', and there was a copy of it in my own home, as in many other similar homes throughout the Highlands and Islands. Indeed, I remember seeing a wonderful Gaelic edition with woodcuts which showed Christian fighting Apollyon. Its pages were becoming damp and mouldy, and I can still recollect its smell and texture. I might add that, when I came to Edinburgh in 1979, I noticed that a coal-merchant called John Bunyan had a yard close to Haymarket Station, and I used to reflect wryly on how another John Bunyan, far removed in time and place, was a major supplier of fuel for sermons and books in the Highlands and Islands – and far, far beyond.

In the course of my forays into Highland church history, I came to realise that John Bunyan was perhaps the religious writer who had been most frequently, and most consistently, translated into Gaelic. Interestingly, the translation of his works had been undertaken mainly in the first half of the nineteenth century, at a time when the evangelical movement, spearheaded by ministers and missionaries of various kinds, but especially by schoolmasters, was touching the farthest corners of the Highands and Islands. Evangelicalism did not make a noticeable impact on the island of Lewis until the 1820s. As part of the burgeoning evangelical movement, literacy in Gaelic was spreading, particularly through the labours of the Gaelic School Societies, the first of which was established in Edinburgh in 1811. These societies aimed to make the Gaelic people sufficiently literate in Gaelic to be able to read the Gaelic Bible, which had been completed in 1801. The Gaelic Bible was the key text in these schools, but it is clear that a taste in reading beyond the Bible was also stimulated. The translation of Bunyan texts reflects, and accompanies, the vigorous indigenisation of evangelicalism in the Highlands and Islands, and it seems to me that the easy-flowing, natural style of the Bunyan translations, and especially of *Pilgrim's Progress*, matched the increasing appeal of the evangelical movement to the general mass of the Gaelic people. The Bunyan books, in their Gaelic forms, represent a critical stage in the important exchange between donor and receptor cultures in a missionary context. Even today, the original Gaelic text of *The Pilgrim's Progress* is easily accessible, and it is very different in texture from the general run of Puritan translations into Gaelic. It avoids what I sometimes call 'Puritanese' and its accompanying Highland counterpart, 'Westminster Gaelic', which is stiff and rigid and doctrinally precise. It is much closer to the everyday Gaelic of the people themselves (Meek 2002a).

The history of the Gaelic version of *The Pilgrim's Progress* will set the scene. It was translated as *Turas a' Chrìosdaidh*, and it first appeared in Edinburgh in 1812. The work was undertaken by Patrick MacFarlane, a schoolmaster in Appin, Argyll, who lived from 1758 to 1832. Schoolmasters were very important figures, not only in spreading the evangelical message, but also in translating key works of the evangelical movement. In this respect, they were more important than the ministers. They had a zeal for routine translation which the ministers, on the whole, lacked. To put it another way, ministers were more inclined to translate high-prestige works, such as the Gaelic Bible, which was undertaken by a succession of ministers. Ministers preferred to write Gaelic prose, rather than translate it, and they made a massive contribution to original Gaelic prose writings. Schoolmasters, on the other hand, undertook the more mundane tasks of translating catechisms and Puritan texts, though the distinction is not entirely rigid, as we shall see. MacFarlane, as a representative of the 'typical' translator, had a considerable range of interests and abilities. He was the translator of two of Philip Doddridge's works, *Rise and Progress of Religion in the Christian Soul*, and *One Thing Needful*, which were both published in Edinburgh in 1811. In addition, he produced a collection of Gaelic poetry in 1813, and a Gaelic vocabulary in 1815. This in itself is sufficient to show that evangelicalism was paying attention to the secular, as well as the spiritual, needs of the Gaelic people. Because of his various excursions into Gaelic culture, MacFarlane had a particular sensitivity to Gaelic language levels. Once in print, his translation became a firm favourite in the Highlands and Islands. It went through thirteen editions in the course of the century, and has retained its pre-eminent place to the present day.[1]

There were, of course, further translations. In 1865 a translation by Dr T. R. MacGillvray was published in Glasgow, a tome of some 940 pages, which included some of Bunyan's other works. This was the work that contained the woodcuts which I remember from my boyhood. In the twentieth century, *Pilgrim's Progress* was also translated by the Rev. Dr Malcolm MacLennan, and published in Edinburgh in 1929. It was reprinted in 1953 with a memoir of the translator by the Rev. T. M. Murchison. This illustrates the continuing appeal of *Pilgrim's Progress* to the Gaelic

[1] For dates and details of early Gaelic Bunyan texts, see Maclean 1915: 40–46.

people. As Murchison points out, MacLennan's translation uses the dialect of Uig, his native part of Lewis (MacGhillinnein 1953: 3–4). In this translation, then, the tinker of Bedford speaks with the cadences of a Lewisman! What greater honour could possibly be bestowed upon him? His cultural apotheosis is most surely complete!

Several other Bunyan texts were translated into Gaelic in the first half of the nineteenth century, and it is instructive to observe the pattern. These were as follows:

Life and Death of Badman	1824 (Inverness)
The Barren Fig Tree	1824 (Inverness)
World to Come	1825 (Tain)
Sighs from Hell	1829 (Inverness)
	1846 (Edinburgh)
Heavenly Footman	1829 ((Inverness)
Water of Life	1835 (Inverness)
	1846 (Edinburgh)
Holy War	1840 (Inverness)
Come and Welcome	1844 (Edinburgh)
Grace Abounding	1847 (Edinburgh)

It will be evident that the Bunyan texts were translated mainly in two periods – in fact, two different decades. The first period was in the 1820s, in the wake of the creation of the Gaelic school societies and the triumph of evangelicalism in the Outer Hebrides, and the second phase was in the 1840s, immediately before and immediately after the Disruption of 1843, when the Free Church of Scotland emerged from the Church of Scotland (Meek 1998). There was a quickening pulse, so to speak, in both of these periods, and each seems to have been marked by the translation of Bunyan texts. This in itself would suggest that, in times of heightened religious enthusiasm or 'revival', Highlanders were inclined to turn to Bunyan as one of the key interpreters of the evangelical experience, and as a guide to spiritual expression. The post-Disruption period witnessed the retranslation of two of the works, *Sighs from Hell* and *Water of Life*. Thereafter there were no significant translations of Bunyan until the twentieth century, although the earlier translations were regularly reprinted.

It is worth noting who translated some of these texts. One of the translators was a certain Robert MacDonald (b. 1795), a Gaelic schoolmaster from Sutherland, who was responsible for the translation of *Life and Death of Badman* (1824) and the first of the translations of *Sighs from Hell* (1829). MacDonald was schoolmaster in different parts of the northern Highlands – Arnisdale (Loch Hourn), Inverness, Keils and Dingwall; a collection of his own verse, published in 1836, contained some satirical sermons. But perhaps the most remarkable of all the translators was the man who undertook the translation of several of the volumes published in the 1840s, including *Grace Abounding* – John MacKenzie. This was none other than the celebrated John MacKenzie (1806–48), from Gairloch, who collected much Gaelic verse, and produced the fine anthology called *Sar Obair nam Bàrd Gaelach: The Beauties of Gaelic Poetry*, which was first published in 1841, and is still regarded as a major source of Gaelic poetry and information about the poets. MacKenzie also wrote a Gaelic account of the adventures of Bonnie Prince Charlie, and compiled a Gaelic dictionary (Maclean 1915: 246–50).

It is one of the more curious aspects of modern Gaelic scholarship that, although MacKenzie's massive achievement in producing the *Beauties of Gaelic Poetry* is regularly and rightly applauded, his role as a translator of John Bunyan's work has hardly ever been noted. This fits conveniently with the general scholarly perception – a modern misperception in my opinion – that there was some sort of unbridgeable gulf between the evangelical movement and the secular world, and that evangelicals helped to destroy Gaelic culture. I cannot comment at this stage on John MacKenzie's commitment to evangelicalism, but it is self-evident that he saw considerable benefits in translating

Bunyan and also in collecting Gaelic song and verse composed by the secular and sacred bards of the Highlands. My own view is that the supposed antipathy of evangelicals to Gaelic culture has been greatly exaggerated, largely because of the effect of the quarrels within the Free Church in the later part of the nineteenth century, and the narrowing of spiritual horizons caused by the creation of the Free Presbyterian Church in 1893. Whatever evangelicals may have thought about the more decadent aspects of Gaelic culture which they tried to eradicate, they participated in literary creativity and in Gaelic scholarship throughout most of the nineteenth century (Meek 1996: 34–53). That there was two-way traffic between Gaelic culture and the evangelical movement is splendidly evidenced by the work of John MacKenzie of Gairloch. I should add that MacKenzie was also the editor of Patrick MacFarlane's fine translation of *Pilgrim's Progress* of 1812, and that he produced a new edition of it in 1845. All in all, MacKenzie's role as a Bunyan editor and translator of Bunyan texts into Gaelic is one of the best-kept secrets of the Gaelic world.

We should also note that the creative interest in Bunyan which is evident by the 1840s is connected with the northern Highlands, and particularly Ross-shire, as the work of John MacKenzie so clearly indicates. The first translation of a Bunyan text, however, was made in Appin, Argyll, by Patrick MacFarlane, and published in 1812. Enthusiasm for Bunyan had thus moved north by 1850, probably because of the popularity of the 1812 text. As Ross-shire was a focus of evangelical Calvinism in the seventeenth and eighteenth centuries, it is fascinating to see Bunyan finding such a firm place in that quarter in the first half of the nineteenth century. Inverness also stands out very prominently as a publication centre for Bunyan texts, producing as many translations as Edinburgh.

The influence and appeal of Bunyan in the Highlands and Islands can be detected in ways other than the citation of places of publication and the names of translators. It can be seen in poetry and in preaching too, especially in the first half of the nineteenth century. In the field of hymnology, for instance, the influence of Bunyan can be detected on Peter Grant (c. 1783–1867), the pastor of the Baptist Church at Grantown-on-Spey (Meek 2002b). Grant, who was an ardent evangelist and itinerant preacher who travelled the length and breadth of the northern Highlands and Islands on preaching tours, became perhaps the most popular of all composers of Gaelic hymns in the nineteenth century. One of the themes that he pursues fairly frequently in his compositions is the journey of the Christian from the fragile and perishing world of humanity to the Heavenly City. The path is strewn with snares and difficulties of all kinds. It is hard to believe that Bunyan's *Pilgrim's Progress* did not mould the thoughts of the Gaelic hymnwriter as he constructed his concept of spiritual itineration. The journey of life is a common metaphor, of course, but Bunyan's work invested it with a special significance for the Christian believer. The believer becomes the Christian pilgrim, making his or her way through the desert of this world, avoiding fleshly temptations and Satan's darts wherever possible. Ioan Williams' comments on the influence of the Welsh translation of *Pilgrim's Progress* are applicable to both Grant's hymns and wider self-perception in the Christian communities of the Scottish Highlands and Islands (Williams 2000: 50):

> Well before the end of the eighteenth century, Welsh Calvinism had developed a characteristic system of social and psychological structures. At the centre of this system was the concept of the Christian as pilgrim, inherited from Bunyan, whose *Pilgrim's Progress* (1676) had long been assimilated into Welsh culture in its translated version as *Taith y Pererin* (1688).

The modes and styles of Bunyan, and in particular the personification of attitudes and arguments, in such characters as Mr Valiant for Truth and Giant Despair, worked their way into the sermons of some Highland preachers. Perhaps the most conspicuous of these was the Rev. Robert Finlayson (1793–1861), a native of Latheron in Caithness. After study at King's College, Aberdeen, Finlayson ministered in the Gaelic Chapel in Aberdeen for three years. Thereafter he became minister of Knock in Lewis, and then moved to Lochs. As a young boy, he had been influenced by his father's library, which included Thomas Boston's *Four-fold State* and Dyer's *Christ's Famous*

Titles (both of which were translated into Gaelic), but which also had copies of Bunyan's works. (Note again, in the bygoing, the northern location of Bunyan, this time in Caithness and Lewis.) In the course of his ministry in Lewis, Finlayson earned the nickname of 'the John Bunyan of the Highlands', because of his Bunyanesque techniques. Finlayson's great gift was his ability to bring characters to life in his sermons, in such a way that his listeners were treated to what might be regarded nowadays as dramatic renditions. As Dr Roderick MacLeod notes in his fine paper on Finlayson (MacLeod 1986):

> Finlayson's method preaching must have been like a breath of fresh air to congregations who had been accustomed to the rather dry, dull and scholarly sermons of the Moderates. He had the intriguing habit of addressing Biblical characters by name in the course of his sermons. Preaching on the Flood, he cried, "Ho, ho, Noah! What a wonderful Admiral you, of this Ark! Many an old crock has floated the seas, but yours was the strangest of all the ships of the world's fleets, and your cargo the most amazing." Another device employed by the minister of Lochs to make personalities from Biblical history more meaningful to his audience, was to place them in a Hebridean setting...A bull from the Butt of Lewis and a ram from Uig feature in his colourful sermon on Noah's Ark.

Finlayson's Bunyanesque style is even more evident in his sermon on Peter's denial of Christ, in which he personifies Zeal and Knowledge:

> Out went Zeal after Christ, and when Jesus said, "You will all be offended in me tonight," Zeal replied, "Though all others are offended in you, I shall not be." But Jesus said to him, "Verily I say unto you today, on this very night, before the cock crows twice, you will deny me thrice." Zeal ran home to Knowledge in tears.
>
> "What has come over you now, Zeal?" asked Knowledge. "Woe is me," said Zeal, "I was foolish. I provoked my Lord and He claimed that I would be guilty of denying Christ!"

Bunyan, then, provided a homiletic model for Gaelic ministers with a creative approach to evangelism and a desire to convey their teaching through forms of ecclesiastical drama. Again, we can cite Welsh parallels, most noticeably in the case of the North Wales Baptist preacher, Christmas Evans (1776–1838), who was regularly compared with Bunyan because of the 'long-sustained parables and pictures alive with allegorical delineation of human character'. In his sermons, it is said that Evans himself was both 'playwright and actor' (Shenton 2001: 398–99).

Bunyan also provided a model for individual believers, by offering a paradigm for faith – and perhaps even for revolutionary politics. We can observe this in Lewis, in comments made by the Gaelic poet, John Smith (1848–81) of Iarsiadar in Lochs, one of the finest of the many Gaelic poets of the nineteenth-century Highlands, and a radical voice in the reaction to oppressive landlordism. Smith composed a couple of major poems in which – perhaps under Bunyan's influence – he personified (not unlike Finlayson of Lochs) virtues such as Kindliness and vices such as Pride, and addressed these in his verse. In his song *Spiorad a' Charthannais*, 'The Spirit of Kindliness', he examines the impact of imperialism and economic determinism on the contemporary Highlands, arraigning alike the militaristic war-mongers of his day and the ruthless landlords whose agents are intent on emptying the glens and the islands of their people. He also turns his spotlight on the contentious, introverted and gloomy kind of religious experience with which he was apparently familiar in Lewis by the 1870s. He provides a word picture of the Christian who is committed to that sort of creed:

> That surly, gloomy Christian
> who meditates so hard,

who assumes a holy countenance
like a prophet in a trance,
who makes a terrible slaughter
of all horror in his breast –
by his dealings you would never know
that Apollyon now was dead.[2]

The reference to Apollyon indicates that Smith has Bunyan's *Pilgrim's Progress* in mind, and he is keen to point out the contrast between the supposed solace of internal meditation and the outward action which lacks love and kindliness – the contrast between profession and practice, the inward and the outward. This is of particular interest in the context of the nascent crofters' rebellion, given the connection which certain historians have identified between the growth of radicalism in Britain and the foundational significance of *Pilgrim's Progress*. The English historian E. P. Thompson states (1986: 34–35):

> And it is above all in Bunyan that we find the slumbering Radicalism which was preserved through the eighteenth century and which breaks out again and again in the nineteenth. *Pilgrim's Progress* is, with *Rights of Man*, one of the two foundation texts of the English working-class movement: Bunyan and Paine, with Cobbet and Owen, contributed most to the stock of ideas and attitudes which make up the raw material of the movement from 1790–1850. Many thousands of youths found in *Pilgrim's Progress* their first adventure story, and would have agreed with Thomas Cooper, the Chartist, that it was their 'book of books'.

As Thompson indicates, for English dissenters Apollyon was not only a symbol of repressive earthly magistrates, he was also a cunning spiritual enemy who could insinuate himself into the lives of Christians. Both strands of interpretation may lie behind Smith's sentiments in this song.

Smith was obviously familiar with Bunyan, and implies that certain – probably many – Christians in Lewis were likewise familiar with him, and perhaps using him as a model, as well as being influenced by his narratives. Can this be substantiated from the surviving evidence anywhere in the Highlands? To what extent did Bunyan's paradigm of the godly life influence Highland evangelicalism at the personal and spiritual level?

To answer that question, and to round off this contribution, I would like to step back a century, to the middle years of the eighteenth century, between the 'Forty-five Rebellion and approximately 1750. In that year the first Gaelic translation of a Puritan text appeared. As we noted at the outset of this paper, it was a translation of Richard Baxter's *Call to the Unconverted*, and it was undertaken by the Rev. Alexander MacFarlane, who was then minister of the parish of Kilninver in Argyll. The translation is an indicator of a growing level of interest in Puritan texts in the southern Highlands. It is clear that Puritan influence had been entering the Highlands for some years previously, and that Bunyan was being read alongside Baxter, but in English, not Gaelic. The most remarkable evidence for Bunyan's influence on the early Highland missionary movement is found in the surviving work of the Gaelic hymnwriter, Dugald Buchanan (1716–68).

Buchanan, a native of Ardoch, in Strathyre, Perthshire, became a schoolmaster with the Forfeited Estates, serving in Kinlochrannoch, Perthshire, from the early 1750s until his death. Buchanan was a highly accomplished writer in both Gaelic and English, and, alongside the hymns for which he is famous, he wrote a diary of his early spiritual experiences. He went through a deep personal crisis in the 1740s, and, even after his conversion, he had great doubts about his state of grace, and agonised over his lack of assurance. His personal crisis is graphically recorded in his diary, where he notes the following in relation to his spiritual search during his teenage years (MacBean [1919]: 140):

[2] For Gaelic text and English translation, see Meek 1995: 90–97, 213–20.

> Not long after this I met with a book called, Grace Abounding to the Chief of Sinners. The title page suited me very well, for I thought that was surely I. In reading this book I found that its author had been a great sinner, and yet obtained mercy. Then I said, peradventure the Lord will be merciful to me also, since mercy is offered to the chief of sinners. This greatly encouraged me to go the Lord in prayer and confess my sins; in doing which, I found such great meltings of heart, that sometimes I would be in floods of tears, and resolved never to forsake the Lord all my days.

Buchanan does not name Bunyan, but he does not need to, as the title of the book tells us all we need to know. This was Bunyan's autobiography, written when he was undergoing twelve years of imprisonment in Bedford jail, and first published in 1666. When Buchanan wrote his own diary in the late 1740s – it remained unpublished until 1836 – he used the standard Puritan model of spiritual autobiography. The influence of Bunyan can be detected there particularly clearly, and, in the early stages of the work, the characters and experiences of Bunyan and Buchanan seem to merge. Like Bunyan, Buchanan is terrified at the prospect of the Day of Judgement; like Bunyan too, he has close shaves with death in his unregenerate days, and narrowly escapes drowning (twice). And like the majority of Puritans who have recorded their spiritual pilgrimages, his greatest struggles are after his conversion, as he strives to find marks of grace which would assure him of his salvation. The material world is almost totally erased in this great quest; we are at a loss to gain meangingful biographical details from Buchanan's diary, since he records only those events which have contributed to his spiritual development. In short, Buchanan epitomises in the Highland context what Owen Watkins (1972) has called the 'Puritan Experience'.

The model of Buchanan's life was hugely influential, particularly through his hymns. He became the archetype of godly living in the southern Highlands, and his influence spread northwards through the Perthshire glens, transmitted by print and by word of mouth, and by song, until it reached such men as Peter Grant of Grantown-on-Spey. Like Bunyan, Buchanan became a living legend, a man whose legend was greater than his life.

Even the most cursory look at the place of John Bunyan in the Gaelic spiritual context is enough to underline the Puritan – and English – dimension in what is sometimes loosely termed 'Highland religion'. 'Highland religion' was not a particularised, essentialist, self-contained Gaelic – or 'Celtic' – phenomenon. It was an extremely complex 'collection' of religious ideas. It was driven by external impulses such as those that were experienced by Dugald Buchanan, and some of those impulses originated not in Beauly or in Back, but in far-away Bedford. They intermingled with indigenous perspectives in such a way that Buchanan's diary contains more than one 'voice': there is Buchanan's own voice, but there is also the voice of Bunyan, and the voice of Scripture, to name but three. There are similar questions with regard to the Gaelic translations of John Bunyan's works. Who speaks through them? Bunyan of Bedford? Or another Bunyan, remade to fit the Highland and Gaelic context? What has been lost and gained in translation, in terms of both the words and the ideas? These are intriguing questions, worthy of much further examination.

Just occasionally, Dugald Buchanan drops his Puritan guard, and he does relate some interesting personal snippets in his diary. Rather unexpectedly, he tells us that he wore 'a Highland dress' on one occasion when he was in Edinburgh, and that someone asked him on that occasion 'what were [his] principles' (MacBean [1919]: 156–57).

It was a good question. Sometimes I wonder who Buchanan really was, and what his principles were (Meek 2009). Was he his true self as he wrote his diary, and tried to accommodate himself to the Puritan paradigm? Or was he, in fact, the first of many John Bunyans in the kilt?

Even if Buchanan were to plead guilty to identity theft, he would not, of course, be alone in his 'confessions', nor would he be doing John Bunyan a disservice. In an era when 'postcolonial studies' are increasingly fashionable and scholars are aware of the significance of key texts which were translated from English into other languages within the former British Empire, the study of the translation of Bunyan's principal works has particular importance. These works were personal in their application, but they were also highly 'portable' and transnational in their appeal. They became part of the bedrock of a new self-definition which accompanied the penetration of previously 'isolated' regions by an English-based majority culture. The evidence provided by Gaelic translations of Bunyan, which appear most prominently after 1800, is but a small part of the international picture of the ready acceptance of a Protestant 'authority figure' who had an uncanny knack of reinventing himself happily in many different cultures (Hofmeyer 2010).

Sources

Dunan-Page, Anne (ed.).

2010 *The Cambridge Companion to Bunyan*. Cambridge.

Hofmeyer, Isabel.

2010 'Bunyan: colonial, postcolonial'. Anne Dunan-Page, *The Cambridge Companion to Bunyan*. Cambridge: 162–76.

MacBean, Lachlan (ed.).

[1919] *Buchanan, the Sacred Bard of the Scottish Highlands; his confessions and his spiritual songs*. London.

MacGhillinnein, Calum.

1953 *Turus a' Chriosduidh*. Lunnainn.

Maclean, Donald.

1915 *Typographia Scoto-Gadelica*. Edinburgh

MacLeod, Roderick.

1986 'The John Bunyan of the Highlands: the life and work of the Rev. Robert Finlayson (1793–1861)'. *Transactions of the Gaelic Society of Inverness* 54 (1984-86): 240–268.

Meek, Donald E.

1995 (ed.) *Tuath is Tighearna: Tenants and Landlords: an anthology of Gaelic poetry of social and political protest from the Clearances to the Land Agitation (1800–1890)*. Edinburgh.

1996 *The Scottish Highlands: The Churches and Gaelic Culture*. Geneva.

1998 'Gaelic Bible, revival and mission: the spiritual rebirth of the nineteenth-century Highlands'. James Kirk (ed.), *The Church in the Highlands*. Edinburgh: 114–45.

2002a 'The pulpit and the pen: clergy, orality and print in the Scottish Gaelic world'. Adam Fox and Daniel Woolf (eds), *The Spoken Word: oral culture in Britain, 1500–1850*. Manchester: 84–118.

2002b '"The Glory of the Lamb": the Gaelic hymns of Peter Grant'. D. W. Bebbington (ed.), *The Gospel in the World: Studies in Baptist History and Thought*, vol. I. Carlisle: 129–164.

2009 'Evangelicalism, Ossianism and the Enlightenment: the many masks of Dugald Buchanan'. Christopher MacLachlan (ed.), *Crossing the Highland Line: cross-currents in eighteenth-century Scottish writing*. Glasgow: 97–112.

SHARROCK, ROGER.

1968 *John Bunyan*. London.

SHENTON, TIM.

2001 *Christmas Evans: the life and times of the one-eyed preacher of Wales*. Darlington.

THOMPSON, E. P.

1986 *The Making of the English Working Class*. Harmondsworth.

WATKINS, OWEN.

1972 *The Puritan Experience*. London.

WILLIAMS, IOAN.

2000 'Gwilym Hiraethog (William Rees, 1802–83)'. Hywel Teifi Edwards (ed.), *A Guide to Welsh Literature c. 1800–1900*, vol. 5. Cardiff: 48–68.

The Great Caledonian Forest of the Mind: Highland Woods and Tree Symbolism in Scottish Gaelic Tradition

MICHAEL NEWTON

John MacInnes's brief but penetrating article 'Samhla na Craoibhe' ('The Symbol of the Tree') begins with the observation *Chan eil samhla nas bitheanta ann am bardachd na Gàidhlig na samhla na craoibhe* ('There is no more common symbol in Gaelic poetry than the symbol of the tree') (Mac Aonghuis 1983: 64-9). The cumulative weight of this imagery should alert us to its importance. Our scientific knowledge about the physical environment of Scotland – the flora, fauna, soil quality, carrying capacity of the land, and so on – has developed extensively since the 1990s, not least due to the leadership of T. C. Smout. Our understanding of the social, cultural and imaginative dimensions of aspects of the landscape has not, however, kept pace with the historical and scientific data.

The title of my contribution is intentionally mischievous. The Great Caledonian Forest is a symbol, an archetype, deeply rooted in the Gaelic imagination which has triggered scepticism, even derision, in recent publications about the history of Scottish woods. Smout has implied, for example, that the modern scholar needs to clear the imaginary woods of literature from the scientific record of real trees: 'Let us begin with the Great Wood of Caledon. It is, in every sense of the word, a myth' (C. Smout 2000: 37).

If we are to take the word 'myth' seriously in all of its facets, we must consider what the narratives and symbolic expressions about the Great Wood meant to the people who told them, and why they created and told them. Although Smout has invited 'the ecologist and the historian' to 'plan a partnership of research and interpretation' (1997: 21), he has overlooked the importance of the anthropologist, linguist and literary scholar who can address questions of meaning for human communities.

It is not that Smout is unaware of the literary record or its potential for unravelling the development of conceptions about the Caledonian Forest or of trees generally: he examines Roman sources and their influence on anglophone antiquarians musing about the Scottish landscape, and recognises that trees were potent icons in Scotland's poetry, English and Gaelic, well before the Romantic movement (2000: 15–18, 41–6, 59–61). It is, then, jarring when he claims that 'In its modern form, the Caledonian Forest is a product of German Romanticism, mediated through the excitable and fantasy-filled minds of the Sobieski Stuarts' (44). He makes the mistake of equating 'modern' with 'anglophone', denying the possibility that Gaelic literature and tradition has had its own trajectory of development.

These cavils are not intended to devalue Smout's contributions, but are meant to highlight the neglect of Gaelic sources and perspectives in the field generally, issues which are crucial if we are to understand the mindsets and cultural expressions of the people who actually lived in such environments.

Scholarly efforts to date have generally focused on biological data or documents recording tree cover, financial transactions, claims of ownership of woodland resources and contentions over them, and have primarily led to conclusions about the élite of Scottish society and the commodification and exchange of resources. By directing our attention to lexical items, idioms, oral tradition, folklore and literature, we can more broadly address the cultural and social dimensions of human ecology: What did forests, tree species, and even individual trees, mean to people? What motivated them to claim, defend, or exploit them? How did their political institutions, cultural values, religious impulses and literary expressions inform and direct their interactions with the environment? When did they accept responsibility for ecological degradation – and when, and why, did they blame others? What did they understand about connections between the vitality of the environment and the human community? I hope to demonstrate in this short article, amongst other things, that the history and economic exploitation of woods as physical commodities often contrasts with their role as social signifiers, cultural landmarks and literary devices in Gaelic tradition.

Arboreal symbolism is pervasive in Gaelic literature, epistemology and cosmology, as it is in many parts of the world. I have examined tree symbolism in detail elsewhere (1998; 2009: 114, 237–42), but will summarise some salient points here. The Gaelic language uses overlapping terms, and offers homologies, between human body parts and the elements of trees (foliage as hair, sap as blood, bark as skin, limbs as arms, legs and fingers, etc.), between human individuals and entire trees (the terms *crann, craobh, faillean, fiùran, fleasg(ach), gallan, gas(an), geug,* and *ògan(ach)* can be used for either), and between groves and forests on the one hand, and families and clans on the other (*doire, coille, craobh-ghinealaiche, craobh-sheanchais*, etc.). Other tree terms are used, both positively and negatively, to describe different human qualities and characteristics. The metaphorical potential of these tropes has been exploited extensively throughout the history of Gaelic literature, oral and written, and the semantic parallels reinforce the notion that humankind is inextricably a part of nature and can be understood within the same terms and in the same frames of reference (Bateman 2009; Newton 2009: 290–6). An excerpt from the eulogy by the wife of Major Alasdair MacLeod of Steinn of the Isle of Skye to Sir John MacPherson (c. 1770) will serve as an illustration (MacLeòid 1811: 104–5):

Chunnaic mise as mo chadal
A' chraobh ùrail bu taitnich
'S a duilleach cur fasgaidh air ceudan;

As na freumhaichean sùghmhor
A ghineadh o thùs i:
Gur brìghmhor an ùir ás na dh'éirich.

I saw in my sleep / the flourishing, most pleasing tree / with its foliage sheltering hundreds; From sap-laden roots / was it begotten from the start: / virile is the soil from which it rose.

This text has a fairly explicit representation of a healthy ecosystem: the tree is rooted in a particular locale, drawing nutrients from the soil which are carried by networks of sap through its limbs, allowing the tree to flourish and foliage to grow, which in turn provides the benefit of shelter to other organisms around it. This ecological awareness is implicit in many other texts.

It is worth noting that this repertoire of literary devices is paralleled by the iconography of sculpture for the Gaelic élite. A recent survey notes: 'The most prevalent type of design or pattern in West Highland sculpture is foliage, normally stylised leaves arranged in scrolls or trellises. There is no apparent significance to this' (Caldwell, McGibbon, Miller and Ruckley 2010: 39). The ubiquity of tree imagery in poems to these same patrons gives me cause to doubt the authors' claim that foliage imagery of this kind is insignificant.

This symbolic system extends at a more abstract level to comment upon the structure and operation of the social order and the relationship between the human order and the cosmos. It might easily be assumed that the relative paucity of expository prose and the marked preference for narrative forms in Gaelic literature hints at some intellectual deficit, but John Carey's comments about symbolic expression in Irish tradition, and its ability to explore ideas and reveal truths, holds equally true for Scottish Gaelic (1992: 102):

> The literature is as rich in metaphor and image as it is poor in theory and abstraction, and it is surely here that the key is to be found. The indigenous Irish mentality tends to find expression in symbolic rather than in analytic terms: concepts are not extracted from phenomena in order to be manipulated on the plane of 'pure reason', but are instilled and contemplated in concrete entities. [...] A symbol, unlike an abstract concept, is alive and therefore inexhaustible: it can embrace contraries, point the way into deeper or subtler realms of thought, or be itself transformed and reinterpreted by the unfolding of history.

The material experience of trees and forests informed Gaelic literary symbolism, especially those which were considered sacrosanct in the Scottish landscape: 'The power of the tree kenning is ultimately derived from the great legendary trees of Gaelic tradition' (MacInnes 2006: 284). Some of the names of the sacred woods in Scotland retained the P-Celtic element *neued*, cognate with the *nemeton* of the ancient continental Celts: Barrow has identified an impressive 27 candidates (1998: 56–9).

Many such archaic beliefs were resilient enough in indigenous Gaelic tradition to survive virtually within living memory, and to manifest themselves in literary expression. The inauguration of rulers was often conducted at a sacred tree (*bile*) from which a rod of sovereignty was cut and given to the new leader. Place names and oral tradition attest to the presence of *bilean* near seats of power associated with several dynasties in the *Gàidhealtachd* (Newton 2009: 132–4). One anecdote from the late nineteenth century inextricably ties the life of a sacred tree to the MacDonalds of Glencoe (John Cameron 1894):

> The magnificent family representative tree in front of Glencoe House fell on the memorable Saturday night's storm. Although there was great destruction among other trees by previous storms, the giant of the forest suffered no damage. On the night referred to, however, it and the gable of a mansion-house which was built the year before the massacre of Glencoe, and which was set fire to at the time, were thrown down. This was taken as a bad omen. The news of the heir's death and the other occurrences taking place on the same week-day, completed the reading of the omen.
>
> Air fonn :— *Flowers of the Forest*
>
> *Tha sgeul an-diugh air Dhòmhnach*
> *Do Chomhunnaich tha brònach*
> *Gun d' leagadh Craobh nan Dòmhn'llach:*
> *'S o-chòn, cha bu chlìth!*
>
> *Ged leag an doinionn mhillteach*
> *An doire tiugh 's a mìlltean*
> *Sheas gallan nan seachd linntean*
> *Deas dìreach gun dìth.*

Bu shoilleir geur an saobhadh
Nuair a thuit an gallan aobhach
'S bha cuid againn a smaoinich
Air taghadh chrann na frìth.

Thug sgeula bàis an oighre
Sgal 's a' chluais as buidhre
Is deòir o'n t-sùil as duibhre
Nach c<e>ill,[1] *ach daoine, 'bhrìgh.*

We have a tale today about Sunday which is sorrowful for the people of Glencoe: that the Tree of the MacDonalds was brought down; alas, it was not weak!

Although the devastating storm felled the dense grove and thousands like it, the stalk of seven generations stood straight and elegant without defect.

The omen was clear and concise when the lovely stalk fell: and some of us thought about the pick of the trees in the forest.

The tale of the death of the heir has brought a shriek to the deafest ear and tears from the toughest eye – it will not hide the significance of it [this omen], even if people will.

The centrality of tree symbolism in Gaelic literature and tradition seems to bear scant relationship to the physical landscape of the Scottish Highlands and Western Isles: many areas have had little or no tree cover for centuries; few non-élite Gaels are likely to have been mobile enough to have experienced a variety of tree types; and humans have intervened in diverse ways in the depletion and/or regeneration of woodlands and specific trees. So what is the relationship between the physical environment and the literary representation of woods and use of arboreal symbolism in Gaelic tradition? Do these tropes arise from the direct experience of trees, or are they just 'pre-packaged' poetic conventions?

The Irish law-tracts categorised trees into four grades based on human social classes (Kelly 1976). Using similar logic, Scottish Gaelic tradition divided trees into noble and non-noble classes. Creating an exhaustive classification requires a thorough knowledge of tree species and their different qualities, a familiarity demonstrated by Sìleas MacDonald of Keppoch, Lochaber, in her c.1721 elegy to Alasdair MacDonald of Glengarry (Ó Baoill 1972: 70–5). Even though there is considerably more surviving Gaelic poetry composed by Hebridean poets than by mainland poets, nearly all of the references to the noble / non-noble division are from texts composed on the mainland of Scotland. Thomas Sinton's collection of Gaelic poetry from Badenoch (1906) contains references to practically the full arboreal diversity of the Highlands. By contrast, there is hardly any tree imagery in the surviving song-poetry from the island of St Kilda (MacFhearghuis 1995).[2] Although the professional poetic order developed a sophisticated framework for tree symbolism (McManus 2006) and their literary productions were highly influential in their own and lower social ranks, only those poets who had a first-hand knowledge of trees tended to employ these devices to good effect.

---

[1] This letter is unclear in the original microfilm: it is likely either 'a',' 'e', or 'o' and I have chosen 'e' and interpret the word as 'ceil' as this seems to make the most sense.

[2] Even if what survives is a small and perhaps unrepresentative sample of what once existed.

The emigrant experience in North America offers another scenario against which we may measure the significance of the tree and forest in the Gaelic world view. The notoriety of the song popularly known as *A' Choille Ghruamach* (or *Òran do dh'Ameireaga*) by the Bard MacLean (Dunbar 2008: 44–5) has cast a long and unnecessarily negative shadow over the relationship between immigrant Gaels and the 'unimproved' landscape. The woods are given far more positive treatment in other song texts, composed before and after emigration (MacDonell 1982: 42, 60, 142; Dunbar 2008: 66–7).

In 1802, well before the appearance of the Sobieski Brothers, the Rev. Augustin McDonald commented from Pictou, Nova Scotia, 'The landscape around and position of the forms are very handsome. But the whole country is as covered with the beautifullest woods of every description and variety as we may suppose old Caledonia to have been…' (Macinnes, Harper and Fryer 2002: 185). A Skye emigrant in the Canadian Maritimes, writing in 1848, not only demonstrated appreciation for the trees native to his adopted country, but also displayed a thorough knowledge of the Gaelic terms for them (Sgitheanach: 236):

> *Do thaobh àireimh agus gné nan craobh, cha fhreagair e ach beagan a labhairt anns an àite seo. Cha lugha na ceithir seòrsa deug giubhais, còig seòrsa beithe, agus ceithir seòrsa daraich, a gheibhear anns a' cheart eilean seo. 'Se an giuthas buidhe as luachmhoire, oir chan e a-mhàin gum bheil e 'na dheagh fhiodh, ach tha e fàs gu meud anabarrach mór. Is minic a gheibhear craobhan de'n ghiuthas seo a thomhaiseas còig troighe deug mu'n bhun, sia fichead troigh ann an àirde, agus ceithir fichead troigh dhiubh sin, air nach faighear aon mheur no meanglan. A-measg nan seòrsa eugsamhla fiodha tha fàs 's a' Cheap, feudar na leanas ainmeachadh: giubhas, darach, aiteann, faighbhile, leamhan, uinnseann, caorann, beithe, feàrna, maple (às an dèanar an siùcar), critheann, agus mar sin sìos. A thuilleadh air gach fiodh dhiubh seo, tha iomadh seòrsa eile ann air nach eil Gàidhlig […]*
>
> *Chan eil teagamh sam bith nach taitneach an sealladh na coillte[an] seo gu léir do na Gàidheil a chaidh air imrich do dh'America, á ceàrnaibh àraid de'n Ghàidhealtachd, agus ás na h-eileanaibh an iar, far nach robh a bheag sam bith de'n choillte a' fàs, agus far am b' éiginn daibh dol gu minic air bàtaichean astar cheudan mìle a dh'iarraidh beagan mhaidean cama crotach air son cheangal agus chabar d'an taighibh. Bu mhath, dà-rìreabh, anns an Eilean Sgitheanach fhéin agus anns an Eilean Fhada, o Rudha na Circe gu Barraigh, beagan de'n bharrachd fiodha a tha aig muinntir a' Cheap. Dhèanadh iad sòlas nach bu bheag ri nì a tha 'nan crìochaibh fhéin cho luachmhor agus cho gann.*
>
> Regarding the number and species of trees, it is only suitable to say a little here. There are at least fourteen different species of pine, five species of birch, and four species of oak that are found in this same island. The yellow pine is the most valuable, because it is not only excellent timber, it grows to be exceedingly big. Very often trees of this species of pine are found that measure fifteen feet around the base, one hundred and twenty feet in height, and eighty feet of that height are free of branches and limbs. Amongst the different kinds of wood that grow in the Cape the following can be named: pine, oak, juniper, beech, elm, ash, rowan, birch, alder, maple (from which syrup is made), aspen, and so on. Besides each of these woods, there are many others for which there is no Gaelic term […]

> There is no doubt whatsoever that the Gaels who immigrated to North America from particular parts of the Highlands and from the Western Isles, where there was hardly any forest growing, and from which they often had to go on boats for distances of hundreds of miles in order to seek a few crooked and bent sticks for the couples and rafters of their homes, thoroughly enjoy the sight of these forests. It would be good, indeed, for some of the excellent wood that the people of the Cape have [to be] on the Isle of Skye itself and in the Long Island from Point to Barra. They would greatly celebrate having something that is so valuable and rare in their own territory.

This is not to assert that all Canadian Gaels – especially those attempting to make a space in the 'wildwood' to build houses and conduct agriculture – waxed lyrical about the forest. In reality, Gaels had a wide variety of attitudes about and perceptions of trees: there are Gaelic narratives and song-poems about immigrants whose impatience to clear unwanted woodlands by lighting fires ended in disaster, for example (Dunn 1968: 29). What we see in immigrant literary expressions are not necessarily explicit commentaries about ecological integrity or the aesthetic evaluations of woods, but rather the use of tree symbolism to express a variety of personal feelings and experiences. In other words, poets used arboreal images and metaphors as rhetorical devices and environmental backdrops upon which to project messages about their own individual aspirations and concerns.

Just as we project our current values and preoccupations into our readings of history, so do Gaelic historical narratives which incorporate the forest primeval – the 'Great Caledonian Forest' in the Scottish context – reveal perceptions of and values related to woodlands from the contexts of their authors. No later than the twelfth century, Gaelic literati fashioned an historical narrative accounting for the origins of the Gaelic people which demonstrates an intuitive understanding of the connections between agriculture, a stratified, patriarchal social order, and the clearing of the forests: in other words, the essence of 'civilisation' in a technical sense (Bitel 2002; Newton 2003: 189–90).

By the late medieval period, an alternative narrative to explain the loss of the primeval forests had taken hold in Gaelic vernacular tradition, shaped by the polarisation between Gael and Norse: jealous of Scotland's resources, which they are not able to exploit, the Norse decide to destroy them (Newton 2003: 185-8; 2009: 284–6, 289). Although this tale (found in many variants) has been dismissed as lacking rational merit (Smout, MacDonald and Watson 2007: 36), it tells us that Gaels saw the destruction of the forests – the remnants of which they found in bogs and deep in the soil – as a tragic loss perpetrated by enemies. The narrative, which has counterparts in Ireland (Ó Catháin and O'Flanagan 1975: 74), indicates the intrinsic value of woodlands, the need to account for the loss of primal integrity and a subconscious desire to deflect blame away from self and onto the Other.

Another significant item in Gaelic oral tradition relates to the *Cailleach Bheur*, the female personification of wild nature and creator of the landscape. In this brief anecdote, the Cailleach is found dethroned and keening the destruction of the forest, bringing us back to the correlation between agriculture, patriarchal desacralisation and the loss of woodlands implied in the earlier Irish myth of origins (Newton 2009: 324).

Every culture in every age is liable to glamorise or deprecate natural environments in ways that contradict how people actually live and earn their sustenance. Such disparities are the stuff of modern debates about ecological sustainability ('Do we exploit the resources of the landscape or preserve its beauty?') and we might ask if medieval Gaels were aware of the inconsistencies between their own attitudes and practices. I believe that there are clues in Gaelic tradition that indicate a consciousness of the inherent contradictions of idealising forests while still needing to exploit them and 'keep them at bay' for agriculture.

A proverb which first appears in a collection written by the early eighteenth-century antiquarian Uilleam MacMhurchaidh illustrates such tensions: '*Mol an lom-thìr is na ruig i; dì-mhol a' choille is na trèig i*' ('Praise the bare-land and don't go to it; dispraise the forest and don't leave it') (Alexander Cameron 1894: 502). The first printed collection of Gaelic proverbs contains a close variant of this: '*Mol am mona[dh] is na ruig e; diomoil a' choille 's na fàg i*' ('You may extol the bleak hill but go not thither; you may vilify the wood, but quit it not'). This is given the gloss 'Analagous to "praise the sea but keep on dry land" ' (Macintosh 1785: 54–5). These two variants are complemented in the later Nicolson collection by '*Mol a' mhachair is na treabh; diomoil a' choille is na tréig*' ('Praise the plain and plough it not, &c.') (Nicholson 1882: 318). These aphorisms clearly reflect ambivalence about contrasting environments and probably also the social classes associated with them: Gaelic warrior-aristocrats had the privilege of hunting in the woods, but the peasantry was tied to working the soil of the fields (MacInnes 2006: 27). The élite maintained their noble status by both avoiding such agricultural drudgery and ensuring that it was safely delegated to reliable trustees.

Literary resources supplemented the physical environment in maintaining ecological diversity in the cultural imagination. On the one hand, the arboreal diversity of any particular Gaelic community was in fact reflected in its literary expressions; on the other hand, the cosmological and literary inheritance of Gaeldom rooted the human experience in a world view which valued trees highly and perpetuated their presence conceptually in an idealised landscape of the mind, even when they were poorly attested in the local environment.

In a broad study of cognitive models derived by cultures from environmental experience, James Fernandez suggests that

> the landscape offers, among other contiguous experiences of human life, primary images out of which or on the basis of which men and women, turning contiguities into similarities, can construct their senses of themselves, of their social relations and of their world – of their moral obligations, in short, in the widest sense of the term (1998: 104).

It is tempting to read something of this affection for woodlands much further back into Gaelic history and identity. It is well established that the ethnonym *Goídil*, which the Gaels used for themselves, was actually a borrowing from their Brythonic neighbours meaning something like 'forest-people' or 'wildmen'. John Koch has recently argued that *Goídil* originated in a cluster of narratives that the Gaelic literati appropriated in the late seventh century for their own purposes (Koch 2000). Although the original Brythonic ethnonym did not present Gaelic speakers in a flattering light, could the adoption of this term indicate some subversive attitude on the part of the literati who were willing to embrace this association with trees and the wild?[3] Does this lead us back to the idea of the nature-loving Gaelic monk-poet, who recent scholars have insisted is a chimera of the modern literary imagination (Ó Corráin 1989) as illusory as the Great Caledonian Forest? Perhaps scientists and poets will only find common ground on these matters in the imagination itself.

---

[3] It is worth pointing out that the ethnonym *Féni* – which could be used restrictively to refer to a particular descent group, but also more broadly to refer to all of the Irish – may be derived from the same Proto-Celtic root **wēdu*. See Koch 2006.

Sources

BARROW, G. W. S.

1998 'The Uses of Place-names and Scottish History – Pointers and Pitfalls'. Simon Taylor (ed.), *The Uses of Place-Names*. Edinburgh: 54–74.

BATEMAN, MEG.

2009 'The environmentalism of Donnchadh Bàn: pragmatic or mythic?' Christopher MacLachlan (ed.), *Crossing the Highland Line: Cross-Currents in Eighteenth-Century Scottish Writing*. Glasgow: 123–36.

BITEL, LISA.

2002 'Landscape, Gender, and Ethnogenesis in Pre-Norman Invasion Ireland'. John Howe and Michael Wolfe (eds), *Inventing Medieval Landscapes: Senses of Place in Western Europe*. Gainsville, FL: 171–91.

CALDWELL, DAVID, FIONA MCGIBBON, SUZANNE MILLER AND NIGEL RUCKLEY.

2010 'The image of a Celtic society: medieval West Highland sculpture'. Pamela O'Neill (ed.), *Celts in Legend and Reality: Papers from the Sixth Australian Conference of Celtic Studies*. Sydney: 13–59.

CAMERON, ALEXANDER (ED.).

1894 *Reliquae Celticae*, vol. 2. Inverness.

CAMERON, JOHN.

1894 'On the Death of the Heir of Glencoe'. *Oban Times* 30 June 1894.

CAREY, JOHN.

1992 'Symbol and Thought in Irish Religious Thought'. *Temenos* 13: 101–11.

DUNBAR, ROBERT.

2008 'Poetry of the Emigrant Generation'. *Transactions of the Gaelic Society of Inverness* 64 (2004–6): 22–125.

DUNN, CHARLES W.

[1943] 1968 *Highland Settler*. Toronto.

FERNANDEZ, JAMES.

1998 'Trees of Knowledge of Self and Other in Culture: On Models for the Moral Imagination'. Laura Rival (ed.), *The Social Life of Trees: Anthropological Perspectives on Tree Symbolism*. Oxford: 81–110.

KELLY, FERGUS.

1976 'The Old Irish Tree List'. *Celtica* 11: 107–24.

KOCH, JOHN.

2000 'On the Origins of the Old Irish Terms Goídil and Goídelc'. Geraint Evans, Bernard Martin and Jonathan Wooding (eds), *Origins and Revivals: Proceedings of the First Australian Conference of Celtic Studies*. Sydney: 3–15.

2006 'Féni.' John Koch (ed.), *Celtic Culture: A Historical Encyclopedia*. Santa Barbara, CA: 738–9.

MAC AONGHUIS, IAIN.

1983 'Samhla na Craoibhe'. An Comunn Gàidhealach and the Gaelic Society of Inverness, *Sàr-Ghàidheal: Essays in memory of Rory Mackay*. 64–9. Inverness.

MACDONELL, MARGARET (ED.).

1982 *The Emigrant Experience*. Toronto.

MAC FHEARGHUIS, CALUM.

1995 *Hiort: Far na laigh a' ghrian*. Stornoway.

MACINNES, ALLAN, MARJORY-ANN HARPER AND LINDA FRYER (EDS).

2002 *Scotland and the Americas, c. 1650–c. 1939*. Edinburgh.

MACINNES, JOHN.

2006 *Dùthchas nan Gàidheal: Selected Essays of John MacInnes*. Michael Newton (ed.). Edinburgh.

MACINTOSH, DONALD.

1785 *Gaelic Proverbs and Familiar Phrases*. Edinburgh.

MACLEÒID, DOMHNUL.

1811 *Orain Nuadh Ghaeleach*. Inverness.

MCMANUS, DAMIAN.

2006 '"The smallest man in Ireland can reach the tops of her trees": Images of the King's Peace and Bounty in Bardic Poetry'. Joseph Nagy (ed.), *Memory and the Modern in Celtic Literatures: CSANA Yearbook 5*. Dublin.

NEWTON, MICHAEL

1998 The Tree in Scottish Gaelic Literature and Tradition. Unpublished Ph.D. dissertation, University of Edinburgh.

2003 'Coille Mhòr Chailleann ann am Beul-aithris nan Gàidheal'. Wilson McLeod and Máire Ní Annracháin (eds), *Cruth na Tíre*. Dublin: 180–94.

2009 *Warriors of the Word: The World of the Scottish Highlanders*. Edinburgh.

NICOLSON, ALEXANDER (ED.).

1882 *A Collection of Gaelic Proverbs and Familiar Sayings*. Edinburgh.

Ó BAOILL, COLM (ED.).

1972 *Bàrdachd Shìlis na Ceapaich / Poems and Songs by Sìleas MacDonald.* Edinburgh.

Ó CATHÁIN, SÉUMAS, AND PATRICK O'FLANAGAN.

1975 *The Living Landscape: Kilgalligan Erris, Co. Mayo.* Dublin.

Ó CORRÁIN, DONNCHADH.

1989 'Early Irish Hermit Poetry?' Donnchadh Ó Corráin, Liam Breatnach and Kim McCone (eds), *Sages, Saints and Storytellers: Celtic Studies in Honour of Professor James Carney*. Maynooth: 251–67.

SGÌTHEANACH.

1848 'Cunntas air Ceap Bretoin an America mu Thuath'. *Fear-Tathaich nam Beann* 8 (An Lùnasdal): 231–41.

SINTON, THOMAS (ED.).

1906 *The Poetry of Badenoch*. Inverness.

SMOUT, CHRISTOPHER.

1997 'Highland Land-use before 1800'. T. C. Smout (ed.), *Scottish Woodland History*. Dalkeith: 5–22.

2000 *Nature Contested: Environmental History in Scotland and Northern England since 1600*. Edinburgh University Press.

SMOUT, T. C., ALAN MACDONALD AND FIONA WATSON.

2007 *A History of the Native Woodlands of Scotland, 1500–1920*. Edinburgh.

Seán Bán Mac Grianna and 'Christine Keeler'

LILLIS Ó LAOIRE

The locally-based poet who composes on traditional themes is, or was, a fairly widespread phenomenon in Gaelic communities on both sides of *Sruth na Maoile*. In Scotland such a poet is often called a *bàrd baile*. Although some women made songs in this tradition (Neat & MacInnes 1999), these poets were mostly male, like their Irish counterparts. These poets made songs that encompassed a wide range of topics, some intimately local, others dealing with more prominent national or international events. In Ireland, by 1993, in excess of a hundred songs had been made in the Connemara Gaeltacht by over forty poets (Ó Conghaile 1993: 7–10), and the tide of song shows no sign of ebbing. Themes could include 'homeland, war, love, local and national events, new technology, religion, philosophy, humour and songs relating to individual members of the community' (Kidd 2006: 174). Despite this range, however, 'poetry derived from the verse tradition of the past'(*ibid.*) has often been considered narrow in scope and limited by traditional conventions. Such views were advanced by those wishing to access more contemporary, up-to-date and modern genres as found in English and other languages more influenced by print culture (MacAulay 1976: 46). The term *bàrd baile* is problematic, as it suggests that such poets' views of the world are confined, limited and consequently inferior. This lack of respect has been attributed to the 'tradition-innovation wars of the 1960s' (Black 1999: lxi).

Recent research, however, has led to a new appreciation of the work of local poets (*e.g.* McKean 1997). The elegies composed by John Morrison of Scalpaigh, Harris, for example, have been described as the literary equivalent of a 'renaissance cathedral' (Black: lxi). The mock-heroic vein, which is strong and well-developed in both Scottish Gaelic and Irish song poetry, can be traced at least to the eighteenth century in Irish Gaelic verse, and is related to the poets' loss of status in that period (Ó Laoire 2009). In this paper, I will discuss a song in this style by a twentieth-century Donegal poet, much of whose work is still popular. However, for reasons that will become clear, the particular song in question has not previously been published. It reveals many of the best characteristics of topical song poetry in Irish, and underlines the close connections between the two related traditions.

Seán Bán Mac Grianna (1905–1979) was the youngest surviving child of Feilimí Dhónaill Phroinnsiais Mac Grianna and Máire Sheimisín Ní Dhomhnaill of Rann na Feirste, Co. Donegal. Both parents were noted tradition-bearers in a Gaeltacht area renowned for the richness of its oral traditions. Seán Bán had ten siblings, two of whom, Séamus (1889–1968) and Seosamh (1901–1991), achieved lasting fame as writers in the twentieth-century efflorescence of Gaelic writing in Ireland. Both he and his sister, who was known as Annie Bhán (1893–1963), were recognized as skilled storytellers.[1] Seán Bán was also a singer and fiddle-player (Mac Grianna & Mac Corraidh 2010), but his most outstanding achievement was as a *file* – a song-maker, akin to the *bàrd bhaile* of Gaelic Scotland.

Mac Grianna's song 'Christine Keeler' shows how a rural Irish-language poet living far from London was able to engage with contemporary events of considerable sophistication, and do so in a sharp, intelligent and comedic manner. The song is firmly rooted in a present where the scandal is

---

[1] 'MAC GRIANNA, Seán Bán (1905–1979)'. *Ainm.ie: Beathaisnéisí Gaeilge* (http://www.ainm.ie/Bio.aspx?ID=448). Consulted on 27 December 2012. *Ainm.ie* also contains biographies of Seán Bán's siblings Annie Bhán, Séamus (1889–1968), Domhnall (1894–1962) and Seosamh (1901–1991). See also MacLennan and Harrison 1997.

still a recent happening. It demonstrates the poet's awareness of the Cold War and its influence on the unfolding of events. As was common in Gaelic poetry, the song borrows an air and some lyrics from another song. The borrowing is not a matter of chance, however, and reveals the clever deployment and extension of references in the source to emphasize and augment the points the poet wishes to make in his own work.

Ióseph Ó Searcaigh, a school teacher from Anagaire, Co. Donegal, collected twenty of Mac Grianna's songs, including two translations of English language songs, and published them in a little book, *Seághan Bán Mac Grianna: Ceoltaí agus Seanchas,* which appeared in 1976 in connection with the Golden Jublilee celebrations surrounding the founding of Coláiste Bhríde, the local Gaelic College in Rann na Feirste, Co. Donegal, where Mac Grianna taught for nearly fifty years. Mac Grianna's online biography is probably correct in observing of his poetry, *tá cuid mhór nach raibh i gcló riamh* 'there is much that has never been published'.[2] Like many oral poets, Mac Grianna did not function in a milieu where publishing was the norm, and unsurprisingly many of his songs have, over time, been lost.

Censored or Private Songs

The well-established idea that songs must be taken up by a community in order to ensure dissemination and survival will always hold true. What is not often considered is how songs that are taboo are transmitted and performed. Kenneth Goldstein researched sectarian songs in religiously-mixed communities in Newfoundland, where he discovered that such songs were sung only in private, and when members from the group being criticised in the song were not present. Goldstein encountered reluctance on the part of his informants to perform them for him, prevailing upon them only after some persuasion (Goldstein 1991). Elsewhere my co-writer Sean Williams and I have shown that a similar dynamic obtained in the case of 'Johnny Seoighe', a song from Carna, Co. Galway, and we have suggested why these restrictions operated in relation to that song (Williams and Ó Laoire, 2011, 71–88). In a Scottish context, one might also mention the incendiary potential attached to the singing of the waulking song *'Cha déid Mór a Bharraidh Bhrònaich'* in Cape Breton communities of Barra and Uist descent, where performance of this item 'could start a fight', and was consequently forbidden at social gatherings (Campbell and Collinson 1977: 112–120; 226–232). Peadar Ó Ceannabháin has remarked on similar conventions among song poets in Conamara. Speaking of some songs he states (Ó Ceannabháin 164):

> *Cé gur amhráin phobail a thugtar orthu ba mhinic gur ar chuid bheag den phobal a bhídís dírithe agus ar phobal beag éisteachta. Is iomaí amhrán a cumadh agus a casadh nár chuala ach dream áirithe, dhá theach nó beagán lena chois ar aon bhaile, b'fhéidir. Amanta, ní bheadh an dream a chum iad ag iarraidh go gcloisfí iad ná go gcasfaí go poiblí iad.'*
>
> Although they are called community songs, they were often meant for a very small part of the community and for a small audience. Many songs were made and sung that only certain people heard, perhaps [the inhabitants of] two houses or a little more than that in one township. Sometimes, those who made them did not want them to be heard or to be sung publicly.

Proinsias Ó Maonaigh, the well known Donegal fiddler (1922-2006), first told me about Mac Grianna's 'Christine Keeler,' a song which falls into this category.[3] Christine Keeler was the young woman at the centre of the infamous Profumo Affair, which rocked British political life when the

---

[2] Mac Grianna, Seán. Ainm.ie.

[3] Ó Maonaigh, Proinsias. Ainm.ie http://www.ainm.ie/Bio.aspx?ID=1916. Consulted 3 July 2013.

story broke in 1963. Given its theme, Ióseph Ó Searcaigh and those involved in the organisation of the Golden Jubilee activities may have decided that the song was unsuitable for inclusion in the 1976 volume. I had often asked about this song, and many people told me they knew of it, but I was unable to get the words until September 2012. I had asked my colleague Micheál Ó Domhnaill, himself of Rann na Feirste stock, a son of the late and well-known singer Caitlín Ní Dhomhnaill (1940–2005), if he had heard of it. He had not, but he enquired and finally managed to procure the text from Tony Mac Ruairí, a Rann na Feirste native who has researched Seán Bán Mac Grianna's songs. Here is the note Micheál attached to the lyrics:

> *Seo leagan den amhrán* 'Christine Keeler' *a fuair mé ó Tony Mac Ruairí an lá faoi dheireadh. Deir sé liom go bhfuair sé ó Phádraig Chonaill Mac Grianna é. Chuir mé ceist fán amhrán i dtrátha an ama adaí ar cheistigh tú mé féin faoi, ach ní raibh a fhios ag aon duine a dhath faoi – tháinig sé seo chun solais agus faoi mo dhéin díreach ar an Luan.*
>
> Here is a version of the song 'Christine Keeler' which I got from Tony Mac Ruairí the other day. He says he got it from Pádraig Chonaill Mac Grianna. I asked about this song around that time you questioned me about it, but nobody knew anything about it – it came to light and to me only on Monday.

Clearly, the song has been remembered by some of the people in Rann na Feirste. However, like the songs mentioned above, where an element of privacy or censorship prevailed with regard to their performance, it is clear that the song has followed less than obvious modes of transmission. Because of its potential for controversy, 'Christine Keeler', like the others, seems to have been deliberately hidden, and sung only in restricted gatherings.

Since its subject matter would have been considered risqué, 'Christine Keeler' was not published with the poet's other songs, and many people remained unaware of its existence. As Micheál Ó Domhnaill's note indicates, however, the song was preserved and kept in good order, as can be seen from the version published here. This is no decaying fragment, but a full and complete version that indicates that the item has been actively and carefully retained and, presumably, enjoyed for its satirical, comedic sentiments.

Údar an amhráin – The Story behind the Song

Mac Grianna composed 'Christine Keeler' in response to a British political scandal that erupted in the early sixties. The reporting of this affaire marked a new era. Such matters could now be aired in public by a press which refused to collude with codes of reportage that had previously sheltered the lives of politicians from public scrutiny. The story itself is a convoluted and intricate one that has been the subject of a number of books. All the details need not detain us here, but a summary of the main points is required for an understanding of the song's text. Like so many Gaelic songs, it alludes to the events of the story, rather than narrating them. Consequently, the accompanying narrative becomes a focal point of the whole, and augments the often brief references made in the lyrics (Shields 1993).

In 1963, John Profumo (1915-2006) was Secretary of State for War in Harold Macmillan's Conservative Government. He was married to actress Valerie Hobson. In 1961 he was introduced to Christine Keeler (1942–) by Stephen Ward (1912–1963), an osteopath and socialite, at a party at Cliveden, the Buckinghamshire residence of Lord Astor. Profumo and Keeler had a brief affair. The following year, rumours of the relationship began to leak out, along with others linking Keeler to Yevgeny Ivanov, a senior Soviet diplomat with the Russian Embassy in London, who was strongly suspected of espionage. In 1962, the year of the Cuban Missile Crisis, Cold War tensions were at their height, and the story attracted considerable interest, especially from members of MI5. They became convinced that the Russians had plotted to use Keeler to procure classified information from Profumo. In fact, Stephen Ward had been assisting MI5 in order to entrap Ivanov. Profumo initially denied any irregularity in his relationship with Keeler, but later, in June 1963, he publicly admitted having lied to the House of Commons. He resigned his cabinet position on 5 June 1963. A few months later, Prime Minister Macmillan, citing ill-health, retired from office and was replaced as leader of the Conservative Party by Sir Alec Douglas-Home. The Tories, however, continued to lose credibility with the electorate, and because of this scandal and other unfavourable circumstances they were defeated in the General Election of 1964 by Harold Wilson's Labour Party. Charged with living off earnings from prostitution, Stephen Ward committed suicide on the last day of his trial in August 1963 (Irving 1963; Young 1963; Brown 2001).

'Christine Keeler' – a reading

Mac Grianna was not the only artist to be inspired by the Profumo Affair. Many other works were based on the story over the years, including the film *Scandal* (Caton-Jones, 1989). Mac Grianna's poem portrays a first-person narrator, an anti-heroic figure who goes to London and encounters Stephen Ward in a pub. He meets people from every race there, including some from France and, tellingly, Russia. He gains access to one of Ward's parties and, surveying all the women present, promptly falls in love with Christine Keeler. He approaches her and whispers in her ear, but she escapes instead with John Profumo. Not to be deterred, however, the narrator takes full advantage of Ward's invitation to his apartment, and enjoys himself to the full with *spéirmhná caoine* – 'beautiful, gentle women'. A reference to a broken mirror in verse six appears to allude to the two-way mirrors in Ward's Wimpole Mews flat (Irving 1963: 198). The scandal spreads throughout the country and becomes the talk of the nation, and Macmillan suffers because of it. Eventually the song refers to Henry the Eighth's fondness for women, declaring that, had he lived, the King would have had an attractive, fun-loving harem. Moreover, he would have needed no permission from clergy to elope with them into the bracken. The song finishes with the dejected narrator declaring that, notwithstanding the many beautiful, gentle women who have spent blissful nights in his company, he will remain in love with Christine Keeler even if he lives forever.

Intertextuality and its import

An interesting aspect of this song is the song's obvious intertextual engagement with *'An Poc ar Buile',* a song composed around 1940 by Múscraí (Cork) poet Dónall Ó Mulláin (1880–1965), which won a prize at the Gaelic League's Oireachtas festival and subsequently became well-known in Gaelic circles.[4] It was even exported by at least one priest and enjoyed immensely by his African congregation.[5] This now iconic song gained widespread popularity through the performances of the well-known tenor, Seán Ó Sé, singing with Seán Ó Riada's Ceoltóirí Chualann, whose 1962 recording was widely disseminated over the national airwaves.[6] Indeed, Seán Ó Sé was nicknamed 'the Pucker' because of his close association with this song. The song has retained its popularity, has been frequently recorded, and remains widely known in Ireland to this day.

Mac Grianna's choice of this air for his song was deliberate. The subject matter of *'An Poc ar Buile',* which concerns a rampaging billy goat and its victims, is so inconsequential as to be considered frivolous. This charge was indeed levelled against it by a correspondent for *Comhar*,

[4] 'Ó MULLÁIN, Dónall (1880–1965)'. *Ainm.ie: Beathaisnéisí Gaeilge* (http://www.ainm.ie/Bio.aspx?ID=537). Consulted on 27 December 2012.

[5] '"An Poc ar Buile" delights Africans, says Priest.' *Irish Independent,* 24 September, 1963, 8. In this article the song's composer is said to be Seán Eoghan Ó Súilleabháin, another noted Cúil Aodha poet. Neither the priest nor the location of his African congregation are named in the article.

[6] Nicholas Carolan, Director, Irish Traditional Music Archive, personally confirmed to me the release date of this recording.

reporting on a concert held at the annual Irish cultural festival, Oireachtas na Gaeilge, in November, 1950:

> *Thairis sin, sa chás so, ní ceart amhrán de shaghas 'An Poc ar Buile' bheith ar an chlár. An gcuirfí 'The Dingle Puck Goat' ar chlár Chuirm Cheoil i mBéarla? Ná tuigtear go bhfuilim in éadan amhráin den tsórt, ach iad do bheith ina suíomh ceart i measc cóluadair shuairc i dteach tábhairne, an piunt ar láimh agus an béal agus an croí ar leathadh gan chosc. Ach ar stáitse fuar i mBaile Átha Cliath mara bhfuil togha na healadhn Gaeilge ar taisbeáint!*[7]
>
> Furthermore, in this case, a song like 'An Poc ar Buile' should not be on the programme. Would 'The Dingle Puck Goat' be put on an English language Concert programme? Let it not be thought that I am opposed to songs of this kind, but that they ought to be in a proper context amongst a happy company in a public house, pints in hand and both mouth and heart open without restraint. But on a cold stage in Dublin where the best of Gaelic art is on show!

This disapproving review condemns the item as unsuitable for serious listeners. However, the very frivolity of *'An Poc ar Buile'* was undoubtedly the source of its appeal for Mac Grianna, with the song's national popularity acting as an additional incentive. He could easily see that the subversive qualities in his fellow poet's song were ideally suited to his own purpose. As a result, his intertextual references are especially effective. His deliberate choice of air and use of the chorus of *'An Poc ar Buile'* intentionally underline the irreverent, Rabelaisian humour. The reference to the goat obliquely emphasizes the sexual nature of the scandal, the goat being considered, in folklore and popular culture, an unusually lecherous animal.[8] The poet's reference to Henry the Eighth adds to the satire here. The King's defection from Roman Catholicism and his fondness for illicit relationships was commonly invoked by Catholics in sectarian debates.

Mac Grianna pokes fun not only at the British establishment and their hypocritical ways, but also at the Gaelic movement. His choice of theme was hardly likely to meet the stringent cultural standards of *Comhar's* reviewer, any more than his model did. In doing so, he destabilises official attempts to promote a monolithic image of a high-minded, serious Gaelic culture without any humorous dimension. The serious image was important for nation-building purposes, especially to counter ingrained stereotypes of fun-loving (but ultimately shiftless) Gaels in opposition with stolid Anglo-Saxons with a dependable, if humourless, work ethic. But while Mac Grianna was committed to the ideals of the movement, he also recognized the futility of attempts to control and manipulate Gaelic cultural expression in a one-sided manner. Mac Grianna's playful but mordant satire fits well with Bakthin's idea of the carnivalesque's questioning of all authority (Bakthin, 1984).

---

[7]Anonymous ('Len Ár dTuairisceoir' – 'From Our Reporter'), *Comhar* 9/11 (1950): 6.

[8]See, for example, Edmund Spenser's *The Faerie Queen,* Book I Canto IV, where lechery is portrayed riding a goat:

> *And next to him rode lustful Lechery*
> *Upon a bearded Goat, whose rugged Hair*
> *And whally Eyes (the sign of Jealousy)*
> *Was like the Person self, whom he did bear:*
> *Who rough, and black, and filthy did appear,*

This imagery ultimately derives from the last judgement in Christian tradition, where the sheep and goats are divided – the sheep being saved and the goats damned. Billy goats are considered especially obsessed with mating; see Black, Conolly and Flint (2011): 582.

Implications

The example of 'Christine Keeler' shows how a rural Irish language poet was able to engage with modern phenomena in an intelligent and unselfconscious manner. His engagement with current events reveals a keen and sophisticated observation of international politics and current affairs. The song is certainly traditional in format and style, but tradition here functions as an 'enabling referent' that enhances, rather than stifles, the creative impact of the song. The poet's access to modern mass media having enabled his engagement with the news of the day, his song is firmly rooted in a present where the event has only just occurred. Reference to the Russian in the first verse shows Mac Grianna's awareness of the Cold War and its influence on the unfolding of events, and his borrowing of air and chorus from another contemporary Gaelic poet is another stroke of brilliance entirely apposite to his theme. Certainly, the song is in character with the poet's well-known persona of *'An Banaí Drabhlásach'* – the profligate womanizer (Mac Grianna & Ó Searcaigh 1976: 61/2) – on which he based other songs. Certainly the song is traditional in its use of motifs and imagery. Nevertheless, tradition here is an enabling force, not a dead weight that limits the poet's creativity. Indeed, Mac Grianna's 'Christine Keeler' bears out the idea that oral poetry 'does not divorce entertainment from instruction, artistic craft from cultural work' (Foley 2002: 28). It therefore seems fair to conclude that, as has been argued in the Scottish Gaelic context, *bardachd bhaile* need not be characterized as narrow, nor need it be doomed to disappear.

Christine Keeler
Seán Bán Mac Grianna (1963)

Ar a ghabháil go Sasain domh ar dtús *Is é a casadh domh na mílte cineadh* *As an Fhrainc is as an Rúis* *'Gus as gach dúiche ar fud na cruinne.*	When I first went to England I met thousands of races From France and from Russia And from every region of the world
Loinneog:	**Refrain:**
Aililiú puililiú, aililiú tá an poc ar buile Aililiú puililiú, aililiú tá an poc ar buile.	*Ailliú Puililiú*, the billy goat is gone mad *Ailliú Puililiú,* the billy goat is gone mad
Chuaigh mé isteach i dtigh an ósta *Is bhí na slóite a' déanamh grinn ann,* *Cé casadh orm ach Stephen Ward* *Is bhí sé rannpháirteach mar dhuine ann.*	I went into the pub And there were crowds having fun there Who should I meet but Stephen Ward Who participated like everyone else.
Thug mé spleáchadh fríd na mná *Agus bhí siad mánla maiseach gnaíúil* *Is go maithe Dia domh mo chás* *Thit mé i ngrá le Christine Keeler.*	I looked among the women They were gracious, elegant and comely And may God forgive me my case I fell in love with Christine Keeler
Chuir mé cogar ina cluais *Nuair a mheas mé go raibh sí súgach* *Ach mo léan géar d'fhág sí mise i nguais* *Is d'éalaigh sí le John Profumo.*	I whispered in her ear When I thought her mellow But alas she left me dismayed And went off with John Profumo.

Thug Stephen cuireadh domh chun tí
Agus chaith mé an oíche ansin gan chodladh
Ní raibh orm easpa bí ná dí
Is bhí spéirmhná caoine 'o mo mhealladh.

Stephen asked me to the house
And I spent the night with no sleep
I didn't want for food or drink
With refined beauties seducing me.

Bhí scáilí ann a mheall mo shúil
Nuair a bhí mé ag súgradh le mo ghrá geal
Ach ba mhaith an mhaise do mo rún é
D'éirigh sí agus bhris sí an scáthán.

Reflections there seduced my eyes
As I played with my bright love
But to give my darling credit
Up she got and broke the mirror.

Thug siad scainnir mhór don tír
Is d'fhág sin gléas éagcaoin ar lucht faille
Chuaigh an scéal go síor i mbéal na ndaoine
Is cé a bhí thíos leis ach Macmillan.

They gave the country great scandal
And an opportune moment for complaint
People talked incessantly of it
And Macmillan paid the price.

Dá maireadh sean-Anraí i réim
Bheadh aige harem *aerach dathúil*
Ní bheadh sé a' dréim le ceangal cléir'
Ach cead a fháil éaló leo fán raithneach.

If old Henry still ruled
He'd have a cheerful, handsome harem
He'd not expect a cleric's tie
But permission to go off into the bracken.

Is iomaí spéirbhean álainn chaoin
A chaith seal oíche liom gan mhairg
Ach tá mé i ngrá le Christine Keeler
Agus beidh le saol na saol dá mairfinn.

Many's the beautiful, gentle woman
Who spent a happy night with me
But I'm in love with Christine Keeler
And so I'll be should I live forever.

Sources

http://www.ainm.ie.
Gaelic (Irish) Biography website.

ANONYMOUS.
1950 'Caighdeán Éagothram in Imeachtaí an Oireachtais'. *Comhar* 9/11 (November): 4–6.

BAKTHIN, MIKHAIL.
1984 *Rabelais and His World.* Bloomington.

BLACK, JOSEPH, LEONARD CONOLLY AND KATE FLINT.
2011 *The Broadview Anthology of English Literature* (2nd ed.). Peterborough, Ont.

BLACK, RONALD.
1999 *An Tuil: Anthology of 20th century Scottish Gaelic Verse.* Edinburgh.

BROWN, DEREK.
2001 '1963: The Profumo Scandal.' *The Guardian,* 10 April 2001.

CATON-JONES, MICHAEL.

1989 *Scandal.* UK.

CAMPBELL, JOHN LORNE & FRANCIS COLLINSON.

1977 *Hebridean Folksongs* II. Oxford.

FOLEY, JOHN MILES.

2002 *How to Read an Oral Poem.* Illinois.

GOLDSTEIN, KENNETH S.

1991 'A Report on the Continuing Research into Treason Songs: A Private Newfoundland Tradition'. G. Thomas and J. D. A. Widdowson (eds), *Studies in Newfoundland Folklore*. St. John's: 126–53.

IRVING, CLIVE.

1963 *Anatomy of A Scandal: A Study of the Profumo Affair.* New York.

KIDD, SHEILA.

2006 'Bàrd Baile'. John T. Koch (ed.), *Celtic Culture: A Historical Encyclopedia* I. 173–4.

MCKEAN, THOMAS A.

1997 *Hebridean Song-Maker: Iain Mac Neacail of the Isle of Skye.* Edinburgh.

MACAULAY, DONALD.

1976 *Nua-Bhardachd Ghàidhlig / Modern Scottish Gaelic Poems: A Bilingual Anthology.* Edinburgh.

MAC GRIANNA, SEAGHÁN.

1976 *Seaghán Bán Mac Grianna: Ceoltaí agus Seanchas.* Ióseph Ó Searcaigh (eag.). Rann na Feirste.

MAC GRIANNA, SEÁN BÁN.

2010 *Seán Bán Mac Grianna: Scéalta agus Amhráin.* Seán Mac Corraidh (eag.). Baile Átha Cliath.

MACLENNAN, GORDON W.

1997 *Seanchas Annie Bhán.* Alan Harrison and Mairi Elena Crook (trans.). Dublin.

NEAT, TIMOTHY, AND JOHN MACINNES.

1999 *The Voice of the Bard.* Edinburgh.

Ó CEANNABHÁIN, PEADAR.

2011 'An Samhradh sa bhFuacht idir Nollaig is Cáisc: spléachadh ar fhilithe in Iorras Aithneach san 19ú céad.' *Bliainiris 10,* 147–168.

Ó CONGHAILE, MICHEÁL.

1993 *Gnéithe d'Amhráin Chonamara ár Linne*. Indreabhán.

Ó LAOIRE, LILLIS.

2009 '"Is mé go déanach i mBaile Sheáin": Donnchadh Rua Mac Conmara i dTalamh an Éisc.' *Léann* 2: 105–28.

SHIELDS, HUGH.

1993 *Lays, Ballads, Come-All-Yes and Other Songs: Narrative Singing in Ireland.* Dublin.

WILLIAMS, SEAN AND LILLIS Ó LAOIRE.

2011 *Bright Star of the West: Joe Heaney, Irish Song Man.* New York.

YOUNG, WAYLAND.

1963 *Scandal 63.* London.

Am Buadhfhacal Meadhan-Aoiseach *Meranach* agus *mearan*, *mearanach*, *dàsachdach*, *dàsan*(*n*)*ach* na Gàidhlig

ROIBEARD Ó MAOLALAIGH

ABSTRACT. The epithet *meranach* is found in Irish sources from the eleventh century. The same element may be present in the Irish surname *Merna*(*gh*) and perhaps also in the early thirteenth-century Scottish epithet *Marrenah*. It is suggested that the underlying element is *meránach* ('delirious, mad, insane'), which survives in Scottish Gaelic *mearan*(*ach*). The rich variety of forms which survive (or survived until recently) in Scotland are discussed. Parallels are drawn with the use of *dásachtach* as an epithet of the Scottish king Domnall mac Causaintín (†900AD) and the survival of *dàsanach*, *dàsannach* and related forms in Scottish Gaelic. These epithets may in origin have referred to the persons classified as *mer* and *dásachtach* in early Gaelic law. The epithet *méránach* / *méranach* from *mér* ('finger') is also considered in the context of the name *Gofraidh Crovan* / *Gofraidh Mérach*; the epithet *Crovan* is explained as deriving from *crobh+án* rather than *crobh+bhán* as has been previously suggested.

Meranach bho shean

Gheibhear am buadhfhacal *meranach* airson a' chiad uair ann an tùsan Èireannach bhon aonamh linn deug. Mar a chì sinn, theagamh gu bheil an aon eilimeid ri fhaighinn cuideachd mar bhuadhfhacal ann an ainm Albannach tràth anns an treas linn deug agus faodaidh gu bheil teist air an aon eilimeid ann an sloinneadh Èireannach bhon t-siathamh linn deug air adhart. Chan eil cinnt mu bhrìgh no thinnsgeadal a' bhuadhfhacail, a tha connspaideach, agus is e cuspair na h-aiste goirid seo a shealltann gu bheil fianais na Gàidhlig, anns an glèidhear tric feartan a bhoineadh dhan t-seann chànan ach a chailleadh anns a' Ghaeilge agus a' Mhanainnis, gar cuideachadh ann a bhith a' toirt duinn lèirsinn air a' bhrìgh a dh'fhaodadh a bhith aig an eilimeid annasaich a tha seo.

Gheibhear an sloinneadh Èireannach *Merna*(*gh*) ann an ear-dheas na h-Èireann – air a chuingealachadh gu ìre bhig ri Siorrachdan Loch Garmann, Cheatharlach agus Chill Mhantain (MacLysaght 1964: 112). Cho fada is is fiosrach mi chan fhaighear an t-ainm an Alba. Tha teist againn air an ainm ann am barantasan Eideard VI agus Ealasaid I bhon t-siathamh agus an t-seachdamh linn deug:

> John Merranagh (1550), Melaghlin mc Shane Meranagh (1583), Donogh roe mc Teige Meranaghe (1598), Callogh Merrenagh (1598), Philip mc Shane Varenagh (1599), Donogh Meranegh (1600–01), Donogh roe Meranagh (1601), Dermod meranagh O Birne (1601), Dallogh meranagh O Birne (1601) (Ó Tuathail 1950: 161).

Bha Edward McLysaght a' cumail a-mach gur h-ann bhon bhuadhair *meirtneach* ('dispirited') (*DIL*: s.v. *meirtnech*) a chinnich an eilimeid anns an ainm seo (MacLysaght 1964: 112) ach chan eil fianais idir ann airson an *t* eadar-fhuaimreagach anns na cruthan eachdraidheil agus cha mhotha na sin a tha na cruthan gu h-àrd anns a bheil trì lididhean a' tighinn ri *meirtneach*, agus air sàillibh sin feumar cùl a chur ris a' bheachd sin. Chuir Éamonn Ó Tuathail air adhart gur h-ann bhon bhuadhair **meireanach* no *mearanach* a chinnich an t-ainm o thùs ged nach eil e buileach cinnteach mu bhrìgh an fhacail: 'the exact meaning of *meranach* is uncertain' (Ó Tuathail 1950: 162). Tha Ó Tuathail (1950: 162) a' moladh, anns an dol seachad, gum faodadh suaip a bhith aig *Mer*(*a*)*na*(*gh*) ris a' bhuadhfhacal *meranach* a gheibhear ann an tùsan eachdraidheil na h-Èireann, leithid Annalan Uladh, air am beachdaichear anns na leanas.

Tha teist air *meranach* mar bhuadhfhacal ann an dà ainm phearsanta ann an Annalan Uladh aig deireadh na h-aonamh linn deug. Seo na h-earrannan maille ris an eadar-theangachadh aig Mac Airt agus Mac Niocaill (*AU*: 516, 517, 528–31):[1]

> Aedh **Meranach** do bath*ud* oc Luimniuch. ('Aed méranach [*sic*, 'é' fhada] was drowned at Luimnech.') (1083.4)[2]
>
> Slog*adh* la Muircertach H. mBriain co Ath Cliath coro innarb Goffraigh **Meranach** a righe Gall ⁊ co ro marb Dom*nall* H. Maelsech*lainn* ri Temhrach. ('An army [was led] by Muirchertach ua Briain to Áth Cliath, and he expelled Gofraidh Méranach [*sic*, 'é' fhada] from the kingship of the foreigners, and killed Domnall ua Mael Sechlainn, king of Temair.') (1094.2)
>
> Goffraigh **meranach** ri Gall mortus *est*. ('Gofraidh Meranach [*sic*, 'e' ghoirid], king of the foreigners, died') (1095.11).[3]

Bha Aedh Meranach na rìgh air Ultaibh agus tha e nochdadh ann an tùsan eile mar: 'Aed **Meranach**' (*LL*: 5845) agus 'An **Meranach** .h. Eochadha, Rí Uladh do badhadh a Luimneach' ('The Meranach, Ua Eochadha, King of Uladh, was drowned at Luimnech') ann an *Chronicum Scotorum*, ann an Annalan Thighearnaich agus Annalan Inis Faithleann (Hennessy 1866: 294; cf. Stokes [1895–97] 1993: 307; Mac Airt 1951: 234, s.a. 1078.5).[4] Is fheàrr aithnichear an dàrna duine dhiubh seo mar Ghofraidh Crovan, an Gall-Ghàidheal a bha na thighearna air Àth Cliath agus na rìgh air na h-Innseachan. Canar ris ann an Annalan nan Ceithir Maighstirean: 'Gofraidh **Meránach**, tighearna Gall Atha cliath, ⁊ na nInnsedh' ('Godfrey Meranach, lord of the foreigners of Ath-Cliath and the islands') (O'Donovan 1848–51, II: 950, s.a. 1095.4). Is e 'Gofraid, ríg Átha Cliath' ('Gofraidh, king of Áth Cliath') agus 'Gobraith, ríg Atha Cliath 7 Inse Gall' ('Gofraid, king of Áth Cliath and Insi Gall') a chanar ris ann an Annalan Inis Faithleann (Mac Airt 1951: 246–47, s.a. 1094.2; 250–51, s.a. 1095.13). Tha Gofraidh air ainmneachadh mar 'Gwrthryt **mearch**' ('Gofraidh Mearch') ann an ginealach Cuimreach Raghnaill (†1229), rìgh Mhanainn agus nan Innseachan (Bartrum 1966: 99; Broderick 1980: 35; Sellar 2000: 251). Feumaidh gu bheil suaip aig *mearch* ri *meranach* ann an dòigh air choreigin mar a chì sinn gu hìosal.

Tha an t-ainm *Malbride Marrenah* (i.e. *Máel Brigte 'Marrenah'*) a' nochdadh tràth anns an treas linn deug ann an cairt Albannaich a bhoineas do Shiorrachd Aonghais (MacQueen 2006: 26).[5] Tha Hector MacQueen a' moladh a' bhuadhair Ghàidhlig *maireannach* ('long-lived') airson a' bhuadhfhacail '*Marrenah*' anns an ainm seo (MacQueen 2006: 13) agus dh'fhaodte coimeas a dhèanamh ris a' bhuadhair *sáeglach* (i.e. *saoghlach* 'long-lived') a gheibhear ann an *Cóir Anmann* mar bhuadhfhacal leis an ainm *Sírna*, a mhair fad ceud gu leith bliadhna: 'Sírna Sáeglach' (Arbuthnott 2005, I: 116; II: 27). Mas e 'saoghalach' as ciall do 'marrenach', chan urrainnear a bhith gu tur cinnteach an e an cruth Albannach *maireannach* no an cruth meadhan-aoiseach *marthanach* a th' ann (*DIL*: s.v. *marthanach*). Mas e *maireannach* a th' ann, is e a' chiad eisimpleir a th' againn

---

[1] Is ann leamsa a tha an clò trom feadh na h-aiste seo.

[2] Tha seo ri fhaighinn ann an Annalan nan Ceithir Maighstirean mar: 'Aodh **Meranach**, rí Uladh, do bháthadh i l-Luimneach no i Loch Eachach' (O'Donovan 1848–51, II: 907, s.a. 1074.10).

[3] Tha an dà chruth *méranach* agus *meranach* aig Mac Airt agus Mac Niocaill anns an eadar-theangachadh aca. Faic shìos.

[4] Is e 'In **Meranach** Húa hEochadha, rí Ulad' a gheibhear ann an Annalan Thighearnaich (Stokes [1895–97] 1993: 307) agus is e 'in **Meranach** h-Ua Eochada' a gheibhear ann an Annalan Inis Faithleann (Mac Airt 1951: 234, s.a. 1078.5).

[5] Faic *PoMS*, pearsa 11638 aig <http://poms.cch.kcl.ac.uk/db/record/person/11638/> [leughta, 27 Faoilleach 2013].

dhen chruth thoiseannach Albannach. Is dòcha gur h-e cothlamadh dhen t-seann chruth *marthanach*, an gnìomhair *mair* agus / no an cruth gnìomhaireach *maireann* a th' ann am *maireannach* na Gàidhlig.[6] Mas e *marthanach* (no **mairtheanach*) a tha air cùl '*marrenah*', tha e suaicheanta nach eil sgeul air an t-suathach dheudach *th*, agus dh'fhaodadh sin a bhith cudromach airson eachdraidh *th* ann an Gàidhlig Alba – anns a' chàrn *rth* co-dhiù; cf. Ó Maolalaigh (2008: 225–28). Air an làimh eile, dh'fhaodadh e bhith gur h-e am buadhfhacal *meranach* a tha ga riochdachadh ann an '*marrenah*'. O thaobh 'a' a bhith a' riochdachadh na fuaimreig /e/ (no /ɛ/) nuair a thig e ro 'r', faodaidh sinn coimeas a dhèanamh ris na riochan seo leanas a tha nochdadh ann an cairtean Albannach a bhoineas dhan treas linn deug: *F**a**rchar Macholf* (1231 x c. 1233) (Easson 1947, I: àireamh 39)[7] airson *Ferchar*; *Duncano filio F**a**rgus* (1259 x c. 1272) (Neville 1983, II, àireamhan 59, 59a)[8] airson *Fergus*; cf. cuideachd *V**a**renagh* shuas (ann an Ó Tuathail 1950: 161).

méránach

Tha Brian Ó Cuív ag ràdh gu bheil a' chiad fhuaimreag 'e' ann an *meranach* fada anns an ainm Gofraidh Meranach mar a tha e nochdadh ann an Annalan Uladh: 'it is marked long in A.U. s. anno 1094', i.e. 'Goffraigh **Méranach**'(Ó Cuív 1957: 284, n. 6). Ach chan eil rian nach e deasachadh Mac Carthy (Hennessy agus Mac Carthy 1887–1901, II (1893): 52) a chuir air iomrall e. Tha cruthan fada agus goirid a' nochdadh ann an deasachadh Mac Carthy: 'Goffraigh **Méranach**' agus 'Goffraigh **Meranach**' (Hennessy agus Mac Carthy 1887–1901, II (1893): 52, 53, 54, 55).[9] Ach is e cruthan goirid a tha a' nochdadh anns an deasachadh a rinn Mac Airt agus Mac Niocaill air an teacsa Ghaeilge: 'Goffraigh **Meranach**', 'Goffraigh **meranach**' (*AU*: 528, s.a. 1094.2; 530, s.a. 1095.11); cf. 'Aedh **Meranach**' far a bheil an 'e' goirid (*AU*: 516, s.a. 1083.4). Faodaidh mi dearbhadh an seo nach eil an 'e' ga sgrìobhadh mar 'e' fhada ann an gin dhe na làmhsgrìobhainnean anns an tàinig Annalan Uladh a-nuas thugainn, i.e. LS 1282 (H.1.8) ann an Colaiste na Trìonaid (CnaT), Baile Àtha Cliath agus LS Rawlinson B 489 ann an Leabharlann Bodleian ann an Oxford.[10] Seo fianais an dà làmhsrìobhainn:[11]

Bliadhna	Rawlinson B 489	CnaT 1282 (H.1.8)
1083	meranach (fo. 44ʳ)	meranach[12] (fo. 62ʳa)
1094	meránach (fo. 45ʳ)	meranach[13](fo.62ʳb)
1095	meránach (fo. 45ᵛ)	meranach (fo.62ʳb)

[6] Is dòcha gur h-e a th' ann an *maireann* na Gàidhlig, a nochdas anns an abairt *nach maireann*, an aon eisimpleir a th' againn sa Nua-Ghàidhlig dhen chruth eisimileach làithaireach *–ann* a chinnich ann an Gàidhlig na h-Èireann (O'Rahilly [1932] 1976: 132); faic cuideachd Murphy 1940: 75, Ó Buachalla 1988: 56–58, agus na tùsan air a bheil iomradh ann am Breatnach 1994: 293, §12.12.

[7] Faic *PoMS*: pearsa 5631 aig http://db.poms.ac.uk/record/person/5631/ [leughta, 27 Faoilleach 2013].

[8] Faic *PoMS*: pearsa 7018 aig http://db.poms.ac.uk/record/person/7018/ [leughta, 27 Faoilleach 2013].

[9] Is e 'e' ghoirid a tha nochdadh ann an 'Aed **Meranach**' ann an deasachadh Mac Carthy (Hennessy agus Mac Carthy 1887–1901, II (1893): 36, 37).

[10] Chithear LS Rawl. B 489 air-loidhne air 'Early Manuscripts at Oxford University', http://image. ox. ac.uk/ [leughta, 27 Faoileach 2013]. Tha mi an comain luchd-leabharlainn Colaiste na Trìonaid ann am Baile Àtha Cliath a thug cead dhomh sùil a thoirt air LS 1282 (H.1.8).

[11] Tha fo-loidhne ag innse gu bheil litir ga chur an cèill sa làmhsgrìobhainn le comharradh no giorrachadh fa leth seach litir slàn.

[12] Air a sgrìobhadh le 'e' àrd.

[13] Ann an LS 1282 (H.1.8) (s.a. 1094) tha mar gum biodh comharradh aotrom crochte os cionn cuid deiridh 'm' agus toiseach 'a' ach tha an dubh nas gile agus dh'fhaodadh e bhith gur h-e smal a bhoineas dhan mheamram a th' ann. Chan eil e idir coltach ris na sìnidhean fada a lorgar anns an làmhsgrìobhainn.

Tha seo a' fàgail nach eil teist làmhsgrìobhainnean Annalan Uladh a' dearbhadh taobh seach taobh cò dhiubh an robh an fhuaimreag 'e' goirid no fada anns a' bhuadhfhacal *meranach* oir chan ann tric a tha fuaimreagan fada gan comharrachadh anns na làmhsgrìobhainnean seo.

Ged a tha an fhuaimreag 'e' goirid aig Mac Airt agus Mac Niocaill, an luchd-deasachaidh as ùire air Annalan Uladh, anns an teacsa Ghaeilge aca, tha 'é' fhada a' nochdadh dà thuras anns an eadar-theangachadh Bheurla aca: 'Aedh Meranach' ('Aed **méranach**'), 'Goffraigh Meranach' ('Gofraidh **Méranach**') ach 'Goffraigh meranach' ('Gofraidh **Meranach**', le 'e' ghoirid) (*AU*: 516, 517, 528–31). Is fheudar, uime sin, gun robh iad dhen bheachd gur h-ann stèidhichte air *mér* (i.e. *meur* 'finger') a bha am buadhfhacal *meranach* anns an dà ainm seo, i.e. gur h-e *méránach* bu chòir a leughadh annta.[14] Bhiodh sin a' fàgail gun robh *méránach* a' cur an cèill feart a bhoineadh do chorragan no do làimh no làmhan an duine air an robh an t-ainm.[15] A' togail air a leithid de thinnsgeadal, tha de Bhulbh a' moladh 'dexterous' no 'deft' mar eadar-theangachadh air *méránach*, an cruth, ar leis-san, a bha air cùlaibh an t-sloinnidh Èireannaich *Mernagh* (de Bhulbh 1997: 304).

O thaobh Ghofraidh Crovan co-dhiù, tha fianais ann a chumadh taic ris' bheachd gur h-e *méránach* (le 'e' fhada) a tha air cùl an ainm *Goffraigh meranach* (*AU*: 1095.11) air a bheil iomradh gu h-àrd. Anns an dàn dìreach ainmeil, 'Baile suthach síth Emhna', a chaidh a sgrìobhadh airson Raghnaill (†1229), Rìgh Mhanainn, iar-ogha Ghofraidh Crovan, is e 'Gofraidh **Mérach**' a chanar ri Gofraidh:

> A ua ghil Gofraidh M**é**raig
> a fhir do lothraig l**ú**irigh,
> do móit, a rí, ri r**í**ghain
> do dígail sí ar a s**ú**ilib

'O fair descendant of Gofraidh **Méarach**, though who destroyed a coat of mail, thy wrath, o king, against a queen, she has avenged upon her eyes.' (Ó Cuív 1957: 292, §25).

Tha meadar an dàin (Rannachd Bheag) a' daingneachadh na fuaimreig fada ann an 'Méraig[h]' (< *Mérach*) oir ann an Rannachd Bheag feumaidh uaithne ('consonance') a bhith eadar na faclan mu dheireadh anns gach rann (Knott [1928] 1994: 13–14). Tha fad nan ciad fhuaimreagan ann an *l**ú**irigh*, *r**í**ghain* agus *s**ú**ilib* a' dearbhadh gur h-e *M**é**raig* le 'é' fhada an cruth ceart anns an rann gu h-àrd. Is dòcha gur h-e *mérach* / *méarach* a tha air cùl 'mearch' a gheibhear le ainm Ghofraidh ann an ginealach Cuimreach Raghnaill:

> Rhanallt m. Gwythryg ap Afloyd m. **Gwrthryt mearch** m. Harallt ddu (m.) Ifor gamle m. Afloyd m. Swtrig ('Ragnall son of Godfrey son of Olaf son of Godfrey Mearch son of Harald Dubh son of Ivar Gamle son of Olaf son of Sihtric') (Bartrum 1966: 99, §6[c]; Broderick 1980: 35; Sellar 2000: 251).

Tha Ó Cuív ag rádh: 'the epithets [i.e. *méarach* agus *méaránach*], derived from *méar* "a finger," presumably referred to some peculiarity or distinguishing feature of Godred's hands.'[16] Agus tha sin a' tighinn ris a' bhuadhfhacal eile a chleachdar le ainm Ghofraidh, seadh 'Crovan', ma ghabhar ris gu bheil e stèidhichte air *crobh* ('hand, claw') (*DIL*: s.v. *crob*) (faic, mar eisimpleir, Ó Cuív 1957:

[14] Ged nach eil Mac Airt agus Mac Niocaill a' sgrìobhadh *–ánach* le 'á' fhada anns an dara lide, tha mi gabhail ris gur h-e *–ánach* a th' ann an deireadh an fhacail – deireadh a tha cumanta anns a' chànan (faic Russell 1990: 88, 191–92). Chan urrainn gur h-e 'a' ghoirid a bh' ann oir a rèir riaghailt Mhic Nèill, is e '**mera**nn**ach*' le *nn* theann ris am biodh dùil (faic MacNeill 1909: 347; Ó Buachalla 1988: 39).

[15] cf. *meuranda* ('tender, weakly, delicate') agus *meurach* ('nimble-fingered') na Gàidhlig (Armstrong 1825: s.vv.).

[16] Tha Broderick (1980: 35) agus Duffy (1992: 106, n. 66) a' gabhail ri beachd Uí Chuív gur h-e *méránach* a tha air cùl a' bhuadhfhacail *meranach* anns an ainm Gofraidh Meranach.

284, n. 6). Eadar dhà sheanchas, tha Ó Cuív a' cur air adhart na barail gum faodadh *crobh-bhán* ('white hand') a bhith air cùl a' bhuadhfhacail *Crovan*, agus e dèanamh coimeas ris a' bhuadhfhacal *Croibhdhearg* ('red hand') a gheibhear leis an ainm Cathal, bràthair Ruaidhrí Uí Chonchubhair anns an dara linn deug (Ó Cuív 1957: 284, n. 6).[17] A rèir riaghailtean eachdraidheil 'cadad' na Gàidhlig, bhiodh dùil ri **crobán* le dì-shèimheachadh mar thoradh air *crobh+bhán* ge-tà, ged a dh'fhaodadh *crobh-bhán* cinneachadh gu nàdarra ann an cainnt. Ar leamsa gu bheil e a cheart cho coltach gur h-e am meanbhan *crobhán* ('hand, little hand', *crobhan* ann an Gàidhlig Alba) a th' ann an 'Crovan', agus bhiodh sin a' tighinn gu snog ri *méránach*. Is math dh'fhaodte gur h-e ainm meafarach a bh'ann an *crobhán* airson làmh mhòr no làmh chearbach.[18]

Tha taobh eile air a' ghnothach air am bu chòir dhuinn breithneachadh is beachdachadh. Saoil an gabhadh e bhith gur h-e *mérach* a bh' ann an ainm Ghofraidh bho thùs ach gun do dh'atharraicheadh e gu *méránach* no *meránach* fo bhuaidh buadhfhacal a bha gu tur eadar-dhealaichte ach a bha glè choltach ris ann an sgrìobhadh? Co-dhiù no co-dheth, ged a bhiodh 'mér' air cùl an ainm Gofraidh Meranach, chan urrainnear a bhith cinnteach an e *méránach* no *meránach* a tha air cùl an ainm Aedh Meranach. Anns na leanas bheirear seachad fianais airson an fhacail *meránach*, anns an robh 'e' ghoirid, a dh'fhaodadh a bhith anns an ainm Aedh Meranach agus a dh'fhaodadh buaidh a thoirt air an ainm Gofraidh Meranach.

meránach

Is e 'The Wanton' an t-eadar-theangachadh a tha Hennessy (1866: 294, n. 1) a' toirt seachad airson 'An Meranach' ann an *Chronicum Scotorum*, agus is e 'Aed the furious' a tha aig MacCarthy (Hennessy agus Mac Carthy 1887–1901, II (1893): 1893: 36, n. 2) airson 'Aed Meranach' ann an Annalan Uladh.[19] Tha sin a' toirt far comhair gur h-e *mer* ('demented; spirited, lively, agile') an eilimeid a dh'fhaodadh a bhith air cùl an ainm *Meranach* (i.e. *Meránach*) (cf. *DIL*: s.v. *meranach* (*-ánach*?); Ó Cuív 1957: 284, n. 7). Bhiodh sin a' toirt leis gur h-e 'e' ghoirid a bh' anns a' bhuadhfhacal seo o thùs. Tha fianais an t-sloinnidh Èireannaich *Meranagh* a' tighinn ris sin (faic gu h-àrd).

***mearan* agus *mearanach* na Gàidhlig**

A' fàgail fianais a' bhuadhfhacail *meranach* agus an ainm *Merán* an dàrna taobh (*DIL* s.v. *meranach*),[20] chan eil teist air *mearán* no *mearánach* ann an Gàidhlig na h-Èireann no ann an tùsan

[17] cf. 'Óengus crobderg' ('Angus the Redhand') (O'Brien [1962] 2005: 204) agus 'do choin croíbhderga' [*sic !*] ('your redfooted hounds') ann an Leabhar nan Ceart (Dillon 1962: 152, 153); cf. *DIL* (s.v. *crob*).

[18] Tha na cruthan *crobhan* agus *crobhanach* a' nochdadh ann am faclair Robert Armstrong mar seo leanas: *crobhan* ('a claw, a paw, a hoof, a little paw, a little claw') agus *crobhanach* ('having (large) hoofs or claws') (Armstrong 1825: s.vv.), ach is e *crodhan* agus *crodhanach* a tha aig Dwelly (Dwelly [1901–11] 1977, s.vv.). Tha *cròbh* / *crobha* ('a claw, a paw, a hoof, a clumsy hand') agus *cròdh* / *cròdha* ('a claw, a paw, the palm of the hand, a large hand') cuideachd aig (Armstrong 1825: s.vv. *cròbh*, *cròdh*). Tha na cruthan seo uile a' dearbhadh gur dòcha gun robh cothlamadh eadar *cruë* ('hoof') agus *crob* ('hand, claw, grasp') — agus math dh'fhaodte *cròg* ('large or clumsy hand; clutch; palm of the hand; paw; claw; first' (Dwelly [1901–11] 1977: s.v.). Faic Greene 1983: 2–3 airson *cruë* agus *crob*.

[19] Chan eil Stokes ([1895–97] 1993: 415) no Mac Niocaill (2010: T1083.2) ag eadar-theangachadh an ainm anns na deasachaidhean aca air Annalan Thighearnaich.

[20] Tha fianais againn air an ainm phearsanta *Merán*. Lorgar e ann an ginealaichean Ua gColla [Ciarraige] mar: *Merān m. Duib-dūin m. Fairchellaich* (O'Brien [1962] 2005: 306 (Rawl. B. 502, 160 b 2)) agus mar dhuine de thriùr laoch Phartholáin ('*tríthrénfhir*') ann an Lebor Gabála: *Merán* (Macalister 1938–2009, III: 8, §212; 26, §225; 56, §7d; cf. Ó Raithbheartaigh 1932: 42, §66; Comyn agus Dinneen 1902–14, I: 172). Tha *Mearan* a' nochdadh mar ainm mnatha diadhaidh ann an Cataibh anns an laoidh 'Lilidhean Chataoibh' le Dòmhnall Mac an Rothaich (1886: 26), ach dh'fhaodadh e bhith gur h-e Muireann a tha air cùlaibh an ainm seo:

eachdraidheil na Gaeilge. Gheibhear fianais am pailteas ann an Gàidhlig Alba ge-tà airson na dhà. Gheibhear iomradh air na dhà ann an cuid de dh'fhaclairean, leithid faclair Comann Gàidhealtachd na h-Alba (1828), faclair MhicEachainn ([1842] 1922) agus faclair Dwelly ([1901–11] 1977) ach cha lorgar iad ann am faclairean eile, leithid Armstrong (1825) agus MacAlpine ([1832] 1955).[21] Cha mhotha lorgar na faclan ann an nuadh-fhaclairean, leithid MacFarlane (1953), Cox (1991), Mark (2003), agus tha e coltach nach eil am facal air mairsinn ann an cainnt an là-an-diugh.[22] Feumar cumail air chuimhne, ge-tà, gu bheil e doirbh a bhith uile-chinnteach am bheil facal fa leth air a dhol bàs gu tur. Mar a thuirt Iain MacAonghuis:

> It is very difficult in the Gaelic context to define what is unusual, archaic or even obsolete. One may have heard in childhood a word used only once or twice by very old people and have therefore assumed that it was now obsolete only to find it suddenly emerging as a vey active item, not just in a distant dialect but much more disconcertingly in the vocabulary of a neighbour, who may be a teenager. Such at any rate has been my experience. (MacInnes 1977: 429–30)

Tha na faclan seo aig MacAonghuis a' toirt nar cuimhne faclan an Rathaillich:

> A word of caution is especially necessary when dealing with the geographical distribution of Irish words [. . .]. It is easy enough to say that a particular word is in use to-day in a particular dialect; but to say that such and such a word is *not* in use in a particular district may well be risky [. . .]. (O'Rahilly [1932] 1976: 244)

Tha an fhianais a tha ri tighinn gu h-ìosal a' dearbhadh gum b' aithnichte *mearan* agus *mearanach* ann an Gàidhlig Alba gu ruige an fhicheadhamh linn. Seo leanas cuid dhen teist a th' againn air na faclan *mearan* agus *mearanach* ann an Gàidhlig na h-Alba:[23]

Faclairean (1828–1932)
A Dictionary of the Gaelic Language (Highland Society of Scotland 1828: s.vv.)

> *mearan*: 1. Madness, delirium, dementia (*C.S.*); 2. Drunkenness (*C.S.*); 3. Lasciviousness.[24]
>
> *mearanach*: 1. Delirious, insane (*C.S.*); 2. Drunk (*C.S.*); 3. Lascivious; lascivious.
>
> Tha *C.S.* a' cur an cèill cainnt an t-sluaigh ('common speech') agus a' leigeil fhaicinn duinn gun robh am facal fhathast ga chleachdadh anns an t-seagh 'madness, delirium, dementia' rè na naoidheamh linn deug.

Is **Mearan** òirdhearc an Eilbhinn bha,
A tuigs' bha geur, is a cridh' bha blàth,
'S aig caithir gràis, O, bu tric an sàs i,
Oir 's e 'chuir cradh oirre, cor ar là.

[21] Ged a chleachdas MacMhaighstir Alastair 'meirin' agus 'mearan' na bhàrdachd (MacDonald 1751: 187; Mac an Tuairneir 1813: 36), chan eil *mearan* no *mearanach* a' nochdadh na *Leabhar a Theagasg Ainminnin* far am faighear na cruthan seo leanas: *miesg* (*recte meisg*) ('drunkenness'), *aotromas*, *baois* ('a frenzy'), *báni*, *cuthach* ('madness'), *meisg* (drunkenness'), *cuthaichte*, *míchiallach* ('mad') (MacDonald 1741: 24, 26, 36, 140).

[22] Tha dearbhadh agam air seo bho iomadach Gàidheal, Iain MacAonghuis nam measg.

[23] Tha an fhianais seo a' tighinn bho mo chruinneachaidhean fhìn agus bho thasglann DASG (Dàta airson Stòras na Gàidhlig) agus data Corpas na Gàidhlig – dà phròiseact rannsachaidh ann an Roinn na Ceiltis is na Gàidhlig ann an Oilthigh Ghlaschu a tha air am maoineachadh le Acadamaidh Bhreatainn.

[24] Tha an treas brìgh a' tighinn bho cho-chruinneachadh Turner de dh'òrain Ghàidhlig.

Anns an earrainn Beurla-Gàidhlig tha *mearanach* a' nochdadh fo na faclan 'mad': '1. Disordered in the mind, distracted: **mearanach**, thair céille, air a' chuthach, air boil.'; 'delirious': 'breisleachail, **mearanach**, gòrach'; cf. 'deliriousness': '**mearanachd**, mearaichinn'; 'delirium': breisleach, eutromas, **mearan**, mearaichinn, cuthach'; 'dementation': '**mearan**, mearaichinn, cuthach'; 'furious': 'mad, phrenetic: air a' chuthach, **mearanach**, eu-céillidh'. Chan eil *mearan*(*ach*) a' nochdadh fo 'drunk', 'drunkenness', 'lascivious', 'lasciviousness' ged a lorgar '*mear*' fon fhacal 'lascivious' anns an t-seagh 'wanton, soft, luxurious'.

Dictionary of the Gaelic Language (MacLeod agus Dewar [1831] 1909: s.v.)

mearan: madness, delirium; drunkenness; lasciviousness

mearanach: delirious, insane; drunk; lascivious

Anns an earrainn Bheurla-Gàidhlig, tha 'mad' air eadar-theangachadh mar 'air a chuthach, **mearanach**, air boile; gòrach, neo-shuidhichte; feargach, garg' (MacLeod agus Dewar [1831] 1909: s.v. *mad*); cf. 'insane': 'cuthaich, mearanach'. Chan eil *mearan*(*ach*) a' nochdadh fo na faclan 'delirious': 'breisleachail, gòrach, eutrom'; 'deliriousness': 'breisleachd, gòraiche, mearaichinn'; 'delirium': 'breisleach, mearaichinn, eutromas, cuthach'; 'drunk'; 'drunkenness'; 'lascivious'; 'lasciviousness'.

Gaelic-English Dictionary (MacEachainn [1842] 1922: s.vv)

mearan: 1. a delirium.

mearanach: 1. mad, delirious.

Tha MacEachainn a' toirt seachad 'mear-a-chinn' anns a' mhìneachadh a th' aige air *mearan*. Faodaidh sinn coimeas a dhèanamh ri '*mearaichinn*' ann am faclair MhicCoinnich, far a bheil *breisleach* agus *mearaichinn* a' co-fhreagairt ri 'delirium' na Beurla (J. MacKenzie [1845] 1962: s.v. *delirium*). Ged a tha faclair MhicCoinnich stèidhichte air faclair MhicAilpein, chan eil *mearaichinn* a nochdadh ann am faclair MhicAilpein idir. Tha *mearaichinn* ('madness, insanity; drunkenness; giddiness' aig Dwelly ([1901–11] 1977: s.v.) agus *air mhearaichinn* ('insane') aig Armstrong (1825: s.v. *insane*); cf. Dwelly [1901–11] 1977: s.v.). Is e th' ann am *mear-a-chinn* freumh-eòlas an t-sluaigh air a' chruth *mearaichinn*. O thaobh cruth an fhacail faodaidh sinn coimeas a dhèanamh ri *duilichinn* ('sorrow') agus *bochdainn* ('poverty') (Dwelly [1901–11] 1977: s.vv.).

Gaelic Words and Expressions from South Uist and Eriskay (*c*. 1893–97)

Tha an dà chuid *meirein* ('madness, frenzy') agus *meirean* ('delirium') a' nochdadh anns na cruinneachaidhan aig Maighistir Ailean Dòmhnallach (J. L. Campbell [1958] 1991: 177).

The Illustrated Gaelic-English Dictionary (Dwelly [1901–11] 1977: s.vv.)

mearan: [1.] Madness, delirium, brain-sickness; 2. Drunkenness; 3. Lasciviousness.

mearanach: [1.] Delirious, mad, insane, brainish, brain-sick; 2. Drunk; 3. Lascivious; 4. Hypochondriacal.[25]

---

[25] Tha a' cheathramh brìgh a' tighinn bho làmhsgrìobhainn neo-fhoillsichte 'MS'. Gheibhear tuilleadh fiosrachaidh mun làmhsgrìobhainn ann an Dwelly ([1901–11] 1977: viii, s.v. MS): 'MS–Large manuscript English-Gaelic Dict. in possession of Rev. D. Walker MacIntyre, Kilmonivaig. It was revised on Nov. 1,

A Pronouncing Dictionary of Scottish Gaelic (Dieckhoff 1932: s.v.)

mearan: [mäRan].[26] 1. delirium.

Tha fianais Dieckhoff a' dearbhadh gum b' aithnichte am facal *mearan* fhathast ann an cuid de dhualchainntean co-dhiù anns an fhicheadamh linn.

Tùsan eile (*c.* 1690–1994)

Leabhar Fheàrnaig (*c.* 1688–93) (Mac Phàrlain [1923])

Tha *mearanach* a' nochdadh ann an 'Crosanachd de ghnè chomhluadair eadar a' cholainn is an t-anam'. Seo an deasachadh aig Henderson (1898: 268; cf. cuideachd Mac Phàrlain [1923]: 116–17, §26c):[27]

Nuair theid thu steach a'n eaglais
Air fear t'theaguisg bi cuimhneach
Na biodh t'inntinn **mearanach**
Thoir aire air gach ni chluinn thu.

Cleachdar *mearan* cuide ri *misg* ('drunkenness') anns an abairt 'Chan 'eil misg no **mearan** orm' ('I am not drunk or crazed')[28] anns an òran 'Séid na builg sin, ghille, dhom' le Ruairidh MacMhuirich, an Clàrsair Dall (*c.* 1656–*c.*1714). Tha an t-òran seo a' tighinn a-nuas thugainn ann an Leabhar Fheàrnaig far a bheil *mearan* ga litreachadh mar 'merran' (Mac Phàrlain [1923]: 252–53, §2c; Matheson 1970: 20, 21, l. 251).

Tha *mearan* cuideachd a' nochdadh anns an laoidh 'Dallaidh sannt sluagh an domhain' a rinneadh le Sior Iain Stiubhart na h-Apuinn (fl. deireadh na 16mh linn) agus a tha tighinn a-nuas thugainn ann an Leabhar Fheàrnaig far a bheil e air a litreachadh mar 'merrhan': 'mōr am mearan do na daoine' (Henderson 1898: 219, §3a; cf. Mac Phàrlain [1923]: 42–43, §3a). Is e 'madness' an t-eadar-theangachadh a th' aig Henderson air *mearan* an seo (1898: 220).

Ais-éiridh na Sean Chànoin Albannaich (MacDonald 1751)

Tha *meirin* a' nochdadh anns an òran 'Moladh a' Chaimbeulaich Dhuibh' le Alastair MacMhaighstir Alastair anns an abairt 'Mar robh **meirin** ort air tuinneadh' (MacDonald 1751: 187). Is e 'Mur robh **meirein** ort air tuineadh' ('Unless your wits you want') a tha ann an deasachadh A. MacDonald agus A. MacDonald (1924: 284, 185) ach is e *mearan* ('Mar robh **mearan** ort air tuinneadh') a tha aig MacCoinnich ann an *Sàr-Obair nam Bàrd Gaelach* (MacKenzie 1904: 133). Tha e soilleir bho dheasachaidhean na ficheadamh linn gu bheileas air gabhail ris gur h-e cruth

1823, and purchased at the sale of Sir Wm.MacLeod Bannatyne's Library in 1834 by Donald Gregory, Edinburgh, who have it to Angus MacDonnell, Inch. No compiler's or reviser's name is given.' Bhathas dhen bheachd nach robh sgeul air an làmhsgrìobhainn seo ach tha am faclair seo an-diugh ann an seilbh an West Highland Museum anns a' Ghearasdan. Is e 'Pocket Gaelic Dictionary' a tha air a sgrìobhadh air druim an leabhair agus is e 'The Anglo-Gaelic Dictionary' a chanar ris am broinn na làmhsgrìobhainn. Nuair a chaidh mi a choimhead air an làmhsgrìobhainn seo anns an Iuchar 2013, dh'inns Glèidheadair na Tasglainn, Fiona Marwick, dhomh gun robh an Dr Iain MacAonghuis air tadhal air an Tasglainn bliadhnaichean fada romham a thoirt sùil air làmhsgrìobhainn an fhaclair seo agus gun do dh'aithnich esan sa bhad cò an làmhsgrìobhainn a bh' ann.

[26] Is ionann sin agus [mæʀan] ann am foghar-sgrìobhadh an là-an-diugh.

[27] Is e *merranigh* an cruth ann an Leabhar Fheàrnaig (Mac Phàrlain [1923]: 116).

[28] Is ann le Uilleam Mac Mhathain a tha an t-eadar-theangachadh Beurla.

meanbhain a th' ann am *meirin* (seach cruth eascruthach *–inn*) air a litreachadh a rèir àrd-rèim a' chànain; faodaidh sinn coimeas a dhèanamh le leithid *Ailin* / *Ailín* agus *Ailpin* / *Ailpín* airson *Ailean* / *Ailein* agus *Ailpean* / *Ailpein* mu seach (Ó Maolalaigh 2001: 24–27). Airson a' chrutha eascruthaich *mearainn*, faic go h-ìosal.

Comh-chruinneachidh Orannaigh Gaidhealach (MacDomhnuill 1776)

Gheibhear *mearan* anns an abairt 'chaidh mo shlàinte gu **mearan**' ann an 'Cumha Alastair Dhuinn' a lorgar ann an deasachadh Raghnaill MhicDhòmhnaill (MacDomhnuill 1776: 135; cf. Caimbeull 1798: 125; MacKenzie 1904: 395).

Comhchruinneacha do dh'Orain Taghta(Mac an Tuairneir 1813)

Anns an òran 'Diomoladh Chabair Fèidh' aig Alastair MacMhaighstir Alastair, tha *mearan* a' nochdadh anns an loidhne 'air thùs thig do **mhearan** ort' (Mac an Tuairneir 1813: 36); cf. 'Your madness will appear' (A. MacDonald agus A. MacDonald 1924: 306).

Beachd-chomhairlean airson Feum do Thuathanaich 'us Choitearan Gaidh'lach ([F. MacKenzie] 1838)

Tha Sior Francis MacKenzie na leabhar dà-chànanach a' cleachdadh *mearan* ann an suidheachadh misgearachd:

> Faodaidh orainean ruidhtearachd no poitearachd tearc uairean a bheatha a bheothachadh. Faodaidh eifeachdan chaothaicheil na neo-mheasaireachd re seal sonas mac-meamnach [*sic*] a thoirt d'a, ach an uair a dhuisgeas e bho a **mhearan**, ciod a chi e mu' thimchioll ? Bean thruagh 'us mhi-shona [. . .] ('Songs of revelry may enliven a few hours of his existence. The maddening effects of intemperance may for a while give him a fancied happiness, but when awakened from his frenzy, what does he see around him? A miserable and unhappy wife [. . .]') ([F. MacKenzie] 1838: 258, 259).

A Double Grammar of English and Gaelic (Forbes 1843: 340)

Anns an earrainn 'Seollairtean Laidinn' ('Latin Phrases') anns an leabhar ghràmair le Iain Foirbeis, tha *mearanach* a' nochdadh mar seo leanas:

> 'Non compos mentis; not of a sound mind, insane': 'A dhith céille, gun inntinn chruinn; **mearanach**, gòrach'.

Metrical Reliques of "The Men" in the Highlands (Rose 1851)

Tha an abairt '**mearan** na h-òige' a' nochdadh anns an duan diadhaidh 'Ceannach na h-àilgheas' le Iain MacAoidh (Rose 1851: 129).

Carmina Gadelica (Carmichael: 1900–71)

Cleachdar *mearan* ann an seagh a tha coltach ris an fhacal *boile* anns na rannan seo:

Gealach Satharna foghair Gabhaidh **boile** seach tràth	Saturday's autumn moon Will take frenzy seven days.
Gealach ùr Satharna Gabhaidh **mearan** trì ràth (Carmichael 1900–71, IV: 202)	New moon of Saturday Will take madness three days.

Tha '**mearan, mirean.** Madness' a' nochdadh mar cheann-fhacal anns an liost 'Gaelic Words and Expressions Collected by Alexander Carmichael', far a bheil *mearan* a' nochdadh anns an rann seo cuide ris an roimhear *fo*:

> Tha 'n Camaranach dubh air a mhealladh,
> Cha mh'athair a chuir fuil 'sa' fhrìth [LS shrith],
> Ach buachhaille monaidh **fo mhearan**
> A dh'eirmis a mhala gu grinn.
>
> 'The black Cameron is mistaken, it was not my father who drew blood in the hill, but a mountain herd gone beserk who skillfully found the mark in his forehead.' (Carmichael 1900–71, VI: 106)

Mac-Talla (1901)

Tha 'air **mhearainn**' ri lorg ann an co-theacsa misgearachd ann an sgeul mun 'A' Bhanais Mhagaidh' anns an iris *Mac-Talla* aig toiseach na ficheadamh linn mar seo leanas:

> Ma bha 'n deoch làidir pailt ann an taigh a' mhaoir an oidhch' ud, bha i a' cheart cho pailt aigan fheadhainn a bh' air an raonaidh. Agus o nach robh iad a' gabhail bìdh, chaidh na bha iad ag òl cho mòr 'nan cinn 's gu 'n robh iad an impis a bhith **air mhearainn** leis a' mhisg. (Iain [*sic*] 1901: 314, col. 3).

Chan urrainn a bhith gu tur cinnteach, is dòcha, an e [vɛrɪɴ′] le fuaimreag dhoilleir schwa /ə/ no [vɛraɴ′] / [vɛrɛɴ′] (no [vɛr′aɴ′] / [vɛr′ɛɴ′]) le fuaimreag shoilleir anns an lide gun bheum a tha air cùl a' chrutha seo. Chan urrainnear a bhith cinnteach nas motha an e cruth lùghdaichte de 'mearaichinn' a th' ann no ainmear stèidhichte air *mear* + an deireadh eascruthach *–ainn* < *-aine* (cf. *bochdainn*; faic Thurneysen [1946] 1993: 168–69, §262) no an e cruth leis an deireadh meanbhain *–ein* a th' ann (faic Ó Maolalaigh 2001). Is e as coltaiche, ar leam, gur h-e cruth eascruthach a th' ann; cf. *air mhearaichinn* ('insane') (Armstrong 1825: s.v. *insane*).

Guth na Bliadhna (Am. B.A. 1907)

Ann an sgeulachd mu mhurt a ghabh àite ann an Ceap Bhreatainn anns a' chiad leath den naoidheamh linn deug, tha **mearan** a' nochdadh cuide ris an roimhear 'an' ann an co-theacsa misgearachd:

> Thòisich a companach air òl, air dhà an t-àite fhagail, agus 'na dhrongair uamhasach, dh'fhàg e an saoghal so **am mearan**. (Am. B.A. 1907: 291)

The Works of "Fiona Macleod" (1910)

mearanach ('mad')

Tha am buadhair *mearanach* a' nochdadh anns an tiotal 'Cumha Fhir-**Mearanach** Aonghas mhic Dhonuill—the Lament of mad Angus Macdonald' ann an leabhar le 'Fiona Macleod', i.e. William Sharp (1910: 324).

The MacDonald Collection of Gaelic Poetry (A. MacDonald 1912)

Tha *mearan* a' nochdadh anns an loidhne 'cha bhean iad fhèin le **mearan** dha' ann an 'Òran nan Lotaichean' le Dòmhnall MacRuairidh (A. MacDonald & A. MacDonald 1912: 397).

Dàin agus Òrain Ghàidhlig (1929)

Tha *mearan* agus na faclan fillte *mearan-cuthach* / *mearan-chuthaich*/ *mearan a' chuthaich* agus *mearan-uaibhreachais* a' nochdadh tric ann am Bàrdachd Aonghais

Mhoireasdain a rugadh ann an Ulapal, Siorrachd Rois (MacilleDhuibh 1999: 718–19):

> Tha **mearan** do bheairteis cur smuid
> Ri earra-ghloir 'g ad sgaradh o d'cheill. (Moireasadan 1929: 129)
>
> le **mearan-chuthaich** 'gat 'nan tulaich do (Moireasdan 1929: 11)[29]
>
> 'Na **mearan-cuthach** neart a h-airm's a h-uaill (Moireasdan 1929: 170)
>
> Is **mearan a' chuthaich** mar shuaicheantas
> Air na cinn tholmanach mhulanach. (Moireasdan 1929: 114)
>
> Thug **mearan-uaibhreachais** a nuas
> Mar shoitheach briste cré (Moireasdan 1929: 187)

Chan eil e soilleir carson a tha *cuthaich* air a shèimheachadh ann am *mearan-chuthaich*; theagamh gur h-e buaidh *mearan a' chuthaich* as adhbhar dha.[30] Faodaidh sinn coimeas a dhèanamh ri *leum-chuthaich* a chuala mi aig Iain MacAonghuis ach nach eil a' nochdadh anns na faclairean; faodaidh *leum* a bhith boireannn no fireann (Dwelly ([1901–11] 1977: s.v. *leum*).[31]

O na Ceithir Àirdean (1952)

Tha *mearan* a' nochadh co-dhiù dà thuras ann am Bàrdachd Deòrsa Caimbeul Hay:

> eadar ciùine s **mearan** ('between placidity and frenzy') (Caimbeul Hay 1952: 5; Byrne [2000] 2003: 167).[32]
>
> Chuir **mearan** uaibhreach iomrall sinn – ar miann
> a bhith na's treasa ann na Dia s an Dàn (Caimbeul Hay 1952: 63).[33]

Sporan Dhòmhnaill (MacMillan 1968)

Cleachdar *mearan* ann an abairt cuide ri *caoch* (i.e. *cuthach* 'madness, insanity') ann an aoir air Mussolìnidh le Dòmhnall Ruadh Mac an t-Saoir, Bàrd Phàislig (1889–64): 'Leantainn na droch smaoin le **mearan** a' chaoich' (MacMillan 1968.263, l. 7554).

Gairm (1969)

Tha *mearanach* a' nochdadh anns an dàn 'Talamh', eadar-theangachadh a rinn Iain Mac a' Ghobhainn air dàn leis a' bhàrd Ruiseanach, Andrei [Andreyevich] Voznesensky (Mac a' Ghobhainn 1969: 33):

> mar pheucagan, de elevators
> air ròpaichean **mearanach**. (Mac a' Ghobhainn 1969: 33)

[29] Tha Moireasdan (1929: 401) a' mìneachadh *dò* mar seo leanas: 'Fiadhaich, ceannardach. Theagamh giorrachdh de 'n fhacal dobhaidh.' Cf. *dòbhaidh* ('boisterous, stormy, etc.' (Dwelly [1901–11] 1977: s.v.).

[30] Air an làimh eile dh'fhaodadh e bhith gur h-e buaidh *mearainn* a tha boireann a tha air a chùlaibh.

[31] Tha *leum caoich* (= *cuthaich*) a' nochdadh ann an tasglann DASG anns an abairt seo leanas: 'Thainig leum caoich [kwhiç] ann!' ('He flew into a rage. He burst into a fit of temper.') a chaidh a chlàradh bho Alex MacDonald (An t-Allt Beithe) anns an Dùbhlachd 1969.

[32] Is e 'frenzy' an t-eadar-theangachadh a tha nochdadh air an t-slip pàipeir ann an tasglann DASG. Is ann le Michel Byrne a tha an t-eadar-theangachadh Beurla gu h-àrd.

[33] Tha seo tighinn bhon dàn 'Rainn a sgrìobh e anns an album air fhèin', eadar-theangachadh air dàn leis a' bhàrd Chròthaiseach Vladislav Kusan.

Rè na h-Oidhche: The Length of Night (1994)

> Tha *mearain-cadail* a' nochdadh anns an dàn 'Gun Stiùir' le Catrìona NicGumaraid: *Dhùisg mi às a' mhearain-chadail* ('I woke from the delirium') (NicGumaraid 1994: 46).[34] Tha Catrìona a bhoineas do Dhùn Bheagain an Eilein Sgitheanaich ag innse dhomh (conaltradh pearsanta, Sultain 2013) gu bheil *mearain* ga fhuaimneachadh mar [mɛrɪɴ′] (i.e. *mearainn*), gu bheil e fireann aicese agus gu bheil e ciallachadh 'delirium' agus gur h-e seòrsa de throm-laighe a th' ann. Chanadh duine cuideachd: *bha mearain(n) orm* ('I had a bad dream') nuair nach biodh e a' faireachdainn gu math mar gun deach an cadal ceàrr air. Tha e soilleir gur h-e cruth eascruthach a th' anns a' chruth seo.

Iain MacAonghuis (2013)[35]

> Ged nach cuala Iain MacAonghuis na faclan *mearan* /mɛran/ no *mearanach* /mɛranəx/ (le 'a' shoilleir anns an dara lide) ann an cainnt riamh, bha cuimhne aige air a' chruth iolra *meirean* /mɛr′ən/[36] (a chuala e aig tè de pheathraichean a athar) a mhìnich e dhomh mar seo leanas. Is e bhiodh anns 'na meirean', 'daoine air an tàinig galar inntinn'. Tha sin a' toirt nar cuimhne am *mer* a dh'aithnichte ann an seann laghan na Gàidhlig (faic shìos). Bha e cinnteach gun cuala e 'bha e sna meirean aig an àm' agus bha e a' smaoineachadh gun cuala e an leithid seo cuideachd: 'bha e fo na meirean aig an àm' agus / no 'bha e leis na meirean aig an àm'. Anns na suidheachaidhean seo tha e toirt leis 'manic tendency', 'chaos of mind', 'frenzy' no 'madness', ach 'chan e galar leantaileach a th' ann', 'tha e glacadh duine ach tha e falbh'.

Geàrr-iomradh air na Cruthan Gàidhlig

Tha fianais againn air iomadh cruth anns a' Ghàidhlig:

> *mear**an*** (-/an/)
> *meir**ean*** (-/ən/) (iolra)
> *mear**ain(n)*** (-/ɪɴ′/); cf. *meirin*?
> *mear**an**ach* (-/an/-)
> *meir**ein*** (-/ɛ/-), *meir**ean*** (-/an/-); cf. *meirin*?
> *cf. mearaichinn*

Is e *mearan* as cumanta agus fianais am pailteas ann airson deiridhean meanbhain *-an*, *-ein* / *-ean* / -*in*(?). Tha fianais Iain MhicAonghuis a' cur air shùilean duinn gun robh cruth iolra *meirean* -/ən/ ann cuideachd. A thuilleadh air na cruthan sin, fhuaras na cruthan eascruthach *mearain*(*n*) agus *mearaichinn* (cf. *meirin*?).[37] Tha fhios gun do chinnich na cruthan anns a bheil 'r' no 'n' chaol tro analachas no cothlamadh le cruthan *mir*(-) agus am meanbhan *-ein*(*n*) ris am biodh dùil às dèidh consan caol (faic Ó Maolalaigh 2001) agus an deireadh eascruthach *-ainn*.

---

[34] Is ann le Catrìona NicGumaraid a tha an t-eadar-theangachadh Beurla.

[35] Còmhradh pearsanta le Iain MacAonghuis (Faoilleach 2013).

[36] Shaoil leis gun cuala e /mer′ən/ cuideachd.

[37] Tha e coltach gu bheil cruth eascruthach, *mearad*, a' nochdadh ann an ainm àite ann an Bàideanach far a bheil cothlamadh eadar an t-ainm *Mairearad* agus *mear*. Tha MacBheathain a' sgrìobhadh:

> *Ciste Mhairearaid* or rather *Ciste Mhearad*, Margaret's kist or chest or coffin, is part of Coire Fhearnagan, above the farm of Achlean. Here snow may remain all the year-round. It is said that Margaret, who was jilted by Mackintosh of Moy Hall, and who cursed his family to sterility, died here in her mad wanderings. (MacBain 1891: 187)

Mer

Tha am buadhair *mer* / *mear* a' tighinn bho **mero-* ('crazy, silly') na Ceiltis (Matasović 2009: 267) ach tha an dàrna brìgh 'spirited, lively, merry' air cinneachadh. Seo na tha aig luchd-deasachaidh *DIL* mun bhun-bhuadhair *mer* (*mear* na Gàidhlig is na Gaeilge):

> o, ā. adj. used chiefly of persons, apparently **off one's head**, **demented**, **crazy**, both of temporary condition due to excitement, intoxication, anger, etc., and of permanent quality; in heroic lit. applied to warriors (often in unfavourable sense **foolhardy**, **rash**); in Laws to the insane or half-witted. In late lit. often used in a complimentary sense **spirited**, **lively**, **agile**; see IGT Dec. § 65 (mear ... ó chéill in mholta). (*DIL*: s.v. [1]*mer*)

Is e 'lively, spirited, etc.' a' phrìomh bhrìgh a tha aig *mear* anns na nua-chànanan ged a gheibhear e cuideachd anns an t-seagh 'quick-tempered, fiery':[38]

The Illustrated Gaelic-English Dictionary (Dwelly [1901–11] 1977: s.v.)

> *mear*. [1.] Merry, joyful; 2. Sportive, playful; 3. Wanton; 4. *poetically* Incited, keen, enraged; 5. Lustful; 6. Apish; 7. Buxom; 8. Agitated, in quick motion; 9. Sudden or quick in motion; 10. Airy; 11. Comical; 12. Very joyful, in high glee.[39]

Foclóir Gaeilge-Béarla (Ó Dónaill [1977] 1998: s.v.)

> *mear*. 1. Quick, fast, nimble, lively, spirited; 2. Precipitate, hasty, rash, quick-tempered, fiery; 3. [Ann an litreachas]: (a) Mad, crazy, (b) Furious, raging, mad, angry.

Tha e soilleir gur h-e an t-seann bhrìgh 'madness, delirium, etc.' a thàinig a-nuas anns na faclan Gàidhlig *mearan* agus *mearanach*.[40]

Ged nach urrainnear a bhith gu tur cinnteach, dh'fhaodadh e bhith gun robh co-cheangal bho shean eadar cleachdadh a' bhuadhfhacail *meránach* agus am *mer* ('one who is confused, deranged') air a bheil iomradh ann an teacsaichean lagha na Seann Ghàidhlig (Smith 1932: 68, 73, 80–82; Binchy 1978, IV: 1276.18–1277.13; Kelly [1988] 1995: 92). Seo mar a mhìnicheas Fergus Kelly an diofar eadar *mer*, *drúth* agus *dásachtach* mar a chleachdar iad anns na laghan:

> The *dásachtach* is the person with manic symptoms who is liable to behave in a violent and destructive manner. The *mer* (lit. 'one who is confused, deranged') poses less of a threat to other people, and is normally permitted into the ale-house [...] The *drúth* appears to be a person who is mentally retarded. (The term *drúth* is also used of the professional clown or buffoon whose act would include imitations of the insane [...]). (Kelly [1988] 1995: 92).

Gheibhear iomradh air na trì faclan seo anns an tràchd 'De Drūthaib ⁊ Meraib ⁊ Dāsachtaibh ('Concerning Fools and Madmen and Lunatics') a tha Liam Breatnach (2005: 307–08) a' cumail a-

---

[38] Is e *mear* (*Mêr*) a chuala Edward Lhuyd bho neach-bhratha bho Earra-Ghàidheal airson 'madness', agus tha sin a' co-fhreagairt ri *cuthaich* (*Kyich*) a fhuaras bho neach-bhratha bho Inbhir Nis (Campbell and Thomson 1963: 152, §XIV.51).

[39] Is e *mear* ('lively, in high spirits, merry') a tha aig Iain MacAonghuis. Mairidh an dà chiall ann am *mire* cuideachd: ged a gheibhear *mire* san t-seagh 'spòrs' no 'suirghe' (m.e. 'Cò nì mire rium?' sna h-òrain), gheibhear *mire-chatha* ('battle frenzy') cuideachd; cf. *mireag nan cruach* agus *mire-mhulan* mar ainmean airson cluich chloinne (Dwelly ([1901–11] 1977: s.vv.).

[40] Gheibhear am buadhair *mearanta* anns an t-seagh 'mirthful' anns a' Ghàidhlig. Mar eisimpleir, tha e nochdadh anns an dàn 'Dàn do 'n Uaigh' le Dòmhnall nan Òran': 'An t-aon is **mearanta** dheth t-shluagh' (MacLeòid 1871: 15); cf. *mearanta* ('mirthful') (Dwelly [1901–11] 1977: s.v.).

mach a bhoineas o thùs dhan tràchd 'Di Brethaib Gaire' ('Concerning Judgements on Maintenance').

Tha e annasach is inntinneach gum bheil *dásachtach* ('mad, insane'; 'one who behaves like a lunatic or who is full of fury, rage or anger') ri fhaighinn mar bhuadhfhacal air an Rìgh Albannach, Domnall mac Causaintín (†900AD). Tha an rann seo leanas air Domnall mac Causaintín a' nochdadh ann am Fàisneachd Bhearchain:

> Nos géabha rí aile ann
> bec do tharba nis comhbrann
> maircc Albain ósin amach
> día-mbia hanim **dásachtach**.
>
> 'Another king will take sovereignty then; little gain, he does not share it; woe to Scotland thenceforth; to him will be the name the madman.'(Hudson 1996: 43, §131; 85, 131)[41]

Ann an rannan eile a chaidh a chur ris an dàn canar 'in garbh' ('the rough one, the fierce one') agus 'athgharbh' ('very rough, very fierce') ris cuideachd agus e ri creach is cogadh fad a rè mar rìgh (Hudson 1996: 45–46, §§143–47; 204). Tha iomradh air Dòmhnall mac Causaintín cuideachd anns an liosta rìghrean aig Flann Mainistreach (†1056 AD) mar 'Domnall **Dāsachtach**' (Skene 1867: 21); cf. Anderson 1922: cxlix, 397–98. Gheibhear *dásachtach* mar bhuadhfhacal ann an ginealaichean Fer Tamnaich Éoganachta cuideachd: '[Lonán] m. Feideilmid Daim **Dāsachtaich**' ('m. Feidlimthi m. Daim **Dāsachtaig**' anns an Leabhar Laighneach) (O'Brien [1962] 2005: 233). Tha an fhianaise a tha seo mun fhacal *dásachtach* mar buadhfhacal a' cumail taic ri cleachdadh *meránach* mar bhuadhfhacal le ainmean pearsanta.

Tha e inntinneach gum faighear *dàsachd*(*ach*) agus na cruthan toiseannach *dàsan*(*ach*)(*d*) (math dh'fhaodte fo bhuaidh *mearan*(*ach*)), *dàsunnach*/ *dàsannach*, *dàsaidh* agus *dàsanta* anns a' Ghàidhlig.[42] Tha luchd-deasachaidh *DIL* a' cumail a-mach gu bheil am facal seo air a dhol à cleachdadh anns na nuadh-chànanan: 'Obs[olete], but given in most mod[ern] Ir[ish] and Sc[ottish] dict[ionaries]' (*DIL*: s.v. *dásachtach*) ach tha an fhianais seo leanas a' dearbhadh gun cleachdte am facal agus na cruthan a thàinig bhuaidhe anns a' Ghàidhlig Albannaich:

dàsachd* / *dásacht

(*mire₇*) *dásacht* ('(madness and) frenzy'), le Niall MacMhuirich ann an Leabhar Dearg Chlann Raghnaill (Cameron 1892–94, II: 192; cf. t.dd. 182, 260).

dāsachd na heaslainti ('virulence'), ann an LS Adv. 72.2.10 (1612 AD) air a sgrìobhadh le Angus Beaton (DASG).[43]

dàsachd ('fierceness, furiousness, madness, rage, fury; impertinence') (Dwelly [1901–1] 1977: s.v.); tha Armstrong (1825: s.v. *dasachd*) ga chomharrachadh mar fhacal a tha air a dhol à cleachdadh.

dàsachd ('wildness, fury') (MacEachainn [1842] 1922: s.v.).

dàsachdach* / *dásachtach

dásachtach ('dauntless') (*c*. 1449–93) (Cameron 1892–94, II: 260).

dásachdach ('pugnacious (non-pejorative)'), ann an LS RIA Av2, fo. 74a) le Cathal MacMhuirich (*c*. 1640) (DASG).[44]

---

[41] Is ann leis an neach-deasachaidh, Benjamin T. Hudson, a tha an t-eadar-theangachadh seo.

[42] Is e *dásacht*(*ach*) agus *dásach* a gheibhear anns a' Ghaeilge (Ó Dónaill [1977] 1998: s.vv.). Chan fhaighear **dàsad*(-), ris am biodh dùil anns an t-sreath -*sacht*- , ann an Gàidhlig Alba; cf. *iasad* < *iasacht*, etc. (O'Rahilly [1932] 1976: 210; Ó Maolalaigh 2005: 112, nn. 24, 25).

[43] Air a thoirt bhon làmhsgrìobhainn le Raghnall MacilleDhuibh.

dàsachdach ('wild') (*c.* 1890) (Gun ainm *c.* 1890: 61).[45]
dàsachdach ('fierce, furious, mad; impertinent, assuming') (Dwelly [1901–11] 1977: s.v.); tha Armstrong (1825: s.v. *dasachdach*) ga chomharrachadh mar fhacal a tha air a dhol à cleachdadh.

dàsach
dàsach ('bold'), Leabhar an Deadhain (Ross 1939: 204, §27d); is e 'Zawsi' a tha nochdadh san làmhsgrìobhainn fhèin (Meek ri nochdadh fhathast)

dàsan
dàsan ('fury, frenzy') (Dwelly [1901–11] 1977: s.v.; Armstrong 1825: s.v.)

dàsanach
dàsanach ('fierce, furious'), ann an *Cath Fionntragha* (LS Adv. 72.2.11, t.d. 27) le Alastair MacMhaighstir Alastair;[46] cf. *dāsannach* gu h-ìosal.
dàsanach ('cunning, wily; presumptuous; furious, fierce, frantic') (Dwelly [1901–11] 1977: s.v.; cf. Armstrong 1825: s.v. *dasanach*).
dàsanach ('without softness or timidity') (J. L. Campbell [1958] 1991: 95).
dàsanach ('bold, cheeky, presumptuous') (Wentworth 2003: s.vv.); o thaobh fuaimneachadh, is e **d̥ɑːsənɔx** a tha aig Wentworth (2003: s.v. *bold*) ged a tha e ag innse gum faodadh **d̥ɑːsanɔx** (le **-an**- soilleir) a bhith ann cuideachd.
dàsannach: 'chaidh e sàs ann gu dāsannach' ('determined') (bho Pheggy Morrison, Kintulavaig, Leverburgh, Harris, DASG [gun bliadhna air a comharrachadh].

dàsanachd
dàsanachd ('furiousness, fierceness, frenzy') (Dwelly [1901–11] 1977: s.v.; cf. Armstrong 1825: s.v. *dasanachd*).

dàsunnach / dàsannach
dàsannach ('bold, fierce') (v.l. *dasunnich*, *daisunnach*), ann am 'Brostughadh-catha Chlann Domhnaill, Là Chatha Gharbhaich' (Thomson 1968: 150, 154).
dāsannach ('furious'),ann an *Cath Fionntrágha* (LS Adv. 72.2.11, t.d. 18) le Alastair MacMhaighstir Alastair; cf. *dàsanach* gu h-àrd.[47]
dàsunach (airson *dàsunnach*?) (MacDomhnuill 1776: 122).
dàsunnach ('cunning, wily, presumptuous') (Highland Society of Scotland 1828: s.v.) far a bheil am facal a'tighinn bho 'C.S.', i.e. 'common speech'; tha *dàsannach* = *dàsachdach* cuideachd anns an fhaclair seo.
dàsunnach = *dàsanach* (Dwelly [1901–11] 1977: s.v.).
dàsannach ('cunning, wily, presumptuous') (MacEachainn [1842] 1922: s.v.).
dàsannach ('trying to do a thing beyond one's power') (J. L. Campbell [1958] 1991: 95).
dàsannach **ˈdɑːsəɴəx** ('audacious'), bhon a' mhnaoi aig Iain MacBeath, a' Chomraich (1966) (DASG).

dàsaidh
dàsaidh ('furiousness; audacious') (Dwelly [1901–11] 1977: s.v.).
dàsaidh (['wild, furious']) (MacEachainn [1842] 1922: s.v. *dàsachd*).

---

[44] Air a thoirt bhon làmhsgrìobhainn le Raghnall MacilleDhuibh.

[45] An t-eadar-theangachadh Beurla bho thasglann DASG.

[46] An t-eadar-theangachadh Beurla le Raghnall MacilleDhuibh, ann an tasglann DASG.

[47] An t-eadar-theangachadh Beurla le Raghnall MacilleDhuibh, ann an tasglann DASG.

dàsanta

dàsanta ('foolhardy') (bho Alexander Nicolson, an t-Eilean Sgitheanach, DASG [gun bliadhna air a comharrachadh].[48]

A-nise, suim an rannsachaidh. Is e a' bharail a thathas a' cur air adhart anns an aiste ghoirid seo gun gabhadh e bhith gur h-e *meránach* tinnsgeadal a' bhuadhfhacail mheadhan-aoisich *meranach* agus, theagamh, *marrenah*, agus gum b' e brìgh *mearanach* na Gàidhlig Albannaich 'delirious, mad, insane' ba chiall da. Tha cleachdadh *dàsachdach* mar bhuadhfhacal a' cumail taic ri sin. Nan gabhte ri sin, bhiodh fianais na Gàidhlig a' dearbhadh dhuinn gur h-e *meránach* (seach *méranach* / *méránach* no *meranach*) an cruth ceart, le *à* fhada anns an dara lide – cruth a tha tighinn ri iomadach facal a tha stèidhicte air a' mheanbhan *-án* agus a' crìochnachadh le *–ach* (Russell 1990: 88, 191–92). Faodaidh sinn coimeas a dhèanamh ris an fhacal *samhanach* ('savage, giant, monster') (Dwelly [1901–11] 1977: s.v.) aig a bheil ceangal ris an ainm *Mac Sam*[*h*]*á*(*i*)*n*.[49] Gheibhear faclan eascruthach eile ann an Gàidhlig is Gaeilge a tha crìochnachadh le *-án* / *-an*, m.e.

Gaeilge
achasán ('reproach, insult'), *béadán* ('gossip, slander; worry anxiety'), *bearrán* ('arrogance, nuisanace'), *cadrán* ('hardness, stubbornness, obstinancy'), *ceatán* ('an awkwardness, annoyance'), *cránan* ('grief, arrogance'), *cumhán* ('(fit of) lonesomeness, anxiety, sorrow'), *díodán* ('giddiness, megrim'), *fiarán* ('anger, petulance, huff'), *gearán* ('complaint, grievance'), *meadhrán* ('diziness'), *meangán* ('wile, deceit'), *míobhán* ('diziness'), *mosán* ('irritation, annoyance'), *piachán* ('hoarseness'), *siabhrán* ('slight derangement, delusion, mental confusion'), *seolán* ('fit of sorrow') (Ó Dónaill [1977] 1998: s.vv.).

Gàidhlig
achmhasan ('rebuke'), *amhartan* ('luck'), *arraban* ('distress'), *cachdan* ('vexation'), *carrasan* ('hoarseness, wheezing'), *dàsan* ('fury, frenzy'), *diùdan* ('giddiness'), *docran* ('anguish'), *dorran* ('vexation, anger'), *driongan* ('slowness'), *faspan* ('difficulty, embarrassment'), *forgan* ('keenness, anger'), *furan* ('welcome'), *gearan* ('complaint'), *imreasan* ('controversy'), *ìogan* ('deceit, fraud'), *luaran* ('diziness, faint'), *smuairean* ('grief, dejection'), *tacan* ('a while, short time') (Dwelly [1901–11] 1977: s.vv.).

Tha an aiste seo a' cur air shùilean duinn aon uair eile luach cudromach is tàbhachdach teist is fianais Gàidhlig Alba ann an rannsachadh nan cànanan Gàidhealach is Ceilteach. Is tric a tha faclan is feartan air mairsinn anns a' Ghàidhlig Albannaich (a tha uaireannan air a dhol à bith anns a' Ghaeilge agus sa Mhanainnis) a tha toirt lèirsinn luachmhmhor dhuinn air eachdraidh na Gàidhlig agus air dualchas nan Gàidheal anns an fharsaingeachd; faic, mar eisimpleir, Fraser (1928), Gillies (2004), Jackson (1951), Kelly (1986), MacAonghuis (1986), MacInnes (1977), Ó Maolalaigh (2005; 2006; 2008: 241–59; 2013), O'Rahilly (1926; 1927, 1929), etc. Mar a thuirt Iain MacAonghuis fhèin bho chionn còrr is fichead bliadhna ar ais, 'tha raointean farsaing ri an

[48] Tha A. O'Henley ag innse: 'Made available courtesy of Mrs Alexander Nicolson and Dr Alistair MacLean, Bernisdale, Isle of Skye.'

[49] Tha an t-ainm *Mac Samá*(*i*)*n* a' nochdadh ann an seann litreachas na Gàidhlig mar fhiadh-dhuine no geilt a tha tighinn beò anns a' choille (Jackson 1935: 113, n. 1; Jackson 1990: 48; Clancy 1992: 84, 88–89). Gheibhear *Mac Samhain* agus *samhanach* cuideachd ann am beul-aithris na Gàidhlig mar ainm a chuireas an cèill uilebheist no fuamhair (Nicolson [1881] 1996: 48, 160; Carmichael 1900–71, II: 347; MacKay 1935: 2–4; Ó Baoill and Bateman 1994: 192, 234; Black [2005] 2008: 509); cf. *sadhanach* ('big sturdy fellow') (J. L. Campbell [1958] 1991: 266). Dh'fhaodadh e bhith gu bheil (air neo gun saoilte gun robh) suaip aig *samhan*(-) ris an fhacal *sam*[*h*] ('sorrel') (*DIL*: s.v. ^{3}*sam*), biadh a dh'itheadh leithid Suibhne Geilt sa choille (faic O'Keefe [1931] 1975: 12, 62).

treabhadh fhathast ann an sgoilearachd na Gàidhlig – agus a cuid cainnte' (MacAonghuis 1990: 25; MacInnes 2006: 128) – tuairisgeul a tha fhathast fìor anns an là-an-diugh ged as saibhride ar tuigse na sgrìobh agus na dh'innis Iain dhuinn mu chainnt is cànan nan Gàidheal. Guma fada beò e.

GIORRACHAIDHEAN

AU — *The Annals of Ulster (to A.D. 1131)*. Seán Mac Airt agus Gearóid Mac Niocaill (eds.). Dublin, 1983.

DASG — Dàta airson Stòras na Gàidhlig / Digital Archive of Scottish Gaelic, Roinn na Ceiltis is na Gàidhlig, Oilthigh Ghlaschu. http://www.gla.ac.uk/schools/humanities/research/celticgaelicresearch/currentresearchprojects/digitalarchiveofscottishgaelicdasg.

DIL — *Dictionary of the Irish Language*. E. G. Quin (ed.). Dublin, [1983] 1990.

LL — *The Book of Leinster*, vol. 1. R. I. Best, Osborn Bergin and M. A. O'Brien (eds). Dublin, 1954.

PoMS — *People of Medieval Scotland: 1093–1314*. www.poms.ac.uk [leughta, 27 Faoileach 2013].

TÙSAN

AM B.A. (*SIC*.)

1907 — 'Taigh na Croise-Shlighe'. *Guth na Bliadhna* 4.3 (Samhradh): 286–92.

ANDERSON, ALAN ORR.

1922 — *Early Sources of Scottish History A.D. 500 to 1286*. Edinburgh and London.

ARBUTHNOTT, SHARON (ED.).

2005 — *Cóir Anmann: A Late Middle Irish Treatise on Personal Names*. 2 vols. London.

ARMSTRONG, R. A. (ED.).

1825 — *A Gaelic Dictionary*. London.

BARTRUM, P[ETER] C. (ED.).

1966 — *Early Welsh Genealogical Tracts*. Cardiff.

BINCHY, D. A. (ED.).

1978 — *Corpus Iuris Hibernici*. 6 vols. Dublin.

BLACK, RONALD (ED.). [= MACILLEDHUIBH, RAGHNALL].

[2005] 2008 — *The Gaelic Otherworld: John Gregorson Campbell's Superstitions of the Highlands & Islands of Scotland and Witchcraft & Second Sight in the Highlands & Islands*. Edinburgh.

BREATNACH, LIAM.

1994 'An Mheán-Ghaeilge'. Kim McCone, Damian McManus, Cathal Ó hÁinle, Nicholas Williams agus Liam Breatnach (eag.), *Stair na Gaeilge in Ómós do P[h]ádraig Ó Fiannachta.*. Maigh Nuad: 221–333.

2005 *A Companion to the Corpus Iuris Hibernici.* Dublin.

BRODERICK, GEORGE.

1980 'Irish and Welsh Strands in the Genealogy of Godred Crovan'. *Journal of the Manx Museum* 8: 32–38.

BYRNE, MICHEL (ED.).

[2000] 2003 *Collected Poems and Songs of George Campbell Hay (Deòrsa Mac Iain Dheòrsa).* Edinburgh.

CAIMBEUL HAY, DEÒRSA.

1952 *O na Ceithir Airdean.* Edinburgh; London.

CAIMBEULL, DONNCHADH.

1798 *Nuadh Orain Ghailach* [...]. Cork.

CAMERON, ALEXANDER (ED.).

1892–94 *Reliquiae Celticae.* 2 vols. Alexander MacBain and John Kennedy (eds). Inverness.

CAMPBELL, J. L. (ED.).

[1958] 1991 *Gaelic Words and Expressions from South Uist and Eriskay.* Dublin.

CAMPBELL, J. L. AND DERICK THOMSON (EDS).

1963 *Edward Lhuyd in the Scottish Highlands 1699–1700.* Oxford.

CARMICHAEL, ALEXANDER (ED.).

1900–71 *Carmina Gadelica: Hymns and Incantations.* 6 vols. Edinburgh and London.

CLANCY, THOMAS OWEN.

1992 'Mac Steléne and the Eight in Armagh: Identity and Context'. *Éigse* 26: 80–91.

COMYN, DAVID AND PATRICK S. DINNEEN (EDS).

1902–14 *Foras Feasa ar Éirinn / The History of Ireland.* 4 vols. London.

COX, RICHARD A. V. (DEAS.).

1991 *Brigh nam Facal: Faclair Ur don Bhun-Sgoil.* Glaschu.

DE BHULBH, SEÁN.

1997 *Sloinnte na hÉireann: Irish Surnames.* Limerick.

DIECKHOFF, HENRY CYRIL.

1932 *A Pronouncing Dictionary of Scottish Gaelic.* Edinburgh and London.

DILLON, MYLES (ED.).

1962 *Lebor na Cert: The Book of Rights*. Dublin.

DWELLY, EDWARD (ED.).

[1901–11] 1977 *The Illustrated Gaelic-English Dictionary.* Glasgow.

DUFFY, SEÁN.

1992 'Irishmen and Islesmen in the Kingdoms of Dublin and Man, 1052–1171'. *Ériu* 43: 93–133.

EASSON, D. E. (ED.).

1947 *Charters of the Abbey of Coupar-Angus.* 2 vols. Edinburgh.

FORBES, JOHN.

1843 *A Double Grammar of English and Gaelic.* Edinburgh.

FRASER, J.

1928 'Some Terms of Old Scots Law'. *Scottish Gaelic Studies* 2/2: 233–34.

GILLIES, WILLIAM.

2004 'Varia II: Early Irish *lía*, Scottish Gaelic *liutha*'. *Ériu* 54: 253–56.

GREENE, DAVID.

1983 '*Cró, crú* and Similar Words'. *Celtica* 15: 1–9.

GUN AINM.

[c. 1890] *Filidh nam Beann: The Mountain Songster.* Glasgow.

HENDERSON, GEORGE (ED.).

1898 *Leabhar nan Gleann.* Edinburgh.

HENNESSY, WILLIAM M. (ED.).

1866 *Chronicum Scotorum: A Chronicle of Irish Affairs*. London.

HENNESSY, W. M. AND B. MAC CARTHY (EDS).

1887–1901 *Annála Uladh: Annals of Ulster Otherwise Annala Senait, Annals of Senat: A Chronicle of Irish Affairs from A.D. 431 to A.D. 1540.* 4 vols. Dublin.

HIGHLAND SOCIETY OF SCOTLAND.

1828 *Dictionarium Scoto-Celticum: A Dictionary of the Gaelic Language.* Edinburgh.

HUDSON, BENJAMIN T.

1996 *Prophecy of Berchan: Irish and Scottish High-Kings of the Early Middle Ages*. Cardiff.

IAIN [*SIC*].

1901 'O Chionn tri Fichead Bliadhna: "A Bhanais Mhagaidh" [I]'. *Mac-Talla* IX, àir. 41 (12/4/1901): 314–15.

JACKSON, KENNETH (HURLSTONE).

1935 *Studies in Early Celtic Nature Poetry*. Cambridge.

1951 *'Common Gaelic': The Evolution of the Gaelic Languages*. London. Also in *Proceedings of the British Academy* 37.

1990 *Aislinge Meic Con Glinne*. Dublin.

KELLY, FERGUS.

1986 'Old Irish *creccaire*, Scottish Gaelic *kreahkir*'. *Ériu 37: 185–86.*

[1988] 1995 *A Guide to Early Irish Law*. Dublin.

KNOTT, ELEANOR.

[1928] 1994 *An Introduction ot Irish Syllabic Poetry of the Period 1200–1600.* Dublin.

MAC A' GHOBHAINN, IAIN.

1969 'As gach Àird: Eadartheangaichean le Iain Mac a' Ghobhainn'. *Gairm* 69 (An Geamhradh): 29–33.

MAC AIRT, SEÁN (ED.).

1951 *The Annals of Inisfallen.* Dublin.

MACALISTER, R. A. STEWART (ED.).

1938–2009 *Lebor Gabála Érenn: The Book of the Taking of Ireland*. Vol. 6: Pádraig Ó Riain (ed.). Dublin.

MACALPINE, NEIL (ED.).

[1832] 1955 *A Pronouncing Gaelic-English Dictionary.* Glasgow.

MAC AN ROTHAICH, DOMHNULL.

1886 *Marbhrainn air Dr. Begg, Bha'n Dun-Eidin; 's air Dr. Ceanadaidh Bha'n Inbhirfeorathain; agus air Daoinibh Diadhaidh Bh'anns an Airde-Tuath.* [gun àite foillseachaidh].

MAC AN TUAIRNEIR, PARUIG (DEAS.).

1813 *Comhchruinneacha do dh' Orain Taghta, Ghaidhealach* [. . .]. Dùn Èideann.

MAC AONGHUIS, IAIN (= MACINNES, JOHN).

1986 'Baird is Bleidirean'. *Féilscríbhinn Thomáis de Bhaldraithe*. Seosamh Watson (deas.): 94–110. Baile Átha Cliath. Ri fhaighinn cuideachd ann am MacInnes (2006: 340–56).

1990 'Cainnt is Cànan'. *An Tarbh* 1: 23–25. Ri fhaighinn cuideachd ann am MacInnes (2006: 120–30).

MACBAIN, ALEXANDER.

1891 'Badenoch: Its History, Clans, and Place-Names'. *Transactions of the Gaelic Society of Inverness* 16: 148–97.

MAC DOMHNUILL, RAONUILL (DEAS.).

1776 *Comh-chruinneachidh Orannaigh Gaidhealach le Raonuill MacDomhnuill ann 'N Eilean Eigg*. Dùn Èideann.

MACDONALD, A[NGUS]. AND A[RCHIBALD]. MACDONALD (EDS).

1912 *The MacDonald Collection of Gaelic Poetry.* Inverness.
1924 *The Poems of Alexander MacDonald (Mac Mhaighstir Alasdair).* Inverness.

MACDONALD, ALEXANDER [=MACDOMHNUILL, ALASDAIR (MAC MHAIGHSTIR ALASDAIR)]

1741 *A Galick and English Vocabulary.* Edinburgh.
1751 *Ais-éiridh na Sean Chànoin Albannaich* [. . .]. Dùn Èideann.

MAC EACHAINN, EOBHAN (ED.).

[1842] 1922 *Gaelic-English Dictionary.* Inverness.

MACFARLANE, MALCOLM.

1953 *A Gaelic-English Dictionary.* Inverness.

MACILLEDHUIBH, RAGHNALL (DEAS.) [= BLACK, RONALD].

1999 *An Tuil: Duanaire Gàidhlig an 20mh Ceud.* Edinburgh.

MACINNES, JOHN [= MAC AONGHUIS, IAIN].

1977 'Some Gaelic Words and Usages'. *Transactions of the Gaelic Society of Inverness* 49: 428–55.
2006 *Dùthchas nan Gàidheal: Selected Essays of John MacInnes.* Michael Newton (ed.). Edinburgh.

MACKAY, J. G.

1935 'An Tuairisgeal'. *Transactions of the Gaelic Society of Inverness* 34: 1–112.

[MACKENZIE, FRANCIS.]

1838 *Hints for the Use of of Highland Tenants / Beachd-chomhairlean airson Feum do Thuathanaich 'us Choitearan Gaidh'lach.* Inbhir Nis.

MACKENZIE, JOHN (ED.)

[1845] 1962 *An English-Gaelic Dictionary.* Glasgow.
1904 *Sàr-Obair nam Bard Gaelach: The Beauties of Gaelic Poetry*. New edition. Edinburgh.

MACLEOD, NORMAN AND DANIEL DEWAR.

[1831] 1909 *Dictionary of the Gaelic Language*. Edinburgh.

MAC LEOID, DOMHNULL.

1871 *Dain agus Orain*. Glaschu.

MACLYSAGHT, EDWARD.

1964 *Supplement to Irish Families*. Dublin.

MACMILLAN, SOMERLED (ED.)

1968 *Sporan Dhòmhnaill: Gaelic Poems and Songs by the Late Donald MacIntyre, the Paisley Bard*. Edinburgh.

MACNEILL, JOHN.

1909 'Notes on the Distribution, History, Grammar and Import of the Irish Ogham Inscriptions'. *Proceedings of the Royal Irish Academy* 27C: 329–70.

MAC NIOCAILL, GEARÓID.

2010 'The Annals of Tigernach'. Unpublished translation. *CELT: The Corpus of Electronic Texts*. http://www.ucc.ie/celt/published/T100002A/index.html. [27 Faoilleach 2013].

MACQUEEN, HECTOR L.

2006 'Some Notes on Wrang and Unlaw'. Hector L. MacQueen (ed.), *The Stair Society: Miscellany Five*. Edinburgh: 13–26.

MAC PHÀRLAIN, CALUM (DEAS.).

[1923] *Dòrlach Laoidhean do Sgrìobhadh le Donnchadh Mac Rath, 1688*. Dùn Dè.

MARK, COLIN.

2003 *The Gaelic-English Dictionary*. London and New York.

MATASOVIĆ, RANKO.

2009 *Etymological Dictionary of Proto-Celtic*. Leiden and Boston.

MATHESON, WILLIAM (ED.)

1970 *The Blind Harper (An Clarsair Dall): The Songs of Roderick Morison and His Music*. Edinburgh.

MEEK, DONALD E. (ED.)

Forthcoming *The Book of the Dean of Lismore*. Online edition, Scottish Gaelic Texts Society.

MOIREASDAN, AONGHAS.

1929 *Dàin agus Òrain Ghàidhlig / Gaelic Poems and Songs*. Edinburgh.

MURPHY, GERARD.

1940 'Notes on Analogy in Middle Irish Conjugation'. E. Ua Riain (ed.), *Féilsgríbhinn Eoin Mhic Néill*. Dublin: 72–81.

NEVILLE, CYNTHIA J.

1983 'The Earls of Stratheran from the Twelfth to the Mid Fourteenth Century, with an Edition of their Written Acts'. 2 vols. Unpublished dissertation, University of Aberdeen.

NIC GUMARAID, CATRÌONA.

1994 *Rè na h-Oidhche: The Length of Night*. Edinburgh.

NICOLSON, ALEXANDER.

[1881] 1996 *A Collection of Gaelic Proverbs and Familiar Phrases*. Malcolm MacInnes (ed.). Edinburgh.

Ó BAOILL, COLM AND MEG BATEMAN (EDS).

1994 *Gàir nan Clàrsach: The Harp's Cry: An Anthology of 17th Century Gaelic Poetry*. Edinburgh.

O'BRIEN, M. A. (ED.).

[1962] 2005 *Corpus Genealogiarum Hiberniae*. Dublin.

Ó BUACHALLA, BREANDÁN.

1988 'MacNeil's Law and the Plural Maker *-(e)an*'. *Proceedings of the Royal Irish Academy* 88 C 3: 39–60.

Ó CUÍV, BRIAN.

1957 'A Poem in Praise of Raghnall, King of Man'. *Éigse* 8: 283–301.

Ó DÓNAILL, NIALL (ED.)

[1977] 1998 *Foclóir Gaeilge-Béarla*. Dublin.

O'DONOVAN, JOHN (ED.).

1848–51 *Annala Rioghachta Eireann: Annals of the Kingdom of Ireland, by the Four Masters*. 7 vols. Dublin.

O'KEEFE, J. G. (ED.).

[1931] 1975 *Buile Ṡuibhne*. Dublin.

Ó MAOLALAIGH, ROIBEARD.

2001 'Forás na nDeirí Díspeagtha *-ean* agus *-ein* i nGaeilge na hAlban'. Brian Ó Catháin agus Ruairí Ó hUiginn (deas.), *Béalra: Aistí ar Theangeolaíocht na Gaeilge*. Maigh Nuad: 1–43.

2005 'A Gaulish-Gaelic Correspondence: *S(o)uxt-* and *suac(hd)an*'. *Ériu* 55: 103–17.

2006 'On the Possible Origins of Scottish Gaelic *iorram* "rowing song"'. Michel Byrne, Thomas Owen Clancy agus Sheila Kidd (deas.), *Litreachas & Eachdraidh: Rannsachadh na Gàidhlig 2, Glaschu 2002*. Glaschu: 232–88.

2008 'The Scotticisation of Gaelic: A Reassessment of the Language and Orthography of the Gaelic Notes in the Book of Deer'. Katherine Forsyth (ed.), *Studies on the Book of Deer*. Dublin: 179–274.

2013 'Mythonyms in Scottish Gaelic: *Fomóir, fomhair*, *famhair*, *fuamhair*(*e*) ('giant') and Related Forms'. *Scottish Gaelic Studies* 29: 172–243.

Ó RAITHBHEARTAIGH, TOIRDHEALBHACH (ED.).

1932 *Genealogical Tracts I.* Dublin.

O'RAHILLY, THOMAS F.

1926 'Etymological Notes [I]'. *Scottish Gaelic Studies* 1.1: 28–37.

1927 'Etymological Notes II'. *Scottish Gaelic Studies* 2.1: 13–29.

1929 'Etymological Notes III'. *Scottish Gaelic Studies* 3.1: 52–72.

[1932] 1976 *Irish Dialects Past and Present with Chapters on Scottish and Manx*. Dublin.

Ó TUATHAIL, ÉAMONN.

1950 'Varia. 4. Meranagh'.*Éigse* 6.2: 161–62.

ROSE, JOHN (ED.).

1851 *Metrical Reliques of "The Men" in the Highlands: or, Sacred Poetry of the North* [. . .]. Inverness.

ROSS, NEIL (ED.).

1939 *Heroic Poetry from the Book of the Dean of Lismore*. Edinburgh.

RUSSELL, PAUL.

1990 *Celtic Word-Formation: The Velar Suffixes*. Dublin.

SELLAR, W. D. H.

2000 'The Ancestry of the MacLeods'. *Transactions of the Gaelic Society of Inverness* 55: 233–258.

SHARP, WILLIAM [= 'FIONA MACLEOD'].

1910 *The Works of "Fiona Macleod"*. Vol. IV. *The Divine Adventure: Iona: Studies in Spiritual History*. London.

SKENE, WILLIAM F. (ED.).

1867 *Chronicles of the Picts, Chronicles of the Scots, and other Memorials of Scottish History*. Edinburgh.

SMITH, ROLAND.

1932 'The Advice to Doidin'. *Ériu* 11: 66–85.

STOKES, WHITLEY (ED.).

[1895–97] 1993 *The Annals of Tigernach*. 2 vols. Felinfach. Reprinted in *Revue Celtique* 16–18.

THOMSON, DERICK S.

1968 'The Harlaw Brosnachadh: An Early Fifteenth-century Literary Curio'. James Carney and David Greene (eds), *Celtic Studies: Essays in Memory of Angus Matheson 1912–1962*. London: 147-52.

THURNEYSEN, RUDOLPH.

[1946] 1993 *A Grammar of Old Irish*. Dublin.

WENTWORTH, ROY.

2003 *Gaelic Words and Phrases from Wester Ross / Faclan is Abairtean à Ros an Iar*. Inverness.

The Significance of Music in the Gàidhealtachd in the Pre- and Early-Historic Period

JOHN PURSER

Ata an saoghal & gach beó-chreatuir da bfuil ann, na chlarsigh:[1]
'The world & every living creature in it is a harp.'

As Robert Kirk's heading for his introduction to the Psalms reminds us, the Gaels' love of music is legendary. The Psalter was the ideal place for Kirk's 1684 assertion, for the Psalms – the three fifties – were the Biblical home of the bard. David, portrayed with striking frequency in early mediaeval Scottish stone carving, represented an ideal: a great king who was a poet and musician. Kirk's assertion is not only Biblical but Pythagorean, the relevant texts of music theory being well known to the Gaels (Purser 2006b: 305).

The Gàidhealtachd has made a significant contribution to European archaeo-musicology, including pre-historic artefacts, some of the earliest vernacular texts about music, and a remarkable range of sculptural evidence. Much of this evidence crosses boundaries that currently separate the societies which produced it, but the early Bronze Age pan-pipes found in County Wicklow (O'Dwyer 2004:141–5) may be as relevant to the Scottish Gaels as the Iron Age bridge for a stringed instrument found on Skye may be to the Irish Gaels (see below). Pre- and early-historic evidence is necessarily patchy, but there is sufficient to propose a degree of continuity, and the quality of the evidence supports the suggestion that high value attached to music and musical instruments, including lip-reed, reed and stringed instruments.

If the Bronze Age seems too early to be relevant to the Gàidhealtachd, we should remember that the inhabitants of a place are not subject to the divisions imposed upon them by linguists, archaeologists, geneticists, or anyone else. Dental analysis has shown that the woman buried close to and roughly contemporaneously with the bridge, found on Skye, lived locally, but we do not know what language she spoke or sang (and these might not necessarily be the same). We also know that the site was in virtually continuous use from the Stone Age to the early mediaeval period, and there is no evidence of sudden change.[2]

Fig. 1: Ballater rock gong. *(Photo: J. Purser)*

1.0 Rock Gongs

The earliest known musical instruments in the Gàidhealtachd are rock gongs (Purser 2007: 23–5). Cup marks feature on rock gongs on Tiree and the southern slopes of *Sìdh Chailleann* – the fairy hill of the Caledonians.[3] The rock gong at Ballater *(pictured)* has a pattern in relief and apparently also incised, running the length of the rock, though whether man had a hand in this is not

[1] Robert Kirk, from his introduction to the Psalms of David (1684), quoted in R. Black 2008: 80.

[2] The full report of the excavations is still being written up. Meanwhile, the team have published some of their interim findings at www.high-pasture-cave.org.

[3] This rock, identified as resonant by the author, is situated at NN 750 554.

known.[4] The rock gong at Port Appin is stated to have been used to gather the clan (MacLeod 1981). Several of these rock gongs have names showing that their potential function was still understood: they are 'the iron stone' at Arn Hill (the recumbent of a stone circle), 'the singing stone' at Ballater, 'the bell stone' at 'Ringing Craig' near Cabrach, and *clach a' choire* ('the kettle stone') at Baile Pheudrais on Tiree (Macdonald and MacKinnon 1899: 289; Beveridge 1903: 115). A reference to what was probably a rock gong known as *Clach a' Ghlagain* (meaning 'rattling' or 'talking'), is also associated with a prophecy – in this case that of Mac a' Chreachaire, who declared that when this stone was found, Kishmul Castle would become *càrn dhruidheachan* – a cairn for thrushes (Black 2005: 144). Part of *Clach Oscar* at the head of Loch Slapin on the Isle of Skye, which is broken into three large rocks, is also a rock gong.[5] Such evidence suggests that the use of such gongs continued over four thousand years.

2.0 Hand Bells

In a previous article, I have discussed the early Christian quadrangular hand-bells of Scotland and their connections with rock gongs, including the use of rock gongs and bells for identical functions (Purser 2006a: 267–91). In the same article, I underlined their relationship with the round towers and the fact that these bells (both iron and bronze) are uniquely associated with the Celtic church, and nearly all the Scottish ones with the Gàidhealtachd. At least one place-name would seem to be associated with such a bell – *Eas nan clag* at the headwaters of the river Nant, though how or why the waterfall acquired this name is not known.[6] The bells feature in the dialogues between Oisin (who did not care for them) and Patrick, as well as in early Gaelic poetry. The subsequent production of beautiful bell-shrines (*e.g.* the Guthrie bell-shrine), further underlines their significance.

3.0 Horns and Trumpets

I have argued elsewhere that the magnificent cast bronze Bronze Age horns found in Ireland were probably known in Scotland (Purser 2007: 25–7). Their number, the amount of bronze they require, and the complexity of their manufacture represent an astonishing investment in music on the part of the society which produced them.

Such investment is far from being isolated in the archaeological record in Scotland and Ireland. From the late Iron Age (200 BC–200 AD), the Irish Loughnashade horn and the Deskford Carnyx found in north-eastern Scotland, both made of beaten bronze, are near contemporaries. Parallels with the Torrs pony cap and Battersea shield indicate a number of similarities in the manufacture of these instruments; indeed, it has been suggested that the surviving Loughnashade horn was Brythonic in manufacture (R. and V. Megaw 1994: 23). In addition, the cast-bronze Caprington horn, found in Ayrshire, and the Ard Brinn trumpet from Ireland show that within the single category of bronze lip-reed instruments there was considerable variety.

That these were instruments of the highest status can be deduced from the skill and expense of their manufacture as well as from their ritual deposition. The Ard Brinn trumpa has over one thousand rivets so tight that the instrument can still be played (O'Dwyer 2004: 78–80 and 125–30). While a very similar trumpet, recently presented at the Royal Society of Antiquaries, is of uncertain provenance, its bell-end is original, and is identical with that of the Ard Brinn trumpa.[7] If these are

[4] The Ballater rock gong is at NO 2997 0162. Catherine Fagg (1997: 82) suggests the marks are glacial grooves, but one of the lines is proud of the surface and, taken as a whole, they are difficult to reconcile with glacial activity.

[5] The latter rock, identified as resonant by the author, is situated at 57 14 30 N by 6 3 30 W.

[6] Information from Brigadier John MacFarlane.

[7] 'A newly discovered Irish Iron Age riveted horn', presented at the *Finds and Exhibits Meeting,* Society of Antiquaries, London, by Maurice Byrne and Michael Wright, 4 February 2010.

the sorts of instruments referred to in stories, as in the following from *Táin Bó Fraích,* then literary tradition clearly indicates the status not only of the instruments but also of the musicians:

> *Mórfesser cornaire leo co cornaib órdaib agus argdidib, co n-étaigib ildathachaib, co mongaib órdaib sidbudib, co lennaib étrachtaib.* (Meid 1974: 2)
>
> There were seven horn players with them, with horns gilded and silvered, wearing many-coloured garments; their hair was fairy yellow, and they wore shining mantles.

I do not suggest that the carnyx itself was known in Ireland, but merely that instruments such as the Loughnashade horns would have been able to fulfil similar musical functions, and that they had high status.

3.1 The Deskford Carnyx

These instruments had a strong visual, indeed sculptural, presence and, in the case of the late Iron Age Deskford Carnyx, this is reflected in its appearance in other art forms. The carnyx is a trumpet-type instrument, two metres long, held vertically, and made largely of beaten bronze. The refinement of its manufacture, including bronze and brass as contrasting colour elements at the bell end in the form of a totemic wild boar's head, has been closely studied (Hunter 2001: 77–108; Piggott 1959; Purser 1998: 325–36; Maniquet 2008: 57–76). The fineness of the workmanship; the thinness of the metal (markedly affecting its sound); the incorporation of structural rivetting into the design 'which mimicked flesh folds of the boar's head'; the stylisation of the lie of the hair surrounding the eyes, are all managed with superb rhythmic control. The reconstruction required, and found in John Creed, a craftsman of the highest calibre, who wrote, 'As a visual artist, it has a particular attraction for me, as being the only instrument I know of where visual appearance is as important as sound.' (Creed 1998: 347–49). These characteristics strongly imply high status for the instrument and, presumably, its music. But there is also a mythological aspect to the significance of the carnyx.

Fig. 2: Deskford Carnyx. *(Photo: J. Purser)*

It has been suggested that the famous image on the Gundestrup bowl, which shows instruments of the type of the Deskford Carnyx, relates to the *Táin Bó Cúailnge* (Olmsted 1976: 95–103 and figures 1–9; also Olmsted 1992: 5–17). This tale, known throughout the Gaelic-speaking world, has echoes through the centuries, as does the totemic character of the wild boar, so magnificently represented on this instrument. We know from *Táin Bó Fraích* that:

> *A chornairi iarum remisium dochum in dúine. Sennait di conid abbad tricha fer di sainchaemaib Aillella ar sirechtai.*(Meid 1974: 9)
>
> His horn-players went in front of him into the dun. They blew so that thirty of Aillil's finest men died of ecstatic grief.

Fraoch hears then the lament of his mother and her people – the people of the *sith*, the fairies – and he is taken into their mound and returned whole. From this event, the story tells us, 'comes the Fairies' Lament of the musicians of Ireland'.

> *Atnagat a ngol oc dul uad co corastar na daíni bátar isind liss tar cend. Is de atá golgaire bad síde la aes ciuiil Hérenn.* (Meid 1974: 10)

> They uttered their lament as they left him, so that the people in the enclosure were prostrated by it. Hence comes the Fairies' Lament of the musicians of Ireland. (Byrne and Dillon 1937: 9)

The manuscript tradition of *Táin Bó Fraích* is early mediaeval Gaelic, but the story is based on material that may be as early as 700 (Meid 1974: xxv). Many of the tale's motifs are ancient and widespread, and can be associated with a scene such as that on the Gundestrup bowl, which features carnyx players, warriors, and a possible healing ceremony associated with the otherworld. Consider the bowl's lavish depiction of horse-harness and of the careful plaiting of the horses' tails – details paralleled in the story itself by the lavish accoutrements of Fraoch's horses, whose harness included little bells; also the possibility that the warriors processing in front of the carnyx players are singing, a detail which brings to mind a sixteenth-century Gaelic text containing parts of the original sixth-century *Amra Choluimb Chille* by Dallán Forgaill, in which the Fenian band is described as singing around a silver bowl (Stokes 1899: Appendix, 422–3. Text: Ms. Egerton 1782).

Given that the Gundestrup bowl and *Táin Bó Fraích* are high points in the visual and the literary canon of the Celts, the significance of the carnyx on the one and the vital presence of possibly similar horns in the other strongly indicates that such instruments were profoundly significant and had a variety of functions.

Evidence relating to the totemic importance of boars further supports such a conclusion. Consider, from *c.* 200 BC, the silver Gundestrup bowl with warriors, cauldron and three carnyx players whose instruments resemble and can imitate the sound of wild boar; from *c.* 0 AD, the mixed burial, in a ritual context, of foetal human bones, pig bones, and the skull of a wild boar, at Uamha an Ard Achadh, a district whose totemic animal is the wild boar; from *c.* 200 AD, the Deskford carnyx with wild boar image including moving jaw and tongue; from 575 AD, the totemic imagery of the Knocknagael boar; and from the 7th-century AD, King Aillil's musicians, and the Celtic warrior band described with a silver cauldron. All of these combined not only leave a powerful impression of interconnectedness and of continuity, but above all underline the symbolic significance of the carnyx in a mythological context, and its use in ceremony, including possible healing, which take it well beyond its martial significance as evidenced by its depictions by the Romans.

3.2 Horns in the early Mediaeval period

The tradition of horn- and trumpet-playing did not end with the Bronze or Iron Ages. In a poem to St. Brigid, thought to have been written by Orthanach, Bishop of Kildare in the first half of the ninth-century, we have a description of horns in battle describing famous 'Alenn' under which many a king is buried:

> *Gáir a ilaig iar cach mbúaid*
> *im chúail claideb, comtaig drend;*
> *bríg a fían fri indna gorm,*
> *gloim a corn cor cétaib cend.*
>
> The shout of its triumph after each victory round a tangle of swords, a fiery encounter; the strength of its mercenary bands against the great battle array, the shriek of its horns over hundreds of heads (Greene and O'Connor 1967: 68–70).

Horns could, however, also be played sweetly, as in this poem, attributed to Muireadhach Albanach Ó Dálaigh – an attribution which, if correct, 'would mean it was already composed by the thirteenth century' (Gillies 2007: 33):

> *Scéalaigheacht ann, duanaigheacht scol, fianaigheacht;*
> *cabhlaigheacht chiúil, chornaigheacht chiúin is cliaraigheacht.*

> [There is] story-telling there, recitation of poems of learned poets, fian-lore; harp-playing by way of music, gentle horn-playing and choral singing. (Gillies 2007: 39)

This poem was included in *The Book of the Dean of Lismore* (Quiggin 1937: 64–5), and its attribution to Muireadhach Albanach, reputed ancestor of the Scottish MacMhuirich bardic family, adds to its significance in a Scottish Gaelic context.

Two Pictish stones (Hilton of Cadboll and Aberlemno III) show pairs of trumpeters blowing straight cylindrical instruments. By contrast, the Lough Erne trumpet is conical rather than cylindrical, thus closely mirroring the trumpets included in the image of David from the eighth-century 'Vespasian' Psalter from Canterbury, in Hiberno-Saxon style (Purser 2002: 17–25), an image showing two musicians blowing straight wooden instruments of similar length to those shown on the Pictish stones, but manifestly conical. That the instruments are wooden is clearly shown by their colour and by the fact that metal rings have been used to contain any tendency they might have to split open. Opposite them are two other musicians playing curved horns such as one sees on the Pictish stones. In this context, the Gaelic literary evidence from the tenth-century AD is significanct:

Ettal seisidach Cruitheantuath inso i cloich Locha Comru:
Gilla padraig plagh mellghaile *noconhuair slan troid seanmaire*
tlam dotharr agmuilt fidhnaigi
Cisdi nach roichet foglaidi *adarc bó rodraide*
cornaire istí ibraighi.[8]

A six-phrase Pictish metre here in the stone of Loch Comru.
Gille-Phádraig, plague of versecraft,
Has not found the musicians' sound measure:
A handful of a wether's belly-wool for bedding;
A treasure-chest bandits can't get at;
The horn of a cow, snarling fiercely;
A horn player, inside, on a yew-wood instrument.[9]

The yew (a sacred tree) was used for musical instruments, and to play this particular instrument indoors was not welcome. Here, a different word *cornaire* is used, perhaps to distinguish it from the word *adarc* which clearly means the curved animal horn: *adarc* literally means 'arc' (Downey 1997: 136). The trumpeters on the Pictish slabs are shown in a Christian and/or hunting context. Downey lays emphasis on their secular aspect in particular (Downey 1997: 139–55), and they share the significance of such instruments in the hunt with many cultures right up to the present day.

4.0 Stringed Instruments

A recent find at Uamha an Ard Achadh at Cille Bhride on the Island of Skye, conservatively dated to the fourth-century BC, provides early evidence for stringed instruments in the Gàidhealtachd.[10] The object is a wooden bridge for a seven- or eight-stringed instrument, and is the oldest to be discovered in Western Europe. Fragments of a tortoise-shell Greek lyre from the sixth-century BC excepted, it is also the oldest find of any part of a stringed instrument in Western Europe, although images of lyres from the Hallstatt culture precede it by two or three centuries (Steinmann and Reichlin 2006: 241; Musée de Préhistoire d'Ile-de-France de Nemours 2002: 119–23; Roberts 1981:

[8] Thurneysen, in Stokes and Windisch 1891: 104.

[9] Adapted from Clancy 1998:145. See Purser 2004: 225.

[10] This dating will be published in the reports of the excavation in due course. The author is indebted to Steven Birch, Dr Graeme Lawson, and other members of the team, of which the author is a member, for this and related information.

303–12). The significance of the find is further emphasised by the fact that any bridge is organologically significant and revealing, allowing one to posit the number of strings, the likely size of the instrument, and the likely manner of its playing. With the bridge were discovered other fragments of charred wood, one being a possible corner of a lyre-type instrument; and parts of a human skull. All had been scorched and only survived because they were at the very base of the fire. The implication is that the skull parts were those of the owner/player of the instrument, and that the person (the sex is undetermined) and the instrument were a motivation for the fire, suggesting that they were of considerable importance – an importance sustained through many centuries (Lawson 2001: 114–6 and 213; Bischop 2002: 215–36, esp. 223–4).[11]

The bridge, about two-thirds of which survives, has notches for the strings, all in the same plane, suggesting that the strings would have been plucked or struck. They could not have been bowed; and in any case, the date is too early for any likelihood of a bowed instrument. A second-century BC stone carving from northern Brittany depicting a seven-stringed lyre may give an indication of what the Uamha an Ard Achadh instrument was like, although the presence of the double yoke (possibly a capo) on the Brittany carving remains controversial (Musée de Préhistoire d'Ile-de-France de Nemours 2002: 120–22; Vendries 1993–4: 38–9).

Other finds of parts of stringed instruments include an antler wrest plank from Dùn an Fheurain in Argyllshire (*c.* 100AD); a possible tuning peg from Cnip in Lewis (first-century BC–first-century AD); and possible peg and wrest planks from Skaill in Orkney, the latter probably Pictish.[12] The context of other organological evidence for the existence of stringed instruments in Scotland, from Castle Sween and Finlaggan, suggests that the instruments were used in high-status environments (Sanger and Kinnaird 1992: 64–5).

The ninth/tenth-century *Scéla Cano* provides literary evidence for the significance of stringed instruments in the same region of the Gàidhealtachd as Uamha an Ard Achadh. It describes the retinue of Cano MeicGartnáin, whose main residence was probably Dùn Cana on Raasay (MacLean 1997: 174–5), including fifty gillies, each carrying a tiompan:[13]

> *Fithchell for muin cach gilla[i] co feraib óir 7 airgid; timpán créda i(n) láim chlí in gilla[i]; da mílchoin ar slabra[i]d airgit ina láim deis* (Binchy 1975: ll. 35–7).
>
> On the back of each gillie, a chess-board with its men of gold and silver; in his left hand a bronze tiompan, in his right hand, two deerhounds on silver leads.[14]

While the report of fifty instruments may be an exaggeration, it is worth remembering that twenty-six bronze horns were found in a single hoard at Dowris, representing an enormous expenditure in bronze (Waddell 1998: 225 ff.). MacGartnáin was on his way to Ireland, and the argument for artistic interaction between Scotland and Ireland in relation to high-status objects is supported by written and material sources, with both Cormac's *Glossary* and an eighth-century law tract specifically mentioning Pictish brooches (Isaac 2005: 73–82; Etchingham and Swift 2004: 31–48). It is from the eighth and the following two centuries that images of triangular framed harps first appear on Pictish cross-slabs, the player sometimes seated on a high-status zoomorphic chair, or associated with Davidic imagery but, in all cases, in a Christian context; these images are further considered below in relation to triple pipes.

---

[11] The chronological list of archaeological evidence for lyres omits all the Scottish examples.

[12] J.V.S. Megaw in Appendix 1 of Ritchie: 1970-71:106-107; also Buteux 1997: 114, 116, 100-101; and Hunter and Kitchener 2006:136-151.

[13] The form of the tiompan has been widely discussed, but certainly designates a sweet-sounding plucked string instrument; see Purser 2007: 35 and notes.

[14] The translation is the author's. Thurneysen translates *créda* as 'tin'. The more likely meaning is 'bronze' – referring either to bronze decoration on the instrument and/or to its strings.

4.1 Harps and their decoration

The significance of the harp or *clàrsach* in the Gàidhealtachd has been well researched and requires little further demonstration. Sanger and Kinnaird have, in particular, outlined its vital role in Gaelic society (Sanger and Kinnaird 1992). Many performers and researchers have followed up their work, and a few have begun to re-introduce it as an accompaniment to, or equal partner in the performance of *òran mòr* and even Fenian lay. The quotation which heads this article, coming from a work published during the decline of the *clàrsach*, insists on its fundamental significance, particularly in a Christian context.

But there may be more to Kirk's quotation than meets the eye of the non-performer, with the identification of the instrument with living organic form. Because the *clàrsach* is traditionally played on the left shoulder, with the left hand playing the higher strings and the right, the lower, Ann and Charlie Heymann suggest that its form was symbolic, in that the left side of the body represented the female, thus the treble range, while the right side represented the male. They also see symbolism in the three parts of the *clarsach*. The box is the female belly, while the fore-pillar is the male phallic member, which both stands up in front of the player, and penetrates the female box. The two are joined in harmony by the curve (Heymann 1991: 82–95). William Drummond makes a not dissimilar anthropomorphic identification for his lute in a sonnet from his *Commendatory Verses* (Drummond 1832: 292).

Of further significance is the evidence for a variety of types of harp. Early mediaeval stone carvings from both eastern and western Scotland clearly depict different sizes and morphology of triangular framed harps, and later mediaeval texts indicate a division between harps strung with gut, and *clàrsachs* with metal. In the case of the latter, strings of bronze, silver and gold are mentioned in manuscript sources, and have been successfully applied to replicas (Purser 2007: 34 and notes).

The tradition of decorating musical instruments is international, but it was a tradition of long standing in Gaelic culture, as evidenced by this passage, again from *Táin Bó Fraích:*

> *Crottbolg di chrocnib doborchon impu cona n-indenam do phartaing foa n-indénam di ór agus argut. Bíann n'errad impu a mmedón; ba gilidir snechta. Sella dubglassa inna medón aide. Bruit lín gilidir fúan ngéssa imna téta. Crota di ór agus arccut agus findruine co ndelbaib nathrach agus én agus mílchon di ór agus arccut. Amal no glúaistís na téta sin, immreithitis ne delba sin íarum imma firu imme cúaird.*(Meid 1974: ll. 91–8).
>
> They had harp-bags of otter-skins covering them, with red ornament overworked with gold and silver. Deer-skin around them in the middle as white as snow, with dark grey spots in the centre. Coverings of linen, white as the plumage of swans around the strings. Harps of gold and silver and white bronze with figures of serpents and birds and hounds on them in gold and silver. When those strings moved, the figures would move all about.[15]

The riches of this description are borne out by subsequent evidence. A poem from the thirteenth century by Giolla Brighde Albanach (the Scottish servant of Brigid) shows that the beauty of the harp was valued equally in Ireland and Scotland. The poem praises an O'Brien of Thomond, and the harp is in Scotland and is not to be returned at any price:

> *mac allmurdaig ni ragaib*
> *an slabradaig siodamail!*
>
> No son of a foreigner shall obtain
> The graceful, gem-set, fairy instrument! (O'Curry 1893: 272–3)

[15] Byrne & Dillon 1937: 4, with slight alterations taken from Henderson 1911: 5-6.

Centuries later, beauty was still a fundamental aspect of the manufacture of harps, as evidenced by the fifteenth-century Lamond and Queen Mary harps in the National Museum of Scotland, and by George Buchanan, who wrote in the late sixteenth-century of the Scottish Gaels that 'their grand ambition is to adorn their harps with great quantities of silver and gems, those who are too poor to afford jewels substituting crystals in their stead'(Watkins 1822: 6).

5.0 Triple Pipes

Another instrument associated with the Celtic church was the triple pipes, consisting of a drone and two chanters, each pipe having its own reed. No actual instruments have been found, but surviving images indicate that these pipes clearly parallel the Sardinian launeddas. The launeddas, still played today, has a history going back to the Bronze Age. Unlike the triple pipes, however, it is not associated with stringed instruments of any kind (Bentzon 1969; Paulis 1994:137–55). Images of triple pipes appear, in association with harps or lyres, on the late eighth-century St Martin's Cross in Iona as well as on tenth-century cross-slabs at Lethendy and Ardchattan in Scotland and at Monasterboice and Clonmacnoise in Ireland. Five later depictions of triple pipes sustain the association with stringed instruments: in the 12th-century York Psalter;[16] a 12th-century English bestiary;[17] a 13th-century Spanish manuscript, *Cantigas de Santa Maria*;[18] and a carving of a triple piper in Westminster Cathedral.

Fig. 3: St Martin's Cross, Iona. *(Photo: J. Purser)*

Fig. 4: Hooded players of clarsach and triple pipes on the Ardchattan cross slab. *(Photo: Tom E. Gray)*

An early thirteenth-century stone-carving at St John, Hawkchurch, in Devon, shows a goat playing triple pipes, opposite a ram playing a fiddle (Montagu 1998: 24). This image would, of course, reinforce the assertion that the triple piper on Muiredach's Cross at Monasterboice is playing for the devil (Ramsey 2002: 31–3). But while the association of pipes with the devil and Pan, and with a lower aesthetic and moral class, in medieval mythology, religion and even law is unchallenged, the depiction of triple pipers in the Scottish and Irish contexts suggests no such clear association. On St Martin's Cross, the musicians face each other; on the Ardchattan stone the three musicians are depicted on the same side and with the same hoods – possibly clerical hoods; and on the Lethendy stone they are playing immediately beneath two clerics. There too, the musicians face each other and play simultaneously – as they do on the Monasterboice cross, the piper also being placed on a zoomorphic chair (suggesting high status) and with his back to the devil. The depiction on the Clonmacnoise cross is in the context of the desert fathers, St Paul and St Anthony. Images of this theme appear on Pictish cross-slabs, notably that at Nigg, where they are depicted with two lions and a raven providing food (Henderson and Henderson 2004: 139–40).

[16] Glasgow University Library, Hunterian Add.f11.

[17] Oxford, MS Bodl 602 f.10r.

[18] Madrid, Real Biblioteca del Monasterio, MS B.1.2, f.49v.

By the time the early laws were being formulated, we see the classically-derived hierarchy of strings over wind partly in operation: according to the *Uraicecht Becc*, the only entertainer with an honour-price is the *cruit* player. The eighth-century *Bretha Nemed déodenach*, however, accords an honour price (*eneclann*) to the piper also (Kelly 1988/91:64, n. 198). It could be that these rankings were primarily designed to fit in with imported Christian hierarchies based on biblical references; unfortunately, the precise nature of the instruments mentioned in these biblical sources is not that clear. What is clear is that the Psalms refer to a variety of instruments, and they mention dance as a proper way to praise the Lord. One can only read Psalm 150 as being deliberately all-inclusive and, it being the ultimate psalm of the three fifties, it must have carried weight with the Gaels. Given the value accorded to the pipes in Gaelic Ireland and Scotland, and taking into account that the word *ceòl* ('music') may be derived from the Latin for a pipe,[19] it may be that the Gaels of Ireland and Scotland ranked the triple pipes in accordance with what they took to be their standing in holy scripture, and were reluctant to accept a lower status for them, especially if such status derived from an argument that pipes were associated with the devil.

English manuscript sources bear out this argument. If the character playing the triple pipes on the Canterbury bestiary is a devil, who, if not a devil, is playing the harp behind him?[20] What, then, is one to make of their supposedly opposed status? And how can one separate the triple piper on the York Psalter from the rest of the musicians accompanying David – musicians who are part of an ensemble portrayed without any judgmental elements?[21] And what of the *Cantigas de Santa Maria*, whose evidence unequivocally supports the pipes being used in honour of the Virgin, thus directly associating the pipes with the idea of absolute purity?

The tenth-century narrative *Inní díatá cuslinn Brighde agus Aidhed mic Dhíchoíme* contains a description of the making and significance of 'forked' pipes (Meyer 1903: 46–54; full text in Thurneysen 1933: 120). This is a version of the widespread story of the King with Ass's Ears, in which the king's secret is made known to a plant (reed or tree) which subsequently reveals it to a musician through the medium of a musical instrument. The musician is then impelled to reveal the secret in the presence of the King (Milin 1989).[22] In this Gaelic version, Mac Dichoime collapses under the burden of keeping the secret, which he has discovered when shaving the king. Three streams of blood soak into the ground from his nostrils and mouth and, from these, three saplings subsequently grow. When Mac Dichoime re-visits the site, he sees the trees and makes pipes out of them:

> *Luid immorro [mac] Dichoime cosna flescaibh iar d[t]ain, co ndergenai cuislind ndègabail dib.*

Meyer translates this as 'Then Mac Dichoime went to the saplings and made a double pipe from them'. *Dègabail* means 'bi-furcated' but as there were three trees, and Celtic mythology tends to group things in threes including types of music, three pipes seems a more likely number – a possibility confirmed later in the tale:

> *At.berat araile dno conad buinne tregabail do.ronadh donaib chuisslennaib tredaib, ro.fassater triasin run.*

[19] McBain (1896 and 1982: 80). *Pìob>cìob>cìol>ceòl*, is a rough-and-ready way of following the possible transition., but the etymology remains obscure.

[20] MS Bodl 602, f.10r.

[21] Ann Buckley's doubts as to whether the York Psalter shows a triple piper or a pan piper are not convincing (Buckley 1991: 180-181).

[22] Milin's comprehensive study unfortunately omits any reference to the latter part of the story as provided by Thurneysen.

> But others say that from the three-forked saplings that grew from the secret a triple pipe was made. (Thurneysen 1933:120)

Besides revealing that triple and double pipes were both known to the tenth-century scribe, the story reveals both the pagan power of the pipes and the Christian status of their music, for St Brigid forces Mac Dichoime to choose between his pipes and a noviate who has run off with him. Mac Dichoime surrenders the pipes. The scribe also records a version which has St Brigid splitting up the pipes and giving away two of them. This suggests that their status meant more to her than their music, and the one pipe she retains features on her battle banner, thereby asserting her episcopal status as well as confirming its visual significance. Mac Dichoime, however, dies of grief without his instrument and the music it made.

The story counteracts any suggestion that the musical instruments depicted on Irish and Pictish stones were merely copies taken out of pattern books or from psalters or other iconographic sources. It also suggests that, just as is the case for bagpipes today, their status in an ecclesiastical context was equivocal. However, in the wider Gaelic context, reed instruments retain as high a status as any musical instrument can claim, and it is suggested here that the iconography associated with triple pipes commonly acknowledges their acceptance as appropriate for the praise of God.

Conclusion

There is yet much work to be done. It is only recently that archaeologists have turned their attention to the Gàidhealtachd in any numbers, and discoveries such as that at Uamha an Ard Achadh challenge many assumptions. There has, for instance, been a tendency to regard the north-west of Scotland as incapable of supporting a society that might have a use for such refined objects as the Lewis chess men. Only recently has this assumption been seriously questioned (Caldwell, D. H., Hall, M. A. & Wilkinson, C. A., 2009). Similarly, the evidence that the people living in 300 BC, in what is now the Gàidhealtachd, were making and using stringed musical instruments requiring refined techniques of both manufacture and musicianship, sheds new light on the relative significance of the Greek lyre and on notions of technological and artistic dissemination derived from its dominance in the literature. Music archaeology is a young discipline. Even the identification of musical artefacts is in its infancy, and the systematic study of early Gaelic texts still offers many opportunities.

Dedication

Ever since the launch of my first radio series of *Scotland's Music* in 1991, John MacInnes has been a source of encouragement and a wonderful breadth of scholarly generosity. I will not forget visiting Callanish with him and a large group of singers from Ireland and Scotland. I had brought replica Bronze Age horns with me, to try them out *in situ*. Nearly all the company retired to the visitor centre at that point, no doubt for a variety of motives. John stayed behind to listen, to investigate and to evaluate; and instead of leaving me feeling like some eccentric fool, he supported me. How does one adequately thank someone for support of that nature? One cannot. But this meagre offering is by way of a very small thank-you to a gem of a man.

Sources

BENTZON, ANDREAS F. W.

1969 *The Launeddas. A Sardinian Folk-Music Instrument.* Copenhagen.

BEVERIDGE, ERSKINE.

1903 *Coll and Tiree: Their Prehistoric Forts and Ecclesiastical Antiquities.* Edinburgh.

BINCHY, DANIEL (ED.).

1975 *Scéla Cano Meic Gartnáin.* Dublin.

BISCHOP, DIETER.

2002 'Die älteste Leier Nordeuropas einer germanischen Siedlung in Bremen-Habenhausen'. *Studien zur Musikarchäologie III.* (Orient-Archäeologie 10). Rahden: 215–36.

BLACK, RONALD.

2005 (ED.) *The Gaelic Otherworld: John Gregorson Campbell's Superstitions of the Highlands and Islands.* Edinburgh.

2008 'Gaelic Religious Publishing 1567–1800'. *Caindel Alban: Scottish Gaelic Studies* 24: 73–85.

BUCKLEY, ANN.

1991 'Music-related imagery on early Christian insular sculpture: Identification, context, function'. *Imago Musicae: International Yearbook of Musical Iconography* 8: 135–99.

BUTEUX, SIMON.

1997 'Settlements at Skaill, Deerness, Orkney'. *British Archeological Reports* (British Series) 260. Birmingham.

BYRNE, MARY E. AND MILES DILLON.

1937 'Táin Bó Fraích'. *Études Celtiques* II: 1–27.

CALDWELL, D. H., M. HALL AND C. A. WILKINSON.

2009 'The Lewis Hoard of Gaming Pieces: A Re-examination of their Context, Meanings, Discovery and Manufacture'. *Medieval Archaeology* 53: 155–203.

CLANCY, THOMAS.

1998 *The Triumph Tree.* Edinburgh.

CREED, JOHN.

1998 'Reconstructing the Deskford Carnyx'. *Studien zur Musikarchäologie II.* (Orient-Archäeologie 7). Rahden: 347–50.

DOWNEY, PETER.

1997 '"If music comes from many horns, then the sound is sweeter": Trumpets and Horns in Early Medieval Ireland'. *Historic Brass Society Journal*: 139–55.

DRUMMOND, WILLIAM, OF HAWTHORNDEN.

1832 *The Poetical Works of William Drummond of Hawthornden.* Edinburgh.

ETCHINGHAM, COLMÁN AND CATHERINE SWIFT.

2004 'English and Pictish Terms for Brooch in an 8th-Century Irish Law-Text'. *Medieval Archaeology* 48: 31–49.

FAGG, CATHERINE.

1997 *Rock Music.* Oxford.

GILLIES, WILLIAM.

2007 'A Poem on the Land of the Little People'. Sharon Arbuthnot and Kaarina Hollo (eds), *Fil súil nglais: A Grey Eye Looks Back – A Festschrift in honour of Colm Ó Baoill.* Ceann Drochaid, Perthshire.

GLASGOW UNIVERSITY LIBRARY.

Hunterian Add.fl1.

GREENE, DAVID AND FRANK O'CONNOR (EDS).

1967 *A Golden Treasury of Irish Poetry.* London.

HENDERSON, GEORGE.

1911 'The Geste of Fraoch and the Dragon'. J. F. Campbell (ed.), *The Celtic Dragon Myth.* Edinburgh.

HENDERSON, GEORGE AND ISABEL HENDERSON.

2004 *The Art of the Picts: Sculpture and Metalwork in Early Medieval Scotland.* London.

HEYMANN, ANN AND CHARLIE.

1991 'Clairseach: The Lore of the Irish Harp'. *Eire / Ireland – Journal of the Irish-American Cultural Institute,* Fall 1991: 82–95.

HUNTER, FRASER.

2001 'The Carnyx in Iron Age Europe'. *The Antiquaries Journal* 81:77–108.

HUNTER, FRASER WITH ANDREW KITCHENER.

2006 'Bone and Antler'. I. Armit, *Anatomy of an Iron Age Roundhouse: The Cnip Wheelhouse Excavations.* Edinburgh: 136–151.

ISAAC, GRAHAM R.

2005 'A Note on Cormac's Pictish Brooch'. *Journal of Celtic Linguistics* 9: 73–82.

KELLY, FERGUS.

1988, 1991 *A Guide to Early Irish Law.* Dublin.

KIRK, ROBERT.

1684 *Psalma Dhaibhidh an Meadrachd, &c.*

LAWSON, GRAEME.

2001 'Musical relics'. K. L. Mitchell, K. R. Murdoch and J. R. Ward (eds), *Fast Castle – Excavations 1971–86*. Edinburgh: 114–16 and 213.

MACBAIN, ALEXANDER.

1896 (1982) *An Etymological Dictionary of the Gaelic Language*. Glasgow.

MACDONALD, JAMES.

1899 *Place Names of West Aberdeenshire*. Aberdeen.

MACLEAN, D.

1997 'Maelrubai, Applecross and the Late Pictish Contribution West of Druimalban'. D. Henry (ed.), *The Worm, the Germ and the Thorn: Pictish and Related Studies Presented to Isabel Henderson*. Balgavies, Angus: 173–87.

MACLEOD, IRIS.

1981 'The Ringing Stone'. *Tales of Argyll: Lismore and Appin Edition*. British Red Cross Society.

MADRID, REAL BIBLIOTECA DEL MONASTERIO.

MS B.1.2, f. 49v.

MANIQUET, CHRISTOPHE.

2008 'Le sanctuaire laténien et gallo-romain des "Arènes de Tintignac" (Naves-Corrèze) et la découverte d'un dépôt d'armes et d'objets gaulois exceptionnels". *Studien zur Musikarchäologie VI* (Orient-Archäologie 22). Rahden: 57–76.

MEGAW, RUTH AND VINCENT.

1994 *Early Celtic Art in Britain and Ireland*. Princes Risborough.

MEID, WOLFGANG (ED.).

1974 *Táin Bó Fraích*. Dublin.

MEYER, KUNO.

1903 'Stories and songs from Irish manuscripts'. *Otia Merseiana* 3: 46–54.

MILIN, GAËL.

1989 Beroul et le Conte AT 782 du Roi aux Marques Animales. Unpublished dissertation. Université de Haute-Bretagne (Rennes 2).

MONTAGU, JEREMY AND GWEN.

1998 *Minstrels and Angels: Carvings of Musicians in Medieval English Churches*. Berkeley.

MUSÉE DE PRÉHISTOIRE D'ILE-DE-FRANCE DE NEMOURS.

2002 *Préhistoire de la musique: Sons et instruments de musique des ages du bronze et du fer en France*. Exhibition catalogue. Nemours.

O'CURRY, EUGENE.

[1873] 1996 *On the Manners and Customs of the Ancient Irish*, III. Dublin.

O'DWYER, SIMON.

2004 *Prehistoric Music of Ireland.* Stroud.

OLMSTED, GARRETT S.

1976 'The Gundestrup Version of *Táin Bó Cuailnge*'. *Antiquity* 50: 95–103.

1992 'The earliest narrative version of the Táin: Seventh-century poetic references to *Táin Bó Cuailnge*'. *Emania* 10: 5–17.

OXFORD UNIVERSITY.

MS Bodl 602 f.10r.

PAULIS, GIUILO.

1994 'I nomi delle *launeddas:* origine e storia'. G. N. Spanu (ed.), *Sonos, Strumenti dell amusica popolare sarda*, Nuoro: 137–55.

PIGGOTT, STUART.

1959 'The Carnyx in Early Iron Age Britain'. *The Antiquaries Journal* 39.

PURSER, JOHN.

1998 'The Sounds of Ancient Scotland'. *Studien zur Musikarchäologie II.* (Orient-Archäeologie 7). Rahden: 325–336.

2002 'Reconstructing the River Erne Horn'. *Ulster Journal of Archaeology* 61: 17–25.

2004 'Listening to Picts'. *Studien zur Musikarchäologie IV.* (Orient-Archäeologie 15). Rahden: 325–336.

2006a 'Hand Bells of the Celtic Church in Scotland'. *Transactions of the Gaelic Society of Inverness* 63: 267–91.

2006b 'Ogam and Interlace Notation, Fact or Fiction?'. *Studien zur Musikarchäologie V.* (Orient-Archäeologie 20). Rahden.

2007 *Scotland's Music.* Edinburgh.

QUIGGIN, E. C.

1937 *Poems from the Book of the Dean of Lismore.* Cambridge.

RAMSEY, GREER.

2002 'The Triple Pipes on Irish High Crosses: Identification and Interpretation. *Ulster Journal of Archaeology* 61: 26–36.

RITCHIE, J. N. G.

1970–71 'Iron Age Finds from Dùn an Fheurain, Gallanach, Argyll'. *Proceedings of the Society of Antiquaries of Scotland*: 103.

ROBERTS, HELEN.

1981 'Reconstructing the Greek Tortoise–shell Lyre'. *World Archaeology* 12/3: 303–12.

SANGER, KEITH AND ALISON KINNAIRD.

1992 *Tree of Strings.* Temple, Midlothian.

STEINMANN, CONRAD AND PAUL J. REICHLIN.

2006 'Instruments and their Music from the 5th century BC in Classical Greece'. *Studien zur Musikarchäologie V.* (Orient-Archäeologie 20). Rahden: 237–54.

STOKES, WHITLEY.

1899 'The Bodleian Amra Choluimb Chille'. *Revue Celtique* 20: 31–55, 132–83, 248–89, and 400–437.

STOKES, WHITLEY AND ERNST WINDISCH (EDS).

1891 *Irische Texte.* Dritte Serie, I Heft, Text III.

THURNEYSEN, RUDOLPH.

1933 'Die Flöte von Mac Dichoeme'. *Zeitschrift für Celtische Philologie* 19: 120.

VENDRIES, CHRISTOPHE.

1993–94 *Le Carnyx et la Lyre.* Besançon-Orléans-Évreux.

WADDELL, JOHN.

1998 *The Prehistoric Archaeology of Ireland.* Galway.

WATKINS, JOHN (ED.).

1822 *Buchanan's History of Scotland.* London.

‘Có às don Chorra-Ghiullan Ghlas?’

IAIN SEATHACH

ABSTRACT. In oral tradition, as well as in literature, the theme is well known of the young man who takes leave of his betrothed or spouse, with the agreement that she is free to (re)marry if he does not return within a specified period of time. Upon his return after many years, unrecognized, he is told that her wedding will take place that night. He sends the bride a concealed message, they are reunited and he takes possession of his former holdings. The story is central to the Odyssey of Homer, and is likely even older. In its oral versions it is widespread, particularly in Europe from medieval times, and has been given the international tale classification ATU 974 ‘The Homecoming Husband’. Interesting variants of the story have been recorded from Scottish Gaelic storytellers by Lady Evelyn Stewart Murray in Perthshire in 1900, and by the present writer in Cape Breton, Nova Scotia in 1978. The Gaelic variants are described, and situated within their international tale context.

Anns a’ Ghearran ’sa bhliadhna 1891 thòisich a’ Bhaintighearna Eilidh Stiùbhart Mhoireach, nighean Diùc Athaill, air trusadh a dheanadh do bheul-aithris ann an Siorramachd Pheairt, far an d’rugadh i. Mun tànaig ceann na bliadhna sin bha sreath do leabhrain aice air an lìonadh leis na ceudan do stòireannan is òrain ionadail bho dhualchas beò an t-sluaigh: aon dhe na co-chruinneachaidhean as luachmhoire a tha ri fhaotainn an diugh ann am beul-aithris na Gàidhlig. Tha na stòireannan sin a’ gabhail astaigh a’ mhór-chuid dhe na gnèithean-seòrsachaidh as aithne dhuinn ann an Albainn: sgeulachdan móra eadarnàiseanta; eachdraidhean air sithichean, tàcharain, famhraichean, bòcain, each uisge is creutairean osnàdarra eile; naidheachdan air ainmeannan-àite, agus eachdraidhean ionadail. Ged a bha na gnèithean seo air aithne ’san àm anns gach ceàrnaidh dhen Ghàidhealtachd, tha roinn mhath dhen dùthchas a tha an tasgadh as na leabhrain obrach sin sònraichte a thaobh susbaint is cruth, agus air leth feumail dhan rannsaiche.

Cha robh a’ Bhaintighearna ach mu mhìos a’ trusadh ’sa raon nuair a thug i sios an naidheachd a leanas, le ceathramhan òrain ’na cois. Tha mi ’ga toirt an seo *literatim* (Stewart Murray 2009: 160–64):

[AN] CORRA GHIULAN GLAS
Mrs. MacPherson [Nether Invervack, Wed. 18.3.1891]

Bha baintighearn’ aig an robh aona mhac, agus bha e fhèin agus ’bhanaltradh aige ’mach latha ’gabhail sràide. Chaidh a’ bhanaltradh ’staigh da bhùth ’bha anns a’ bhail’, agus dh’fhàg i an giullan car beagan aig an doras. Ghoid ’n fheadhainn a bhios ‘sguab’ nan similearan e. Chuir ’bhaintighearn’ forais anns a h-uile àit’ air son a leinibh ach cha d’fhuair i sgeul air. Chaidh mòran bhliadhnaichean seachad agus cha d’fhuair ì sgeul riamh air. Ach bha comharr’ ann an craiceann an leinibh gum fainicheadh a mhàthair fhèin e c’àite air bith am faiceadh i e.

Chaill a’ bhaintighearn’ dùil gum faiceadh i seall’ gu bràth tuille dheth, agus rinn i ’n àird a h-inntinn gu pòs’ a rithistich. Chaidh i latha ’ghabhail sràide ann an coill’ suas bhon taigh aice agus thachair gille oirre anns a’ choill’, agus labhair i ris ann an còmhradh garbh, “Cò às dona’ chorra ghiullan ghlas?” agus seo mar a fhreagair an giullan.

Mas glasa mise, ’s glas am feur,
’S glas a’ choill’ fo duibh neul,
’S glas am badan tha ’m bàrr a’ chroinn,
’S their leam fhèin gur glas an cuileann.

'S glas an claidheamh thèid anns an truaill,
'S glas an tuadh thèid anns a' chois,
Ach mar bhios am faobhar gu tana geur
Gu dè 's misd' a gnè bhith glas.

'S geal am bainne 'thig bhon a' bhuaile,
'S geal a shnuadh 's gur ro mhath 'bhlas,
Ach nuair a sgathas an gruth on mheug,
Cailleas e a shnuadh 's bios e glas.

'S dearg an earbag thig bhon a' phreas
Ri am samhraidh agus teas
Ach nuair thig an geamhradh fada, fuar
Caochaileas i snuadh is fàsas i glas.

Thuig a' bhaintighearna air a' chainnt aige gum b'e a leanabh fèin a bh'ann, agus 'thuillieid air sin, choimhid i air cùl an amhaich aige, 's dh'aithnich i air a' chomharr' a bha anns a' chraiceann gum b'e 'leanabh fhèin a bh'ann. Chaidh i dhachaigh 's rinn i cuirm mhòr air son gun d'fhuair i air ais e, 's dh'fhuirich iad cuideachd fhad' 's bha iad beò. Agus cha do phòs i idir.

All remember of song, may be more.

Seachdainn as deaghaidh sin (25.3.91) fhuair a' Bhaintighearna tuilleadh dheth – 'rann eile' – bho phiuthar na bana-bheulaiche, Sìne NicUilleim, Sruthan:

A bhean thachair orm san dùn
'S an tùr tha shuas bhon eas,
Labhair i le còmhradh borb
'Cò às don chorra' ghiullan ghlas?' (Stewart Murray: 162–64, 's faic td. 574, 583).

A nunn ri deireadh nan 1970s chaidh òran fon aon ainm àraid a recórdadh ann an Ceap Breatann, Alba Nuadh, bho Iain MacNìll ('Iain mac Dhòmhnaill Bhàin') a thogadh ann am Parraiste a' Chamais Leathain, Siorramachd Inbhirnis, aois mu 88.[1] Air réir aithris 's ann à Barraigh a thànaig an sliochd sin do Chloinn Nìll:

'S e gille bochd a bh'ann. Bha athair 's a mhàthair bochd. Agus an nighean, bhiodh iad a' dol dhan sgoil còmhla 's cha d'fhalbh an darna duine gun an duin' eile. Bhiodh iad còmhla air ais 's air adhart a h-uile latha riamh. Mu dheireadh rinn iad suas ri chéile gum pòsadh iad. Thuirt e gu feumadh esan falbh matà, agus gun tugadh e seachd bliadhna air falbh mun tilleadh e airson airgead a dheanamh, 's dar a thilleadh e gum pòsadh iad. Dh'fhalbh e, thug e na seachd bliadhna air falbh ag obair 's deanamh airgid 's an oidhche a thànaig e dhachaidh thuirt a mhàthair ris gu robh an nighean a bha seo, a' bhainis aic' ann an nochd 's i dol a phòsadh air la'r-na-mhàireach.

---

[1] 88A8. Air a chlàradh leis an ùghdar 10/6/78. Ged a tha facal neo dhà 'sna ceathramhan a' togail duilgheadas a thaobh aisig is fuaimneachaidh, tha an seagh soilleir gu leòr. Thugadh an t-siathamh ceathramh agus corra fhacal eile bho sheinn Ailig Iain 'Ic Ìosaig (AIM), Ste. Rose, a bha 'na choimhearsnach do dh' Iain mac Dhòmhnaill Bhàin.

Cha tuirt e guth. Dh'fhalbh e 's dhreas e e-fhéin anns an t-seann aodach a bh'air mun do dh'fhalbh e riamh. Chaidh e ann dh'ionnsaigh na bainnseadh. Ghnog e aig an dorus. Có thànaig dh'ionnsaigh an doruist ach a' bhean òg. Dh'iarr i air a dhol astaigh 's chaidh e astaigh. Bha iad a' gabhail òran, a' gabhail òran. Mu dheireadh dh'fhoighneachd e am faodadh esan òran a ghabhail, 's O, dh'fhaodadh. Thòisich e air deanamh an òrain:

'S an t-seachdamh bliadhna dhan eun
'G obair le bheul anns a' chraoibh;
Obair [dhaor], a' chairt bhith dian
Dhan eun gus na tholl e a' chraobh.

'S glas am fochunn, 's glas am feur,
'S glas an gleann ud thall fo neul,
'S glas an duilleach air a' chraoibh,
'S ar leam fhìn gur glas an ailm.

'S glas an claidheamh théid 'san truaill,
'S glas an tuagh as an téid cas;
Ach ma bhios i tana, geur
Cha mhisde a feum a bhith glas.

Sin dar a labhair a' bhean ùr,
'Lig astaigh [e] bho thùs gu grad';
Labhair bean-an-taighe borb,
'Có às tha'n Corra-Ghiullan Glas?'

['S lasadh teine fo phloc,
Tiormachadh clòimhe ann an cuan,][2]
Comhairle thoirt air bean bhorb,
Mar bhuill' ùird air iarunn fuar.

[Iasgach an lochain gun lìon
Sìol a chur air tìr 's i fliuch,
'S breith air easgann ann an sruth,
'S mairg a thug gaol riamh do dh'fhear.][3]

Éiridh fiùran òg amach,
Cha till astaigh air an uair;
Éiridh bean òg as a dhéidh
'S théid iad le chéil' an taobh tuath.

Thuig ise gura h-e a bh'ann. Dh'fhalbh esan amach. Dh'fhalbh i astaigh do *bhathroom*, chuir i oirre 's thog i uinneag 's chaidh i amach air an uinneag. 'S choinnich i esan amuigh 's thog iad rith'.

Tha caoin annasach aig Iain mac Dhòmhnaill Bhàin air na ceathramhan; caoin nach cuala mi 'ga gabhail air òran eile thall neo bhos:

---

[2] Air réir AIM. Teip: *'S fhad tha teine fo phloc / Tiormachadh clòimheadh fo shruth.*

[3] Air réir AIM.

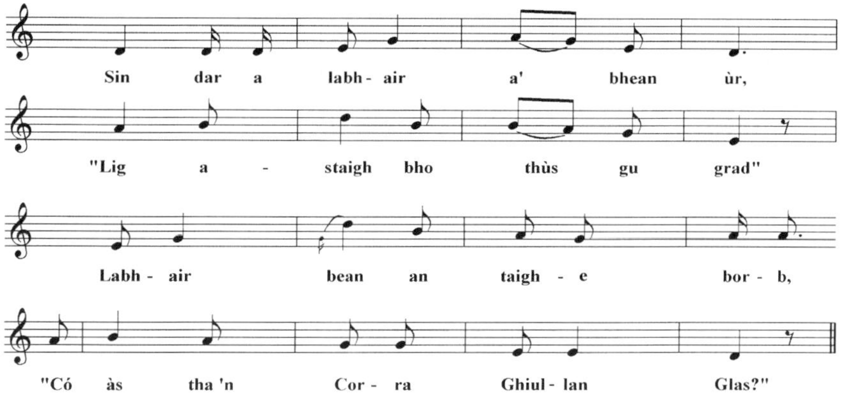

Ann an saoghal Gàidhlig na h-Alba air fad, chan fhiosrach mi air aon eisimpleir eile dhen òran is naidheachd amach bhon dà innse a tha seo, 's iad air an trusadh air astar mór bho chéile. Ma's ann às na h-Eileannan an Iar, airneo à Mùideart/Mórar a thànaig an darna fear – rud a tha dualach gu leòr 'sa cheàrnaidh sin do Cheap Breatann – bhiodh an sgaradh astair sin ann eadar an iar-thuath agus Siorramachd Pheairt 'san earra-dheas, agus móran dhen Ghàidhealtachd eatorra. Gun fhios le cinnt gu dé thachair 'san eachdraidh a thaobh siubhal is lìonsgaradh gach òrain is naidheachd, tha seo a' cur romhainn gu faodadh 'An Corra-Ghiullan Glas' a bhith air a shuidheachadh ann an Albainn fad iomadh linn.

Dé is ciall dhan ainm 'Corra-Ghiullan'? Fhuair mi am beachd a's fheàrr liomsa bho Iain MacAonghuis, am measg nan iomadh còmhradh a bh'againn air dha bhith air sgrìob oirnn ann an Alba Nuadh aig deireadh nan 1980s; tha seo ann, suidhichte ann am farsaingeachd-inntinn bhuan a thug buaidh air aon ghinealach is còrr – gun ghuth air faochadh anama – ann an sgoilearachd na Gàidhlig 's a tha a' leanaid chun a' latha an diugh. Air réir seo, faodar a ghabhail mar 'fhacal fillte' – coltach ri faclan dhen t-seòrsa a tha bitheanta gu leòr ann am bàrdachd – 'sa bheil 'corr(a)- a' ciallachadh 'air leth, sònraichte'.[4] Mar a chithear 'san òran againn fhìn agus anns na seòrsachan eile dheth a bhuineas dhan lìon dùthchais air feadh na Roinn Eòrpa, dh'fheumadh an 'giullan' a bhith air leth dàna, teòma ma shoirbhich leis 'san t-saoghal a bh'ann. Air réir seinneadair eile 'san aon pharraiste bha na ceathramhan 'lasadh teine fo phloc…iasgach an lochain gun lìon', *etc.* a' tarraing air gnìomhan a bha doirbh a choilionadh, airneo do-dhèanta.[5]

'S fhiach sùil a thoirt air cruth an dà innse againn agus mar a tha iad a' gabhail astaigh òran is rosg le chéile. A nist, aithnighidh luchd beul-aithris a th' air ùine a thoirt a' clàradh ann an coimhearsnachdan Gàidhealach nach eil seo 'na annas buileach; bidh an t-òranaiche gu tric ag aithris naidheachd a tha ceangailte ris an òran a tha e gabhail, gu h-àraid do neach a thànaig bho thaobh amuigh na coimhearsnachd 's gun fhios aige air na daoine 's an 'àrd-chotheacs' shòisealta a tha an cois nan ceathramhan. A thuilleadh air sin, tha cuid do dh'òrain ann nach tuigeadh duine beò buileach as aonais na naidheachd tha fuaighte riu. Uaireannan, bidh an t-òranaiche eadhon a' faighinn tlachd ann a bhith a' deanadh feum dhen naidheachd ann am fianais neach ùir mar mheadhon oideis: a' gluasad air n-ais 's air n-adhart eadar rosg is bàrdachd agus a' sealltainn cho snasail 's a bha obair a' bhàird. Air sàilleabh seo, gheobhar suas ri leth-cheud naidheachd dhen t-seòrsa ann an cairt-lann seòmbair nan sgeulachd aig Sgoil Eòlais na h-Alba, cuspair obrach a tha airigh air tuilleadh rannsachaidh, gu h-àraidh air na ceanglaichean a tha beò 'san dùthchas eadar

[4] *Pace* Murray: 164 gl. 'little'.

[5] Faic nota 1.

bàrdachd nan òran agus rosg nan sgeulachd. A nist, air a' cheud sealladh 's ionnan seo agus cruth a' Corra-Ghiullain Ghlais. Gun teagamh, 'san innse a thug sios a' Bhaintighearna Mhoireach à Siorramachd Pheairt, tha na ceathramhan fhéin na's coltaiche ri dubh-fhacail na bhith a' toirt freagairt choileanta air a' cheist bho mhàthair, 'Có às don chorra ghiullan ghlas?', agus as aonais na naidheachd cha bhiodh annta ach fuigheall gun bhuintealas. Tha barrachd seagh ann an innse Iain 'ac Dhòmhnaill Bhàin à Ceap Breatann: tha an càs-éiginn 'sa bheil an Corra-Ghiullan Glas air a dheanadh soilleir gu bheil riatanas air seòltachd is cainnt dhìomhair. Gu ìre mìnichidh an naidheachd na ceathramhan dhuinn – ach chan ann buileach. 'San dà innse seo tha na ceathramhan ann *mar phàirt* dhen naidheachd, agus 's e seo a tha 'gan sònrachadh bhon chòrr dhe na h-òrain a th' air am mìneachadh le pìos rosg bhon bheulaiche. Gu dearbh, tha na ceathramhan a th' air an suidheachadh anns an naidheachd seo coltach ris na duain a gheobhar ann an eachdraidhean gaisge na Féinneadh, cleachdadh a tha a' toirt 'nar cuimhne a' mheasgradh àrsaidh sin do rosg is bàrdachd ris an can cuid *prosimetrum* agus a nochdas as na h-eachdraidhean gaisge as sine a gheobhar ann an làmhsgrìobhannan meadhon-aoiseil na h-Éirinn.

Ged nach eil An Corra-Ghiullan Glas a' nochdadh ach dà thurus thall 's a bhos ann an saoghal Gàidhlig na h-Alba tha e buinntinn do ghnè eadarnàiseanta a tha sgaoilte air feadh cuid mhòr dhen Roinn Eòrpa, le freumhaichean a tha sìneadh air n-ais chon nan linntean roimh-eachdraidheil, agus amach 'san fharsaingeachd gu ruige na h-Aisia mheadhonaich. Mar ghnè, tha e air ainmeachas 'san t-siostam sheòrsachaidh sgeulachd mar ATU 974 'Turus Tillidh a' Chéile Phòsda' ('The Homecoming Husband'), agus air réir choimeasan luchd-rannsachaidh eadar caochladh thionndaidhean a chaidh a thrusadh 'sna dùthchannan 's na cànanan céine, tha am bun-sgeul mar leanas:

> As deaghaidh dha céile pòsda a bhith air falbh air turus céin, neo air a chumail an greim, fuirghidh a' bhean òg gu dìleas aig an taigh air réir gealltanas a rinn iad 'san dealachadh, gu ceann ùine àraid – mar as trice seachd bliadhna. Nuair a bhios sin suas 's gun a céile a thilleadh, 's fheudar dhi céile ùr a ghabhail, 's cuirear bainis air dòigh. 'S ann air latha na bainnseadh, gun fhiosda dhi fhéin neo dhan t-sluagh, a thilleas a céile pòsda far a thuruis, 's e air a sgeadachadh ann an seann aodach giobagach, coltach ri dìol déirce, air dòigh nach gabh e aithneachadh tuilleadh le muinntir a' bhaile. Ann an caochladh sheòrsa dhen ghnè sgeula seo, tha coltas corporra an fhir shiubhail air atharrachadh air thàilleabh aois 's a' chruadail thron deach e air a thurus. Ann an iomadh dreach dhen naidheachd, nuair nochdas an taistealach seo aig dorust taigh na bainnseadh, bidh 'bean bhorb' (màthair bean na bainnseadh) airneo fear dhen chòmhlan astaigh a' feuchainn air bacail a chur air le mì-mhodh is buirbe. Ach tha comharraidhean ann – air réir cànan is cultair – a tha fo dheireadh a' ligeil fhaicinn có e: fàinne a thug a chéile dha mun do dh'fhalbh e; cù 'san lùchairt a dh'aithnigheas e; seann chreuchd; airneo iomlaid is cluich-cheathramhan eadar e fhéin 's a chéile, mar a chunnaic sinn shuas. Tha barrachd air aon char ann an deireadh an sgeòil: taghaidh a bhean a' cheud chéile 's gun an còrr ann mu dheidhinn; teichidh an dithist le chéile; bheir am fear-tillidh amach aichbheil air na suirghichean 's gheobh e air n-ais sealbh air céile is oighreachd (faic Uther 2004: 1, 607–608; Brednich 1990: 702–704).

Aithnighidh gach leubhadair gura h-ionnan an geàrr-chunntas seo agus brìgh a' chunntais 'san dàn ainmeil sin, *Odysseia* Hómair, agus gun teagamh cha robh obair litreachais ann a thug barrachd buaidh air an t-saoghal chlasaigeach 'na h-àm ach an *Iliad* fhéin (Casson 2001: 54). A thaobh turus ànraidh Odysseus, tha na coimeasan ri naidheachd a' Chorra-Ghiullain Ghlais an dà cuid follaiseach agus bunaiteach. Mun do sheòl Odysseus amach gu cogadh na Troidhe, gheall a bhean, Penelope, nach gabhadh i céile 'na àite gus an tigeadh feusag air aodann a' ghille aca, Telemachos. An déidh a' chogaidh, 's e mì-chòrdadh is aimhreit eadar na diathan 'sna speuran a thug air Odysseus làn deichead eile fhulang air fògradh, a' sìor strì gus a bhean 's a dhachaidh a bhuannachd. Air dha eilean àraich a ruigsinn, cuir e air seann aodach 's nochd e aig dorust an talla mhóir ann riochd leth-sheann dìol déirce. Nuair thug cuid dhe na bha astaigh dùbhlan dha air sàilleabh a choltais, thànaig a shàr-chomasan am follais, gu h-àraid le bogh' is saighead, cho math ri sheòltachd a' còmhradh ri Penelope. 'San eadar-àma, dh'aithnicheadh e le Eurycleia, a bhan-altruim aosda, air seann chreuchd-lot air a shliasaid nuair nigh i a chasan; fhuair e creideas cridhe Penelope mu dheireadh nuair dh'innis e dhi mar rinneadh an leabaidh-phòsda, rud a bha eadarra fhéin amhàin. 'San t-sabaid a dh'éirich, chaidh na suirghichean 's an luchd leanmhainn a chur 'sa ruaig le Odysseus 's a mhac, 's bha Odysseus air ceann-uidhe a thuruis a ruigsinn le bhean ri thaobh 's le làn shealbh air oighreachd shinnsearail.

Mar sin dheth 's léir dhuinn gu bheil an naidheachd againn 'na cruth bunaiteach a' leantail air n-ais co-dhiubh gu ruige linn Hómair, agus 's e sin an sampla as àrsaidhe a th'againn dhi. Aig aon àm air thàilleabh choimeasan ghnathasan bheòil eadar na gheobhar 'san *Odysseia* agus seann litreachasan eile (m.e. dàin a' *Rig Veda* às na h-Innseachan) bhite a' gabhail ris gura h-ann bhon t-saoghal Indo-Eòrpach a tha prìomh-thùs a' chuspair-sgeòil ri fhaighinn. 'Sa cheud 's a chaidh, ge-tà, tha rannsaichean 'sa Ruis air fianaisean susbainteach a thogail gura h-iad na treubhan siubhlach Turcach is eile feadh mhór-raointean na h-Aisia Mheadhonaich a dhealbh an tèama bho thùs, agus gun do thogadh an dìleab sin le muinntir na Roinn Eòrpa mar iasad 'sna linntean meadhon-aoiseil, airneo na bu tràithe na sin.

'S na 1960s thànaig anailis gheur-chùiseach amach leis an Ruiseanach Victor Zhirmunsky a' toirt sealladh farsaing air eachdraidh is sgaoileadh na tèama 's na tha fuaighte rithe air feadh Aisia 's an Roinn Eòrpa. Tha i seo a' toirt am follais gu bheil 'tèama an òrain tillidh' air a riarachadh ann an dà roinn leathan. Tha a' cuid as sine dhith air taobh an ear na h-àrainn-sgaoilidh, m.e. *Odysseia* Hómair agus na duain fhada às Aisia, a' cumail ri saoghal na gaisge agus spàirn mu cheannas na treubha. Air taobh an iar 'san Roinn Eòrpa, tha gnè ùr air tighinn air lom le sealladh agus cumadh-inntinn romansachail, caran coltach ri nobhail. Ged is léir dhan leubheadair gu bheil a' ghnè Eòrpach seo dhen tèama air móran dhe na cuspairean a chumail a tha fillte astaigh ann an dàn Hómair, a dh'aindeoin buaidh an litreachais sgrìobhte chan ann bhon taobh sin a thàrmaich i. Tha sgoilearachd choimeasan bhon fhicheadamh ceud a' deanadh soilleir gura h-e aithris bheòil fhuadain an t-sluaigh ('Märchen'), a' tighinn anuas bho linn ro-eachdraidheil 's dòcha, bu bhun dhi (Zhirmunsky 1966: 272–80). Gun teagamh, 'na chruth 's 'na susbaint tha An Corra-Ghiullan Glas mar phàirt dhen taobh Eòrpach seo do ATU 974 – an taobh as motha a th' air a riochdachadh ann an leabhar-seòrsachaidh sgeulachd Uther. Gheobhar ann an iomadh dùthaich e: 'sa Ghearmailt, 'san Fhraing, 'san Ungar, 'san Eadailt, 'sa Spàinn 's as na h-àrainnean Slàbhach, gu h-àraid anns na duain mhóra gaisge a chlàradh 'san fhicheadamh ceud ann an Serbo-Croatia (cf. Lord 1960: 242–59). Chan eil fianais air 'sna dùthchannan fada mu thuath (m.e. 'san Nirribhidh agus 'san t-Suain) ach fìor chorra uair, neo fiù 's ann an Éirinn (Uther 2004: 1, 607–608 Christiansen 1992: 215; af Klintberg 2010: 412; Ó Súilleabháin 1963: 193). Tha an t-eisimpleir sgrìobhte as tràithe a' tighinn às an 11mh linn; tha na sgrìobhannan romansachail seo buailteach air cudthrom a chur air tursan fada 'thar chuain', gaol agus dìlseachd. Bha seo ri linn Chogaidhean na Croise, cuspair fasanta, tha e coltach, a chuidich leis lìonsgaradh cho fada 'san àm, 's tha seòrsachan dheth ri fhaotainn ann an cuid dhe na leabhraichean ainmeil sgeulachd mar *Gesta Romanorum* (àir. 193) agus *Decamerone* Bhoccaccio (Tolstoi 1934: 261–62: Brednich 1990: 703). Tha an naidheachd air a h-aithris ann an caochladh chruthan beul-aithris 'sa Roinn Eòrpa: òrain an t-sluaigh, baileadan, naidheachdan ionadail, sgeulachdan eadarnàiseanta, romansachan, *novella*n sgrìobhte: iomadaidheachd a dh'fhàg a comharra, 'nam bharail, air structar neo-chumanta a' Chorra-Ghiullain Ghlais aig na Gàidheil.

Bho na meadhon aoisean anuas tha sruth làidir dhen dìleab Eòrpach seo ann am Breatainn 'sna baileadan Beurla 's Albais *Hind Horn* 's *King Orfeo* (àir. 17 is 19 ann an Child); fhuaireas gabhail dhen darna fear 'san naoidheamh ceud deug bho sheinneadair Sealltainneach. Bhon tha cuspair tèama an òrain tillidh cho measail agus buan aig an t-sluagh, ma dh'fhaoidte gura h-ann bho thùsan ann am Breatainn a thug Gàidheil na h-Alba i. 'S tric a leum a leithid fairis air crìochan cànain is cultair air tìr mór na Roinn Eòrpa, agus 's gann gun gabh fianaisean coltach dhen tèama romansachail lorg ann an Éirinn neo as na dùthchannan mu thuath, far a bheil an riochdachadh cho lag. Ach chan eil sinn ann an suidheachadh tighinn gu fuasgladh neo làn dearbhadh le cinnt.

Am feasgar sin a ghabh Iain mac Dhòmhnaill Bhàin An Corra-Ghiullan Glas, bha fear eile còmhla rinn: Lachlann Dhòmhnaill Nìll, sàr òranaiche le eòlas domhainn is farsaing air dùthchas an àite. Neo'r-thaing nach do dh'éist Lachlann gu dlùth ri gach ceathramh is car dheth. Aig deireadh na sgeòil gun guth a ghràdhainn lig e fhaicinn an tlachd agus an gluasad cridhe a thànaig air, agus cha b'iongnadh linn sin.

TÙSAN

BREDNICH, ROLF WILHELM (ED.).

1990 *Enzyklopädie des Märchens*. Band 6. Berlin, New York.

CASSON, LIONEL.

2001 *Libraries in the Ancient World.* New Haven and London.

CHILD, FRANCIS JAMES (ED.).

1956 *The English and Scottish Popular Ballads.* Vol 1. New York.

CHRISTIANSEN, REIDAR TH.

1992 *The Migratory Legends*. FF Communications No. 175. Helsinki.

AF KLINTBERG, BENGT.

2010 *The Types of the Swedish Folk Legend.* FF Communications No. 300. Helsinki.

LORD, ALBERT B.

1960 *The Singer of Tales.* Cambridge, Mass.

MCLAUGHLIN, JOHN.

1975 'The Return Song in Medieval Romance and Ballad: King Horn and King Orfeo'. *The Journal of American Folklore*, Vol. 88, No. 349: 304–307.

Ó SÚILLEABHÁIN, SEÁN.

1963 *The Types of the Irish Folktale.* FF Communications No. 188. Helsinki.

STEWART MURRAY, LADY EVELYN.

2009 *Tales from Highland Perthshire.* Translated and edited by Sylvia Robertson and Tony Dilworth. Aberdeen.

TOLSTOI, J.

1934 'Einige Märchenparallelen zur Heimkehr des Odysseus'. *Philologus* 89: 261–74.

UTHER, HANS-JÖRG.

2004 *The Types of International Folktale. A Classification and Bibliography.* FF Communications No. 284. 3 vols. Helsinki.

ZHIRMUNSKY, VICTOR.

1966 'The Epic of 'Alpamysh' and the Return of Odysseus'. *Proceedings of the British Academy* 52: 267–86.

Mì-thuigse, Dìth Tuigse, Tàthagan: Buannachd nam Mearachd ann an Cruinneachaidhean Beul-Aithris Alasdair MhicGille Mhìcheil

DOMHNALL UILLEAM STIÙBHART

ABSTRACT. The field notebooks of Alexander Carmichael (1832–1912), now transcribed, catalogued, and available at www.carmichaelwatson.lib.ed.ac.uk, allow us to eavesdrop on interactions between a major Highland folklore collector and his informants. Carmichael noted names, ages, locations, and occupations of interviewees, along with dates of interviews, allowing us to trace continuities, breaks, and developments in his collecting career over more than half a century. Carmichael's cluttered and sometimes chaotic notebooks free us from the notion of a formal encounter between performer and audience (or collector), and allow us to take in the multiplicity of voices heard in the Highland céilidh house. The paper focuses upon the miscommunications, misunderstandings, mistaken inferences, confusions, and communicative breakdowns recorded in Carmichael's notebooks, and explores what these may reveal about relations between the recorder and his informants.

Tha iomadach neach-cruinneachaidh beul-aithris air a bhith an sàs ann an obair-trusaidh air Gàidhealtachd na h-Alba; 'nam measg, air deagh adhbharan agus air droch adhbharan cho math, tha àite suaicheanta aig Alasdair Gilleasbaig MacGilleMhìcheil (1832–1912). Liosach bho thùs, ris a' ghàidsearachd mar bhith-beò, thòisich e a' clàradh dualchas nan Gàidheal a's t-samhradh 1860, 's e stéidhichte aig an àm ann an Eilean Ìle. As leth Iain Òig Ìle, fear-deasachaidh *Popular Tales of the West Highlands* (4 leabhn, 1860–62), chuir e 'aghaidh air sgeulachdan eadar-nàiseanta agus laoidhean na Féinne; cuideachd, rinn e cruinneachadh cuibhseach farsaing de theacsaichean mhith-òran Gàidhlig airson an Lieut. Donald Campbell, ùghdar *A Treatise on the Language, Poetry, and Music of the Highland Clans* (1862). B' ann eadar 1864 agus 1882, ge-tà, an linn shoirbheachail anns an robh e a' dèanamh còmhnaidh ann an Uibhist, a' togail teaghlaich, agus a' tighinn beò am measg nan daoine, a ràinig e àirde a chomais mar neach-cruinneachaidh. Dh'fhàgadh làrach nam bliadhnachan sin, na cuimhneachain a dhealbhaich e asda, buaidh mhaireannach air stoidhle-chruinneachaidh agus dòighean-clàraidh Alasdair, air an t-seòrsa caidreachais a mhiannaicheadh e a bhith eadar e fhéin agus na h-aithrisichean, agus air na bun-bheachdan agus na seallaidhean eachdraidheil agus litreachail a dhealbhaich na modhannan-deasachaidh a chuireadh e gu feum ann an *Carmina Gadelica* (Stiùbhart 2008a: 13–15).

Tha a' cheud dà leabhar de *Charmina Gadelica,* a' mhór-chuid dhiubh air a lìonadh le beannachdan, orthachan, agus ùrnaighean, 'nan càrn-cuimhne buan air saothair Alasdair MhicGilleMhìcheil, an dà chuid mar fhear-cruinneachaidh agus mar fhear-deasachaidh. Cha bheag na trioblaidean a dh'éireas asda, ge-tà, 's e cho nochdaidh an-diugh gun deach na chruinnich e ath-obrachadh agus a dhealbhadh às ùr airson a' chlò. Mar a sgrìobh Iain Latharna Caimbeul, cha sheas *Carmina Gadelica* mar taisbeanadh litireil air na chruinnich MacGilleMhìcheil, ach mar taisbeanadh litreachail (Campbell 1978–81a: 13; cuideachd Black 2008; Bruford 1983; Meek 2007; Robertson 1971-76). Am measg an tasglainn gléidhte ann an Leabharlann Oilthigh Dhùn Éideann, tha a-nis lorg againn air leabhraichean-raoin, air leabhraichean tar-sgrìobhaidh, agus air na tha air fhàgail de phàipearan deasachaidh Alasdair MhicGilleMhìcheil (Stiùbhart 2008a: 22–4). Le seo f'ar comhair, dh'fhaodadh e bhith gu bheil cothrom ann breith chothromach a thoirt a-mach m'a dhìleab. Fad a réis leanadh MacGilleMhìcheil comhairle Iain Òig Ìle. An clàradh a bhith facal air an fhacal. Mion-fhiosrachadh 'na lùib mu cuine agus có: ceann-latha, ainm, sloinneadh, aois, àite-fuirich, obair (Stiùbhart 2008a: 3–5). 'S urrainnear a-réisde cùrsa beatha an fhir-chruinneachaidh a leantainn gu mionaideach anns na pàipearan, chan e a-mhàin có ris a bhruidhneadh e agus càite, ach mar a dh'atharraicheadh, agus mar nach atharraicheadh, na gnèithean beul-aithris agus na cuspairean a bu mhiannaichte leis, agus na dòighean-cruinneachaidh cho math. 'S urrainnear coimhead gu mionaideach air na deifir sheòrsachan de dhàimh agus de chonaltradh eadar MacGilleMhìcheil agus iadsan a thug seachad an cuid dualchais – gun luaidh orrasan nach tug a bharrachd. Anns na leabhraichean-raoin, 's urrainnear mion-sgrùdadh a thoirt a-mach air amannan sònraichte agus air tachartais shònraichte ann an cùrsa-cruinneachaidh MhicGilleMhìcheil. Mu dheireadh, 's urrainnear, an-dràsda agus a-rithist, ar n-aire a thoirt do na h-amannan 'nuair a dh'fhàillich an tuigse, 'nuair a chaidh an caidreachas a mhilleadh, amannan nan tàthag agus nam facal anns a' ghuth thàmh.

Sin na buinn-còmhraidh a bhios fainear dhuinn anns an earrainn ghoirid seo, cuspairean aig a bheil mar chinn-uidhe caochladh roinnean-eòlais ùrail torrach inntinneach, roinnean a ghabhas gnothaich ri mì-thuigse, ri mì-mhìneachadh, agus ri mì-bhreithneachadh: sosiochànanachas, teoiric conaltraidh-cànain, agus pragmatachas.[1] Dh'fhaodadh e bhith nach eil na cunnartan a dh'fhaodadh éirigh an lùib mì-thuigse ann an obair-chruinneachaidh beul-aithris buileach cho da-rìribh 's a bhios iad ann an gnothaichean leighiseachd, stiùireadh eitealan, no comannd anns a' bhlàr; ach gheibhear innte a cuid thubaistean fhéin: nàire, magadh, tàir, droch chliù, agus, air uaireannan, fiù's nas miosa buileach.

Tha cuspairean de'n leithid a' cur air chuimhne dhuinn an astair fhada eadar duilleagan clòbhuailte *Charmina Gadelica*, grinn soilleir so-thuigseach, agus an ruth-ràth de sgròbalaich dhoilleir chabhagaich a lìonas na leabhraichean-raoin. Tha iad sin loma-làn de dh'othail iomadach guth, iad uile a' farpaisich ri chéile gus ar n-aire a ghlacadh ann an cabadaich far a bheil air uaireannan a' chiall fhéin an impis ciaradh às. Tha fianais nan leabhraichean-raoin a' dol às àicheadh gu bheil a' bheul-aithris stéidhichte air aon aithrisiche a-mhàin agus an clàraiche. Am broinn nan taighean-céilidh pàipeir sin gheibhear sgaoilteachd de dheifir ghuthan, a' toirt a-steach oirnn mar a bha an dualchas aig an àm ud fhathast beò, aig cridhe na coimhearsnachd. Ann a bhith a' toirt sùil gheur bhreithneachail air pàipearan MhicGilleMhìcheil, feumar beachdachadh mu dé is ciall dha-rìribh do bhriathran leithid clàraiche no aithrisiche, dé cho eadar-dhealaichte no co-ionnan a tha iad. Tro obair dlùth-leughaidh, bheirear an aire don chaidreachas eadar-mhìneachail eadar aithrisiche agus éisdeachd, agus don phròiseas robach mhì-fhoirmeil anns an téid dualchas a bhuain, a dhealbhadh, agus a dheasachadh. Tuigear mar a chaidh Alasdair MacGilleMhìcheil agus an luchd-cuideachaidh ann an Dùn Éideann gu mionaideach tro na ceudan de ghuthan eadar-dhealaichte, agus na mìltean de phìosan beul-aithris eadar-dhealaichte, 'gan deasachadh, agus le mór-shaothair, mac-meanmna, agus neart inntinn, a' cruthachadh fear de na leabhraichean-ealain a bu chudromaiche r'a linn, *Carmina Gadelica* (Black 2008; Campbell 1978–81b; Macdonald 2008).

Cha b' ann a-mhàin air a chuid obair-chlàraidh a tha cliù euchdan MhicGilleMhìcheil stéidhichte, ach air na h-oidhirpean a rinn e gus brìgh an dualchais a thoirt am follais. 'S tric a bhios sgoilearan conaltraidh a' cur an céill gur ann ciogailteach meachranach, fiù's mearachdach, 's a tha còmhradh 'nar measg. Le iomadach gnè de bheul-aithris, gnèithean air an compàirteachadh am measg coimhearsnachdan beaga, drùidhte le eòlas ionadail, gheibhear briathran, gnàthasan-cainnt, gràmar, céisean-mìneachaidh, creideasan, agus seallaidhean cultarach, 's iad cho tric às an àbhaist, air an dìtheadh còmhla ann an cruthan lìomhte làidir loma-làn brìgh, eòlais, agus bheachdan do na cluasan a thuigeas. Faodar a ràdh gu bheil na beàrnan-céille agus na leumannan tuigse a nochdas cho tric ann an cuid de na gnèithean beul-aithris – gu seachd àraid anns na h-òrain – mar mheadhan brosnachaidh don éisdeachd an coitheacs a lìonadh air an ceann fhéin. Mar a chunnacas, airson iomadach bliadhna bha Alasdair MacGilleMhìcheil gu domhainn an sàs anns an dualchas, rud a

[1] Am measg nan iomadach obair-rannsachaidh mun chuspair, mar thoiseach tòiseachaidh faodar coimhead air Bosco *et al.* 2006; Briggs 1984; Carr 2010; Dascal 1999; Dascal & Berenstein 1987; Fabian 1995; Thomas 1983; Verdonik 2010; agus Weigand 1999.

bhuilich air an comas iongantach a dhearbh e gus na beàrnan a lìonadh, gus na bloighdean sgapte a thrusadh 's a thàthadh còmhla. Ach far an robh an tàlant, bha cuideachd cunnart gun cuirteadh gu droch bhuil e: leis na caraidean aige 'ga mhisneachadh, agus 'aigne air a lasadh le aisling gum b' urrainn dha còirichean cultarach agus poilitigeach nan daoine aige fhéin a sheasamh agus fhìrinneachadh, chuir MacGilleMhìcheil cruth às ùr air an dualchas d'an do choisrig e a bheatha.

Aig cridhe a' phàipeir seo a-réisde tha gnìomhan-cainnt mì-shoirbheachail: mì-chonaltradh, mì-thuigse, iomraidhean air mhearachd, cunntasan troimhe-chéile, seanchas a' fàilligeadh, fiù's cainnt agus caidreachas a' briseadh sìos. Tha fhios nach dèan trioblaidean mì-thuigse dragh do na h-uile; air uaireannan 's dòcha nach bi iad fiù's mothachail dhaibh. Faodaidh gum bi an t-aithrisiche riaraichte gun deach am fiosrachadh a chompàirteachadh. Aig an aon àm, ge-tà, faodaidh gum bi an clàraiche a' strì ri mìneachadh ceart a ruigsinn, gun ghréim aige air na gnàthasan, na bun-bheachdan, agus na breacaidhean sònraichte as dual don choimhearsnachd. Nas miosa buileach, dh'fhaodadh gu bheil suidheachadh a' ghnìomh agus gu dearbh a shuidheachadh sòisealta fhéin ag adhbhrachadh nach eil e am fàsach don chlàraiche soilleireachadh a shireadh aig an àm.

Fàgaidh sinn gu rithist an t-saothair gus oidhirpean-cruinneachaidh Alasdair MhicGille-Mhìcheil a shuidheachadh ann an coitheacs nas fharsainge, gu sònraichte tro choimeas leis na rinn muinntir sgioba Iain Òig Ìle ann an iomairt *Popular Tales of the West Highlands*. Tha raon nas cumhainge f'ar sròin: ruith ghoirid a thoirt air na deifir sheòrsachan de mhì-thuigse a dh'éireas eadar aithrisiche, clàraiche, agus éisdeachd, le fianais bho phàipearan MhicGilleMhìcheil. Dé dh'innseas fianais nam facal sgrìobhte mu cuine agus carson a dheidheadh tuigse a lagachadh agus a chur gu neo-bhrìgh?

MacGilleMhìcheil a' tionndadh do ghnèithean 'pearsanta'

Mu thimcheall air deireadh nan 1860an chì sinn Alasdair MacGilleMhìcheil a' tionndadh air falbh bho na sgeulachdan fada foirmeil eadar-nàiseanta agus na dàintean Oiseanach, aig an robh cliù cho àrd anns na taighean-céilidh agus am measg luchd-cruinneachaidh bho muigh, gu sònraichte aig sgioba Iain Òig Ìle. 'S ann a bha e a-nis a' gabhail barrachd ùidh anns na h-òrain, anns na naidheachdan eachdraidheil, ann an làraichean airceòlach, agus anns na h-orthachan, beannachdan, agus ùrnaighean a lìonas a' cheud dà leabhar de *Charmina Gadelica*. Cuideachd, bha MacGilleMhìcheil a' tionndadh gu pìosan beul-aithris a bha tòrr na bu ghiorra (Stiùbhart 2008a: 13–14; idem 2010: 129–32; idem 2013).

Dé a b' adhbhar air a' bhun-atharrachadh seo? An toiseach, bha an ùidh aig MacGilleMhìcheil 'na dhualchas fhéin ag atharrachadh, 's e a' cur cùl ris na sgeulachdan cliùiteach, a' tionndadh gu teacsaichean na bu phrìobhaidiche, na bu phearsanta, na bu spioradail, fiù's. Bha tòrr de na seanchaidhean a bu chomasaiche a bh' ann 'nuair a ràinig e na h-eileanan an toiseach a-nis air bàsachadh. A-rithist, bha am pòsadh a rinn e le Màiri Frangag NicBheathain ann an Faoilleach 1868, breith a' cheud mhic, Ailig, aig deireadh an Dàmhair, dranndan àbhaisteach na h-obrach làitheil aige, agus an t-saothair a bha an lùib dachaigh a thogail agus a chumail suas, ag adhbhrachadh nach robh a-nis na h-uibhir de thìde-chruinneachaidh 's a bh' aige roimhe. Cha robh e furasda an ùine a lorg gus pìosan fada a chlàradh, mar a thuigear bho bhriathran a sgrìobh e air 22 Màirt 1871, aig deireadh teacs sgeòil fhada leis an t-seanchaidh bharraichte Alasdair MacNéill, Ceann Tangabhal:

> Heard this from his father when a boy. [*del*: l] Al[e]x[ande]r MacNeill is 72. Wrote this tale while granting tax Licences at Castlebay during spare minutes & intervals. (CW119/3 [fo.19^{r}])

Ged a bha a bheatha a' sìor lìonadh le dleasdanasan làitheil – obair, teaghlach, dachaigh – ann an dòigh bha na dleasdanasan sin 'ga chuideachadh, a' toirt air pìosan na bu ghiorra a chruinneachadh. Cha b' e fleasgach a bh' ann am MacGilleMhìcheil a-nis ach fear-pòsda, ball den choimhearsnachd, le bean is teaghlach; leis an inbhe ùir aige, tha a thuar gum biodh e tòrr na b' fhasa dha beul-aithris a thogail bho bhoireannaich. Cuideachd, bhiodh e coltach gum biodh barrachd ùidh aige co-dhiù ann an gnothaichean co-cheangailte ri broinn an taighe. Mu dheireadh, bha a bhean Màiri Frangag an sàs ann an obair-charthannais am measg feadhainn de na daoine a bu bhochda anns na h-eileanan, obair a thug cothrom don duine aice aithrisichean ùra a lorg 'nam measg. Gheibhear eisimpleir math air mar a b' urrainn do dh'Alasdair teacsaichean ùra a lorg air sgàth an atharrachaidh 'na chùrsa-beatha, fiù's mus do phòs e, anns a' cheud ortha a chruinnich e a-riamh. B' e seo rann ortha-breith, le cnò àirne Mhoire 'na chois, a fhuair e bho Anna NicÌosaig: 's e bh' ann ach preusant-bainnse d'a caraid òg (Stiùbhart 2013: 34–9).

Bha MacGilleMhìcheil cuideachd a' sìor chur eòlas an dà chuid air cruth-tìre nan eilean agus air na làraichean eachdraidheil fradharcach leis an robh an cruth-tìre air a bhreacadh, eòlas a dhaingnicheadh an greim a bhiodh aige air cuimhne eachdraidheil nan coimhearsnachd 's i cho tric neadaichte, mar gum biodh, anns na làraichean sin (Cheape: 125–30; Stiùbhart 2009: 144–59). A-nis, cha b' e buileach coigreach maol is conadail air faondradh a bh' ann dheth. Co-cheangailte ris a' seo, tha fianaisean nan leabhraichean-raoin a' cur an céill dhuinn gun robh MacGilleMhìcheil a' tionndadh air falbh 'na dhòighean-clàraidh bho chéis an agallaimh fhoirmeil, bhon bheul-aithris mar ghnìomh a-mhàin; gheibhear a-nis dòighean-conaltraidh nas saoire, nas so-lùbte, nas siùbhlaiche. Air cùl nan atharrachaidhean seo, dh'fhaodadh e bhith gun robh an clàraiche fhéin a' gabhail air ròl an aithrisiche 'nuair a mheasadh e freagarrach, 's e ag innse sgeulachdan, ag aithris naidheachdan, a' sradadh cheisteannan, agus, dh'fhaodadh e bhith, air uaireannan fiù's a' gabhail òran mar phàirt de chaidreachas an taighe-chéilidh. Chan urrainnear a ràdh le cinnt gu dé'n ìre 's gun robh Alasdair MacGilleMhìcheil 'na bhall den 'choimhearsnachd ghnàthasaich', ach cha bhiodh e 'na iongnadh idir ged a bhiodh aithrisichean na bu dheònaiche agus na bu chofhartaile bloighdean dualchais eile a thoirt dha seach na sgeulachdan àbhaisteach a dh'innseadh iad do choigrich: earrainnean na bu phearsanta, na bu dhìomhaire. Aig an aon àm, faodaidh sinn a bhith cinnteach gum biodh a dhuaisean fhéin, agus 's dòcha eadhan airgead-cobhair cuideachd, an lùib conaltraidh le Alasdair MacGilleMhìcheil, fear proifeiseanta a bhuineadh do dh'àrd-choluadar an eilein, le bean aig an robh sgilean sòisealta thar tomhais. Mar bu mhotha de dh'eòlas a chuireadh eileanaich air Alasdair MacGilleMhìcheil, 's ann bu mhotha de dh'earbsa a chuireadh iad ann cuideachd. Mar a dh'aidicheadh e fhéin, cha chuireadh an gàidsear móran dragh air a' mhór-shluagh: cha robh ann ach aon turas, mar eisimpleir, far an robh e 'na fhear-fianais ann an Cùirt an t-Siorraim ann an Loch nam Madadh.

Ré'n tràth seo, cha b' e a-mhàin gun robh MacGilleMhìcheil a' cur eòlas air aithrisichean nan eilean; 's ann a bha e cuideachd a' dèanamh caidreachas ri feadhainn air an taobh a-muigh, feadhainn trom b' urrainn dha a chuid rannsachaidh a thoirt am follais. Thar nam bliadhnachan, chum e suas lìonrath sgapte de dh'eòlaich, 's e a' trusadh sgaoilteachd mhath de chuspairean dhaibh: tuilleadh dhàintean Oiseanach do dh'Iain Òg Ìle agus do Ghilleasbaig Mac a' Chléirich; naidheachdan agus orthachan airson colbh pàipeir-naidheachd an Urr. Alasdair Stiùbhart ('Nether-Lochaber') anns an *Inverness Courier*; iomraidhean air eòin do John Harvie-Brown; sean-fhacail don t-Siorram Alasdair MacNeacail; agus tuairisgeulan mu làraichean airceòlach don Chaiptean Frederick Thomas (ap Rheinallt 2010; Cheape 2008; Stiùbhart 2008a, 2009, 2013). Mar thoradh air an seo, thàinig mùthadh air leabhraichean-raoin MhicGilleMhìcheil. An àite a bhith coltach ri clàr cuirm-chiùil no cuirm-aithris, 's ann a dh'atharraicheadh iad gu bhith 'nam bolgan-solair, loma-làn chuspairean eadar-dhealaichte, letheach slighe eadar am beul agus an teacs. Bha buaidh aig an dòigh-chruinneachaidh thruimeach thar shearrach seo air an fhear-cruinneachaidh fhéin: uaireannan bha e mar nach b' urrainn do MhacGilleMhìcheil stad a chur air fhéin, mar a chithear bhon turas a thòisich e ri sgeulachd a chlàradh:

> a story of Rocabarray. 3 others & I went to Kill ([*air a dhubhadh às*: bioraich] here poor old Donald [*air a dhubhadh às*: Macphie] MacInnon fell on the floor off his stool in a swoon & I thought he was dead. There were only two little children in a boy & a girl & I request[ed] them to run for the neighbours I raised the old mans head & plac[e]d a bag with some [*loidhne foidhe*: diasun] bere heads under his head.

> He vomited [*air a dhubhadh às*: spe] A neigh[bouring] woman came but she seemed as scared as myself I placed 2/- in his hand & left. Poor man! [*air a dhubhadh às*: So] Death would be a relief from such wretched poverty & rags & disorder & dirt. Wretched! wretched! wretched! (CW119/16 [fo.43^{v}])

'S ann gu math amh neo-lìomhte a-réisde a tha deagh chuid de leabhraichean-raoin Alasdair MhicGilleMhìcheil, a' leigeil leis an leughadair gorradaireachd thar gualainn a' chlàraiche fhad's a bhios an duilleag 'ga lìonadh. Air an adhbhar seo, tha luach thar tomhais aig na leabhraichean-raoin seo ann a bhith a' leigeil ris dhuinn cuid de na dùbhlain agus na cunnartan a dh'éireadh agus a dh'éireas fhathast an lùib obair clàradh agus eadar-mhìneachadh an dualchais.

Mì-thuigsean

Faodar deifir ìrean de mhì-thuigse a shònrachadh ann an clàraidhean Alasdair MhicGilleMhìcheil, feadhainn a dh'éireas bho luaths còmhradh an aithrisiche, feadhainn eile bho neo-shoilleireachd na cainnte. Air uaireannan cha ghreimich an clàraiche air ciall litireil briathran an aithrisiche; uaireannan eile cha téid an coitheacs cultarach eadar-mhìneachadh gu coilionta; agus an-dràsda 's a-rithist faodaidh amharas a bhith againn nach do thuig an clàraiche a' mhiann bhunaiteach air cùl briathran an aithrisiche, gu h-àraid 'nuair a bhios ìoranas, cùl-cainnte, no sgaiteachd anns a' cheist. Obraichidh mì-thuigse aig deifir ìrean, agus an clàraiche a' dèanamh a dhìchill dòighean-labhairt an aithrisiche a mhìneachadh, agus breithneachadh pongail a thoirt a-mach eadar na deifir chiall a dh'éireas asda.

Airson deagh eisimpleir air duilgheadasan mar thoradh air aithris ro chabhagaich, faodar coimhead air Anna, an nighean aig Aonghas Guinneach, an seanchaidh iomraiteach à Dail fo Thuath, Sgìre Nis ann an Eilean Leòdhais. Ann an Dàmhair 1873, bha MacGilleMhìcheil trang a' cruinneachadh, air a' cheud uair a-riamh, anns an eilean a b' fhaide gu tuath ann an Innse Ghall. Gu mì-fhortanach, ge-tà, air sgàth dìth eòlais mu chruth-tìre agus eachdraidh an àite, cho math (dh'fhaodadh e bhith) ri trioblaidean leis an dual-chainnt ionadail, chan eil na notaichean aige ach mabach agus troimhe-chéile an taca ris na chlàradh e mar bu trice ann an Uibhist. Leis mar a bha Anna Ghuinneach ag aithris sgeulachd Charain mhic Fhitheall aig peilear a beatha, chan eil ann an teacs MhicGilleMhìcheil ach bloighdean sgeòil a bhriseas às a chéile gu tur aig an deireadh:

> Caran mac Fitheall
> (Ann Gunn – a woman who talks like a machine) Was a mas[ter] build[er] of temples and castles – He had 3 sons. He had a joiner re-fit[in]g his son a man building dyk[e]s. He was susp[icious] of his wife in his abs[ence] & he wished to test his sons – A river past his house. He asked his eld[est] not to take sion a bhurn a clais d aon gara mor thogail. (CW115/7 [fo.4^{r}])

Air an ath dhuilleig tillidh MacGilleMhìcheil gu sgeulachd nas iomraitiche, sgeulachd mun naomh ionadail Rònan. Tha tachartais mar sin, far a bheil beàrnan ann an eòlas a' chlàraiche mu chruth-tìre agus mu eachdraidh na sgìre anns an robh e a' cruinneachadh gu ìre bheag no mhór a' tighinn eadar e fhéin agus tuigse cheart phongail mun dualchais ionadail, a' cur air shùilean dhuinn gur dòcha gum bu chòir a bhith caoimhnteach leis na gearainean gnàthaichte nach do rinn am fear-cruinneachaidh barrachd chuairtean do dh'àiteachan na b' fhaide air falbh leithid Eilean Leòdhais. Bha soirbheachadh MhicGilleMhìcheil ann an Uibhist agus Barraigh stéidhichte air iomadach bliadhna a' toirt a-steach na talmhainn, mar gum biodh, a' cur dlùth-eòlas air cruth na tire agus a' cosnadh 's a' buannachadh earbsa nan daoine.

Aig amannan eile anns na leabhraichean-raoin, a-réir coltais 's ann mar thoradh air sgìths a' chlàraiche a thachras am briseadh-conaltraidh. As déidh làn latha a' straibhéigearachd timcheall air feadh Eilean Mhiughlaigh an cuideachd an t-seanchaidh ainmeil Ruairidh an Rùma, 's e air 's dòcha deich duilleagan ar fhichead uile gu léir a lìonadh leis an stòras de dhualchas a bha 'na sheilbh, teannaidh MacGilleMhìcheil ri sgeulachd eile a chlàradh bhuaithe. Ach cha luaithe a thòisicheas e na gu h-obann – le tomhais math de dh'fhaochadh, dh'fhaodadh e bhith – leigidh e seachad an sgeul. Tha e coltach gun cuala e a cheana e:

> Bha mac aig mac Nill agus dh fhag ad an Duart e &c &c
> [*nota*: niean Fear Bhororay] (CW114/67 [fo.79^{v}])

Cha b' e a-mhàin nach b' ionnan Gàidhlig Liosach Alasdair MhicGilleMhìcheil agus cainnt muinntir Uibhist agus Bharraigh. Gus cùisean a dhèanamh na bu thoinnte buileach, thàinig grunn de na h-aithrisichean a bu chomasaiche agus a b' fheàrr leis do na h-Eileanan A-muigh mar shearbhantan bho cheàrnaidhean eile leithid Chinn Tàile agus an Eilein Sgitheanaich. 'S tric a chithear anns na leabhraichean-raoin trioblaidean ag éirigh agus MacGilleMhìcheil a' dèanamh 'uile-dhìchill gus an dual-chainnt a thuigsinn agus a' chiall a réiteachadh. Bha saothair a' chlàraiche eadhan na bu dhùbhlanaiche 'nuair a b' fheudar dha strì le teacs 'ga bhreacadh le briathrachas agus le gnàthasan-cainnt a bha gu tur às an àbhaist. Mar aon eisimpleir, 's ann gu math follaiseach a tha am meas mór a bh' aig MacGilleMhìcheil air Màiri NicRàth, ach bha saothair nach bu bheag aige a' gleachd ris an dual-chainnt Thàilich a bhruidhinn i, mar a chithear bho thoiseach an laoidh foidhe:

> Fhir a chruthaich fhir (air?) fhir a chrì
> Chruthaich a chre air an t-sluagh (CW87/66 [fo.37])

Cha do rinn MacGilleMhìcheil steama den fhacal 'criùbh', fuaimneachadh 'craobh' air taobh siar Cheann a Tuath na Gàidhealtachd. Leis mar nach do dh'aithnich e an ìomhaigh thùsail – Crìosd a chaidh a chrochadh air a' chraoibh – b' i an tuairmse a ràinig e gum b' e 'chruthaich' a bu chiall don tritheamh fhacal an àite 'chrochadh'. Chaidh na loidhnichean sin an dubhar air a' chlàraiche. Chithear an trioblaid cheudna a' togail ceann ann an dà chlàradh de laoidh eile, *Crìosda Cléireach os ar cionn*, far an cuala MacGilleMhìcheil am facal 'crann' mar 'ceann' air a' cheud dol a-mach:

> Noc[hd] oi[dh]che chrechar a chruai
> Ceann [*supra*: Crann?] cruai[dh] ris na chroch[adh] Criost
> Criost cleireach os an cionn (CW116/118 [fo.38^{v}])

> Noc oiche chrochaidh chruaidh
> Ceann cruaidh ris na chroch[adh] Criost
> Criost[a] cleir[each] os ar cionn (CW111/40 [fo.9])

Tuigear gu bheil deagh shuaip eadar na trioblaidean a dh'éireas anns na h-eisimpleirean shuas agus na mì-thuigsean a gheibhear cho tric an lùib briathrachais bho roinn-eòlais shònraichte, air neo ann an còmhraidhean le sàr-eòlaichean.

Tha na h-eisimpleirean shuas cuideachd a' cur an céill cho bitheanta 's a bhios na h-adhbharan litireil agus na h-adhbharan meafarach air cùl mhì-mhìneachaidhean sònraichte air an amladh ri chéile. Faodar tionndadh a-nis gu ceist eile: 's i sin, an robh aig amannan sònraichte ciall àraid air cùl nam briathran a chleachd an t-aithrisiche seach a' chiall litireil? Ann an *Carmina Gadelica*, is tric a bhios ealain is sgeadachaidhean na dòigh-riochdachaidh a' cur coitheacs a' chruinneachaidh am falach air an leughadair. Chan e sin do na làmh-sgrìobhainnean, far a bheil fianaisean gu leòr ann a bheir deagh chothrom dhuinn beachdachadh mu có ris a dh'fhaodadh an conaltradh eadar aithrisiche agus clàraiche a bhith coltach ann an da-rìribh.

Bu chòir dhuinn toirt an aire gun robh cuid de na h-eileanaich a' diùltadh gabhail ri luchd-cruinneachaidh beul-aithris a-muigh 's a-mach. Ri linn an earraich agus àm na buana, mar eisimpleir, dh'fheumte brath a ghabhail air na làithean geala mar a thigeadh iad. Bha saothair anns an acha-dubh na bu bhuannachdaile na bhith a' caitheamh nan cairtealan ag aithris do choigreach naidheachdan caithte bho shean.

Tha fianais làmh-sgrìobhainnean Alasdair MhicGilleMhìcheil a' toirt dhuinn eisimpleirean de dh'innleachdan na bu caraiche gus faighinn réidh de neach-cruinneachaidh. Air 7 Giblein 1875 bha e anns a' Bhaile Shear, Uibhist a Tuath, a' dèanamh còmhraidh ri Fionnghal NicLeòid, Fionnghal nighean Chaluim, boireannach aig an robh ainm fad is farsaing anns an eilean. Cha b' e sin a-mhàin, ach gun robh aice, gun teagamh, stòras de dh'orthachan a dh'ùisnicheadh i 's i air a cuairt ann an Uibhist. Cha do chlàraich MacGilleMhìcheil ach an t-aonan dhiubh, an ortha 'cnàimh ri cnàimh' air am biodh eòlas sgapte aig cha mhór a h-uile duine anns an eilean (CW111/87 [fo.20]). Bhiodh e coltach gun tug i dha té de na h-orthachan a bu chumanta a bh' ann mar dhòigh gus faighinn cuidhteas e.

Bheir Dòmhnall Mac a' Phì dhuinn leasan eile 's e a' cur ruaig air an fhear-chruinneachaidh. 'S e bh' ann am Mac a' Phì ach an seanchaidh a bu chliùitiche ann an Uibhist air fad aig an àm, sgeulaiche a chaidh a chlàradh le Iain Òg Ìle agus le 'fhear-chuideachaidh Eachann MacGillEathain ann an 1859 agus 1860. 'S ann gu math saoghalta 'nan nàdar a bha an dithis mu dheireadh ud, agus bha iadsan agus Mac a' Phì gu math réidh. Cha b' e sin do dh'Alasdair MacGilleMhìcheil, òganach romansach, a-réir coltais, rud beag stòlda leis – agus, feumar cuimhneachadh, 'na ghàidsear cho math. Thàinig MacGilleMhìcheil air chéilidh air Dòmhnall Mac a' Phì air 21 Gearran 1866. Chuir an seanchaidh gu deuchainn e, 's dòcha air beulaibh éisdeachd mhór: tha e coltach gun còrdadh a' chùis riutha math dha-rìribh. Leis a' cheud sgeulachd a dh'innis e, chlàraich MacGilleMhìcheil cho fada ri:

> Dh-innis an cuillein breac odhar do mhac an Righ gum bitheadh madadh nan seac[hd] cas na mheasan aig nighean Righ rioghac[hd] an Domhain an oi[dh]che sin eadar a da chìch. (CW104/9 [fo.35])

agus an uair sin leig e seachad e. An ath stòraidh a dh'aithris Mac a' Phì, 's ann a-mach air rìgh a bha e, a dh'iarr air duine bochd innleachdail làn sreath de rudan iongantach fhaighinn dha. Aig deireadh gnothaich, faighnichidh an rìgh:

> An tug thu leat [del: do] amadan an duine chionta? Thug ars an duine boc[hd]. Chai[dh] e mach gus fuasgail a bhri[o]g[a]is agus thainig e staigh a stealladh feadh an taighe. Gu dearbh gu dearbh is math a chuile dad a th agad a dhuine bhoc[hd] ars an R[igh] (CW104/14 [fo.37])

A-réir coltais, cha do sheas MacGilleMhìcheil air stairsnich Dhòmhnaill Mhic a' Phì a chaoidh tuilleadh.

Fiù's 'nuair a chaidh aig MacGilleMhìcheil air beul-aithris a chruinneachadh, chan eil sin ri ràdh nach cluinn a' chluais a dh'éisdeas beachdan mar gum biodh anns a' ghuth-thàmh mun chlàraiche 'na lùib. 'S i a' cheist, an robh an clàraiche fhéin a' gabhail ealla mu na barailean sin, 's e a dh'aona ghnothaich 'gan leigeil seachad, air neo nach do dh'fhidir e idir dhaibh air a' cheud dol a-mach?

Seo Alasdair MacGilleMhìcheil air chuairt ann an Miughlaigh ann an Lùnasdal 1867:

> Fulling at Miulay. Heard a fulling song sung while pas[sing] a hut and went in. Found six good looking comely girls waulking cloth One sung the verses the rest the chorus and all took their turn at this. All the songs suited the body made in ful[ling] and all to my ear wild weird and beautiful.
>
> One was a fairy song and fairy like.
>
> Measured the arms of two of the girls. Each meas. 11½ inches in circ. The rest seemed to be gen[er]ally stout and yet they did not seem to me to be any sup[erfluous] flesh about them.
>
> The ful. song com first slowly and ma? and all keep time to this in their mov[ements]. Then it becomes 'fast and fun['] till the whole as by have frel? a dif? in rest[ing] their prop. The cloth is sent round with the sun. upon no ac[count] would they attempt the con[verse]. The cleith luai is a a [sic] plank a fair in[ch] thick 1½ bro[ad] & 10 f long. /

> It must have been tossed ab[out] in the At[lantic] for a time for it is perfor[ated] all over by teredo
>
> One of the songs sung was a comp[osition] one made to myself the Stranger all the rest gun the chorus.
>
> I asked them to sing the fairy song again. They hesi[tated] and when I pressed them they said that did they repeat a song twice at a clei luai they the cloth would become as thin as before and in[tantly] lose all its col[our] and become pure white!
>
> I did not then press.
>
> M eudail an t uacran cluitach
> Nach dean an tua a spuileadh
> Nuar thug an cro bho chuntaobh?
> Reach eir mo ghlun duit
> Nam fhiach mi fhin dhiult?
> Saod fada us
> Mum teid thu la a na ?cuntai
> Cha n e tigh[earna] no diuc e. (CW114/31 [fos.62^{v}–63])

Tha mi air iomradh a thoirt ann an àiteigin eile mu dheagh rath MhicGilleMhìcheil, mar a thàinig e tarsainn air luadhadh ann am baile Mhiughlaigh, eilean beag far an robh na taighean cruinn còmhla seach a bhith sgapte ann an sreath fada cleas a' mhór-chuid de na bailtean croitearachd; agus seo aig àm 'nuair a bha luadhadh a' dol air adhart co-dhiù; agus gun robh e ann an cuideachd 'rìgh' an eilein, Ruairidh an Rùma, cuideigin a b' urrainn dhol a-steach don taigh, stad a chur air an obair, agus am fear-cruinneachaidh a chur an aithne air a' phannal. Do MhacGilleMhìcheil, b' e seo tachartas a dh'atharraich na cleachdaidhean-cruinneachaidh aige; thairis air na bliadhnachan ri tighinn dhèanadh e clàradh de dh'iomadach òran-luaidh 'na leabhraichean-raoin.

Ach bheirear an aire don òran a ghabh mnathan a' phannail: 'M' eudail an t-uachdaran cliùiteach/Nach dèanadh an tuath a spùilleadh'. A bheil iad a' dèanamh feum den òran seo, 's e gu math mì-chumanta a-réir coltais, gus beachd a phàirteachadh 'nam measg fhéin mu Alasdair MacGilleMhìcheil, an gàidsear a thàinig thuca gus cìsean a chruinneachadh cho math ri beul-aithris? Tha deagh choltas air a' chùis gum b' e seo a thug MacGilleMhìcheil don eilean: bhiodh gu leòr chon aig muinntir Mhiughlaigh, 's iad 'gan ùisneachadh air obair eunadaireachd. An rud as cudromaiche buileach an seo, bheirear an aire nach eil am fear-cruinneachaidh a' tighinn am measg nan eileanach agus a' goid an cuid òran; 's ann a tha muinntir na coimhearsnachd iad fhéin a' dèanamh feum de na h-òrain gus beagan magaidh a dhèanamh air a' choigreach.

Airson eisimpleir car dramatach de mhì-thuigse, an turas-sa de chaidreachas a' briseadh sìos, faodar dhol air ais dà bhliadhna don cheud chuairt a thug MacGilleMhìcheil a dh'ionnsaigh Hirt, ann an Céitean 1865. Bhiodh dà dheichead ann mus tadhaileadh e air an eilean a-rithist. Tha na notaichean goirid a rinn e air a' cheud turas a' toirt sanas dhuinn carson:

> Arrived at St Kilda about 12 noon. Fine open bay. Bold rocks and remarkably grand. Landed in first boat. Was at manse. Poorly furnished but good house. Cameron the missionary oldish and common looking. St Kildans good looking s[t]out fellows with pale complexions. Woman good [*air a dhubhadh às*: ruddy] looking and ruddy complexions. Women high shoulders and crouched figures and bad ankles and feet. Beautiful white teeth. Pronunciation peculiar and lisping. People seem to be spoiled not polite. Bought cloth [*air a dhubhadh às*: 3] 10¼ yards. / Price 14/- Bottle ful[*supra*: m]ar oil 1/- Kissed a St Kilda lassie. A [*supra*: little] beauty with dark brown eyes and fresh complexion about ten or eleven years. Kissed her so as to have

> to say that I Kissed a St Kilda lassie. Saw men going on rocks. Fearful sights. The deep blue fathomless ocean roaring many hundred feet beneath them. Took out two fulmars and some [*air a dhubhadh às*: egs] eggs. Birds vomiting oil – painful sights. (CW113/17 [fo.55^{v}])

Cha bhiodh taobh ro bhlàth aig na Hirtich do choigreach sam bith 's e a' gabhail gréim air cloinn-nighean an àite agus a' toirt dhaibh pòg gun iarraidh. Ged a choinnich MacGilleMhìcheil ris an té a bu shine air an eilean aig an àm, Oighrig NicCruimein, a-réir coltais cha do dhearg e air barrachd air dà òran a-mhàin a chlàradh. As déidh dha tilleadh à Hirt, air 25 Céitean 1865, sgrìobh am fear-cruinneachaidh sìos òran bho Choinneach MacCalmain (1845–78), marsanta òg far na Comraich, ach a bha a' dèanamh còmhnaidh ann an Uisgebhagh air taobh sear Bheinn na Faghla. Feumaidh gun robh MacCalmain air cluinntinn mu thrioblaidean a charaid ann an Hirt: ghabh e dà rann bhon òran *Nam biodh agam bàta biorach* le Dòmhnall MacMhathain, Fear Atadail (bh. 1763):

> S gun taoghainn a' mhaighdinn a bheusach
> A leum a h-oc[hd] blia[dh]n[a] diag
> 'S cha bu chall gad bhiodh i fichead
> 'S doigh nach am bu mheasa ciall
>   Hi hiuri bhi hoirnn o
>   Hi hiuri bhi hoirinn an
>   Hi huiri bhi hoirinn eile
>   Mo run fhein duit 's d' fhaicinn slan (CW113/19 [fo.57])

Gus a' chiall a sparradh air a' ghàidsear – agus feumaidh gun robh e làn aithreachais – dh'aithris MacCalmain an uair sin dha 'Comhairle a Aoide do Mhac an Toisich', sreath de shean-fhacail ag innse mun bheusachd a bu chubhaidh do dh'òigear d'a leithid.

Mar eisimpleir mu dheireadh, aithrisiche a' cosnadh a chliù air ais air beulaibh éisdeachd, faodar tionndadh gu Alasdair MacNéill, Ceann Tangabhal ann am Barraigh, aon uair eile. 'S gann gun robh co-sheise Alasdair mhic Ruairidh Bhàin airson seanchas anns an eilean air fad. Tha e follaiseach gun robh MacGilleMhìcheil a' dèanamh fiughair ris a' chonaltradh a bhiodh eatorra: thug e leis a dh'aona ghnothaich leabhar-raoin bàn ùr, 's e an dùil, tha e coltach, gun sgrìobhadh e na h-ultaichean de dhualchas bhon bhodach. Ach mar a thaisbeanas na beàrnan geala air feadh na cheud duilleig, chaidh aithris Alasdair MhicNéill gu tur am mearachd: chaidh e air iomrall leis an dàn Oiseanach *Laoidh na Ceàrdaich*, agus dh'fhairtlich air a chrìochnachadh (CW119/2 [fo.5$^{r–v}$]). B' e seo adhbhar-nàire dha-rìribh don t-seanchaidh, gu seachd àraid leis mar a thachair e, a-réir coltais, air beulaibh sluagh mór de dh'eileanaich 's iad a' feitheamh gus cìsean ('tax Licences') a phàigheadh. Eadar dhà sgeul, chan eil fhios nach robh MacGilleMhìcheil a' sùileachdainn gum biodh an seanchaidh a' cur seachad an tìde don fheadhainn eile. An ath latha, thill MacNéill do MhacGilleMhìcheil a-rithist, agus an turas-sa dh'innis e sgeulachd. Bha fios aige gum biodh *An Gruagach Bàn, mac Rìgh Éireann* soirbheachail, chionn deich bliadhna roimhe bha e an déidh an aon sgeul ìnnse do dh'Eachann MacGillEathain, fear-cuideachaidh Iain Òig Ìle; chaidh a chlòbhualadh anns an dàrna leabhar de *Popular Tales of the West Highlands* (CW119/3 [fos.6–19]; Campbell 1860–2: ii, 410–35). Tha againn a-réisde cothrom luachmhor coimeas a dhèanamh eadar dà dheifir tharraing den aon sgeulachd, leis an aon seanchaidh. Ged nach e seo an t-àite làn choimeas coilionta a dhèanamh eatorra, faodar a ràdh gu bheil barrachd fealla-dhà anns an tarraing as anmoiche, 's dòcha mar thoradh air suidheachadh na h-aithrise fhéin, agus, dh'fhaodadh e bhith, cho cofhartail 's a bha MacNéill leis an dàrna chlàraiche.

Gnè

Faodaidh sinn crìochnachadh le bhith a' toirt sùil nas fharsainge air cho teis-meadhanach 's a tha gnéithean agus fo-ghnèithean 'litreachail' ann an roinn na beul-aithrise, agus gu dearbh do chonaltradh a' chinne-daonna air fad. Tha gach gnè le a cuid riaghailtean ciallachail agus pragmatach fhéin, agus le a cuid chomharraidhean sònraichte cho math. Tha na riaghailtean agus na comharraidhean sin a' dealbhadh teachdaireachd an aithrisiche agus tuigse na h-éisdeachd, agus a' toirt buaidh orra. Tha seo 'gar tilleadh do na raointean ùra cruinneachaidh a dh'fhosgail MacGilleMhìcheil air an robh mi a-mach roimhe.

Bha Iain Òg Ìle an sàs ann an dà ghnè gu sònraichte: cruinneachadh sgeulachdan eadar-nàiseanta no *Märchen*, a chaidh a chlòbhualadh ann am *Popular Tales of the West Highlands*; agus na dàintean Oiseanach a nochd ann an *Leabhar na Féinne* (Campbell 1860–2, 1872). 'S dòcha gum b' e sin a thug air Alasdair MacGilleMhìcheil ceum eile a ghabhail, 's e a' rannsachadh ghnèithean den dualchas nach deach an sgrùdadh roimhe, agus nach robh fiù's cho so-ruigsinneach, gu h-àraid do na fireannaich. Gu seachd àraid bha na h-òrain-luaidh ann, òrain gu tric air an gabhail ann an àite a bha toirmisgte do dh'fhireannaich, òrain a bha sònraichte duilich am mìneachadh, neo eadhan an sònrachadh mar theacsaichean fa leth, gun dlùth-eòlas a bhith agad an toiseach air a' choitheacs (Stiùbhart 2010). Le a charaid Frangag Tholmach, bha MacGilleMhìcheil air thoiseach air càch anns an raon seo. Ach ged a chruinnich e na ficheadan de theacsaichean, cha b' urrainn dha an deasachadh don chlò, ged a bha iad mar phàirt den tritheamh leabhar de *Carmina Gadelica* nach deach fhoillseachadh 'na bheatha fhéin. Ann an teacsaichean nan òran-luaidh bha dùbhlan air leth don neach-deasachaidh: bha iad sruthach iom'-fhillte, bha an teachdaireachd neo-dhìreach, gu tric an dubhar eadhan air an éisdeachd, agus bha atharrachaidhean obann iongantach ann an cuspairean agus ann am faireachdainnean. Leis cho tric 's nach robh aon sgeulachd ri faighinn bho cheann gu ceann anns na h-òrain sin, dh'fheuchadh MacGilleMhìcheil ri co-chur fhuaigheil ri chéile às na deifir bhreacaidhean a bha e air a chlàradh, co-chur a dh'fhàsadh na b' fhaide agus na b' fhaide. Cha b' urrainn dha, air a' cheann thall, càil fhàgail às.

Tha cunnartan a-thaobh mì-thuigse agus mì-mhìneachaidh fiù's nas fhollaisiche ann an orthachan. 'S iad seo teacsaichean goirid, doirbh ri thuigsinn a chaidh a ghabhail, a dh'aona ghnothaich, fon anail ann an ceud chabhaig, làn cànain àrsaidh mheafaraich, ma b' fhìor, a dhiùltadh mìneachadh sìmplidh agus a chumadh am brìgh an uaigneas. Bha a' chùis eadhan na bu dhuiliche leis cho tric 's a bha, an lùib na h-aithrise, gnìomhachdan agus nithean 'gan cur gu feum cuideachd.

Dìreach mar a tha dà bhreacadh againn den aon sgeulachd, *An Gruagach Bàn*, bhon aon seanchaidh, Alasdair mac Ruairidh Bhàin, tha cuideachd dà tharraing eadar-dhealaichte againn den aon ortha, agus sia bliadhnachan eatorra, bhon aon aithrisiche. B' ise Màiri Stiùbhart, air neo Màiri Bhreac, seann bhanarach ann am Malacleit, Uibhist a Tuath (faic Stiùbhart 2008b). Tha an dà bhreacadh seo a' cur air shùilean dhuinn cho neo-stéidhichte 's a dh'fhaodadh teacsaichean orthachan a bhith – agus, dh'fhaodadh e bhith, mar nach robh an clàraiche a' greimeachadh air na briathran uile gu léir air a' cheud aithris. Cuideachd, cuiridh iad an céill dhuinn an tlachd 's an tàladh a dh'fhairicheadh cruinniche le mac-meanmna ealanta innleachdach ann a bhith a' tàthadh nan leth-bhreac ri chéile ach am buannaicheadh iad às ùr an riochd a bh' orra bho thùs – mas fhìor.

Aig an àm seo cha robh e 'na nòs aig MacGilleMhìcheil barrachd air aon chlàradh de theacsa a dhèanamh bhon aon aithrisiche, ach lorgar an dàrna tarraing den aon ortha ann an sreath de dh'ochd dhiubh a sgrìobh MacGilleMhìcheil sìos bho Mhàiri Stiùbhart air an aon latha, 19 Màirt 1877. Leis mar a chaochail Màiri dìreach ceithir mhìosan as déidh seo, tha e coltach gum b' e dìleab a dh'aona bhàghadh a bha i a' toirt seachad d'a charaid: na bh' aice de dh'orthachan, a' ghibht mu dheireadh bhuaipe don chlàraiche.

Cuiridh mise 'n spréidh so romham
Mar a dh-òrduich Rìgh an Domhain,
Muire ga'n gleidheadh o fheith' nan coimheach;
Air thùs a Bhrìde mhìn bi mariu,
Le d' bhata 's le d' lorg bi rompa
'S gun glacadh tu cir as d' fhalt,
O rinn thu dhuibh eolas 'as earail,

Gan gleidheadh o chall 's o lochd,
O bhathadh, an oilt 's o gharadh cam,
Na o mhilleadh sluic;
A Bhride mhin fagam h-agad,
Muire tilleadh thugam,
Le luas Dhia 's Challum-Chille
Casan cuiribh fothaibh
'S drochaid Mhuire romhaibh. (Stewart 1872)

Ora na Buachileac

Cuiri mise sprei so romham
Mar a dh'ord. Ri an domh.
Muir ga feth a gli an coidead
Eirich thus a Bhride mhin
Gun glac a tri chir as t-fhast.
Cuiri tu dhaibh eolas gun eanra?
Ga'n glei o chall gun loc
Bride fagam agam
Buach Dhe agus C-chille
Casa-cura fothaibh s drochaid
Car muire romhaibh
O chreig o chabhan o allt
O ghala coin no a mhille sluic
Carra Casacurra = never failing feet. (CW108/10 [fo.4])

Bho anmoch anns na 1860an air adhart, a-réisde, bhiodh Alasdair MacGilleMhìcheil a' cruinneachadh tòrr a bharrachd na dìreach na teacsaichean a b' àirde cliù anns na taighean-céilidh, 's iad sin, sgeulachdan eadar-nàiseanta agus laoidhean na Féinne. Le bean, taigh, agus teaghlach a-nis, cha bhiodh cus ùine aige tuilleadh. Aig an aon àm, dh'fheumadh e fios-freagairtean a chumail ri grunn luchd-eòlais. Mar sin, dh'fheumadh MacGilleMhìcheil clàradh ann an àite sam bith a b' urrainn dha. Ach leis mar a bha e a-nis pòsda le teaghlach òg, agus a' bhean Màiri gu domhainn an sàs ann an obair charthannais am measg nan daoine bochda, b' urrainn dha aithne a chur air aithrisichean ùra, b' urrainn dha gnèithean ùra de dhualchas a ruigsinn agus a sgrìobhadh sìos. Leis cho mì-fhoirmeil siùbhlach 's a dh'fhàsadh an conaltradh càirdeil eadar clàraiche agus aithrisiche – mar bu trice ann an riochd còmhraidh seach agallaimh – agus leis cho siùbhlach saor 's a bha nàdar nan gnèithean beul-aithrise a bhiodh e a-nis a' clàradh agus a' tar-sgrìobhadh co-dhiù, bhiodh Alasdair MacGilleMhìcheil a' sìor fhàs cleachdte ri bhith a' cruinneachadh bhloighdean agus chriomagan.

Bheireadh e an aire cuideachd do cho tric 's a dh'éireadh mì-thuigse agus mì-mhìneachadh ann an conaltradh, cha b' ann a-mhàin eadar aithrisiche agus cruinniche, ach cuideachd, dh'fhaodadh e bhith, eadar deifir ghinealaichean de dh'aithrisichean. Mar sin, bhiodh 'inntinn an sàs a' meòrachadh ciamar a dhèanadh e càradh air na lochdan a bha buailteach don obair-se, ciamar a lìonadh e na beàrnan a dh'fhosgladh anns na teacsaichean. Anns na suirbhéidhean agus na clàdhachaidhean airceòlach a rinn e anns na h-eileanan, b' fheudar do MhacGilleMhìcheil beachdachadh mu ciamar a b' urrainnear bloighdean de chultar dùthchasach a thàthadh ri chéile, agus gu dé dh'innseadh an fhianais a bha taisgte annta mun àm a dh'fhalbh. Fo bhuaidh a mhnatha Màiri Frangag, té a bhiodh a' saothrachadh, mus do phòs i, ann a bhith a' rannsachadh agus a' clò-bhualadh leabhraichean-aifrinn don Eaglais Easbaigich, thòisich Alasdair MacGilleMhìcheil a' coimhead air na h-orthachan Gàidhlig mar bhloighdean theacsaichean aifrinn a thàrr à long-bhriseadh na h-eaglaise Ceiltiche tràth anns na Meadhan Aoisean:

> The poem is curious and at first sight looks very superstitious. Closer inspection, however, shows that it is symbolic, rather than superstitious. Probably it formed part of the ritual of the ancient Celtic Church, as I think the most, if not all these old rhymes did. A.C. (CW131A fo.416)

Mar thoradh air dà fhichead bliadhna de dh'oidhirpean gus beàrnan-conaltraidh eadar aithrisiche agus cruinniche a lìonadh, choisinn Alasdair MacGilleMhìcheil fìor liut ann an tomhais dé bu chiall agus dé bha a dhìth air na teacsaichean a chlàraich e. Tha cuid de sgoilearan a' cumail a-mach nach robh Maighstir Ailein Dòmhnallach buileach ann an da-rìribh anns a' mholadh a rinn e d'a charaid as déidh dha leabhraichean de *Charmina Gadelica* i–ii fhaighinn mar ghibht bhon fhear-deasachaidh:

> The translation is marvellous. It is a puzzle to me how you were able to interpet what I know the reciters themselves would tell you they could not translate, and yet when I read any such piece and look at the translation I say 'Yes, it must be that'. Your Gaelic intuition must be extraordinary. (Campbell 1971–6: 298)

As déidh dhomh coimeas a dhèanamh eadar grunn theacsaichean tùsail agus na chaidh a chlòbhualadh ann an *Carmina Gadelica*, chan urrainn dhomh aontachadh le seo. Saoilidh mi gun do sgrìobh Maighstir Ailein gu h-onarach. Bha comas air leth aig MacGilleMhìcheil ciall a thoirt fìù's às na briathran, na meafaran, na gnàthasan-cainnt a bu mhì-ghealltanaiche a' coimhead a' cheud shùil 'gan tugadh orra.

Cha bu chòir dhuinn idir làn mhaitheanas a thoirt do dh'Alasdair MacGilleMhìcheil airson nan dòighean-deasachaidh a thagh e. Aig an aon àm, chan fhuilear dhuinn aideachadh nach robh iad sin idir 'nan annas am measg a cho-aoisean. Gu dearbh, 's iomadach neach-cruinneachaidh beul-aithris a tha air gabhail ris na prionnsapalan sin suas chon an latha an-diugh, 's iad a' dealbhadh, a' ceangal, a' lìomhadh, agus ag ath-obrachadh theacsaichean tùsail airson ceann-uidhe na duilleig clòbhuailte. B' fhiach aithneachadh cuideachd gum b' e dian-oidhirp a bh' ann an *Carmina Gadelica* fhéin gus seann mhì-thuigsean, mì-mhìneachaidhean, mì-earbsa, agus mì-rùn a shlànachadh ri linn aimsir bhruailleanach ann an eachdraidh: Cogadh nan Croitearan, agus aire nan ùghdarras dìrichte aon uair eile air an 'Trioblaid Ghàidhealaich', air na Gàidheil, air a' chànan, agus air an dualchas. Chaidh *Carmina Gadelica* a chur fo chomhair an t-sluaigh mar phàirt de dh'iomairt tòrr na bu sgaoilte: sgrìobhaichean, sgoilearan, agus luchd-coiteachaidh a' strì ris an dùbhlan a bha rompa, 's e sin mar a dhèanadh iad eadar-theangachadh eadar cainnt-beòil thùsail an t-sluaigh, agus teacsaichean sgrìobhte no clòbhuailte, eadar a' Ghàidhlig agus a' Bheurla, agus, an rud bu chudromaiche buileach, mar a lorgadh iad a' chèis-mhìneachaidh iomchaidh a bheireadh seachad brìgh na céille don choigreach, agus eadhan don nàmhaid fhéin.

Buidheachas

Bu mhath leam taing a thoirt do dh'Urras Leverhulme 's iad cho fialaidh ann a bhith a' maoineachadh an rannsachaidh seo; agus gu dearbh don Dr Iain MacAonghuis airson na thug e dhomh de thaic, de chomhairle, agus de chuideachadh thar nam bliadhnachan.

Giorrachaidhean

CW	LSS Carmichael Watson, Leabharlann Oilthigh Dhùn Éideann.

Tùsan

AP RHEINALLT, TRISTAN.

2010 *Obair gun Duais? Alasdair MacGilleMhìcheil a' tional Ainmean Gàidhlig eun. A Thankless Task?: Alexander Carmichael as a Collector of Gaelic bird names*. Kershader, Isle of Lewis.

BLACK, RONALD.

2008 'I thought he made it all up: Context and controversy'. Domhnall Uilleam Stiùbhart (ed.), *The Life and Legacy of Alexander Carmichael*. Port of Ness, Isle of Lewis: 57–81.

BOSCO, FRANCESCA M., MONICA BUCCIARELLI AND BRUNO G. BARA.

2006 'Recognition and repair of communicative failures: A developmental perspective'. *Journal of Pragmatics* 38: 1398–1429.

BRIGGS, CHARLES L.

1984 'Learning how to ask: Native metacommunicative competence and the incompetence of fieldworkers'. *Language in Society* 13: 1–28.

BRUFORD, ALAN.

1983 '"Deirdire" and Alexander Carmichael's treatment of oral sources'. *Scottish Gaelic Studies* xiv: 1–24.

CAMPBELL, DONALD.

1862 *A Treatise on the Language, Poetry, and Music of the Highland Clans*. Edinburgh.

CAMPBELL, JOHN FRANCIS (ED.).

1860-62 *Popular Tales of the West Highlands*. 4 vols. Edinburgh.

1872 *Leabhar na Féinne*. Edinburgh.

CAMPBELL, JOHN LORNE.

1971-76 Review of *Carmina Gadelica* vi. *Scottish Gaelic Studies*: 290–9.

1978-81a 'Notes on Hamish Robertson's "Studies in Carmichael's *Carmina Gadelica*"'. *Scottish Gaelic Studies* xiii: 1–17.

1978-81b '*Carmina Gadelica*: George Henderson's corrections and suggestions'. *Scottish Gaelic Studies* xiii: 183–218.

CARR, E. SUMMERSON.

2010 'Enactments of expertise'. *Annual Review of Anthropology* 39: 17–32.

CHEAPE, HUGH.

2008 '"Every treasure you chanced on": Alexander Carmichael and material culture'. Domhnall Uilleam Stiùbhart (ed.), *The Life and Legacy of Alexander Carmichael*. Port of Ness, Isle of Lewis: 115–34.

DASCAL, MARCELO.

1999 'Introduction: Some questions about misunderstanding'. *Journal of Pragmatics* 31: 753–62.

DASCAL, MARCELO, AGUS ISIDORO BERENSTEIN.

1987 'Two modes of understanding: Comprehending and grasping'. *Language and Communication* 7: 139–51.

FABIAN, JOHANNES.

1995 'Ethnographic misunderstanding and the perils of context'. *American Anthropologist* 97: 41–50.

MACDONALD, MURDO.

2008 'The visual dimension of *Carmina Gadelica*'. Domhnall Uilleam Stiùbhart (ed.), *The Life and Legacy of Alexander Carmichael*. Port of Ness, Isle of Lewis: 135–45.

MEEK, DONALD.

2007 'Faking the "True Gael"? *Carmina Gadelica* and the Beginning of Modern Gaelic Scholarship'. *Aiste: Rannsachadh air Litreachas Gàidhlig / Studies in Gaelic Literature* 1: 76–106.

ROBERTSON, HAMISH.

1971-76 'Studies in Carmichael's *Carmina Gadelica*'. *Scottish Gaelic Studies*, xii: 220–65.

STEWART, REV. ALEXANDER.

1872 'Nether-Lochaber'. *Inverness Courier*, 1 August 1872: 3.

STIÙBHART, DOMHNALL UILLEAM.

2008a 'Alexander Carmichael and *Carmina Gadelica*'. Domhnall Uilleam Stiùbhart (ed.), *The Life and Legacy of Alexander Carmichael*. Port of Ness, Isle of Lewis: 1–39.

2008b 'Màiri Bhreac agus Gàidsear an Fhèilidh: Màiri Stiùbhart, Alasdair MacGilleMhìcheil, na thug i seachad, agus na rinn e leis'. *Scottish Gaelic Studies*. xxiv: 551–571.

2009 'Alasdair MacGilleMhìcheil agus cultar dùthchasach'. Richard A. V. Cox (deas.), *Dualchas agus an Àrainneachd: Sin am Fearann Caoin*. Ostaig, An t-Eilean Sgitheanach: 134–60.

2010 'Alasdair MacGilleMhìcheil: Fear-cruinneachaidh òran ri linn nan 1860an'. Ruairí Ó hUiginn (eag.), *Foinn agus Focail: Léachtaí Cholm Cille XL*. Maigh Nuad: 109-49.

2013 'The making of a charm collector: Alexander Carmichael in Uist, from 1864 to 1882'. James Kapalo, Éva Pócs, and William Ryan (eds), *The Power of Words: Studies on Charms and Charming in Europe*. Budapest: 21-70.

THOMAS, JENNY.

1983 'Cross-cultural pragmatic failure'. *Applied Linguistics* 4: 91–112.

VERDONIK, DARINKA.

2010 'Between understanding and misunderstanding'. *Journal of Pragmatics* 42: 1364–79.

WEIGAND, EDDA.

1999 'Misunderstanding: The standard case'. *Journal of Pragmatics* 31: 763–85.